AF841165

CONFERENCING AND RESTORATIVE JUSTICE

CONFERENCING AND RESTORATIVE JUSTICE

INTERNATIONAL PRACTICES AND PERSPECTIVES

EDITED BY
ESTELLE ZINSSTAG
INGE VANFRAECHEM

OXFORD
UNIVERSITY PRESS

OXFORD
UNIVERSITY PRESS

Great Clarendon Street, Oxford, OX2 6DP,
United Kingdom

Oxford University Press is a department of the University of Oxford.
It furthers the University's objective of excellence in research, scholarship,
and education by publishing worldwide. Oxford is a registered trade mark of
Oxford University Press in the UK and in certain other countries

© Oxford University Press 2012

The moral rights of the authors have been asserted

First published 2012

Impression: 1

All rights reserved. No part of this publication may be reproduced, stored in a retrieval system, or transmitted, in any form or by any means, without the prior permission in writing of Oxford University Press, or as expressly permitted by law, by licence or under terms agreed with the appropriate reprographics rights organization. Enquiries concerning reproduction outside the scope of the above should be sent to the Rights Department, Oxford University Press, at the address above

You must not circulate this work in any other form and
you must impose this same condition on any acquirer

Crown copyright material is reproduced under Class License
Number C01P0000148 with the permission of OPSI
and the Queen's Printer for Scotland

British Library Cataloguing in Publication Data
Data available

ISBN 978-0-19-965503-8

Printed in Great Britain
CPI Group (UK) Ltd, Croydon, CR0 4YY

Links to third party websites are provided by Oxford in good faith and
for information only. Oxford disclaims any responsibility for the materials
contained in any third party website referenced in this work.

Inge would like to dedicate this book to Ghislaine Michiels-Debrouwer who passed away during the last weeks of writing this book, and who would have been proud of her grandchild.

Estelle would like to dedicate this book to her mother Evelyne Remund Zinsstag and her daughter Charlotte Pavlakos-Zinsstag.

PREFACE

As an intellectual tradition, restorative justice scholarship has been rather dominated by anglophone scholarship. This collection is a nice balance in that regard, even as an English language publication, including distinguished researchers from the anglophone tradition as well as thinkers from spaces that attract less attention.

A good example of the counterbalance is Chapter 10 by Daniela Bolivar et al. on the 'vertical' connection of restorative justice to democracy in South America, for example through conferences that are a platform for citizen critiques of institutional practices. Bolivar et al. speak of a need for a Latin American restorative justice that responds to the context of the tenuous hold of Latin American democracy, to the extremes of inequality, poverty, violence and civil war that are much greater than in the United States and much, much greater than in the rest of the West. Naturally, this is a context where one would think in a very different way about how restorative justice might acquire a useful foothold by giving voice to institutional critiques of inequality. As in many of the contextually attuned chapters of this volume, the authors do this well.

The author of this Preface is one of those anglophone scholars whose writing on restorative justice is cited much more than is deserved. A Nordic scholar whose work is deservedly cited a lot, and not because he has an anglophone orientation, is Nils Christie. Yet how interesting it is that the restorative practice innovations of the 1980s, described by Anna Eriksson in Chapter 13, that were partly inspired by Christie's 'Conflicts as Property', have such a marginal place in the restorative justice literature. Perhaps one explanation is that Nils Christie maintained a critical stance toward the very innovations he inspired, rather than being an uncritical booster of them. Perhaps it was because the Nordic reforms were not marketed with the 'restorative justice' brand in their early decades?

In Finland at least, restorative mediation combined with diversion became part of a package of reforms that very sharply reduced imprisonment rates during the height of Christie's theoretical influence in the Nordic countries. This is not something even New Zealand can claim for adults, though perhaps it can for juveniles as a result of its conferencing reforms. In Australia, one of my deepest disappointments about restorative conferencing is that it has not contributed to a reduction in the shockingly high indigenous imprisonment rates that are cause for such national shame for Australia. Doubtless Anna Eriksson's interpretation of the restorative justice role in the struggle against punitiveness in the Nordic countries is a controversial one in various ways. I do not have the local knowledge to evaluate that. My point is about why debate about the empirical effects of restorative justice in a part of the world where punitive justice has fluctuated more dramatically than elsewhere is not a more central theme in our literature (notwithstanding the interest of some thoughtful anglophones like John Pratt).

A final reason Eriksson's contribution is so interesting overlaps with the appeal of the Bolivar et al. chapter, and with the discussion of empowerment and storytelling in the Northern Ireland restorative justice journey in Tim Chapman's Chapter 5, and with Estelle Zinsstag in Chapter 11. It is the idea that Nordic rationales for restorative youth justice, according to Eriksson, have their roots in a quest for solutions to inequality and exclusion and a rejection of criminalization, at least for younger teenagers, in favour of a welfare model. Those of us who write about this path from within the anglophone tradition of restorative justice research have that aspect of our work dismissed as unworldly. One way into a better conversation on structural inequality, exclusion, and a vision for restorative justice reforms is through reflection on the ups and downs of the Scandinavian welfare model attempts at social democratic transformation of the justice system. It is so instructively different from the anglophone experience of social democratic parties. These parties seek to outdo conservative parties in law and order auctions informed by unsophisticated opinion poll politics that in the long run enfeebles social democratic electoral success.

Joan Pennell and Elizabeth Beck's chapter (Chapter 9) has the instructively different lens of the fear of the State in the United States restorative justice tradition that is so different from Scandinavian harnessing of volunteers to state restorative projects. It is also a chapter that picks up a refreshingly biographical lens to look at the struggles within and without the State by inspiring 'planters' of American restorative justice, Kay Pranis and Lauren Abramson. Even as programmes are shut down from withdrawal of funding support, the planters, the networking of ideas, remain and the programme shut-down becomes an opportunity for 'replanting' with new seeds germinated from the experience of the collapsed program. So long as the network and the conversation is sustained among the folk who are readers of a volume like this, hope of renewal and transformation endures. As one of those network builders with our editors, Lode Walgrave argues in Chapter 3, there is no 'real story' of restorative justice; there are many stories. We can reflect upon different regional, national, and sub-national stories through varied lenses. Then we can ponder options for restorative justice reforms that supply alternatives to 'punitive apriorism' (a term from Walgrave's earlier work with Gordon Bazemore) within a particular space.

There are few things more tedious than a Preface that seeks to discuss every chapter in a book before the reader gets their own chance to digest them in their own way. Perhaps it is better to attempt to whet appetites with morsels of reflection on the kind of insight on offer throughout the text. In this case, I can assure the reader that across all the chapters there are many equally rich engagements with the big questions of restorative justice awaiting them, which will doubtless be richer when viewed through their own lenses, rather than mine. There are also engagements with countless micro-questions of restorative practice that demand critical engagement and much more high quality empirical research. These micro-questions matter a lot. This volume is a rich new resource in relation to them. It is a particularly rich resource on conferencing as an approach to restorative justice that can come in the many forms discussed in this volume. It is a broadened approach with many potential advantages over more dyadic mediation encounters between a victim and offender facilitated by a mediator. Overall, this book is another fine example of a big European contribution to restorative justice that is interested in learning from parts of the world that are very different from Europe.

John Braithwaite
Australian National University

ACKNOWLEDGEMENTS

This edited collection is the result of the collaboration, commitment, and hard work of a number of people, who we wish to acknowledge and show our appreciation to.

First we would like to express our special thanks to Ivo Aertsen for his unwavering support and availability to discuss the work. We would like to thank the European Forum for Restorative Justice for instigating and supporting the important research project on conferencing and therefore allowing this book project to be born. In particular we would like to name Marlies Teunkens, Brunilda Pali, Carmen Borg, and Karolien Mariën, who have all worked with much commitment on the project, as well as all the members of the steering group (some of them writing in the book). In addition we would like to acknowledge the support of Niall Kearney and the board members of the Forum.

We wish to make a special mention of the participants to the expert seminar on conferencing which took place in Leuven in September 2010, where a number of the ideas included in this book first emerged, were discussed, and debated upon.

We would like to thank all the individual authors for their enthusiasm towards the project, their good humour towards our repeated comments and suggestions on their chapters, and for having accepted our time pressures (fairly) diligently!

We would also like to acknowledge the very kind support of John Braithwaite and Shadd Maruna, who both were very helpful guides and supporters in this quite new endeavour for us.

We would like to thank warmheartedly the team at Oxford University Press, in particular Peter Daniell and Lucy Alexander, whose support and enthusiasm for our project, but also patience, have helped us greatly in bringing this book to completion. We would also like to thank the three anonymous reviewers, who made encouraging and helpful comments and suggestions on our book project.

Last but not least, we would both like to thank our respective families. Estelle wants to thank both her husband Georgios and daughter Charlotte for being in her life and making any of this possible. Inge wants to thank her husband Koen and Mirthe, Stinne, and Maurice for bringing laughter in her life and supporting her in her work.

Estelle Zinsstag and Inge Vanfraechem
Leuven, April 2012

CONTENTS

PART III CONFERENCING: EUROPEAN PERSPECTIVES

LIST OF CONTRIBUTORS

Ivo Aertsen is Professor at the KU Leuven Institute of Criminology in Belgium. He holds degrees in Psychology and Law from the same university. His main fields of research and teaching are Victimology, Penology, and Restorative Justice. Within the Leuven Institute of Criminology, he coordinates the Research Line on Restorative Justice. Professor Aertsen has been chair of the European Forum for Restorative Justice from 2000–2004 and has coordinated COST Action A21 on Restorative Justice Research in Europe from 2002–2006. He is editor in chief of *Restorative Justice: An International Journal* and editorial board member of several other journals as well as being involved in various practice and policy oriented partnerships.

Elizabeth Beck is Professor at Georgia State University. Her book *In the Shadow of Death: Restorative Justice and Death Row Families*, is published by Oxford University Press, and received the American Library Association CHOICE award for Outstanding Academic Title of 2007. Her recent book, an edited volume, with Nancy Kropf and Pamela Leonard *Social Work and Restorative Justice: Skills for Dialogue, Peacemaking, and Reconciliation* (also published by Oxford University Press), explores restorative practices in traditional social work settings. From 2006–2010 she was Principle Investigator to the Georgia Council for Restorative Justice, examining Defense Initiated Victim Outreach as a restorative justice strategy often used in death penalty cases. Since 2007 she has been the Director of the Georgia State University School of Social Work Center for Community Social Work.

Daniela Bolivar currently works as the coordinator of the research project, Victims and Restorative Justice at the European Forum for Restorative Justice in Leuven, Belgium. She holds degrees in Psychology and Community-Psychology at the Pontificia Universidad Católica de Chile. Her doctoral dissertation, obtained at the KU Leuven Institute of Criminology, focused on the role of victim-offender mediation in victims' processes of restoration. She has worked on the topic of victimology in both the professional and the academic field, working as a psychologist in victim support programmes in her home country (Chile) and offering lectures at different Chilean Universities on victimology and psychology and law.

Leoberto Narciso Brancher is a district judge and a Professor at the Escola Superior da Magistratura do Estado do Rio Grande do Sul, Brazil, where he is coordinator of the Center in Restorative Justice Studies (Núcleo de Estudos em Justiça Restaurativa). Since 2005, he has worked in the project Justiça para o Século 21 (<http://www.justica21.org.br>) which aims to implement restorative justice practices in the pacification of situations of violence that involve children and juveniles.

Tim Chapman is a Lecturer on the Masters in Restorative Practices programme at the University of Ulster and has contributed to the development of restorative conferencing in both the voluntary and statutory sectors in Northern Ireland. He spent

25 years working in the Probation Service in Northern Ireland. He played an active part in developing effective practice in the United Kingdom particularly through the publication of *Evidence Based Practice*, written jointly with Michael Hough and published by the Home Office. His 'Time to Grow' model for the supervision of young people has influenced youth justice practices especially in Scotland.

Kathleen Daly is Professor of Criminology and Criminal Justice, Griffith University (Brisbane). She was based in the United States (Yale University and the University of Michigan) before going to Australia in 1995 as a Senior Fulbright Scholar to study restorative justice at the Australian National University. She took up her current position at Griffith University in 1996. Her research and writing is on gender, race, crime, and justice; and on restorative, indigenous, and international criminal justice. Her book, *Gender, Crime, and Punishment* (1994, Yale University Press) received the Michael Hindelang Award from the American Society of Criminology. With Lisa Maher, she co-edited *Criminology at the Crossroads: Feminist Readings in Crime and Justice* (1998, Oxford University Press); and with Andrew Goldsmith and Mark Israel, *Crime and Justice: A Guide to Criminology* (2006, Lawbook Company). From 1998 to 2006, she received three Australian Research Council (ARC) grants to research restorative justice and the race/gender politics of new justice practices. In 2008, she launched an international project on innovative responses to sexual violence; and in 2009, as co-principal investigator with Elena Marchetti and Jackie Huggins, a project on sentencing indigenous partner violence in Australia, both funded by the ARC. In addition to books and edited volumes, she has published over 75 journal articles or book chapters. She is a Fellow of the Academy of the Social Sciences in Australia, and immediate past President of the Australian and New Zealand Society of Criminology (2005–2009).

Mélanie Decocq holds degrees in Psychology and Criminology from the University of Liège, Belgium. She is a teaching assistant and researcher at the School of Criminology of the same university. Her current research focuses on conferencing with juveniles and more specifically on the decision making processes of juvenile court judges concerning restorative justice interventions. She also works as a psychologist with juvenile offenders in a youth facility.

Anna Eriksson is a Senior Lecturer in Criminology at Monash University, Melbourne, Australia. She has published on restorative and transitional justice, including the monograph *Justice in Transition: Community Restorative Justice in Northern Ireland* (2009, Willan Publishing), and she was awarded the New Scholar Prize by the Australian and New Zealand Society of Criminology in 2009, for the article 'Challenging Cultures of Violence through Community Restorative Justice' *Restorative Justice: From Theory to Practice, Sociology of Crime, Law and Deviance*, vol. 11 (2008, Elsevier). She is currently involved in a major comparative project together with Professor John Pratt, on contrasts in punishment between Nordic and anglophone countries, to be published with Routledge in 2012. In 2011, she was awarded an Australian Research Council DECRA fellowship for a three year study on comparative penology.

Katrien Lauwaert is a Lecturer at the University of Liège, School of Criminology. She studied law and criminology at KU Leuven, l'Université Catholique de Louvain (Louvain-la-Neuve) (Belgium), the University of Leiden (the Netherlands), and the American University (Washington DC). She obtained a PhD from the University of Maastricht (2008) on the topic of 'Restorative Justice and Procedural Safeguards'. Her main fields of research are victimology, restorative justice, and youth delinquency. Professor Lauwaert is currently a member of the board of the European Forum for Restorative Justice and chair of the Flemish victim-offender mediation organisation Suggnomè.

Gabrielle Maxwell, PhD, is a senior associate of the Institute of Policy Studies and was previously the Director of the Crime and Justice Research Centre at Victoria University of Wellington, New Zealand. Her research focuses on youth justice, restorative justice, family violence, and criminal justice policy. She has authored, co-authored, or edited several books including: *Families, Victims and Culture: Youth Justice in New Zealand* (1993, Social Policy Agency), *Restorative Justice and Practices in New Zealand* (2007, Institute of Policy Studies) and *Addressing the Causes of Offending: What is the evidence?* (2009, Institute of Policy Studies).

Ivan Navarro Papic is a lawyer. He works in the Mediation Unit, at the Ministry of Justice, Chile. Previously, he worked as director of the Mediation Center of Santiago, at Corporación de Asistencia Judicial Metropolitana where he, together with prosecutors and defence lawyers, participated in the design and implementation of mediation projects that involved both adults and young offenders. He has followed studies related to family mediation and restorative justice, and specifically to victim-offender mediation.

Joan Pennell, PhD, is a Professor of Social Work and Director of the Center for Family and Community Engagement at North Carolina State University (United States). She has received funding for work on family engagement in child welfare, juvenile justice, domestic violence, schools, and system of care. She is frequently consulted on implementing the meetings in safe and effective ways in situations of family violence. She co-authored *Community Research as Empowerment* (1996, Oxford University Press) and *Widening the Circle* (1995, NASW Press). She previously chaired the Youth Justice Committee of the (Canadian) National Crime Prevention Council which was instrumental in advancing restorative justice practices in legislation.

Joanna Shapland is Professor of Criminal Justice and Head of the School of Law, University of Sheffield. She has been at Sheffield University since 1988, and was previously at King's College London and at Oxford University. She directed the evaluation of the use of restorative justice (both conferencing and mediation) with adult offenders within the criminal justice system (pre-sentence, during community sentences, and prior to release from prison), funded by the Ministry of Justice, between 2001 and 2008. The results have now been published as a book: *Restorative Justice in Practice* (2011, Routledge), with Gwen Robinson and Angela Sorsby. She was part of the team headed by the European Forum on Restorative Justice looking at conferencing and mediation worldwide. She has also recently co-directed a major project funded by the

Economic and Social Research Council (ESRC) (with Anthony Bottoms), looking at desistance from crime in young adult men. She is Executive Editor of the *International Review of Victimology*.

Ashley Shearar is completing her PhD at Victoria University of Wellington, New Zealand on a comparative analysis of youth justice transformation between New Zealand and South Africa. She has worked on a number of youth justice initiatives in South Africa for various non-governmental organizations (NGOs) as well as for the University of Cape Town, including developing and delivering training to probation officers working with youth in conflict with the law around the country. Prior to that she spent several years working for international NGOs including Save the Children, UNICEF, and Doctors without Borders, implementing programmes for children and families living in countries affected by conflict such as southern Sudan, Sierra Leone, Lebanon, and Indonesia.

Heather Strang is Director of the Centre for Restorative Justice at the Australian National University and Deputy Director of the Lee Centre of Experimental Criminology at the Institute of Criminology, University of Cambridge. She has supervised many experimental tests of the effects of restorative justice in Australia and the United Kingdom and is currently analysing a ten year follow-up of victims and offenders who participated in the Australian study. She has published extensively in this area, including her victim-focused book, *Repair or Revenge: Victims and Restorative Justice* (2004, Clarendon Press).

Inge Vanfraechem is a researcher at KU Leuven Institute of Criminology in Belgium, where she is project manager of the FP7 ALTERNATIVE project. Before that, she coordinated a project for the European Forum for Restorative Justice funded by the European Commission on 'Victims and restorative justice' (2010–2011). She obtained her PhD on Conferencing for Serious Youth Delinquency in 2006 at the same university. In the period 2007–2010 she worked at the National Institute for Criminal Sciences and Criminology of the Belgian Ministry of Justice where she evaluated the Belgian victim policy. Her main fields of research are victimology, restorative justice, and youth criminology. Her research and publications include restorative justice, conferencing for youth delinquents, studies on victims of crime, victim assistance, and victims and the criminal justice system. Doctor Vanfraechem was the vice-chair of the European Forum for Restorative Justice between 2006–2010. She is a member of the editorial team of *Restorative Justice: an International Journal.*

Jan van Lieshout is a former journalist. He was an editor of the *Tijdschrift voor Maatschappijvraagstukken en Welzijnswerk and the Welzijnsweekblad*, the main social work magazines in the Netherlands (1970–1988) and of *Mobiel*, the national journal of foster care (1989–1997). In this period he was part of the team that transferred foster training programs (MAPP, PRIDE) from the United States to the Netherlands. He was responsible for the cultural adaptation of the programmes and worked with prospective and skilled foster parents. From 1972 until the present day he lives as a foster parent with his wife and daughter together with five other children (four brothers and their sister); he has become part of their (extended) family and learned a lot about family groups and their decisions. From his first acquaintance with the model of Family Group Conferencing in 1998 he became a member of the Dutch implementation team for restorative practices. He is member of the editorial board of the *Flemish-Dutch Journal on Restorative Justice.*

Rob van Pagée trained social worker, is governing board member of the Eigen Kracht Centrale in the Netherlands. He has been active in many parts of child care and became a foster care specialist. He has transferred the PRIDE training and assessment programme for prospective foster parents from the United States to the Netherlands and 14 European countries by providing training and consultation for many professionals, foster carers, and administrators. Introduced to Family Group Conference (FGC) in 1996, he recognized the potential of this model to the child care arena and beyond. Together with colleagues he started the introduction of FGC in the Netherlands and created in 2002 the Eigen Kracht Centrale, which became the Dutch Center for Restorative Practices. FGC is now implemented in many arenas of care, welfare, education, and justice. He was one of the founders of the European Network for FGC and instrumental in the introduction of FGC to a number of European countries.

Manyori Vega Gutiérrez is Peruvian and holds a bachelor degree in law. She is part of the team that started implementing, seven years ago, the first experiment of restorative justice with juvenile offenders in Peru. In this practice, Manyori has worked as a mediator, facilitating processes between victims and young offenders, promoting juveniles' processes of responsibilization. Currently, she offers counselling to the prosecutor's office related to the implementation of juvenile restorative justice practices, in response to their interest in promoting restorative justice as a wider practice to deal with crimes. She has participated in training of restorative circles at the Instituto Latinoamericano de Practicas Restaurativas. In 2009, she participated as a volunteer in the first 'Congreso Mundial de Justicia Restaurativa' that took place in Lima, Peru. In 2010, she participated in a comparative study between Peru and Italy about the application of remission and the practice in Bari.

Lode Walgrave is Emeritus Professor in Criminology at the KU Leuven (Belgium), where he taught youth criminology and theoretical criminology. He has been a member of the Research Council of the KU Leuven. He is a former chair of the International Network for Research on Restorative Justice and of the International Association for Criminology of Youth. In 2008, Lode Walgrave received the European Criminology Award. He has given guest lectures and conferences in Australia, Brazil, Canada, China, New Zealand, South Africa, the United States, and in most European countries. He published more than 300 titles in Dutch (which is his mother tongue), in English, and in French. Translations are published in Chinese, German, Portuguese, and Russian. He contributed chapters to most of the recent international works on restorative justice. He is also a member of the editorial team of *Restorative Justice: An International Journal.*

Annemieke Wolthuis is a senior researcher at the Verwey-Jonker Institute in the Netherlands. She defended her PhD on 'Restorative Justice, a Children's Right' in March 2012 at the Open University. Her book has been published by Boom Lemma

Publishers. For ten years she worked with Defence for Children in Amsterdam as a staff member and coordinator of the section youth law. Her law degree is from Maastricht University, followed by an LLM in international law and human rights from the Raoul Wallenberg Institute in Lund, Sweden. She is currently a board member of the European Forum for Restorative Justice, has a seat on the editorial board of the *Dutch/Flemish Journal on Restorative Justice* and is active in the working group on youth law and health law of the Dutch Committee of Jurists for Human Rights. She publishes and lectures on several areas dealing with children's rights, youth law, and restorative justice.

Estelle Zinsstag is a senior researcher on the FP7 project ALTERNATIVE at the KU Leuven Institute of Criminology, Belgium. Previously she lead a project for the European Forum for Restorative Justice funded by the European Commission on 'Conferencing: a way forward for restorative justice in Europe'. She publishes in the fields of sexual violence against women, transitional justice, and restorative justice. Her forthcoming publications include a book co-edited with Martha Fineman on *Feminist Perspectives on Transitional Justice* (2012, Intersentia) and a chapter on 'Wartime Sexual Violence, Transitional Justice and the Possibility of a "Blended Approach"' in S. Parmentier and A. Czarnota (eds) *Transitional justice and the Rule of Law* (2012, Intersentia). She is the managing editor of *Restorative Justice: An International Journal*. In recent years she completed a PhD entitled 'Sexual Violence against Women in Armed Conflict: Towards a Transitional Justice Perspective' at the School of Law, Queen's University Belfast.

1

CONFERENCING

SETTING THE SCENE

Inge Vanfraechem and Estelle Zinsstag

THE CONTEXT

Restorative justice in general and conferencing in particular have in the last two decades developed extensively. They have during this time established themselves as valuable potential alternatives to a problematic criminal justice system, or as an ideal partner through which coordination with a more punitive type of justice attempts to bring a fairer sense of justice to all stakeholders of a crime. However, restorative justice in Europe is still mostly equated with victim-offender mediation (VOM) (Miers and Willemsens 2004). The European legislation passed in early 2001 has encouraged such views, since it referred principally to 'penal mediation'.[1] Nevertheless, the inexorable developments of conferencing around the world, as are discussed in this book, led to a heightened interest for the subject at a European level. Therefore, some years ago, the European Forum for Restorative Justice applied for an Action Grant to the European Commission to encourage a comprehensive reflection on the topic. The grant was awarded and a project entitled 'Conferencing: a way forward for restorative justice in Europe' was conducted between 2009 and 2011, guided by three main research questions:

- To what extent has conferencing been developed internationally?
- What are the processes used in, and outcomes achieved by, conferencing, and how do they compare to victim-offender mediation (sometimes referred to as VOM)?
- How could conferencing practices be developed further in Europe?

In order to get a good overview of conferencing in Europe, partners were found with an extensive knowledge on the topic, namely the Leuven Institute for Criminology (KU Leuven, Belgium), the National Institute of Criminalistics and Criminology (Ministry of Justice, Belgium), the University of Sheffield (United Kingdom), the Youth Justice Agency of Northern Ireland (United Kingdom), and the Eigen Kracht Centrale (Netherlands).

[1] Article 10, Framework Decision on the Standing of Victims in Criminal Proceedings (2001/220/JHA) of 15 March 2001.

The outcomes of the project were a large report (Zinsstag et al. 2011; see also Zinsstag in Chapter 2), a practical guide on conferencing (Shapland et al. 2011), and this book. Indeed, in the context of an expert seminar on conferencing which took place in September 2010 in Leuven (Belgium), this book was conceived: experts from around the world had been invited to present a paper on the state of affairs of conferencing in their respective countries. For the book, we asked selected authors from the seminar and other invited authors to write chapters taking into account the developments in their own countries combined with a specific focus relevant to their country and research interests.[2] The aim was to provide a broad and original picture of conferencing. That is how we came to have 13 unique chapters, some more thematic and some more geographical, but all portraying a different picture of conferencing.

CONFERENCING AS A CONCEPT

Before describing the content of this book, it is important to sketch a framework to the concept: what does conferencing mean? First of all, conferencing is a restorative justice practice. Restorative justice has mainly been described through two approaches: the 'purist' approach focuses on the communication process and refers to Tony Marshall's definition: 'Restorative justice is a process whereby all the parties with a stake in a particular offence come together to resolve collectively how to deal with the aftermath of the offence and its implications for the future'(1996: 37). The 'maximalist' approach considers restorative justice 'as an option for doing justice after the occurrence of an offence that is primarily oriented towards repairing the individual, relational and social harm caused by that offence' (Walgrave 2008: 21).[3] It therefore considers restorative justice as another paradigm compared to the criminal justice system. In the context of the conferencing research project, we have adopted the United Nations definition: 'Restorative justice is a way of responding to criminal behaviour by balancing the needs of the community, the victims, and the offenders' (2006: 6–7). We have decided in this book to focus mainly on conferencing in the framework of criminal justice affairs, while being aware that conferencing has been and still is practised in many other areas such as schools and workplace conflicts.[4]

Family group conferences (FGC) started in New Zealand in 1989, both for youth justice and youth care cases (Hudson et al. 1996). It was the model for various practices throughout the world (Morris and Maxwell 2001) and is therefore often used as a common term (see also Walgrave, in Chapter 3). In this book, we use the more neutral term of 'conferencing' to point to those communication processes that involve victims, offenders, their supporters, and possible others such as professional actors. The European Forum research (Zinsstag et al. 2011; Zinsstag in Chapter 2) shows that, although in theory the restorative justice practices of conferencing and mediation

[2] We would like to acknowledge some colleagues whose contributions to the seminar or project in general also helped shape the final product, in particular Otmar Hagemann, Bas Van Stokkom and David O'Mahony.

[3] For more extensive explanation on the differences, see (Walgrave 2008).

[4] Chapter 14 by van Pagée and colleagues takes a broader approach.

may be relatively easily distinguished (see also Walgrave, in Chapter 3), in practice there are many similarities, for example when mediation includes support persons or when only victim and offender attend a conference (see also Shapland, in Chapter 4). The role of the professionals is seldom described, although large differences occur according to whether the conference includes the police (as a facilitator or as representing society, see Vanfraechem 2009), social workers, and lawyers. In this book, we also devote a chapter to the role of the facilitator (Chapman, in Chapter 5), since he/she has a crucial role to play in order for the conference to take place, run smoothly, and come to an agreement successfully.

OVERVIEW OF THE BOOK

The chapters in this book have different focal points, some being more geographical, some more thematic, but all unique in their arguments and original in their research. We had to exclude topics, such as, for example, policing, or developments in Eastern Europe and Asia, even though we think it is vital that these be studied further. We nevertheless think that the chapters included here give a very good overview of the developments of conferencing as a restorative justice programme worldwide, and explore a number of relevant related topics.

The first part of the book offers a view on some more general and theoretical topics when it comes to conferencing as a restorative justice programme. In Chapter 2, Estelle Zinsstag describes the most important outcomes of a worldwide survey that was carried out in 2010. The chapter first discusses some of the main theoretical characteristics concerning conferencing. She then presents some of the most important findings that emerged from a survey which was constructed, sent out, and analysed in the context of the research project mentioned above. The results enable an accurate and up to date picture of the many aspects which make conferencing. Some of the results for example were that it is clear that practice tends to be much more advanced than theory and that the limits between mediation and conferencing are not clear.

In Chapter 3, Lode Walgrave aims for clarity with regard to conferencing: what are different models and what exactly are we talking about? Empirical research is not always convincing and may even be contradictory. According to the author, these dispersing results are linked to the blurring regarding restorative justice and conferences. When studying different models, the following elements come to the fore: the difference between mediation and conferencing, the specificity of the New Zealand FGCs, the role of the police, and the use of volunteers as facilitators. According to Walgrave, more research is needed to really understand what happens in a conference, although distinguishing criteria to base the research on (restoration, satisfaction,…) are not self-evident.

Joanna Shapland in Chapter 4 undertakes the challenge to compare mediation and conferencing in different countries—this is indeed a challenge since although in theory the differences may be clear-cut (see also Walgrave, in Chapter 3), these practices may lean towards each other and the concrete context within a certain country will need to be taken into account in order to discern what one is really talking about (see also Eriksson, in Chapter 13). In order to make a comparison, Shapland looks at attendance, the stages of the process, the role of the facilitator or mediator, the aims of the practices, and the types of outcomes envisaged as important. She studies practices in Belgium, England and Wales, and Northern Ireland. With regard to attendance, mediation may include support people and conferencing may take place without supporters—the number of people therefore does not seem to be a good demarcation variable. With regard to what actually happens during the meeting, information is rather scarce: this is often not written up in a detailed manner. Reasons to participate are mostly the same for victims and offenders in both mediation and conferencing cases, namely to communicate about what has happened. With regard to the aims of the schemes, it looks like the set-up and context has more influence than the mere fact of the scheme offering mediation or conferencing.

As Tim Chapman (Chapter 5) argues, although the facilitator is considered to have a crucial role in guiding the process, literature with regard to the role is scarce. The author therefore uses Northern Ireland as a case study to dig deeper into the role the facilitator may play when facilitating a conference process. The Balanced Model of Restorative Justice provides a framework to understand the needs of the parties involved, namely victim, offender, and their communities. For facilitation, storytelling is crucial in order for the (full) stories to come out. According to Chapman, 'the effectiveness of the conference depends upon the dialogue being based upon a specific direct experience, shared in relationship with others. This allows stories to "thicken" and to complete.' Therefore, the facilitator needs to show respect for each story and ensure a framing of the problem and possibilities to resolve it. Chapman sees three important stages in the process: inclusion, participation, and transformation. Reparation of the harm is the starting point, but rehabilitation for both victim and offender may be needed. The author concludes that besides the 'professional façade' (which can be relatively easily taught), other skills need to be developed through practice and feedback.

Heather Strang (Chapter 6) studies the position of victims in restorative justice conferences (RJCs). She upholds that restorative justice offers a solution for problems encountered by victims regarding the criminal justice system. The author refers to the theory on procedural justice to confirm that victims want a fair treatment; to emotional processing theory; and to the interaction ritual theory, all theories that may explain why RJCs might work better for victims than the criminal justice system. Empirical research results show that victims can indeed benefit from participating in RJCs, namely through receiving apologies, perceptions of procedural justice, reducing the desire for revenge, reduced levels of post-traumatic stress, and satisfaction with the justice experience. Strang refers to a long-term study that interviewed victims ten years after their participation in RJCs, which shows that victims who participated in RJCs generally rated their wellbeing higher than court-assigned victims, had lower anxiety levels, were less afraid, and showed less feelings of revenge. Strang therefore concludes that RJCs have a capacity to resolve the harm caused to the victims (who choose to participate), especially for victims of violence.

The second part of the book examines some of the original models of conferencing (New Zealand and Australia), points out some of the challenges (ensuring quality, approaching difficult cases such as sexual assault), and refers to some newer developments, such as developing conferencing in Latin America.

Ashley Shearar and Gabrielle Maxwell (Chapter 7) describe the origins and functioning of the New Zealand FGCs, which are used as a model throughout the world (eg Australia, Belgium, Norway, and Northern Ireland), even though it was set up not as a restorative justice practice, but as a culture-sensitive welfare model for youngsters. The practice of FGCs shows that the following elements are important: participation (of both parties, their supporters, and professional actors), empowerment, repairing harm, addressing the causes of offending, re-integration, and effectiveness (reducing re-offending but also other future-oriented outcomes). Challenges faced are a lack of resources, differences between youth justice coordinators (facilitators) and social workers, replacing flexibility with tick boxes (see also Umbreit's (1999) notion of 'McDonaldization' when practices become standard), limited follow up on the execution of the plans, and public pressure for harsher penalties. These are challenges that, we think, will also be faced in other countries implementing conferencing. Shearar and Maxwell further explore some avenues to ensure the continuing and (better) implementation of FGCs: Youth Offending Teams, therapeutic jurisprudence (rehabilitation and re-integration combined with a justice approach), Marae-based youth courts, and Whana Ora (thus creating a link to the Māori culture).

Kathleen Daly (Chapter 8) sketches conferencing in both Australia and New Zealand as the framework for the use of conferencing in cases of gendered violence. Her overview shows that Australia mostly uses the New Zealand model of youth conferencing, while the cases are generally of a less serious nature. With regard to adult conferencing, Australia shows a more scattered picture, but generally victims are freer to choose to attend compared to youth conferencing. With regard to gendered violence, most literature focuses on domestic violence and on principled discussions, since not so much empirical research is at hand. General concerns include the voluntariness, victim safety, and potential problems related to power imbalance. The current professional role of the people interviewed is important: the further away they are from restorative justice, the more sceptical they tend to be. With regard to empirical findings, adult conferences seem to cause the least controversy when applied post-sentence. For youth conferencing, research in Australia shows that conferences may offer more to victims than court and for those offenders with no previous offending, conferences led to lesser recidivism. In Europe, some experiences are known to have taken place with youth conferencing in sexual violence cases both in Manchester (United Kingdom) and Flanders (Belgium). Daly concludes that gendered violence poses challenges to conferencing and restorative justice because of the context and the role of victims, and that one should broaden the array of practices that may offer an answer to cases of gendered violence.

Elizabeth Beck and Joan Pennell (Chapter 9) study conferencing in the United States by interviewing four persons who laid the basis of the introduction of a restorative justice-practice in the context of an individualized society (the authors refer to Hsu's concept of 'rugged individualism') and a punitive system. Restorative justice contradicts this context since it focuses on cooperation, caring, and mutuality. The four examples in the chapter show how practices may emerge from bottom-up and why the people involved may opt to implement it without state control, but rather linked to communities, since this would enhance the collective values and participatory principles of restorative justice.

Daniela Bolivar, Leoberto Narciso Brancher, Ivan Navarro Papic, and Manyori Vega Gutiérrez (Chapter 10) study conferencing in three Latin American countries: Chile, Peru, and Brazil. The emergence can be situated in the context of concerns for human rights and victims, social inequality, and deformalization of criminal procedures. Practices differ between the countries and vary from mediation (Chile) to conferencing (Peru) and circles (Brazil). According to the authors, the practices do have a 'social justice' element in common by ensuring the protection of rights and access to justice. With regard to conferencing and democracy, Bolivar et al. distinguish three elements they deem as important: inclusiveness, the horizontal-vertical role of restorative justice, and the territorial aspect of community. With regard to inclusiveness, availability and true involvement of the parties come to the fore—conferencing in Latin America could be further developed in that regard, especially through taking the community aspect into consideration. The empowering role of restorative justice and the link to social justice could be strengthened by ensuring equal access and voice to the participants and by critically reviewing relations with the society and state. A lot of discussion has taken place in the restorative justice literature with regard to the idea of community (see for example Crawford 2002; Vanfraechem 2007; Walgrave 2008). Bolivar et al. suggest that for Latin America the idea of community as a social group that shares history and culture, and as involving social interaction, will be important. According to them, the link to democracy can be made through the insertion of micro-activities into the local communities.

The third part of this volume consists of European perspectives on conferencing: some countries have developed conferencing more extensively (in Northern Ireland and Belgium it is integrated at the core of the juvenile justice system), others are still in a starting-phase (the Nordic countries) or focus on other spheres than the justice system (the Netherlands).

Estelle Zinsstag and Tim Chapman (Chapter 11) describe the Northern Ireland model of conferencing, which is based on the FGCs and puts conferencing at the heart of the youth justice system, and focuses on the position of the victim from the start. The Balanced Model balances the needs of the victim, community, and offender. Victims participating generally regard the conference as satisfying. Rather than using a script, a robust and flexible model was developed. Some of the challenges include providing follow-up, dealing with multiple conferences, and public credibility.

Inge Vanfraechem, Katrien Lauwaert, and Mélanie Decocq (Chapter 12) study conferencing in Belgium to understand the relationship between rehabilitation and restorative justice: conferencing has been included in the Belgian Youth Justice Act of 2006 which is mostly still oriented towards a pedagogical approach to youth delinquency. Even though mediation and conferencing are the first option at the level of the youth judge/court, referrals have not increased enormously since the implementation of the Youth Justice Act. Some bottlenecks in the relationship between the rehabilitative youth justice system and restorative justice practices include the restorative justice working principles (neutrality, confidentiality, and voluntary participation), the position of the victim, and the role of professionals such as the police, social worker, and lawyer.

Anna Eriksson (Chapter 13) starts with the description of mediation in Nordic countries, stating that it often takes the shape of conferencing since other people are invited to attend. Countries such as Denmark and Iceland do not practice mediation a lot (only at the end of 2011 was a law introduced in Denmark (Asmussen 2012)) and these countries refer to Norway as an example. Therefore, the author focuses her overview on Norway, Finland, and Sweden, with the aim of showing how the national context influences the actual practice and choices made when implementing restorative justice. Eriksson argues that crime in the Nordic countries is seen to have its roots in social inequalities and exclusion, and answers are therefore sought to remedy these inequalities. Restorative justice is then regarded as a pedagogical and preventive tool, rather than an alternative for a punitive system, as is the case in the United Kingdom. According to the author, the risk exists that more juveniles will be labelled as an 'offender' within a restorative justice practice since this is the starting point for the communication process. Furthermore, problems may exist with regard to the position of the victim, especially with regard to compensation by juvenile offenders.

Rob Van Pagée, Jan van Lieshout, and Annemieke Wolthuis (Chapter 14) offer a broader view on conferencing, since the developments in the Netherlands are more focused on various settings (school, communities, neighbourhoods, child care) rather than only criminal justice. Although various mediation models exist and/or have been piloted, the authors consider the restorative justice developments to be rather slow. Because of the national implementation of the so-called 'victim-offender conversations', 'Real Justice' conferences were no longer funded and developments regarding conferencing were focused mostly on other fields. Evaluation shows that conferencing can make a bridge between the people and the institutions they are in contact with, so citizens can take the initiative in the resolution of their conflicts and problems.

In the conclusion (Chapter 15), Ivo Aertsen considers some of the points made throughout this volume by its diverse authors and offers some reflections concerning key points such as facilitation, community, or justice for the further development of conferencing and restorative justice.

REFERENCES

Asmussen, I. (2012), *Victim-Offender Mediation in Denmark*, presentation at the Nordic Conference on Mediation, Helsinki, 9 February.

Crawford, A. (2002), 'The State, Community and Restorative Justice: Heresy, Nostalgia and Butterfly Collecting', in Walgrave, L. (ed.), *Restorative Justice and the Law* (Cullompton: Willan Publishing), pp 101–29.

Hudson, J., Morris, A., Maxwell, G. and Galaway, B. (eds.) (1996), *Family Group Conferences: Perspectives on Policy and Practice* (Monsey: The Federation Press-Criminal Justice Press).

Marshall, T. (1996), 'The Evolution of Restorative Justice in Britain', *European Journal on Criminal Policy and Research*, 4(4), pp 21–43.

Miers, D. and Willemsens, J. (eds.) (2004), *Mapping Restorative Justice: Developments in 25 European Countries* (Leuven: European Forum for Victim-Offender Mediation and Restorative Justice v.z.w.).

Morris, A. and Maxwell, G. (eds.) (2001), *Restorative Justice for Juveniles. Conferencing, Mediation & Circles* (Portland: Hart Publishing).

Shapland, J., Robinson, G. and Sorsby, A. (2011), *Restorative Justice in Practice: Evaluating What Works For Victims and Offenders* (London: Routledge).

Umbreit, M. (1999), 'Avoiding the Marginalization and "McDonaldization" of Victim-Offender Mediation: A Case Study in Moving Toward the Mainstream', in Bazemore, G. and Walgrave, L. (eds.), *Restorative Juvenile Justice: Repairing the Harm of Youth Crime* (Monsey: Criminal Justice Press), pp 213–34.

Vanfraechem, I. (2007), 'Community, Society and State in Restorative Justice: Some Reflections', in Mackay, R., Bosjnak, M., Deklerck, J., Pelikan, C., van Stokkom, B. and Wright, M. (eds.), *Images of Restorative Justice Theory* (Frankfurt am Main: Verlag für Polizei und Wissenschaft), pp 73–91.

Vanfraechem, I. (2009), 'Restorative Policing: In Pursuit of Principles', in Moor, L.G., Peters, T., Ponsaers, P., Shapland, J. and van Stokkom, B. (eds.), *Restorative Policing: Cahiers Politiestudies* (Antwerp: Maklu Uitgevers N.V.), 2(11), pp 39–64.

Walgrave, L. (2008), *Restorative Justice, Self-Interest and Responsible Citizenship*, (Cullompton: Willan Publishing).

Zinsstag, E., Teunkens, M. and Pali, B. (2011), *Conferencing: A Way Forward for Restorative Justice in Europe?* Report to the European Commission (Leuven: European Forum for Restorative Justice).

PART I

CONFERENCING: BROADENING THE SCOPE OF RESTORATIVE JUSTICE

2

CONFERENCING

A DEVELOPING PRACTICE OF RESTORATIVE JUSTICE

Estelle Zinsstag[1]

INTRODUCTION

Conferencing[2] is a restorative justice practice which has started developing quite consistently since the 1990s. The first large scale programme was set up in New Zealand and soon thereafter also in Australia. To this day, conferencing has mostly been developing in anglophone countries such as the two mentioned above as well as the United States, Canada, the United Kingdom, and—with consistently promising results for juvenile justice—in Northern Ireland. Some continental European, Latin American, and African countries are also slowly starting to introduce this alternative or complement to traditional criminal justice, especially in the case of juvenile justice, with some promising results.

In the realm of a research project on conferencing in Europe run by the European Forum for Restorative Justice between 2009 and 2011 we set up a survey on conferencing, and conferencing in comparison to mediation. It was an extensive survey, going into great detail on specific practices and requesting expert responses. The survey was sent out to a number of targeted experts around the world and over 100 useable surveys were sent back representing about 25 countries worldwide where conferencing practices could be identified and analysed. A report was written with a very detailed analysis of the results (Zinsstag et al. 2011). In this chapter I aim only to look at some specific and characteristic points which emerged from the collected information in order to offer a picture of what conferencing may mean at the beginning of the 2010 decade.

I also aim in this chapter to discuss conferencing in a global context, looking both theoretically, but mostly practically, at the developments and advances made up until today with this restorative justice mechanism, showing specifically that practice is actually more advanced than theory, in contrast to common belief.

[1] I would like to thank Inge Vanfraechem, Marlies Teunkens, and Georgios Pavlakos for re-reading and commenting on this chapter.

[2] I will use the term of conferencing as an umbrella term to mean all different types of conferencing, including family group conferencing (FGC), restorative justice conferencing, etc.

CONFERENCING IN THEORY: WHAT ARE THE MAIN CHARACTERISTICS?

This section will discuss some of the main characteristics concerning conferencing from a theoretical and normative point of view.

ORIGINS AND DEFINITION

The very origins of conferencing can be found in the establishment of family group conferencing (FGC), which started in 1989 under the provisions of the Children, Young Persons and Families Act in New Zealand, addressing child welfare and youth justice issues (Maxwell and Morris 2001; Raye and Roberts 2007). It started as a reform to empower Māori people in New Zealand whose youth was over-represented among young offenders. It was based on a social welfare approach rather than, as it soon thereafter developed in Australia, a more criminal justice approach, which involved for example the police in greater portions (see Van Ness and Strong 2010).

Conferencing is as difficult and controversial to define as restorative justice, and many researchers and practitioners have attempted to do so more or less successfully (see eg for restorative justice: Marshall 1996, Zehr 2002; for conferencing: Raye and Roberts 2007; Van Ness et al. 2001) but this is not the aim of this chapter. Instead, as mentioned earlier, I wish to offer some elements which characterize this programme theoretically and which, in coordination with the other main part of this chapter—the results of a large survey on the practice—will make it possible to draw a picture of this developing practice of restorative justice.

For the purposes of our project on conferencing and in particular for the respondents to our survey we developed the following definition: conferencing is a restorative justice process which, with the help of a facilitator, brings together the victim(s) of a crime (directly or not), the offender(s) and their support persons, who may include family members and friends. In a conference a number of other persons may participate such as a police officer, a lawyer, a community worker, and a social worker. They come together in order to find an acceptable resolution for all parties to the above mentioned crime.

There are alternative definitions on the market. Raye and Roberts (2007: 213) for example have written in the context of New Zealand that: 'The process was designed to bring families of victims and offenders together to find their own solutions to conflicts'. Walgrave (2008: 34) explains that:

> a restorative conference is facilitated by an impartial moderator and consists of an inclusive process that brings together the victim, the offender and their 'supporters' in order to find a socially constructive solution to the problems and harms caused by the offence.

Shapland et al. (2011: 9) explain '*conferencing*—involving a face-to-face meeting between offender and victim, with one or more mediators or facilitators, and including one or more supporters of the offender and victim also invited to attend.'

These different definitions show the amount of vagueness one has to preserve in order not to over- or under-determine such a programme. They also demonstrate the breadth of such a programme and the different possibilities that it represents. It is very delicate to define it because each country, service, or programme generates its own type of conferencing. It is a very malleable tool and may be understood very differently as concerns its aims, possibilities, and outcomes. It can be used at different levels of the criminal justice system, as a complement, or sometimes even as an alternative. It may also be employed in a number of non-criminal settings with much success such as in schools, workplaces, or neighbourhoods; all of which will not be addressed here, since we focus on crimes.

MAIN AIMS

The aims of a conferencing programme may vary widely, depending for example on the type of programme or type of offenders, yet there exist some aims which remain constant across schemes. Harris (2003: 123–129) described them as follows: empowerment (for all of the participants to the conference), restoration (it is about addressing the harm both to the victim and the wider community), reintegration (following the reintegrative shaming theories developed for example in Braithwaite and Braithwaite (2001)), and emotional resolution (for both the victim and the offender, as it is an important part of the process).

Conferencing in its broad aims also very much fits the ideas developed by Christie (1977). Some examples include:

- the need to involve the victim in the resolution of their case;
- to take the conflict out of 'professionals' hands in order to allow the actual protagonists to resolve the 'conflict'; and
- to resolve a conflict in finding useful and constructive ways to repair, both physical and emotional, therefore avoiding pure punishment.

All these different aims can and should be found in most conferencing programmes if they are to be truly restorative. Of importance as well is the participation of supporters, most often the family but also the community, as it is key that those affected directly or indirectly by a crime should be invited to participate, encouraged to speak, and should be listened to during the process (see eg Moore and McDonald 2000).

MAIN TRAITS

Conferencing is a restorative justice programme or scheme, which is still less widespread than mediation in many countries and whose main difference from the latter is the presence of supporters for both the offender and victim who are taking part. That is to say that instead of being a meeting between just the two main stakeholders and a mediator, it involves the community of care, which ensures on the one hand that the two main stakeholders receive support during and after the meeting. On the other hand, it also means that the community of care has to take some responsibility for the crime committed and its resolution. As Walgrave (2008: 35) explains:

> Most conferences are organised as a form of diversion at police level or public prosecutor's level; sometimes they are facilitated by a police officer, as a kind of caution to the young offender; some conferences address the welfare problems of the young offender more than the victim's genuine needs. These variations are important. All in all, one could consider most of these versions as extended mediations including the communities of care in the deliberation. Their plus value is that the involvement of the social network may help to strengthen the positive consequences of the deliberation. But such conferences also have more or less the same limitations as mediation.

In a conference there may also be some community representatives, be it a police representative, a probation officer, a social worker, or a community worker, even sometimes a lawyer or any other person that is deemed relevant by the facilitator in his/her preparation of the case.

A conference can deal with a wide variety of crimes, from very low level misdemeanours to very violent crimes such as armed robberies, domestic and sexual violence, and attempted murders. Generally cases of murder are not dealt with by this type of programme. However, that is a general policy decision of each programme and also has to do with the nature of the crime in question and what it implies for the offender and the victim (see discussion in Cunneen and Hoyle 2010).

MAIN TYPOLOGIES

Notwithstanding the variety of typologies of conferencing we shall confine our outline to just the main ones here: for example, FGC in which the role of the family is central. As Connolly and McKenzie (1999: 15) wrote, it is about:

> the participation of family in child protection, the strengthening of families and kinship networks, the connection or reconnection of children to their families and wider kinship group, and the community of care for children.

There is also restorative conferencing, which brings together all direct stakeholders in attempting to find the most appropriate ways of repairing the harm which was committed by the offence (McCold and Wachtel 2002). Models may vary with respect to the involvement of the victim, but also the supporters of both the victim and the offender (McCold 2001).

'Real Justice' conferences are scripted and police-lead, very much in line with what is also called Police Conferencing (Wagga model). A police officer called Terry O'Connell transposed the FGC model from New Zealand to a small town called Wagga Wagga in New South Wales, Australia in 1991. This type of conferencing 'was a natural extension of the cautioning used in countries with British-style policing' (McCold 2007: 33). O'Connell was also influenced by Braithwaite's theory of reintegrative shaming. Conference protocols have been scripted to help the facilitators, who are police officers, through the conference.

In addition, one can also find what is called community conferencing (also called Real Justice conferencing, community accountability conferencing, and restorative conferencing), which according to McCold (2007: 33) 'provides forums for dealing with wrongdoing throughout society as well as peacemaking possibilities in schools, workplaces, communities, youth organisations, college campuses and other settings.'

These are a few of the different types of conferencing which can be identified today, but in many cases they overlap and the objectives or ways to run them are similar from one type to another. Some are more focused on welfare issues while others on the criminal side of the harm depending on who runs them, or whether there is a script or not. But, as we will see from the practice in the next section, these typologies do not seem as important in practice; rather, a theoretical understanding of the main concepts and ideas behind conferencing is crucial for a truly restorative exercise which guarantees the safety of the victim and upholds (or respects) the rights of the offender.

CONFERENCING IN ACTUAL FACTS: RESULTS FROM AN INTERNATIONAL STUDY

As part of the project on conferencing run by the European Forum for Restorative Justice, we developed a survey in 2009–2010, from which I will present some relevant results with an eye to setting the practice of conferencing in a more global context.[3]

The survey was developed by the project's team[4] and concerned the collection of detailed information on two of the most common and current restorative justice programmes, namely victim-offender mediation and conferencing, which we intended to compare in the final report (see Zinsstag et al. 2011). The survey was sent out to 'key stakeholders', a number of persons, both practitioners, academics, and those working from a policy point of view, who have expert knowledge on mediation or conferencing across the world. In total about 260 surveys were sent out and we received over a 100 useable surveys. The importance however was not the number of returned surveys but mostly the representativeness of the information collected: we wanted the survey to really cover all regions of the world, to collect information on as many types of conferencing as possible, and on their institutional settings and their functioning. The results were analysed[5] and some of the facts that emerged will be discussed below.

What is important to remember when reading the beginning of this portrait of current practices of conferencing is that it is based on an average of responses given, on occasion, from very different perspectives. Therefore it is possible that very few programmes would look exactly as described here, however the information that was collected may help provide a reliable outline.

[3] For the full analysis of the survey, see Zinsstag et al. (2011).

[4] Carmen Borg and Estelle Zinsstag with the support of the steering group of the project composed of Ivo Aertsen, Kelvin Doherty, Joanna Shapland, Inge Vanfraechem, and Rob Van Pagée.

[5] The results were analysed by Marlies Teunkens and Estelle Zinsstag with the support of the above mentioned steering group.

GEOGRAPHICAL DATA

In order to put the results of the survey in context it is important to have a quick overview about the origins of the respondents: from the results of the survey we discovered that conferencing practices could be found in one form or another in 26 countries and on all continents (Figure 2.1). The 26 countries represented are 58 per cent European and 42 per cent non-European. There were in total 65 European respondents and 34 non-European respondents.[6] The results showed that forms of conferencing could be found in 76 per cent of the non-European countries (or 26 respondents) and in 42 per cent of the European countries (or 27 respondents).

The relationship between the use of conferencing and the fact that the country is European or non-European was found to be statistically significant ($x^2 = 11.874$; df = 1; $p<0.01$), so it is clear that conferencing is really applied more in non-European countries. Furthermore the results showed that the practice of conferencing is generally more developed and widespread than originally thought, ie when we started the research project and what could be derived from literature.

GENERAL CHARACTERISTICS

First of all, we depict some general characteristics concerning conferencing such as the aims of such a programme, what types of cases can be dealt with, what types of offenders can be involved, and how they can be referred.

Aims of the programme

In the survey we proposed a number of aims which could be ticked and here I cite only those that were ticked by more than half of the respondents by decreasing popularity:

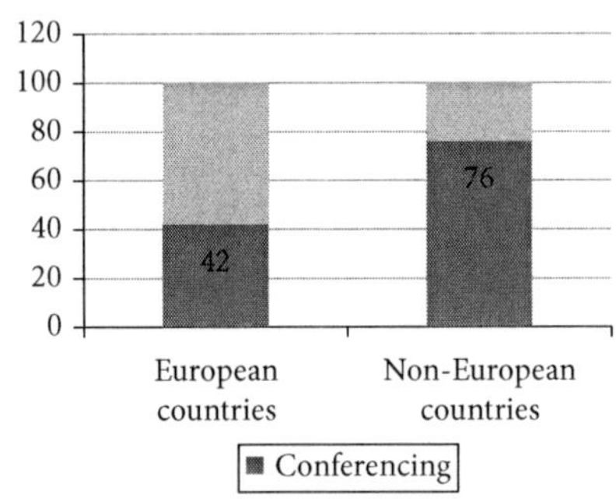

Figure 2.1 Conferencing in European (n = 65) and non-European countries (n = 34) (%)

[6] This adds up to 99 respondents. This is because two respondents did not fill in their country and one declared that no restorative justice was applied in his/her country (Malta).

1. reach an agreement which is acceptable to all participants;
2. increase the offenders' sense of responsibility for the offence;
3. provide an opportunity for the victim to receive reparation;
4. provide an opportunity for the victim to ask questions and receive information from the offender;
5. provide opportunity for the offender's family to participate;
6. reduce re-offending;
7. provide an opportunity for the victim's family to participate;
8. provide an opportunity for other people to participate in the process;
9. leave victim/offender with a greater sense of satisfaction about the criminal justice system;
10. provide an opportunity for the victim to participate in a programme which involves the community; and
11. make the community/society more responsible.

As can be seen for example, 'reduce re-offending' was certainly not considered as the most important aim of such a programme. One reason may be, as Maxwell and Morris (2001) explain, that it tends to be quite difficult to measure. Policy makers tend to think, and mostly want, to evaluate such programmes by taking as a reference whether conferencing affects re-offending (at least compared to traditional criminal justice). In most cases it is seen to do as well or slightly better than the traditional criminal justice system but as practitioners have shown there are many other 'selling' points for this programme, as important if not more so (Doherty 2010). It is clear from the survey that people running such programmes, on average, put it in the sixth place of their objectives. Re-offending seems clearly to be considered more as a side-effect of this type of programme and its focus is directed towards restoring ties in a society, giving the victim a voice, helping the offender to take responsibility for his/her crime, etc.

When looking at aims for the programmes through the specific lens of juvenile offenders, adult offenders, or programmes for both, we come to slightly different results. In the case of programmes dealing specifically with juvenile offenders, the most cited aims are (again in decreasing order and only the responses which were ticked at least by 75 per cent of the respondents):

1. provide an opportunity for the victim to ask questions and receive information from the offender;
2. provide an opportunity for the victim to receive reparation and/or an apology;
3. provide an opportunity for the victim's/offender's family or other people to participate;
4. increase the offender's sense of responsibility for the offence;
5. reach an agreement which is acceptable to all participants; and
6. reduce re-offending.

The aims which were chosen the least by these respondents are 'reduce the caseload of the court' and 'reduce financial costs'. This last aim may not be an important aim for those organizing such programmes but it actually is a reality. In Northern Ireland, for example, it was calculated that a conference is generally much cheaper than a traditional court case for a similar type of crime (see eg Doherty 2010; Zinsstag et al. 2011).

In the case of programmes dealing specifically with adult offenders, the chosen aims were:

1. provide an opportunity for the victim to ask questions and receive information from the offender;
2. provide an opportunity for the victim to receive reparation and/or an apology;
3. provide an opportunity for the victim to participate in a programme which involves the community;
4. increase the offender's sense of responsibility for the offence;
5. leave the victim/offender with a greater sense of satisfaction with the criminal justice system; and
6. reach an agreement which is acceptable to all participants.

The aims marked the least by these respondents are 'reduce the number of adult offenders in prisons' and 'make the community/society more responsible'.

What conclusions can be drawn from these results? What is the picture that emerges? A key conclusion concerns the important place allocated to victims and to their right to be given an explanation and reparation for the harm they have been subjected to. In addition it is also about the place given to the offender taking responsibility for his/her acts. Finally, a very important characteristic of a conferencing programme is that the family and generally the community of care is involved and has to take over some of the responsibility. These few points show how different this alternative justice programme is from traditional criminal justice (see eg Walgrave 2008) and how it differs even from other restorative justice programmes, as McCold (2000) argues, possibly rendering it the most restorative.

Types of cases

Another important characteristic to paint the portrait of conferencing, which the survey inquired about, is the type of cases which conferencing is able and willing to take on. What was interesting to discover was whether conferencing was used more in one type of crime or another, if there were crimes that could not be dealt with through this medium in terms of, for example, severity of the crime or types of victims. Figure 2.2 shows that the range of crime is very wide and conferencing can be used in almost all types of crime. The graph below shows how many of the 52 programmes we had responses from are able to deal with each type of crime. The decimal is the result of the grouping of some categories of crime; indeed when we asked the question in the survey there were more categories of crime available to the respondent than shown in the graph below.

The chart shows that conferencing can actually deal with any type of crime. That does not mean that all conferencing programmes deal with all the crimes cited in the table above. However, it is clear that the majority of crimes dealt with are crimes related to 'theft', followed by 'assault'. It is also interesting to note that 'domestic violence', 'disorderly public behaviour', 'handling stolen goods,' and 'wounding with intent' were all dealt with in about 50 per cent of the cases. Cases of murder are usually the

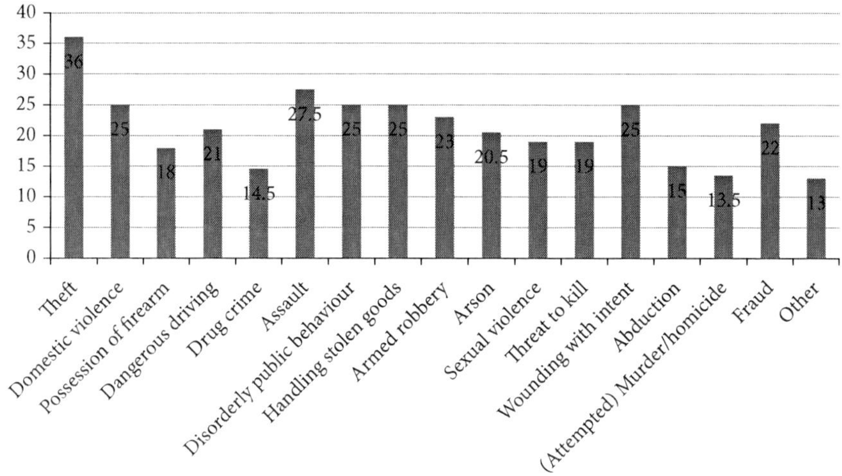

Figure 2.2 Type of cases that can be referred to a conference (n = 52)

only crime not dealt with in such a programme. Another interesting result of the survey was to discover that cases of sexual violence on adults can be referred to 18 programmes and cases of sexual assault on children can be referred to 20 programmes. That does not mean that these programmes deal with such cases on a regular basis, or frequently, but the possibility exists and is used.

The offenders

In the survey we had a number of questions concerning the offenders. We aimed at trying to understand who are the typical offenders referred to such a scheme and whether there was a preference from an institutional point of view.

From this chart (Figure 2.3) it follows that the majority of offenders who are referred to such a programme are juvenile offenders and in slightly fewer cases both juvenile and adult, but that there are very few programmes dealing only with adult cases. It is a fact that conferencing still tends to be considered as a justice programme directed in its majority to juveniles, as the legislation passed in New Zealand, Northern Ireland,

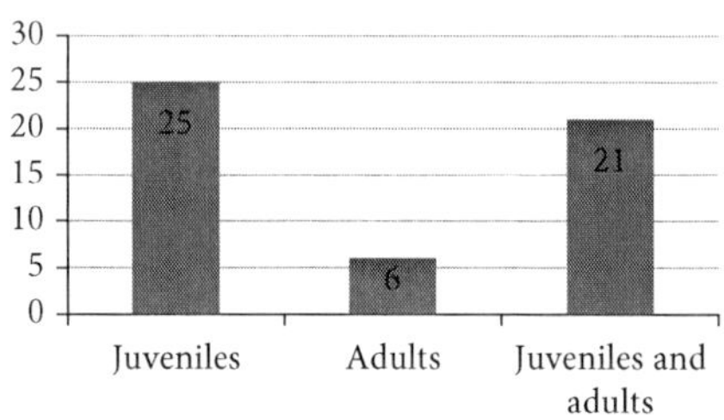

Figure 2.3 The participating offender (n = 52)

or Belgium illustrates. However during the interviews for the project on conferencing (Zinsstag et al. 2011), when the interviewees were asked whether they could imagine that the programme they were running or were commenting on could or should be run for adult offenders as well, the response was irremediably positive.

The referring authority

There are different ways for offenders to be referred to a conference, the survey reported on the three main ones: the police, the public prosecutor, and the court.

According to this chart (Figure 2.4) it is quite clear that in a majority of cases the police are able to refer cases in many programmes even if public prosecutors and judges seem to have an important role in at least half of the programmes. We considered also whether there was a difference between European countries as opposed to non-European countries in this matter and it is interesting to note that courts seem to be the main authority to refer cases in both cases, although the police and prosecution offices seem to play an important role in many cases as well, as shown in the following chart (Figure 2.5).

Furthermore we also approached the question of the referral by investigating whether the admission of guilt was an important factor for cases to be referred to conferencing. We inquired whether a case would generally be referred before or after that admission, and whether there was a difference on this point between civil and common law countries.

The results as shown in Figure 2.6 are quite telling on the latter point. In common law countries, in most cases, guilt has to be proven before the referral can be made

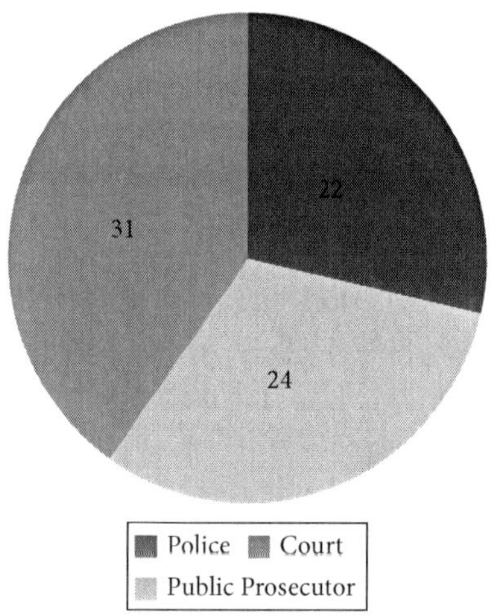

Figure 2.4 The referring authority in case of a conference (n = 52)[7]

[7] The number of respondents is 52 but respondents could give more than one answer and that is why the total of the responses represented in the graph is more than 52.

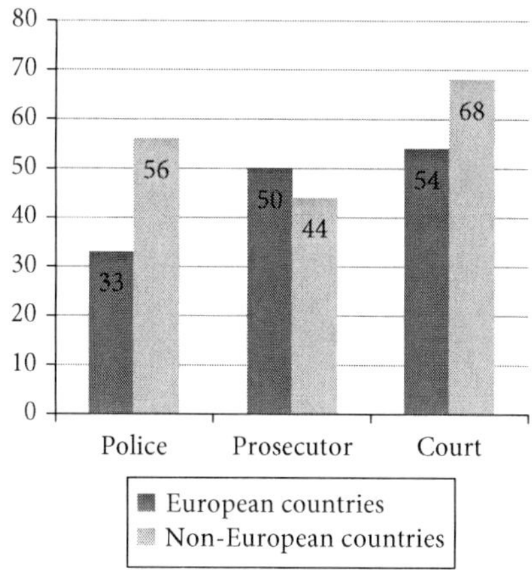

Figure 2.5 The referring authority in European (n = 24) and non-European countries (n = 25) (%)

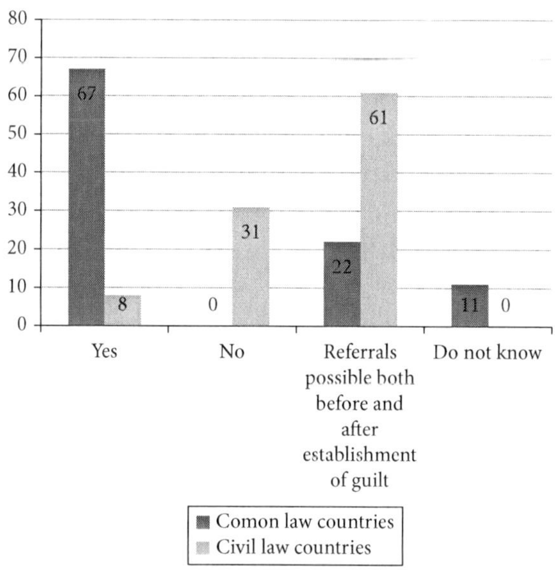

Figure 2.6 Does guilt have to be established for the court to make a referral, in civil law (n = 17) and common law countries (n = 12)? (%)

whereas in many civil law countries referrals can be done before and after the establishment of guilt.

The disparity between the two legal systems seems to be statistically significant ($x^2 = 7.091$; df = 1; $p<0.05$) when only the answers *yes* and *no* are looked at. This shows that there might be a link between whether the offender is found guilty or not *before* his/her possible referral and the country's legal system (common law or civil law).

THE CONFERENCE

The survey also inquired about a number of practical points concerning the running of conferences such as, for example, time limits and how they are regulated, how the parties are prepared, the number of conferences per offender or offences, or who can or has to participate, etc. I turn, next, to examine some of the most characteristic results, starting with who participates.

Participants

The survey tried to discover whether there is a clear distinction between who has to be there, without whom a conference would not take place, and who could be there but whose non-participation would not stop the programme from continuing. In addition it also tried to understand whose participation can be wished for and can be clearly beneficial. We also wanted to inquire about possible replacements: we have seen from the literature that typically the offender and the facilitators are the indispensable participants and victims are encouraged to attend. Other possible attendees may include supporters of the offender/victim, a police officer or police representative, a social worker, a probation officer or probation representative, a public prosecution office representative, a lawyer of the offender/victim, and a community representative. The responses to the survey's question of who 'has to participate' and who 'may participate' are summarized in Table 2.1.

Table 2.1 Possible participants [8] (n = 48)

	HAS to participate	MAY participate
Offender	45	27
Victim	29	35
Facilitator	47	26
Supporter offender	22	37
Supporter victim	14	41
Police officer	12	29
Social worker	5	38
Probation officer	5	26
Public prosecution office representative	1	12
Lawyer offender	4	25
Lawyer victim	1	25
Community representative	1	39
Do not know	1	2
Other	7	12

[8] The numbers in this table should be exclusive. For example: the number of respondents who say the offender *has* to participate and the number of respondents who say the offender *may* participate should add up to 48 (total number of respondents who answered this question). This is not the case, probably because this question was unclear to many of the respondents.

It is clear from Table 2.1 that the above mentioned participants in their great majority are not an indispensable component of the process and therefore do not *have* to take part in a conference, but only *may* participate. This means that despite a conference's aim to encourage that the most relevant people attend and take part in order to increase the chance to have a positive outcome, most programmes do not make their presence a prerequisite. It is a fact that the offender and the facilitator are generally the only ones whose participation is likely to be required if the process is to go forward. The only participants for whom participation is more likely to be required, rather than possible, for the conference to take place are the offender and the facilitator.

In the case of the victim it is less straightforward. In almost 30 programmes the victim also *has* to participate, but there are still more programmes where he/she only *may* participate. The fact is that, as came out from the interviews we conducted (see Zinsstag et al. 2011), there was a consensus that the victim should never be forced to participate and should be offered other ways to participate, should he/she wish to participate without attending physically, for example through a video or audio link or simply through a letter. They may also find a replacement (Figure 2.7) and as we have seen from our survey, this may be done by a number of people, although family, friends, and victim's organizations are clearly favoured.

All these different means to involve the victim in the procedure show that generally efforts are made to ensure that his/her side of the story is heard and that the questions that he/she may have concerning the offence are put forward. It is however clear from the interviews in particular (Zinsstag et al. 2011) that the physical presence of the victim has a special and generally positive effect on the offender and on the conference process itself and that it should be encouraged and strived for.

When we questioned our respondents on the effect of the participation of either the victim or the offender in the conference, the results are as is shown in Figure 2.8.

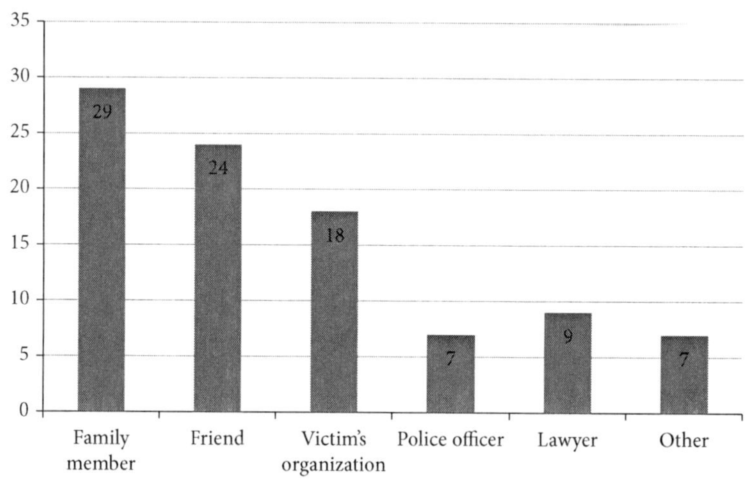

Figure 2.7 Who can replace the victim? (n = 31)

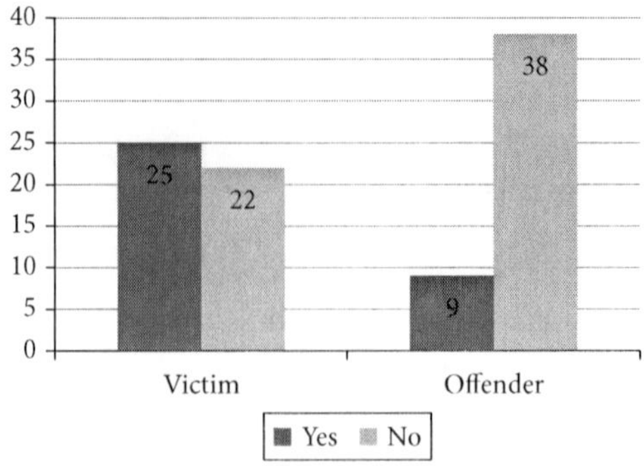

Figure 2.8 Will the conference take place if the victim or the offender is not able to or refuses to participate? (n = 47)

This chart clearly illustrates that about half of the programmes would go ahead with the conference, should the victim not participate, whereas there is a clear difference with the offender's participation. Indeed few programmes would go ahead if he/she is not present. It is interesting to consider then how a programme could go ahead without either a victim or an offender. It became clear from the results we obtained that it is fairly common for a victim to have someone represent him/her, either from his/her family or friends or from a victim's organization, as seen above, whereas it is very uncommon to have a representative for the offender. This is in line with the aims of conference, and restorative schemes more generally, which are directed at achieving a restorative process (see eg Shapland et al. 2011).

Supporters[9]

One of the characteristics of a conference is that the main participants, the offender and the victim, may bring a supporter to the proceedings. The person may be a family member or a friend or someone from social services or victim support services. These persons are there to support the person they came for. Who may come depends very much on the programme regulations. The survey's results are depicted by Figure 2.9.

The results make clear that the people who accompany the victim and the offender to a conference tend to be in the same category. They are mostly, as said above, family members or friends but may also be from social services or the community. Lawyers clearly do not have a preponderant position although in some programmes they are automatically included. There are differences for example between programmes only for juveniles where parents and siblings would be more common supporters and programmes for adults where partners may be chosen more systematically, so it is safe to say that the age of the participant very much influences the type of support network which would be organized for the conference.

[9] The word supporter can be used interchangeably with support person or support network, as the terminology depends on the programme.

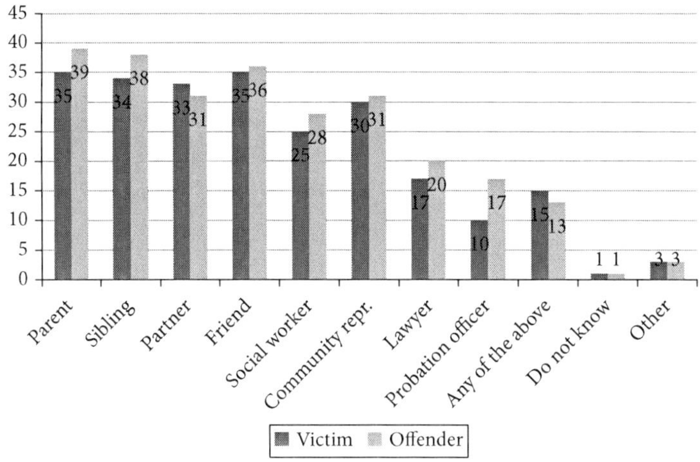

Figure 2.9 Supporters of the victim and the offender (n = 46)

The facilitator[10]

I would like to start this section by saying a few words about the training of facilitators as it is still very variable from one programme and one country to another. In the survey we were interested to understand whether specific training was provided for facilitators to be. The responses showed that the great majority of programmes offer specific training to their future facilitators (38 out of 44) and Figure 2.10 shows the main providers of that training.

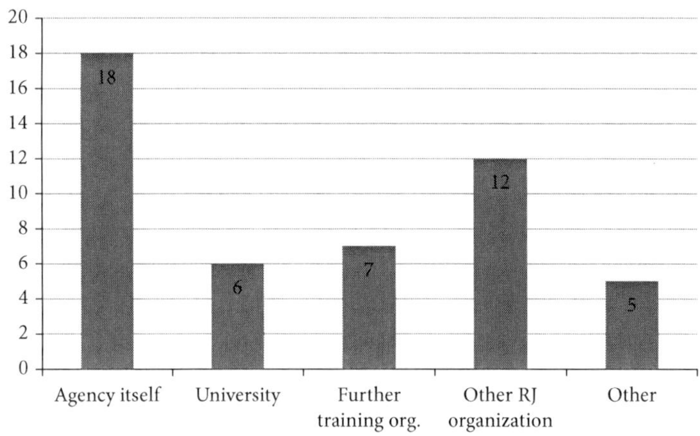

Figure 2.10 Training provided by... (n = 38)

[10] I call this person a facilitator because I think it is most representative of the function and that most conferencing programmes do so, but in I am aware that in some schemes this person may be called a mediator or a coordinator.

Although it is clear that training is provided, mostly by the agency running the programme itself or by another RJ organization, the extent and nature of the training tends to differ greatly (see the examples of Norway and Northern Ireland in Zinsstag et al. 2011). It is clear that in the majority of cases the training is provided before the facilitators start to work but in many organizations there seems to be on-going training. All these differences however may also have a great deal to do with the status of the said facilitator and his/her role in the programme, for instance the number of conferences he/she will have to take on per year, whether he/she has to do the preparation or the follow up, and so on.

When questioned on the topic of the facilitator's status, the responses very clearly showed that people feel quite strongly about what it should be, whether voluntary or paid. Indeed during the interviews for example it became clear that each of the programmes seemed to have very good reasons behind their choice of one or the other. The results, as Figure 2.11 shows, do go quite clearly in one direction: the majority of facilitators are paid employees.

One possible explanation for this result is that it may be explained by the type of conferencing scheme the person is working for, and the more institutionalized the scheme the more the facilitator's status would be established. Indeed the difference whether there is a legal basis for a programme or if the organization remains an non-government organization (NGO) or voluntary organization may have effects on the status of their staff, in particular facilitators, even if it does not follow automatically. But it is clear that in many cases it seems to be a reflected choice, whatever directions they have decided to follow.

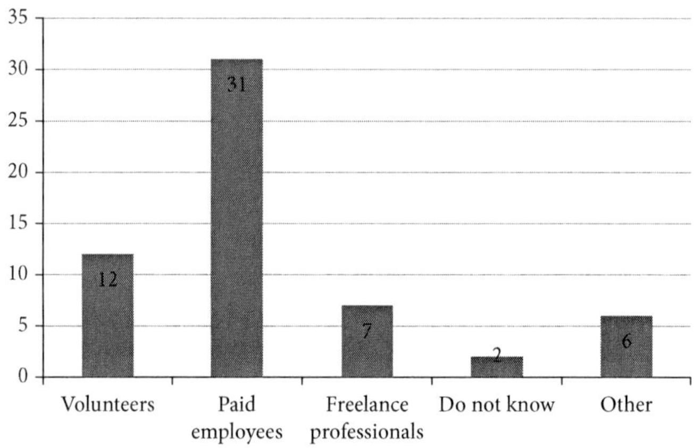

Figure 2.11 The status of facilitators (n = 44)

Preparation of the parties

When constructing the survey we were very interested in getting a precise image of what the preparation to a conference entailed, what participants may be prepared for, etc. We understood from the interviews and the literature that it may vary a great deal but also that it is of crucial importance as it can influence the participation rate, especially

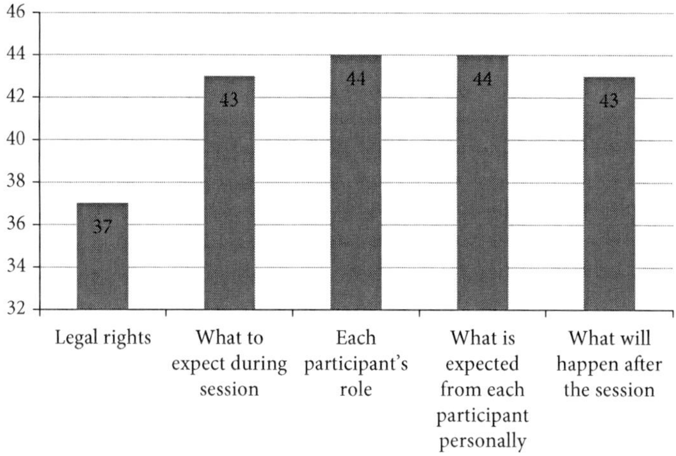

Figure 2.12 Areas where the facilitator prepares the parties (n = 47)

in the case of the victim. Indeed the more a victim understands what the conference is for, what can be gained from it, what are the dangers but also the positive outcomes which can result from it, the more he/she may change their mind concerning a possible participation. It also may help to avoid possible re-victimization. It is also crucial for the offender as it is the time where the rules of the procedure for the conference can be made clear. Indeed for all parties it is the time where the possible advantages and disadvantages can be clearly exposed and this may therefore influence greatly the actual running of the conference. Figure 2.12 shows the result.

This chart shows that the participants are prepared about most topics with a fairly equal focus, with legal rights getting slightly less emphasis.

THE AGREEMENT

Another important aspect which we inquired about in our survey was the outcome of a conference, such as, the number of agreements which have been reached and fulfilled, what they usually entail, who does the follow up, and whether the victims are informed of the progress and final outcome.

Agreements reached and fulfilled

At the end of a conference the aim of most programmes is to find an agreement between the different parties attending. It is mostly about finding acceptable ways for the offender to repair the harm he/she has done to the victim and the community, and to ensure or at least assist him/her in avoiding that it happens again. It could include, among other options, some community work, some anger management classes, an apology, or perhaps substance abuse treatments, etc. The fulfilment part is about whether the offender satisfactorily achieves what he/she has agreed to do. It is clear from the results of the survey (Figure 2.13) that a majority of the conferencing programmes represented in those results aim to reach an agreement (42 out of 46).

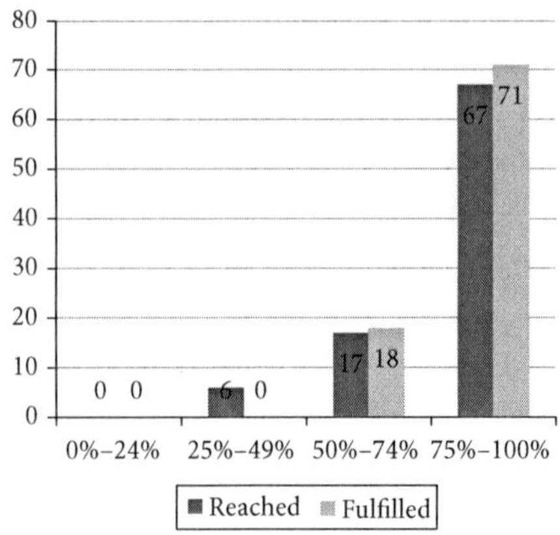

Figure 2.13 Agreements reached (n = 36) and fulfilled (n = 28) (%)

A majority of the programmes have rather good results regarding conferences which reach an agreement and those whose agreement is then completed. The respondents were indeed asked to estimate what percentage of their conferences achieves either of these results. About 70 per cent of the respondents declared that in over 75 per cent of the cases the conference achieves both agreement and its fulfilment.

The consequence of reaching an agreement

Another interesting aspect concerns the possible repercussions of a conference ending in an agreement between the parties. Indeed it may be positive for the offender, victim, and community but it may, depending on how formal the conferencing programme is, also have consequences for the referring authority. Indeed a prosecutor or judge who referred a case must generally be contacted once the conference has taken place, for him or her to agree or disagree with the agreement reached. The referring authority depending on the outcome may then come up with a number of possible decisions concerning the continuation of the case. Figure 2.14 shows the results of this particular set of questions to the respondents.

The results show that in a good half of the cases following an agreement, cases are either dismissed or passed on to a professional. A professional could be a probation officer, a social worker, the police, a victim organization representative, or someone from the conferencing programme, who will follow up the fulfilment of the agreement with the offender.[11] The survey showed that in the great majority of cases someone from the conferencing programme is assigned to the task, followed by a probation officer.

[11] There is a statistically significant relationship between the referral by the public prosecutor and the consequences dismissed ($x^2 = 4.049$; df = 1; $p<0.05$) and handed to a professional ($x^2 = 5.602$; $p = 0.018$). These relationships have a medium strength (Cramer's V = 0.374 and 0.431).

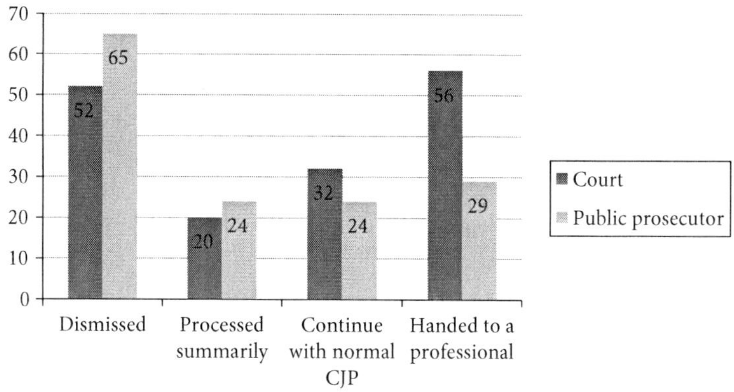

Figure 2.14 The possible legal consequences of reaching an agreement when the case was referred by the court (n = 25) or by the public prosecutor (n = 17) (%)

We were also interested in understanding what would happen from a judicial point of view if an agreement was not actually fulfilled once reached during a conference (Figure 2.15). In our analysis we divided the results between respondents from civil and common law systems since there seemed to be some differences between them.

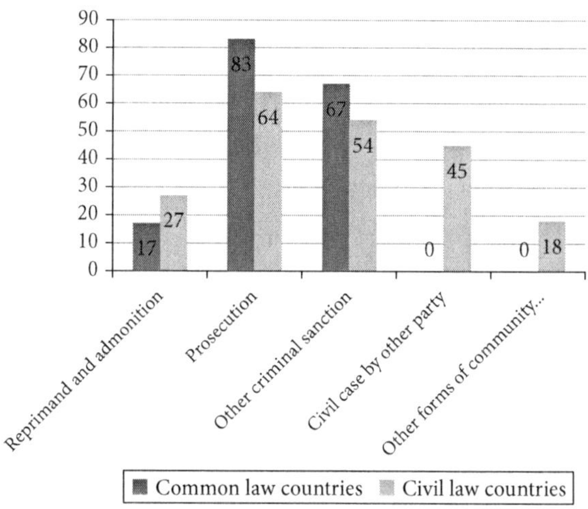

Figure 2.15 What are the possible legal consequences when the agreement is not fulfilled in common law (n = 6) and civil law countries (n = 11)? (%)

In the great majority of cases offenders who do not manage, or intend, to fulfil the agreement that was reached during a conference will be sent back to court. When looking at the results through the lens of the civil vs. common law distinction one can see that both prosecution and other criminal sanction are the most common consequences in both legal systems but in civil law countries there may be a number of other consequences and the results are more spread between them.

Informing the victim

In the survey we also inquired about whether a victim was kept informed about the progress of the offender in the fulfilment of the plan that was agreed at the end of the conference. We believed that to be an important aspect since it would make the process truly restorative, showing to the victim that he/she is part of the process as well as that the offender is keeping his/her promises, thus vindicating the effort to participate to the programme. Figure 2.16 shows the results of the survey concerning this point.

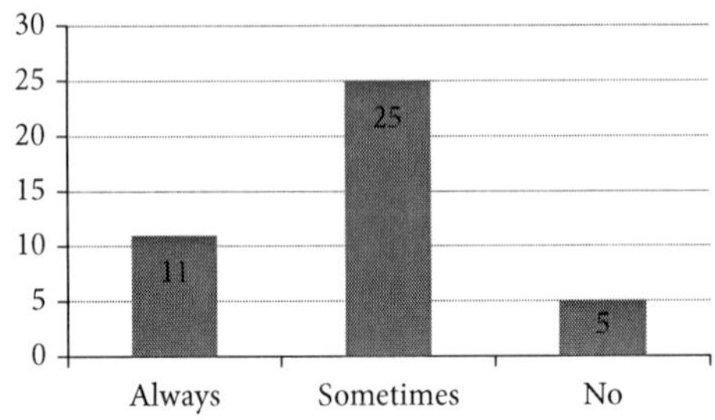

Figure 2.16 Is the victim periodically informed about the progress? (n = 45)

One could start reading the results by commenting that the majority of programmes do mostly inform victims and that only five do not. This is obviously a slightly worrying result but it does reflect the reality. Indeed when interviewing facilitators and programme managers for our research project, this was an area which was quite commonly designated as needing improvement.

CONCLUSION

In the last section we have highlighted some of the interesting results emerging from the survey conducted during the research project on conferencing which allows us to draw the outlines of what a conferencing programme, mostly used in cases of criminal offences, might look like and what it may contain.

We have seen that for the main aims of a conferencing programme to be respected and for it to remain 'truly' restorative it is crucial, for example, for the offender to take responsibility for his/her action, for it to be voluntary for both the offender and the victim, and for the community of care to take an active and constructive role in the process. In this way conferencing may be able to deal with a great variety of crimes ranging from some very low level crime up to sexual assault and attempted murder. The offenders are, in the majority of cases, still juvenile offenders although it is clear that this type of programme may be very well suited for adult offenders as well. Cases may be referred by judges, prosecutors, but also the police. We have also seen that conferences may be attended by a number of people in addition to the main protagonists in a crime, including supporters and representatives of the community. Finally, we have seen that most programmes have the aim to reach an agreement between the parties in the conference and that this agreement will be followed up until it is fulfilled.

Some of the main conclusions of the survey are that it is clear that practice is much more advanced than theory, the latter in many cases is still attempting to find definitions and to classify activities, when in practice 'pure' conferencing does not exist, for, as this volume amply demonstrates, in many parts of the world mediation and conferencing come most often in a mixed form in order to respond to the specific demands at hand.

Indeed conferencing is a developing restorative justice practice and, as we have seen within the last 20 years, it has been spreading rapidly, if unevenly, across countries and continents. In some countries it remains unknown, some pilots have been put in place but no funding or political will has been present to give it a firmer standing. In other countries it has become an integral part of the justice system and still in some others it remains, and will continue remaining, a local, bottom-up initiative, done by communities for communities.

REFERENCES

Braithwaite, J. and Braithwaite, V. (2001), 'Shame, Shame Management and Regulation', in Ahmed, E., Harris, N., Braithwaite, J. and Braithwaite, V. (eds.), *Shame Management Through Reintegration* (Cambridge: Cambridge University Press), pp 3–58.

Christie, N. (1977), 'Conflicts as Property', *British Journal of Criminology*, 17(1), pp 1–15.

Connolly, M. and McKenzie, M. (1999), *Effective Participatory Practice: Family Group Conferencing in Child Protection* (New York: Aldine de Gruyter).

Cunneen, C. and Hoyle, C. (2010), *Debating Restorative Justice* (Oxford: Hart Publishing).

Doherty, K. (2010), 'The Development of Restorative Justice in Northern Ireland', in Taylor, W., Earle, R. and Hester, R. (eds.), *Youth Justice Handbook: Theory, Policy and Practice* (Cullompton: Willan Publishing), pp 243–51.

Harris, N. (2003), 'Evaluating the Practice of Restorative Justice: The Case of Family Group Conferencing', in Walgrave, L. (ed.), *Repositioning Restorative Justice* (Cullompton: Willan Publishing), pp 121–35.

Marshall, T. (1996), 'Criminal Mediation in Great Britain 1980–1996', *European Journal on Criminal Policy and Research*, 4(4), pp 21–43.

Maxwell, G. and Morris, A. (2001), 'Family Group Conferences and Reoffending', in Morris, A. and Maxwell, G. (eds.), *Restorative Justice for Juveniles: Conferencing, Mediation and Circles* (Oxford: Hart Publishing), pp 243–63.

McCold, P. (2000), 'Toward a Holistic Vision of Restorative Juvenile Justice: A Reply to the Maximalist Model', *Contemporary Justice Review*, 3(4), pp 357–414.

McCold, P. (2001), 'Primary Restorative Justice Practices', in Morris, A. and Maxwell, G. (eds.), *Restorative Justice for Juveniles: Conferencing, Mediation and Circles*, (Oxford: Hart Publishing), pp 41–58.

McCold, P. (2007), 'The Recent History of Restorative Justice', in Sullivan, D. and Tifft, L. (eds.), *Handbook of Restorative Justice* (Oxon: Routledge), pp 23–51.

McCold, P. and Wachtel, T. (2002), 'Restorative Justice Theory Validation', in Weitecamp, E. and Kerner, H.-J. (eds.), *Restorative Justice: Theoretical Foundations* (Cullompton: Willan Publishing), pp 110–42.

Moore, D. and McDonald, J. (2000), 'Guiding Principles of the Conferencing Process', in Burford, G. and Hudson, J. (eds.), *Family Group Conferencing: New Directions in Community-Centered Child and Family Practice* (Piscataway: Transaction Publishers), pp 49–64.

Raye, B. and Roberts, A. (2007), 'Restorative Processes', in Johnstone, G. and Van Ness, D. (eds.), *Handbook of Restorative Justice* (Cullompton: Willan Publishing), pp 211–27.

Shapland, J., Aertsen, I., Doherty, K., Teunkens, M., Vanfraechem, I., Van Pagée, R. and Zinsstag, E. (2011), *Conferencing: A Way Forward for Restorative Justice—A Practical Guide* (Leuven: European Forum for Restorative Justice).

Shapland, J., Robinson, G. and Sorsby, A. (2011), *Restorative Justice in Practice: Evaluating What Works for Victims and Offenders* (London: Routledge).

Van Ness, D. and Heetderks Strong, K. (2010), *Restoring Justice: An Introduction to Restorative Justice* (4th edn) (Cincinnati: Anderson).

Van Ness, D., Morris, A. and Maxwell, G. (2001), 'Introducing Restorative Justice', in Morris, A. and Maxwell, G. (eds.), *Restorative Justice for Juveniles: Conferencing, Mediation and Circles* (Oxford: Hart Publishing), pp 3–16.

Walgrave, L. (2008), *Restorative Justice, Self-Interest and Responsible Citizenship* (Cullompton: Willan Publishing).

Zehr, H. (2002), *The Little Book of Restorative Justice* (Intercourse: Good Books).

Zinsstag, E., Teunkens, M. and Pali, B. (2011), *Conferencing: A Way Forward for Restorative Justice in Europe?* Report to the European Commission (Leuven: European Forum for Restorative Justice).

3

THE NEED FOR CLARITY ABOUT RESTORATIVE JUSTICE CONFERENCES

Lode Walgrave

CONFERENCING IS A SUCCESS STORY (AS A STORY!)

Conferencing is a crucial practice of restorative justice. The introduction of family group conferences (FGC) in the New Zealand Children, Young Persons and their Families Act (1989) was considered a great success. Since then, restorative conferences have spread all over the world, in different versions and with varying scope (Umbreit and Zehr 1996; Dignan 2005). They have been called different names, such as 'diversionary conferences', 'youth justice conferences', 'real justice conferences', 'community conferences', etc. In Belgian law they are called, in Dutch, *Herstelgericht Groepsoverleg* and, in French, *Conférences Restauratrices en Groupe*. A much used common denomination is 'restorative conferences'. They exist in different legal statuses and regimes. Most conferences are organized as a form of diversion at police level or public prosecutor's level; sometimes they are facilitated by a police officer, as a kind of caution to the young offender; some conferences address the welfare problems of the young offender more than the victims' genuine needs.

The conferencing model is also used in other social contexts, such as for addressing disciplinary problems in school or welfare problems. In this chapter, I do not speak of these 'extensions of restorative justice', as I have called them elsewhere (Walgrave 2008). For a number of reasons, I focus here on restorative justice conferences meant to deal with the aftermath of an offence.

There is no doubt that conferencing is a success story within restorative justice. But it is a story. In 2002, Daly (2002) wrote a much quoted article 'Restorative justice: the real story'. My position is that the real story of conferencing in restorative justice is that there is not just one story; and that it is crucial to be aware of that and to take into account the differences.

EMPIRICAL EVIDENCE NOT TOTALLY CONVINCING, SOMETIMES CONTRADICTORY

The results of research on restorative justice practices and on restorative conferencing are often mixed and ambiguous. It shows that a more nuanced and differentiated view of restorative conferencing practice is needed. Victims' satisfaction, for example, seems to be a constant finding after conferences, but this general finding hides the observation that a considerable minority of victims are not at all better off after a conference, or are even more in distress after it (Daly 2005; Pemberton et al. 2007).

While reoffending is not the first concern of restorative justice, the bottom line is that restorative justice interventions should not provoke more reoffending than traditional interventions. And the general trend is indeed that recidivism seems to drop after conferencing, but the results are far from being triumphant. Sherman and Strang (2007), for example, conclude their survey of randomized controlled trials that the (mostly police-led) conferences significantly reduced repeat offending among violent offenders under 30 years of age in Canberra, but produced little or no difference among violent males under 18 years in Northumbria. A significant reduction was found among male property offenders under 18 in Northumbria, but little or no difference among property offenders under 18 in Canberra.

A few restorative justice schemes seem to increase reoffending, compared with traditional criminal justice sentencing (Latimer et al. 2001). Sherman and Strang (2007) noted more re-arrests among young Aboriginals for property offences in Canberra, and refer to comparable (but non-significant) observations among young Hispanics in Bethlehem (Pennsylvania) (McCold and Wachtel 1998).

'Good outcomes depend on good practice', Maxwell (2007: 65) summarizes. Shapland et al. (2008) found a significant relationship between less reconviction and the adult offenders' appreciation of the conference (the offenders are made to realize the harm done, the offender was actively involved in the conference, the offender felt the conference was useful). Less reoffending was observed after FGCs that were experienced as 'fair, forgiving, allowing to make up for what they had done and not stigmatizing or excluding them' (Maxwell et al. 2004: 214). When the offender expressed remorse and a consensus was reached, conferences were more effective (Maxwell and Morris 1999; Hayes and Daly 2003). It is not clear, however, whether remorse is provoked by the quality of the conference, or is part of a compliant attitude of the offender which existed prior to the conference: '... where offenders have decided to try to stop offending, a conference can increase motivation to desist (because of what victims and offender supporters said) and provide the support offenders may need to help tackle problems relating to their offending' (Shapland et al. 2008: iv).

THE NEED FOR CLARITY

Parts of these puzzling disparities in the results may be due to the blurring of restorative justice and conferencing in restorative justice literature. Important evaluation studies call police-led conferences simply 'conferences', as if the type of the facilitator did not matter. Surveys name all encounters in a restorative context as 'conferences', including mediation practices and even reparative boards in one notion, as if meeting with a victim alone or with the community of care and being confronted with a board composed of (benevolent) citizens were all the same. Family group conferencing is identified with restorative justice as a whole, as if no other practices were important in restorative justice. Such blurring is detrimental for the development of restorative justice in practice, the quality of restorative justice research, and for the credibility of restorative justice in policy.

Research needs clear definitions of the research object. If there is no view on the variety and complexity of possible restorative processes or of practices in restorative conferencing, conclusions on one practice cannot address the restorative justice practice or the conferencing model as a whole. Mingling all in one notion makes it impossible to distinguish which elements are decisive and which are superficial. If reflection on restorative justice does not differentiate sufficiently among different practices, good practices will be mixed with bad practices, so that it will never be possible to correct what went wrong and to indicate which practice is successful. It will be impossible to link particular problems with specific types of conferencing.

Policy makers need to know exactly what they are involved in. Accuracy and modesty in what can be achieved in the communication aimed towards them and towards the public will increase credibility more than general and vague stories that always end happily.

The currently dominant question is whether restorative justice works or not. It is like asking whether medicine cures diseases or not. More specifically, the question whether restorative conferencing works or not is like asking whether medication cures diseases or not. We must be clearer about the different models and versions, the objectives, and the quality of the implementation. The question is not whether 'restorative justice conferences do work or not', but 'which model of restorative justice conferences may work for what purposes and under what conditions'. We obviously need to become more accurate, more detailed, and more differentiated. In restorative justice conferences, differentiation is to be considered along several lines.

MODELS AND VERSIONS

Conferences exist in many different models and versions.

MEDIATION/CONFERENCING

Literature mostly speaks of mediation and conferencing. Both seem to be clearly different practices. But what actually distinguishes them? Literature in fact is limited in discussing the characteristics that would distinguish mediation from conferencing, and the potentials and risks of each of them. Maybe this is because many countries so far offer only one of either mediation or conferencing. Mediation is largely predominant on the European continent, and conferencing has the monopoly in Australia and

New Zealand. When both are possible, the reason for distinction is unclear. In the Belgian Youth Justice Act of 2006, for example, only mediation is possible at the level of public prosecution, while both mediation and conferencing can be proposed at the court's level (Put et al. 2012). This option is based on a preceding pilot project, where this distinction was made on practical and intuitive grounds (Vanfraechem and Walgrave 2004).

Many mediation programmes with juvenile offenders also include the parents of the juvenile; conferences that bring together only the young offender and (one of) his/her parents with the victim are not exceptional. In fact, many versions of conferencing can be considered as extended mediations, including the communities of care in the deliberation (see also Eriksson in Chapter 13). Their 'plus value' is that the involvement of the social network may help to strengthen the positive consequences of the deliberation. But such conferences also have more or less the same limitations as mediation. Indeed, victim-offender mediation deals with the dispute between the victim and the offender only, whereas settling the aftermath of a crime should also include concern for its public dimensions. Moreover, mediation is excluded when the victim refuses any cooperation. This is not necessarily the case in conferences. In New Zealand, for example (and also in the practice in Flanders), the conference also proceeds when the victim remains absent.

FAMILY GROUP CONFERENCING

In my view, there are reasons to believe that the original New Zealand model offers a particular 'plus value' which distinguishes it clearly from the other—mostly diversionary—models. Family group conferencing (FGC), as carried out in New Zealand, has particular characteristics which allow it to have a broader scope than most other conferencing models (MacRae and Zehr 2004; Vanfraechem 2006). First, FGC is procedurally located at the heart of the public response to crime. Whereas most of the restorative justice conferences are seen as diversionary practices, the New Zealand Children Young Persons and their Families Act makes it obligatory to try to set up an FGC before the court can take any sanction. FGC is thus not a diversionary offer, but fully integrated in the court proceedings.

The second particularity is probably the most crucial difference with mediation: police officers are present in the conference in the typical roles of informant and guardian of public order. This is unique. In other conferencing models, the police act as the facilitator of the conference, which is conceived as a version of police cautioning; or the police presence may be facultative or even not really promoted. The position of the police presence in its proper role brings in the public dimension of the issue to be debated. It makes clear to all participants that the state also has a stake in the consequences of the offence and has an interest in finding a constructive solution to the injustice committed.

Third, lawyers are invited to attend the conference (and the youth advocates mostly do), which offers an additional guarantee for legal safeguards. This is especially important in FGC for serious cases, because they may lead to severe deprivation of liberties.

These particular characteristics enable the original FGC model to deal with serious cases also. Morris (2002) estimates that the most serious youth offences—comprising 15 to 20 per cent of all youth offences—are dealt with through FGC, while the remaining less serious offences are dealt with through cautions or diversion by the police. These particularities are the reasons why the 2006 Belgian Youth Justice Act has opted to preserve conferencing at the level of the court, where the most serious offences are presented (Put et al. 2012). Belgians clearly have opted for copying, as much as possible, the New Zealand model.

Distinguishing the New Zealand model of conferencing from the other conferencing models is in my view crucial because it is, more than the other models, one of the most powerful experiences in support of seeing restorative justice as a maximalist option. Contrary to a diversionist version of restorative justice, the maximalist version has ambitions to replace the current 'punitive apriorism' in criminal justice with a 'restorative apriorism' (Bazemore and Walgrave 1999). In the longer term, penal justice should change drastically into a restorative justice system. Consequently, it is also necessary to present restorative responses to serious crimes and to include it completely within a legal framework (Walgrave 2008). Until recently, the New Zealand model was the only one to respond to these conditions.

POLICE IN CONFERENCING

Conferences may be led by different types of facilitators. In the FGC formula, youth justice coordinators convene and monitor the conference. They are social professionals, who specialize in organizing such conferences. This option has also been adopted in several other countries and districts. In other situations, police officers lead the conference, as a form of caution for—mostly—relatively benign offences or first offenders. The difference between both options is not without consequences.

It is a matter of debate whether police should lead conferences (Braithwaite 1994; Shapland 2009; Young 2001). On the one hand, it is argued that it fits well into the vision of community-oriented policing to work towards restoring or preserving peace in the community. Moreover, the monitoring role of the police seems to enhance feelings of safety among the possible participants. On the other hand, it is feared that police officers leading a conference may have difficulties leaving their typical role of threatening with coercion and may over-dominate the conference in ways that are not in line with the restorative philosophy and the methodology of genuine conferencing. Of course, facilitating a conference can be taught and the way it is carried out also depends on personal capacities and sensitiveness. I personally attended several police-led youth diversionary conferences in Canberra and I appreciated very much how the police officer monitored the processes.

But there are reasons to be sceptical about the adequacy of the police structure and mission to consider facilitating a conference as a mainstream task for police officers. For example, it is interesting to consider here the earlier mentioned finding that ethnic minorities seem to reoffend more after a police-led conference than after a traditional judicial procedure (Sherman and Strang 2007). My hypothesis is that the increases were a direct consequence of the police facilitation of the conference. If ethnic minorities have poor relations with police, which is often the case, police-led conferences may provoke more defiance than compliance. Therefore, you cannot, as the surveyors did, conclude that 'restorative justice' may be less adequate for ethnic minorities, but only that it may be not recommendable that police lead the conferences with ethnic minorities.

Another issue with regard to police in conferencing is whether the police should be present in a conference at all. As mentioned, police officers participate in the New Zealand FGCs in their typical police role. Intuitively, I think this is a good option, especially when the conference deals with serious youth crime where the public dimension is more at stake. Vanfraechem (2006) explored the conferencing practice in the Belgian pilot project, which is a close copy of the New Zealand practice. She found that the great majority of the participants appreciated the police presence. They found it useful. The victims in particular esteemed the police's role in clarifying the facts and some felt more secure due to the police's presence. But this aspect should be explored more deeply and more systematically.

VOLUNTEERS

Some restorative justice programmes rely on volunteers to facilitate restorative conferences. Restorative justice literature has, since its beginning, promoted the active involvement of the local community in restorative justice encounters. Volunteering community representatives are invited into conferences, or take a seat in citizens' boards dealing with (youth) offending in a restorative way. Relying on volunteers to facilitate conferences raises a tension between two reasonable concerns. On the one hand, it is a worthwhile pursuit to commit the community in the search for a constructive and restorative response to an offence (conflict, injustice) which occurred in its midst. It may encourage citizens to take their citizenship seriously and promote inclusive peace in the community. On the other hand, facilitating a conference must be done with all the methodical skills that are indispensable to do this. It is quite something different to set up and monitor a conference than to organize a party with neighbours.

The combination of both concerns is not self-evident. It provokes many doubts and questions. Where more methodical skills are needed, the less chance there is that one can leave conferencing to volunteers. The more volunteers are trained in methods and the more they gradually build experience, the less they remain real volunteers and risk turning into unpaid professionals. Moreover, it is not really clear why people who are trained and are paid for their work cannot be at the same time committed members of their community. Inversely, there is no guarantee that unpaid people being motivated and able to facilitate conferences do really represent the community in which the offence has occurred.

In short, there may be good reasons to refer to volunteering members of the community in dealing with the aftermath of crime (Claes and Van Daele 2011), but it may degrade into a 'sloganesque' rhetoric and lead to bad practice if it is not justified better and examined thoroughly. It must be examined whether conferences led by volunteers have at least the same quality as professionally led conferences do, whether they really enhance the commitment of the wider community, and to which types of problems and under what conditions these results apply.

INTRINSIC QUALITY OF PROCESS

As in prevention and in treatment programmes, a great variety exists in the quality of the restorative justice processes. There are brilliant performers and awful bunglers. Probably, an important part of the variety in the results of restorative justice research is due to the variety in the intrinsic quality with which processes are monitored. I do not know of any research that includes 'quality' as a variable. There is agreement that an adequate selection and training of facilitators is needed, as well as a permanent, critical follow up of the practices carried out. This also applies in cases when volunteers are involved. But to set up such trainings and to orient the follow up of the practices, one must have a clear view on what a good practice is. The training that we organized to start our pilot project with conferencing in the New Zealand-style for serious youthful offending was quite different from the training that is offered by the Echt Recht (Real Justice) organization in the Netherlands.[1] Another question relates to what 'good practice' entails? To decide upon this, one needs a good view on how restorative justice conferences may work and why (and what type of problems the restorative justice conference addresses). This view has to be based on experience, research, but also on good theoretical reflection. Theoretical explanations are needed to orient practice and to evaluate it more accurately. Unfortunately, evaluation research on restorative justice practice which is oriented by theoretical presuppositions is relatively scarce. So far, most research on restorative justice has tried to find out *whether* such processes work, rather than *why* or *how* they may work. It brought McCold (2003: 106) to conclude that 'research on restorative justice practice is a mile wide, but only an inch deep.' From the rich fund of theories on human and criminal behaviour and its treatment, some hypotheses can be advanced to speculate about why and how restorative justice might work as it does. Firstly, since Braithwaite and Mugford's article 'Conditions of Successful Reintegration Ceremonies' (1994), reintegrative shaming theory has been one of the most quoted and used theories to try to understand what is going on in restorative conferences. Since then, several criticisms have challenged the original version of the theory. First, the centrality of the shame emotion in restorative encounters has been nuanced and completed. Other (moral) emotions and dynamics, such as guilt, remorse, and empathy, seem to play an equally important role (Walgrave and Aertsen 1996; Morris 2002; van Stokkom 2002). Secondly, it has been recognized that shame, as such, does not necessarily lead to compliance. That is why later versions have completed the reintegrative shaming concept: it is not shame as such, but 'acknowledged shame', that is the constructive emotion which may lead to accepting responsibility and being prepared to comply (Braithwaite and Braithwaite

[1] That does not mean that one is better than the other. Both may very well apply to the type of problems they want to address.

2001). Thirdly, reintegrative shaming theory focuses on what happens to the offender. Because restorative processes are focused at least as much on emotional and other benefits to the victim, reintegrative shaming is too limited in scope. Programmes relying too exclusively on reintegrative shaming theory risk being less restoration-oriented, and may use victims as 'shamers' or 'props', instead of genuinely focusing on the victims' needs.

It is, however, difficult to avoid an offender feeling shame, if he is personally confronted with the rejection of what he did, as in conferencing or mediation. To reduce the risk that shame remains unacknowledged, the social-emotional climate of the experience is crucial. This is where the theory of procedural justice comes in (Tyler 1990). Procedural justice focuses on the subjective sense of being treated fairly, with respect and equity, being taken seriously, and being listened to by the authorities. It brings about a shift from the motivation to avoid punishment by an external power towards an internal motivation to comply with a legitimate authority. The characteristics of a restorative justice meeting offer better conditions for the stakeholders to feel such procedural justice than traditional court proceedings (Strang 2002; Tyler 2006).

In addition to being treated fairly, the experienced support and confidence of the loved ones provides a strong platform for a new start. Bazemore and Schiff (2005) believe that victims and offenders who can rely on on-going relationships of informal control and support will benefit from a conference. The idea recalls Hirschi's theory of social bonds (1969), especially the attachment bond. There are indeed reasons to believe that a successful conference may help tighten social bonds, so that they are an informal social platform for reparation and for social reintegration afterwards.

If participants experience procedural justice and feel supported by their informal network, shame can be acknowledged and can become reintegrative. For offenders, it may be the starting point for reconstructing their identity in a more socially conformable version. Maruna (2001) found that desistance from further criminality depends most of all on the opportunity to 'make good', meaning to reform the conception of the self as a social-norm-compliant person. Maruna also presents restorative conferences as redemption rituals and sees the opportunity to repair what has been done wrong as a major chance to build a new identity.

Strang et al. (2006) advance a theoretical approach concerning the victim. Cognitive behavioural therapy offers the victims an opportunity to be shown that they were not responsible for what happened to them. The researchers believe that restorative justice encounters present a context wherein the victim can relive and confront the victimization in a safe and respectful climate, which may help to reduce the post-traumatic stress. Strang et al. (2006) also refer to Collins' theory on Interaction Rituals (Collins 2004), which may help to understand the socio-emotional dynamics of a restorative conference. In this theory, interaction rituals are meetings characterized by four features: (1) participants are physically present and influenced by proximity; (2) participation is clearly defined as distinguished from non-participation; (3) all participants focus on a common target; and (4) are moved by a common emotional mood. Restorative encounters clearly respond to these characteristics. Interaction rituals may provoke 'collective effervescence', a high emotional intensity which drags the emotions to be focused on the common goal. It can be applied to the intensive emotional dynamics in a restorative process and help to explain why they so often lead to constructive satisfying outcomes, including apologies and forgiveness. It is these kinds of theoretical presuppositions or hypotheses that may help to understand how restorative conferences may work. It should orient research to check whether it really works as expected and under what conditions. It should orient selection and training of facilitators so that they become more than just good, willing persons, but also well-focused, goal-oriented guiders of processes.

OBJECTIVES

We act or take initiatives with a view to achieve a goal. To improve the action, we need to be sure which objective we are pursuing. To evaluate, clear objectives are indispensable evaluation criteria. To convince policy makers, well defined objectives are promised achievements. That also applies to restorative justice. To implement, to evaluate, and to promote restorative justice in practice, we must be clear about the goals we promise to achieve.

'Restorative justice' means 'justice that restores'. Restoration is an outcome pursued by restorative justice.[2] Defining and measuring restoration is however a challenge that has not been met easily so far. Traditional criminal justice or treatment interventions aim at the offender. Hence, their standard of success is easy to define (yet, not always easy to measure accurately): reoffending must decrease. But as restorative justice does not aim primarily at the offender but at the harm to be repaired, the first standard of success cannot target the offender and his reoffending; it must indicate the degree of reparation of harm, suffering, and social unrest. Material compensation is only a part of it. How to measure psychological, relational, or social restoration? Literature mentions some indications, such as decreasing post-traumatic stress syndrome in victims, as an indication of the degree to which victims have got over their victimization (Sherman and Strang 2007).

Satisfaction of the participants is one of the most researched variables in assessments of restorative justice. While this may seem too superficial and general a concept, it is an important one (Van Ness and Schiff 2001). Because restorative processes put the decision on how to repair the harm in the hands of the direct stakeholders, it is logical to look for subjective criteria that express their feelings. Satisfaction does not mean that they are completely happy or enthusiastic. It is to be understood in relation to what they expected. Satisfaction is often a kind of relief, because the event went better than they feared. Moreover, satisfaction is a container concept that covers a broad diversity of feelings and subjective evaluations, such as the fact that the victimization is taken seriously, that they have been listened to respectfully, and that their own opinion has been taken into account, a feeling of 'procedural justice', the feeling that

[2] Some scholars would resist the idea of 'outcomes' in restorative justice. I have explained elsewhere why I consider restorative justice unavoidably through an outcome based definition (Walgrave 2008: 16–24).

the offender has apologized sincerely, etc. Many projects investigate such elements separately.

Apart from satisfaction, and its components, as indications of subjective contentment, external checks are also needed. The juridical quality of the process is investigated insufficiently, as it should appear through, for example, the rights of the stakeholders and proportionality of the reparative effort in relation to the seriousness of harm (Walgrave 2002). Also reoffending is an external criterion. Influencing the offender is a derived effect of the primary objective to repair, but it must be researched. If more reoffending were observed, the additional harm to peace and safety in community would be contrary to the pursued restoration. Moreover, increased reoffending after restorative processes would be detrimental to the public and political acceptability of restorative justice.

Restorative justice ambitions (or pretentions) are wide and multiple. Bazemore and Schiff (2005) distinguish immediate, intermediate, and long term outcomes. I would rather distinguish four evaluation phases: (1) the quality of the process (respect for rights, mutual respect of stakeholders, empowerment, participation, etc.); (2) the feelings immediately after the process (procedural justice, satisfaction, mutual image of victims and offenders, etc.); (3) evaluation after the execution of the reparative plan (carried out correctly or not, feeling of 'being restored' in the victim, self-image and prospects of the offender, etc.); and (4) in the longer term (reoffending, experiences of victims, etc.). Not all criteria are equally important. Distinction is to be made between indispensable preconditions (respect for human rights), hard core reparation (assessable reparation or compensation of concrete damage and suffering), wider restorative effects (subjective feelings of peace, reintegration of victim and offender, feelings of safety in the local community, etc.), and impact on a wider community and institutional level (growing confidence in restorative justice dealing with offending, extension of restorative model of conflict resolution towards other fields of social life, etc.).

NEED FOR A SECOND GENERATION PROGRAMME OF RESEARCH ON RESTORATIVE JUSTICE

Clarity of concepts and of practices examined is crucial for good research. If clarity is lacking, research is doomed to be blurred by inaccurate research designs, sloppy variables, and impressionistic results. Clarity is also essential for good practice. It must lead to more nuanced indications about what model may work for what problem under what conditions. What are the potentials of conferencing in the FGC-style compared to the 'Real Justice' model? Why are some victims so distressed after conferences? How does one ensure that conferences are facilitated as they are meant to be? These and other questions transcend the rough 'conference' idea as it is predominantly used nowadays. Clarity is indispensable to get credibility in policy. The lack of clarity in conception has made restorative justice vulnerable to scepticism which is based on a misconception or an overly reduced understanding; some criticisms address practices which are in fact caricatures of restorative justice. It is difficult to respond to such wrong understandings and to convince interested policy makers and justice professionals if the response cannot itself rely on a clear conception.

It is therefore time to start up a second generation programme of research on restorative justice practice and on restorative justice conferencing. In comparison to the first generation of research, this new programme must be: (1) more differentiated according to several variables (position in legal and institutional context, the role of the police, type of offenders and victims dealt with, participation rate of victims, process management, quality of implementation, etc.); (2) more steered by theory on the conditions, potentials, and risks of restorative justice processes, based on precise analyses of relevant characteristics and differences in restorative justice conferences, the possible social-psychological dynamics and moral emotions; and (3) including more close observation of actual processes in restorative justice conferences. Therefore the predominant quantitative approach of the first generation research programmes is to be complemented by more qualitative accounts of what really happens in such restorative justice conferences.

REFERENCES

Bazemore, G. and Schiff, M. (2005), *Juvenile Justice Reform and Restorative Justice* (Cullompton: Willan Publishing).

Bazemore, G. and Walgrave, L. (1999), 'Restorative Juvenile Justice: In Search of Fundamentals and an Outline for Systemic Reform', in Bazemore, G. and Walgrave, L. (eds.), *Restorative Justice for Juveniles: Repairing the Harm of Youth Crime* (Monsey: Criminal Justice Press), pp 45–74.

Braithwaite, J. (1994), 'Thinking Harder about Democratizing Social Control', in Alder, C. and Wundersitz, J. (eds.), *Family Conference in Juvenile Justice: The Way Forward or Misplaced Optimism?* (Canberra: Australian Institute of Criminology), pp 199–216.

Braithwaite, J. and Braithwaite, V. (2001), 'Shame, Shame Management and Regulation', in Ahmed, E., Harris, N., Braithwaite, J. and Braithwaite, V. (eds.), *Shame Management Through Reintegration* (Cambridge: Cambridge University Press), pp 1–69.

Braithwaite, J. and Mugford S. (1994), 'Conditions of Successful Reintegration Ceremonies', *British Journal of Criminology*, 34(2), pp 139–71.

Claes, E. and Van Daele, E. (2011), 'Vrijwilligers Binnen een Maximalistische Visie op Herstelrecht' (Volunteers from a Maximalist Point of View on Restorative Justice), *Tijdschrift voor Herstelrecht*, 11(3), pp 24–37.

Collins, R. (2004), *Interactional Ritual Change* (Princeton: Princeton University Press).

Daly, K. (2002), 'Restorative Justice: The Real Story', *Punishment and society*, 4(1), pp 55–79.

Daly, K. (2005), 'A Tale of Two Studies: Restorative Justice from a Victim's Perspective', in Elliott, E. and Gordon, R. (eds.), *Restorative Justice: Emerging Issues in Practice and Evaluation* (Cullompton: Willan Publishing), pp 153–74.

Dignan, J. (2005), *Understanding Victims and Restorative Justice* (Maidenhead: McGraw Hill, Open University Press).

Hayes, H. and Daly, K. (2003), 'Youth Justice Conferencing and Reoffending', *Justice Quarterly*, 20(4), pp 725–64.

Hirschi, T. (1969), *Causes of Delinquency* (Berkeley: University of California Press).

Latimer, J., Dowden, C. and Muise, D. (2001), *The Effectiveness of Restorative Justice Practices: A Meta Analysis* (Ottawa: Department of Justice).

MacRae, A. and Zehr, H. (2004), *The Little Book of Family Group Conferences New Zealand Style: A Hopeful Approach When Youth Cause Harm* (Intercourse: Good Books).

Maruna, S. (2001), *Making Good: How Ex-Convicts Reform and Rebuild Their Lives* (Washington DC: American Psychological Association Press).

Maxwell, G. (2007), 'The Youth Justice System in New Zealand: Restorative Justice Delivered Through the Family Group Conference', in Maxwell, G. and Liu, J (eds.), *Restorative Justice and Practices in New Zealand: Towards a Restorative Society* (Wellington: Institute of Policy Studies, Victoria University), pp 45–67.

Maxwell, G., Kingi, V., Robertson, J., Morris, A. and Cunningham, C. (2004), *Achieving Effective Outcomes in Youth Justice* (Wellington: Ministry of Social Development).

Maxwell, G. and Morris, A. (1999), *Understanding Reoffending: Final Report* (Wellington: Victoria University, Institute of Criminology).

McCold, P. (2003), 'A Survey of Assessment Research on Mediation and Conferencing', in Walgrave, L. (ed.), *Repositioning Restorative Justice* (Cullompton: Willan Publishing), pp 67–117.

McCold, P. and Wachtel, B. (1998), *Restorative Policing Experiment: The Bethlehem Pennsylvania Police Family Group Conferencing Project (Final Report)* (Washington: U.S. Dept. of Justice, National Institute of Justice National Criminal Justice Reference Service).

Morris, A. (2002), 'Shame, Guilt and Remorse: Experiences from Family Group Conferences in New Zealand', in Weijers, I. and Duff, A. (eds.), *Punishing Juveniles: Principle and Critique* (Oxford: Hart Publishing), pp 157–78.

Pemberton, A., Winkel, F.W. and Groenhuisen, M. (2007), 'Taking Victims Seriously in Restorative Justice, *International Perspectives in Victimology*, 3(1), pp 4–14.

Put, J., Vanfraechem, I. and Walgrave, L. (2012–forthcoming), 'Restorative Dimensions in Youth Justice', *Youth Justice* (on file with author).

Shapland, J. (2009), 'Restorative Justice Conferencing in the Context of Community Policing', in Moor, L., Peters, T., Ponsaers, P., Shapland, J. and Van Stokkom, B. (eds.), *Restorative Policing*, (Antwerpen: Maklu), pp 119–38.

Shapland, J., Atkinson, A., Atkinson, H., Dignan, J., Edwards, L., Hibbert, J., Howes, M., Johnstone, J., Robinson, G. and Sorsby, S. (2008), *Does Restorative Justice Affect Reconviction? The 4th Report from the Evaluation of Three Schemes* (London: Ministry of Justice).

Sherman, L. and Strang, H. (2007), *Restorative Justice: The Evidence* (London: Smith Institute).

Strang, H. (2002), *Repair or Revenge: Victims and Restorative Justice* (Oxford: Clarendon Press).

Strang, H., Sherman, L., Angel, C., Woods, D., Bennett, S., Newbury-Birch, D. and Inkpen, N. (2006), 'Victim Evaluations of Face-to-Face Restorative Justice Conferences: A Quasi-Experimental Analysis', *Journal of Social Issues*, 62(2), pp 281–306.

Tyler, T. (1990), *Why People Obey the Law* (New Haven: Yale University Press).

Tyler, T. (2006), 'Restorative Justice and Procedural Justice: Dealing with Rule Breaking', *Journal of Social Issues*, 62(2), pp 307–26.

Umbreit, M. and Zehr, H. (1996), 'Restorative Family Group Conferences: Differing Models and Guidelines for Practice', *Federal Probation*, 60(3), pp 24–9.

Van Ness, D. and Schiff, M. (2001), 'Satisfaction Guaranteed? The Meaning of Satisfaction in Restorative Justice', in Bazemore, G. and Schiff, M. (eds.), *Restorative Community Justice: Repairing Harm and Transforming Communities* (Cincinnati: Anderson), pp 47–62.

Van Stokkom, B. (2002), 'Moral Emotions in Restorative Justice Conferences: Managing Shame, Designing Empathy', *Theoretical Criminology*, 6(3), pp 339–60.

Vanfraechem, I. (2006), *Herstelgericht Groepsoverleg. Op Zoek Naar een Constructief Antwoord op Ernstige Jeugddelinquentie* (Restorative group deliberation. In search of a constructive response to serious youth offending) (Leuven: PhD Criminology KU Leuven—on file with author).

Vanfraechem, I. and Walgrave, L. (2004), 'Restorative Conferencing in Belgium: Can it Decrease the Confinement of Young Offenders?', *Corrections Today*, 66(7), pp 72–5.

Walgrave, L. (2002), 'Restorative Justice and the Law: Socio-Ethical and Juridical Foundations for a Systemic Approach', in Walgrave, L. (ed.), *Restorative Justice and the Law* (Cullompton: Willan Publishing), pp 191–218.

Walgrave, L. (2008), *Restorative Justice, Self-Interest and Responsible Citizenship* (Cullompton: Willan Publishing).

Walgrave, L. and Aertsen, I. (1996), 'Reintegrative Shaming and Restorative Justice: Interchangeable, Complementary or Different?', *European Journal of Criminal Policy and Research*, 4(4), pp 67–85.

Young, R. (2001), 'Just Cops Doing "Shameful Business"? Police-Led Restorative Justice and the Lessons of the Research', in Morris, A. and Maxwell, G. (eds.), *Restorative Justice for Juveniles* (Oxford: Hart Publishing), pp 195–226.

4

COMPARING CONFERENCING AND MEDIATION

SOME EVALUATION RESULTS INTERNATIONALLY

Joanna Shapland[1]

IS IT POSSIBLE TO COMPARE FORMS OF RESTORATIVE JUSTICE?

Attempting to contrast and compare conferencing and mediation, particularly in an international context, is a potentially dangerous exercise for the researcher or evaluator. Restorative justice has evolved in parallel in a number of different countries. The result is that one is comparing not just different restorative justice practices, but also the historical and cultural traditions which have given rise to those practices. Not surprisingly, those traditions are held dear by both restorative justice practitioners and criminal justice professionals who are involved in referring cases. The comparative researcher, then, is liable to be accused of misinterpreting the practices and their context—and potentially of favouring the legal culture in which he or she is most used to working. It is therefore with some caution, and hopefully, some self-awareness of my own cultural assumptions, that I continue on this perilous task.

It is, however, a task which I think is key to the continuing development of restorative justice. Different countries have tended to adopt one particular model of restorative justice. So, for example, the Scandinavian countries have legislated for 'mediation', as in the Mediation Boards set up in Norway and Finland (Iivari et al. 2009; Nergård 1993). Yet the historical background and types of mediators used are different from the police-led and penal mediation practised in, for example, Belgium (Aertsen 2009). In Scandinavia, mediators tend to be drawn from the community in which the offence occurred, rather than being full-time paid mediators or criminal justice personnel. In

[1] The author is very grateful to Gwen Robinson for her insightful comments on the draft of this chapter.

England and Wales, practices termed 'mediation' include both direct meetings between victim and offender ('direct mediation') and cases where the mediator 'shuttles' between the parties ('indirect mediation'), with the latter predominating numerically (Shapland et al. 2011). The question then arises whether practices termed 'mediation' are the same within or between countries—and indeed whether practices termed 'conferencing' are entirely different from 'mediation' or show considerable overlap—it is not possible to simply rely on the names of the restorative justice practices to delineate difference. If we want to know what works well or works well for the particular population it serves, we need to start unpacking those terms and working out what is or is not different between them, and the extent to which it matters. Because each scheme and country tends to be quite wedded to its own type of restorative justice—and nomenclature—this is a contentious exercise.[2]

It is also a difficult exercise, because it depends upon there being sufficient evaluation evidence of what is happening in the different countries and their outcomes. Yet detailed evaluation studies of restorative justice have been rare and tend to have been confined to a relatively small number of countries, many of which work in the English language and have a legal Anglo-Saxon common law culture (ie the United States, Canada, Australia, New Zealand, and the United Kingdom). Though restorative justice is also commonly practised within the mainland European civil law tradition, there has been less detailed evaluation (Shapland 2008; though see Vanfraechem et al. 2010).

Many of these dilemmas are common to other areas of criminal justice research, such as, for example, studies of the relations between police and prosecutor, or sentencing practice (Nelken 2009). There is always the difficult choice between undertaking a wide-ranging but potentially superficial comparison, or engaging in a detailed, culturally relevant description, which is so place- and tradition-bound that it renders almost impossible finding important thematic differences. This is one of the reasons why international comparison between forms of restorative justice is still in its infancy. Yet it is becoming ever more important to try to make such comparisons, as international instruments (such as the United Nations Basic Principles 2002 or Council of Europe 1999) seek to provide international standards, and as practitioners themselves wonder whether they might reach out and experiment with other forms of restorative justice in particular cases.

The EU funded survey of practices of mediation or conferencing, responded to by practitioners in different countries, has shown that old stereotypes of conferencing being 'Anglo-Saxon' but mediation being more 'European' now need drastic re-examination (Zinsstag et al. 2011). Restorative justice schemes can, and do, undertake both for different cases. Countries contain different schemes, sometimes associated with different stages of criminal justice or different offending populations, some of which are described as one, some as the other. This is then, I think, the time to reconsider the old labels and to see what the key parameters are which may differentiate practices.

[2] Schemes with the same name ('mediation' or 'conferencing') may in fact have very different theoretical foundations and aims, as discussed later.

The reader, by this point, may be wondering whether this is a possible task, given the variety of practice and the relative paucity of evaluation. It has long been said that restorative justice is an 'umbrella term'. Is the diversity so pronounced that it is impossible to classify? Is restorative justice simply inchoate, where, as long as one involves both victim and offender, 'anything goes'? No, I think that would also be a false picture. As Howard Zehr (2010) has said, restorative justice proceeds from some similar values and standards (see also Braithwaite and Mugford 1994; van Ness 2003). All restorative justice practices believe there needs to be adherence to human rights, accountability to participants, and feedback to those referring cases. It is not an accident, I think, that the international instruments have centred on those same values and standards, rather than on the minutiae of process and practice. There is a unity within restorative justice practice which enables comparison. However, one needs to be sensitive also to the different traditions and the weight given to different aims (and hence to different outcomes) within those values and standards.

There need to be some boundaries given to what will be considered as examples of conferencing and mediation in this chapter. Two key boundaries will be adopted. The first is that the procedure needs to be restorative justice, rather than a restorative practice—ie it needs directly to engage those considered the victim(s) and offender(s) of the same offence (see Restorative Justice Council 2011; Shapland et al. 2011). Hence areas such as victim awareness (thinking about the effects on victims) or restorative practices using other victims or victim representatives will not be included. The second is that we shall look at restorative justice relating to criminal justice. This may include schemes mainstreamed within criminal justice (as, for example, family group conferencing in New Zealand or youth conferencing in Northern Ireland), or cases referred by criminal justice officials to divert the case from the criminal justice system (whether or not the case or the people return after the restorative justice or the case is diverted). However, it will not include purely 'community justice' done without reference to or referral from criminal justice, even though that community justice may be (and often does) deal with events which could be seen as falling within the ambit of the criminal law.

The chapter will first look at how 'conferencing' and 'mediation' are conventionally defined and then consider what aspects of procedure or practice tend to be different between them. In particular, we shall look at attendance (who comes?), the stages of the process, the role of the facilitator or mediator,[3] the aims of the events used, and the types of outcomes envisaged as important. In looking at these elements, I shall primarily be referring to the evaluation of three restorative justice schemes in England and Wales, which included both conferencing and mediation, and so permitting a direct comparison (Shapland et al. 2011), but also considering evaluations of youth conferencing in Northern Ireland, referral panels for young offenders in England and Wales, and mediation in Belgium.

[3] The terms 'mediator' and 'facilitator' will be used interchangeably, though commonly practices called 'conferencing' tend to use the term 'facilitator' or 'coordinator' and practices called 'mediation' tend to use the term 'mediator'.

WHO COMES TO RESTORATIVE JUSTICE EVENTS?

The definitions of conferencing and mediation classically focus on attendance: mediation is where only the victim(s) and offender(s) of a particular offence are involved, together with the neutral mediator, whereas in conferencing both victim and offender are allowed to bring supporter(s) with them to any meeting. Direct mediation includes a face-to-face meeting between the parties, whereas indirect mediation (or shuttle mediation) involves the mediator passing information between the parties, without any face-to-face meeting between victim(s) and offender(s). These definitions are subject to slight amendment for legal reasons in certain cases. Hence if one party is a young person, then a parent or appropriate adult/guardian has to give their consent to any mediation and will normally attend. Similarly, a professional case worker may attend a mediation involving someone who has mental health difficulties, or is in care or custody. Fundamentally, though, the differentiating idea between mediation and conferencing is that mediations are small, intimate occasions whereas conferences can be large affairs involving all the parties, their supporters and, potentially, members of the community as well.

These stereotypes, like many others about conferencing and mediation, need to be examined using an empirical lens. Is it the case that conferences are large meetings? Who does attend restorative justice events? I shall be looking at them using the results of the evaluation of three restorative justice schemes we carried out, funded by the Ministry of Justice (previously the Home Office) of England and Wales, which also funded the schemes over the 2001–2004 period (Shapland et al. 2006; 2011).

THE THREE SCHEMES

The three schemes were the Justice Research Consortium (JRC), CONNECT, and REMEDI. As outlined below, they undertook restorative justice, primarily with adult offenders and including serious offences, at many stages of criminal justice, but only where there was an individual victim (not a corporate victim).

The three schemes evaluated in England and Wales

1. **JRC** provided only conferencing (with supporters present), using an experimental model involving random assignment of cases after both victim(s) and offender(s) had agreed to take part:

- pre-sentence at the London Crown Court centres with adult offenders convicted of burglary of domestic premises, robbery, theft from the person, and other 'street crime', led by police facilitators;
- pre-sentence in Northumbria, for adult offenders convicted of property or violent offences at the magistrates' court who were not in custody, led by police facilitators;
- as diversion from prosecution in Northumbria, for young offenders who admitted the offence and were being given a final warning for violent or property offences,

and for adult offenders being given a formal caution for violent offences (the latter was not part of the random controlled trial), led by police facilitators;

- pre-release from prison in Thames Valley for adult offenders convicted of violent offences, within about the last year before release, led by probation officer, prison officer facilitators, or community mediators; and
- during a community sentence in Thames Valley (ie supervised by the Probation Service) for adult offenders convicted of violent offences, led by probation officer facilitators or community mediators.

2. **CONNECT** provided direct mediation, indirect mediation, and conferencing (but mostly mediation) for adult offenders pre-sentence at magistrates' courts in inner London, for all types of offence.
3. **REMEDI** provided direct mediation and indirect mediation (mostly indirect mediation) for both adult and young offenders in South Yorkshire, at various stages of criminal justice, including:

- pre-release from prison;
- during community sentences;
- as diversion from prosecution for young offenders (given a final warning); and
- as part of the referral panel's deliberations for young offenders given a referral order by the youth court.

Around 840 restorative justice events (the majority from JRC) were included in the evaluation, which involved observing face-to-face restorative justice meetings, interviewing offenders and victims, and looking at reconviction and the running of the schemes (Shapland et al. 2011).

ATTENDANCE AND PARTICIPATION—WHAT DO THE EMPIRICAL RESULTS SHOW?

In practice, the stereotype of conferences being typically large gatherings seems not to be correct. In our own evaluation, for JRC, the number of participants in the circle (those able to speak[4]) was on average 6.3, including facilitator, victim(s), offender(s), and victims' and offenders' supporters. The range for the random allocation trials was from three (normally one victim, one offender, one facilitator[5]—which is identical to the minimum for mediation) to 15. Supporters who were brought by victims and offenders were typically those close to them—family members, work colleagues, close friends, or on occasion a key worker (social worker, youth worker, probation officer). They were essentially those who have been referred to as the 'community of care' (McCold 2004) or the 'micro-community' (Braithwaite 1993).

[4] Those who sit in the circle can speak during restorative justice events. Those outside the circle (normally only one or two people) might be trainee facilitators, observers finding out about restorative justice—or the researchers. Participants need to agree to the presence of those outside the circle.

[5] Victims might on rare occasions, due to illness, etc. not be present (all victims had originally agreed to take part in conferencing prior to the random assignment to conferencing or control group taking place), but the minimum number of participants was three.

However, diversionary conferences with adult offenders for violence offences, which dealt with neighbourhood disputes or other disputes involving people who know each other (extended family disputes, disputes arising in clubs, workplaces, or local community facilities) were typically much larger (Shapland 2009). They could involve up to 25 participants 'in the circle'. Normally, these would also involve two facilitators in order to cope with participants' needs for time out, breaks, etc.

Relatively small attendances for conferences have not only been found in our evaluation. The evaluation of statutory youth conferencing in Northern Ireland also showed relatively small conferences to be the norm (Campbell et al. 2005). Here, victims and offenders are allowed to bring supporters at the discretion of the conference facilitator, whilst the young offender must be accompanied by an appropriate adult, and his or her lawyer also has the right to attend (though very rarely did). Campbell et al. (2005) found that a second offender supporter (apart from the appropriate adult) was only present in 61 per cent of conferences, a third supporter in 17 per cent. Victims, however, were present at 69 per cent of conferences.

Few evaluations of restorative justice or restorative practices involving meetings have measured the numbers of people attending. It is notable though that referral panels with young offenders in England and Wales have also tended to have relatively small numbers of people attending. Crawford and Newburn's (2003) evaluation of the start of such conferences showed that 15 per cent of the conferences run had no offender supporter attending and 68 per cent had only one (normally the mother of the young offender). Overall very few victims attended these conferences.

Clearly, the number of people attending a meeting will affect its dynamics. However, large conferences seem to be rare and concentrated on neighbourhood matters and disputes. The more typical criminal justice restorative conference seems to contain only a few participants and centres around the victim and offender. One may query, then, whether attendance is—or should be seen as—actually the defining distinction between conferencing and mediation. Is it the people there, or who speaks, and about what, which may be different?

SCRIPTS, TOPICS AND STAGES

In order to consider who participates within face-to-face mediation and conferencing meetings, we need to know about what happens and what it is intended should happen. This is where we tend to run up against a blank wall in terms of information. Apart from a very few case studies (Rossner 2011; Tudor 2000), very little of the voluminous literature on restorative justice seems to have provided precise details of how such meetings are run, who speaks when, and for what amount of time each participant speaks. Nor is it often clear whether there is a precise script which the facilitator uses, whether there is a looser set of questions which may be phrased in different ways for different conferences, or whether there is an understood order of speech for participants. Hence finding out exactly what happens during restorative justice events is difficult.

In terms of the schemes which we evaluated, JRC facilitators were trained by facilitators from Transformative Justice Australia, which has a precise three stage 'script', though the words facilitators might use to pose the three questions might vary (Shapland et al. 2011). The three stages were: (a) what happened? [in relation to the offence], for which the offender is asked to speak first, followed by questions from others and discussion; (b) what were the effects? [of the offence], where the victim is asked to speak first and then each participant in turn is encouraged to contribute; (c) how could things be made better? [a future-oriented discussion in which everyone is invited to contribute, intended to end with an outcome agreement, written by the facilitator, and signed by everyone present]. JRC facilitators were trained to use very little verbal input to this process, beyond saying the next question, prioritizing non-verbal communication and short verbal prompts. From our observations of JRC conferences, this 'script' was followed in all areas.

REMEDI and CONNECT direct mediations which we observed were much more variable in terms of topics and mediator participation. Their philosophy was to follow whatever the participants (victim and offender) themselves brought up, though typically the mediation covered first, what happened, and secondly, what effects did it have. A future-oriented stage would only occur if the victim or offender brought up the need (to either the victim or the offender, or both) for an agreement for the future or to discuss the future. In general, CONNECT and REMEDI mediators took a much more active role than JRC facilitators in putting questions, introducing topics, and suggesting things.

The evaluation which we undertook had the advantage that we were observing direct meetings for all three schemes, using the same observation schedule in which we could record who spoke, about what, when, and approximately for how long. It hence enabled comparison between schemes and practices, and allowed us to see how variable it could be. It is clear from the limited amount of description in others' research that there is considerable variability. This occurs in relation to the extent of intervention by mediators/facilitators;[6] whether participants stay together throughout the meeting or there is separate time for, for example, the offender's family to meet together and discuss potential outcomes (as in family group conferencing run by Youth Offending Teams in England and Wales: Zernova 2007); and in the order of speech at the beginning. Some conferences start with the offender speaking (as with JRC above), some with the victim talking about the effects, and some with a statement by the police or other 'official' person about the facts of the offence (as in Northern Ireland youth conferencing: Campbell et al. 2005).

It is not clear to what extent the different mediation and conferencing schemes around the world have considered the patterns they have adopted in terms of the dynamics and stages of the meetings. The 'accepted' or 'best' practice for each scheme is likely to have been set in place at the beginning of the scheme. It is highly unlikely that it is a spontaneous reaction to what each victim and offender brings to each meet-

[6] Indeed, different schools of mediation have very different theoretical views about whether mediation should be largely non-directed or whether mediators should play an active role in 'moving the participants on'.

ing, with the victim and offender being left to introduce whatever topics they consider pertinent (though if victim or offender wish to discuss a particular matter, it would normally, in all schemes, be included within the restorative justice discussion, unless it was highly inappropriate or would be harming third parties). Instead, I suspect that facilitators and mediators indicate to victims and offenders during the preparation phase what the order and questions should be or could be. We need to remember that restorative justice is still a relatively unknown concept to many members of the general public, whilst it is rare for victims to have had previous experience with either criminal justice or restorative justice—simply because being a victim of crime is a rare event and it is only a minority of cases which proceed to prosecution or court (Kangaspunta et al. 1998). Hence it is highly likely that facilitators or mediators are, during the preparation phase, 'setting the scene' of the process, order, and topics for discussion for lay participants. Restorative justice schemes will have trained their facilitators in one particular process which they will aim for being a good, consistent experience for all their cases. The result is, I suspect, that schemes have not considered in depth or reviewed regularly what the effects are of their 'normal' process and dynamics of the meetings, nor looked at what other schemes are doing (because of the paucity of research in depth and the concerns around confidentiality which restrict videos passing from scheme to scheme). In other words, we have very little data from which to look at the usefulness of different processes or procedures or whether conferencing and mediation differ from each other in these respects.

In our own evaluation of the three schemes, we are able to use the observation material to consider how the three schemes differed in terms of who spoke and whether any participant was more dominant.

For JRC, we have sufficient observations to know that the average conference time was 68 minutes (ie just over an hour: Shapland et al. 2006). Estimations of who spoke for how long provided figures of 27 per cent of the conference time for the offender (the main offender if there was more than one), 21 per cent for the victim (the main victim if there was more than one), 12 per cent for the main offender supporter, 13 per cent for the main victim supporter and 16 per cent for the facilitator. This indicates that:

- offenders were able to speak in the conference and that their input was the principal input in terms of time;
- victims and offenders spoke for about the same amount of time and were the most dominant participants;
- offender and victim supporters also contributed, but to a lesser degree than the victim and offender; and
- the facilitator (there was only one facilitator speaking in the circle) did not play a dominant role in terms of proportion of time spent speaking.

Both CONNECT and REMEDI direct mediation meetings tended to be shorter than JRC conferences overall. Both victims and offenders indicated that they were involved 'a lot' (Shapland et al. 2007), but our observations suggested that mediators spoke for a greater proportion of the overall time than with JRC conferences. REMEDI typically worked with two mediators (who could include volunteer, trained mediators), whilst

CONNECT worked normally with one. The experience of both JRC and REMEDI, who worked with young offenders, was that young offenders tended to speak less than adult offenders—but could be encouraged to speak and say what they wanted to say. Young offenders being able to speak freely is contrary to some of the experience in South Australia (Daly 2004), but in accord with the evaluation of Northern Ireland youth conferencing (Campbell et al. 2005).

Conferencing intrinsically tends to have more participants, even though, as we saw above, conferences still tend to be quite small meetings. Does the number of participants affect who speaks? There is some evidence from our evaluation in England and Wales, and from other research in Australia and elsewhere, that when there are more participants, as in conferencing, the facilitator/mediators speak for a lower proportion of the time and seem to be less dominant—but there are very little quantitative data on participation, as opposed to attendance. Certainly, Strang (2002) has suggested that having more participants can be part of the solutions adopted where there are fears about power imbalances in the conference. If one participant (victim or offender) is likely to be seen by the other as much more dominant, then having supporters there tends to lessen those effects. This is not so much a numerical balancing effect, but that others present are likely to intervene and so tend to moderate the input or impact of one dominant person, whether or not the supporters are those of that party. We found that supporters did play major roles in encouraging taciturn or nervous participants to speak and reminding them about crucial elements they wanted to contribute. We could hence see conferencing, as opposed to mediation, as potentially beneficial in allowing a good balance of contribution between participants, and as rendering facilitators as less dominant—but this is due to the participation of all those present, not merely their attendance.

THE AIMS OF MEDIATION AND CONFERENCING

What happens during restorative justice meetings should be related to people's aims for those meetings. Many people can have expectations and aims for the meeting: the participants themselves, the scheme (in its official remit and purposes), funders, facilitators, those referring cases to the scheme (including criminal justice system decision makers), those with an interest in that scheme more generally (stakeholders), and the wider society, including those living in the local community. Given the many potential aims for restorative justice of different types and traditions (which is why restorative justice is called an umbrella term), there is the potential for divergence between these parties. One key question for schemes is whether they are aware of the expectations and aims of these different parties for their own scheme.

I want to focus here on participants' aims and expectations, and on those of the scheme managers and facilitators. These are perhaps the two most important parties, because managers and facilitators will be governing what actually happens and setting the framework for the scheme's activities in practice. If their aims are divergent from participants' aims and expectations, it is highly likely that there will be some dissatisfaction.

In the three schemes we evaluated, we asked intending participants, just before the restorative justice event (or after they had consented to take part, in relation to indirect mediation) why they wanted to come or to take part in restorative justice. This was to gain an idea of their expectations of what they would encounter and what they wanted to happen. Because our interviews and questionnaires had to be very short (to avoid adding to people's nerves before the event started[7]), we gave victims and offenders a list of possible reasons and asked them to rate them on a scale of one to four (where four is very important, one not at all important) whether each reason applied to them. There were insufficient interviews with CONNECT participants to provide numerical data, but the figures for JRC and REMEDI are shown in Table 4.1 below. For REMEDI participants, two extra items were added at the request of the scheme:

The most obvious result from Table 4.1 is that participants have several reasons why they want to participate in restorative justice. Offenders want to express their feelings, have a say in how the problem is resolved, offer reparation, *and* help the other person, whilst victims want to express their feelings, have a say in how the problem is resolved, help the other person, *and* are coming because they were asked to take part. In fact, offender and victim reasons for participating seem to be quite similar.[8] They stress communication, but not just communication about the past (the offence) and the present (the effects of the offence) but also about the future (solving problems). Principal components analyses, done on these pre-restorative justice interviews and also on answers from interviews with victims after participation, showed a general factor, loading strongly on communicative reasons, for both victims and offenders (Shapland et al. 2006; 2007). Interviewees were also quite clear that they were not participating just because they were told to. This key aspect of communication which participants felt restorative justice was offering them was linked to altruistic, other-directed reasons for participation: wanting to help the other person and prevent reoffending on the part of victims; wanting to answer questions and repay harm on the part of offenders.

Looking at Table 4.1, however, it is difficult to see a different pattern of responses for JRC participants (conferencing) from that of REMEDI respondents (mediation). Both sets of participants emphasized communication and altruistic, other-directed reasons. Both wanted to talk about the past and the present, but also the future.

Our next question must then be whether those expectations were met by the process they then experienced. For this, we need to look first at the aims of the schemes themselves. Taking again as an example the three schemes we evaluated, Table 4.2 shows which aims were acknowledged and stressed by the managers and facilitators

[7] Note that for JRC, interviews before the conference took place were attempted only during the initial phase of the scheme, before the random controlled trial started, so that they could not 'contaminate' the trial.

[8] The major difference was that offenders wished to offer reparation, but victims were not sure they wanted it from offenders. Partly this may be because the offences included serious offences where monetary reparation would not be seen as necessarily appropriate by victims; partly because in England and Wales symbolic reparation seems to be rather more important to victims than monetary reparation (Shapland et al. 1985). In other countries, the wish for reparation from victims may well be higher and certainly reparation plays a far larger role in, for example, restorative justice in Belgium (Aertsen 2009) and in Northern Ireland (Campbell et al. 2005) than in England and Wales (Shapland et al. 2011).

Table 4.1 Why do participants agree to come? *(scale of 1 = not at all important to 4 = very important)*

	JRC (conferencing)		REMEDI (mediation)	
	Offenders	Victims	Offenders	Victims
You wanted to express your feelings and speak directly to the other person	3.44	2.58	3.48	3.23
You wanted a say in how the problem was resolved	3.33	2.86	3.16	2.96
You wanted to repay the harm (Os) or be repaid for the harm you had experienced (Vs)	3.24	2.00	3.61	2.49
You wanted to help the other person	2.98	2.75	3.32	3.12
You felt a duty to attend/take part	2.74	2.35	3.15	2.64
You were asked to attend/take part	2.69	2.29	3.16	2.97
You were told to attend/take part	1.10	1.25	2.50	1.43
You would like some questions about the offence answered	–	–	2.78	3.22
Taking part may affect what happens as a result of the case	–	–	2.77	2.83

Table 4.2 Manager and facilitator aims for the scheme

	JRC (conferencing)	CONNECT (mediation)	REMEDI (mediation)
Meet victim needs	JRC		
Enable the victim to ask questions and receive information	JRC	CONNECT	REMEDI
Enable reparation to the victim		CONNECT	
Enable restoration of the victim	JRC		
Enable victim recovery			REMEDI
Prevent reoffending	JRC	CONNECT	
Increase the offender's sense of responsibility for the offence		CONNECT	REMEDI
Help offenders reintegrate into the community			REMEDI
Leave victim and offender with greater satisfaction about criminal justice		CONNECT	

of each scheme, whom we interviewed both early on in the research and at its end (Shapland et al. 2006). If a particular element was stressed, the name of the scheme is put against it.

It is clear from Table 4.2 that each scheme had more than one aim and that both the numbers and types of aims varied for the different schemes. As would be expected with restorative justice, some aims related primarily to the victim, some to the offender, and each has been grouped separately in the table. Only one aim—to enable the victim to ask questions and receive information—was highlighted in all three schemes.

Were participants' expectations met? We attempted to couch our questions to victims and offenders, in interviews after they had experienced the restorative justice process, to reflect these aims of schemes and expectations of participants. The overall judgements of 'satisfaction' and 'whether participants would recommend the restorative justice to those in a similar position to themselves' obviously meld together participants' reactions to individual expectations. The results of the evaluation showed high ratings on the individual questions and on the overall judgements (Shapland et al. 2007). Where there was any dissatisfaction, it related to difficulties in communication, showing the importance of the overall expectation of communication. As far as we could judge, these schemes, where there were direct meetings, were delivering what they said they would do, which met participants' expectations.

The only real note of concern (apart from rare cases where offenders did not take responsibility or where there were specific difficulties in communication) was with indirect mediation. Here, participants found the rather drawn-out process of posing questions and waiting for the mediator to bring back answers days or weeks later, difficult. Sometimes they did not obtain the answer they wished for or expected from the other party—then they might wonder whether the mediator had properly reported what the other party had said. The overall extent of communication was far less, because the cycle was not repeated many times, so question could not be followed by answer, another question, another answer and so forth, as would have happened in a face-to-face meeting. Were these difficulties, however, symptomatic of the choice of mediation as opposed to conferencing? Or were they primarily about the indirect nature of the restorative justice experienced?

It cannot be assumed that all conferencing schemes will have similar aims or that all mediation schemes will have similar aims. In our evaluation, was it the case that CONNECT and REMEDI (the two schemes primarily using mediation) had similar aims, and that these were different from the aims of JRC, which only offered conferencing? Considering Table 4.2, this does not seem to be so. JRC had aims (such as preventing reoffending) which are clearly linked in to those of criminal justice, but so are those of CONNECT (such as increasing satisfaction with criminal justice). Those of REMEDI, in contrast, seem to prioritize victim recovery and integration into the community, rather than links with criminal justice. Clearly schemes' historical ties and theoretical influences seem to have more relevance than whether they are offering mediation or conferencing. We would also argue that it is not the title which affected participants' more negative reaction to indirect mediation, but the indirect element.

WHICH THEORETICAL MODEL SCHEMES ADOPT AND THE RELATION WITH OUTCOME MEASURES

The scheme's aims should of course themselves be underpinned by the particular theoretical models which that scheme and its practitioners have adopted as to their views on restorative justice. Theoretical models of how restorative justice happens and how it 'works' vary considerably. Let us take, for example, the potential aim of reducing offending (which JRC and CONNECT in our evaluation had as specific aims, but which REMEDI, though desiring it as an indirect outcome, considered might occur through the operation of other intermediate effects). As Gwen Robinson and I have argued (Robinson and Shapland 2008), some theories of restorative justice do not really deal with reducing offending. Theories which stress restoration, reconciliation, or healing (such as that of Zehr 1990) and those which stress problem solving through restorative justice (such as those of Christie 1977 and Shearing 2001) do not specifically address preventing reoffending. They would, if the restoration or problem solving was successful, predict that the particular problem should not reoccur, but they do not widen this to include a specific aim of the reduction of reoffending by that offender in general.

On the other hand, some theories do embody the potential reduction of offending. Procedural justice (Tyler 2006), which is a general theory of justice, encompassing criminal justice, civil justice, and restorative justice (Tyler et al. 2007), would argue that if offenders are treated fairly by decision makers who take their decisions and are seen to take their decisions fairly, then offenders would grant increased legitimacy to such justice mechanisms and to that society, which should pull them further towards conformity to mainstream values and behaviours, including not offending. Reintegrative shaming (Braithwaite 1989) directly addresses preventing reoffending, by suggesting that, if offenders are both shamed in terms of the specific offence committed and then reintegrated, they would be pulled further towards conformity to that society's values and be less likely to reoffend.

Another theoretical mechanism, which is not incompatible with the theories of Tyler and Braithwaite, is that restorative justice brings together key elements to cement offenders' own decisions to desist (Robinson and Shapland 2008; Shapland forthcoming) and that both offenders' agentic decisions and creating appropriate societal spaces for desistance for that individual are vital in terms of offenders' journeys towards desistance (Bottoms and Shapland 2011). Some forms of restorative justice enable that journey because:

- offenders taking part (voluntarily) take responsibility for the offence in front of the victim and (in conferencing) key people in their lives;
- forward-looking restorative justice events provide an opportunity for the offender to think through what it would mean to reduce reoffending and what lifestyle would need to be undertaken by them;
- restorative justice events attended by those versed in what opportunities there are for offenders to tackle factors leading to their offending provide practical support and help as to what offenders could do to change their lives (an individualized 'rehabilitation package' towards desistance);
- the event provides the opportunity and a 'stage' on which the offender can affirm their wish to change their lives, which is then supported by the victim and those close to them (in conferencing). This is a very different sense of 'reintegration into the community' from that originally proposed by Braithwaite (1989) or advocated by those who work in community-oriented restorative justice (where the community is usually seen as a geographic community), but it is, in today's relatively anomic Western society, perhaps a more meaningful reintegration into the community for offenders—reintegration and reaffirmation of their place in their own micro-community.

Clearly, restorative justice schemes around the world currently vary in which of these theoretical traditions they feel they fall. It would be wrong for me arbitrarily to assign schemes to particular theoretical traditions, partly because that is for them to think through themselves, partly because managers, funders, and facilitators may vary as to which tradition they themselves feel they belong. However, it is clear that there is a strong link between schemes' aims, their theoretical traditions, and their desired outcomes.

To take one example, it is only if the scheme wishes to encourage problem-solving for the future, reducing reoffending, or encouraging desistance that it will tend to encourage discussion about the future between participants. A corollary is that future-oriented schemes will tend to be those which emphasize the production of a written outcome agreement and its signing by all participants (so that there is a record to which people can look back and see what they agreed). Schemes which wish to put the emphasis on understanding the past ('truth-telling') or reconciliation in the present have no need for such a future-oriented document in which people agree to do particular elements. However, a scheme which emphasizes problem-solving will want to have set down what participants might do if the problem looks as though it might recur—and it is just such restorative justice events which produced, in our evaluation, outcome agreement elements which considered who should be told and how to diminish that likelihood (Shapland 2009).

In our evaluation, schemes which emphasized the need for participants to have greater satisfaction with the criminal justice system than experiencing the traditional system alone (such as CONNECT) took trouble to find out what criminal justice system decisions about the case had been and to relay them to participants, and also followed up specific problems that participants had. Here, an appropriate outcome measure would not be the presence of a signed outcome agreement or whether the offender undertook programmes to reduce the likelihood of reoffending, but whether victims and offenders felt afterwards that they were more satisfied with criminal justice or saw it as having more legitimacy.

WHAT ARE THE DEFINING ELEMENTS BETWEEN CONFERENCING AND MEDIATION?

We have seen that there will be (or at least should be) a strong link between schemes' aims, theoretical background, and desired outcomes. However, different schemes are likely to have different aims, theoretical backgrounds, and outcomes. The current distinction between conferencing and mediation primarily concerns attendance (who comes), which is linked to the extent to which different kinds of participants participate. To what extent, then, is attendance/participation likely to affect the accomplishment by schemes of the aims and outcomes they wish to adopt? In other words, is conferencing likely to be more successful in accomplishing certain aims and outcomes and mediation others?

As stated earlier, we are very much hampered in answering this question by the paucity of published work which has considered the ways in which schemes actually operate, particularly the extent of participation and processes within face-to-face restorative justice meetings. Given the extent of interest amongst practitioners about whether they should be undertaking conferencing or mediation (or indeed offering one in relation to some types of offence or participants, the other for others), I would see it as imperative that schemes do start documenting what they are doing. It would be very helpful for themselves and for practitioners worldwide if schemes were to video events (obviously with the consent of participants) to illustrate their practice and the range of their practice. It would also be very helpful if they worked through what aims they are pursuing, given that these will be plural, and what kinds of outcomes, and outcome measures, would then be sensible to adopt. We have seen the adoption of almost a 'standard package' of outcome measures, primarily 'satisfaction' overall and some compliance/reoffending measures. However, these bare measures cannot tell schemes whether they are accomplishing what they desire. So, for example, are they aiming at a general reduction in reoffending by those offenders, or that that type of problem, or that specific dispute, does not reoccur? Are they aiming at participants feeling that their distress has been alleviated, or that they are reconciled with that particular offender, or that their material loss has been compensated?

The paucity of work has meant that this chapter has concentrated too much on England and Wales (though where available other countries' evaluation results have been introduced). Conclusions as regards conferencing and mediation must therefore be heavily circumscribed with warnings about their potential non-generalizability. They are only possible pointers, in a very bare field, to the potential advantages of one or other method.

Rashly stepping onto this terrain, I would first argue that the name 'conferencing' or 'mediation' by itself is not necessarily linked to the adoption of particular aims or theoretical background, and so not to particular outcomes. It is the aims/theoretical background/outcomes which are important, not the name. There are currently differences in these aspects between schemes which call themselves mediation and those which call themselves conferencing, because of the parallel development in different parts of the world of theoretical traditions and culture. However, I see no reason why some mediation schemes could not change to become more like current conferencing schemes and vice versa (see also Zinsstag et al. 2011).

However, the evaluation results tend to suggest that the type of attendance in direct meetings leads to certain types of processes, probably encouraged by the currently adopted models of restorative justice which facilitators and mediators stress. Hence, both participants *and* scheme traditions/practitioner practices are important in differentiating what happens and so what is likely to occur. What facilitators/mediators suggest to participants in preparation is what may bind participants' expectations and speech, at least whilst restorative justice is relatively unknown to those being invited to participate. In particular, looking at the differences between conferencing and mediation in the evaluation of the three schemes in England and Wales suggests that having offender and victim supporters present at a direct meeting makes it more likely that:

- the restorative justice event has a future-oriented phase;
- the restorative justice event ends with an outcome agreement signed by all those present;
- supporters contribute to what may happen in the future and may take responsibility for some items or help with some items; and
- the meeting discusses, using the supporters' experiences as well, how the offender may stop reoffending and so may contribute to underlining and supporting the offender's decision to desist or otherwise change his or her life (if that decision has been or is being taken by the offender).

Whether or not those preliminary views are corroborated in future research, it seems vital for restorative justice that individual schemes and practitioners think through what they wish to achieve for individual cases and so what kind of process should be encouraged and who should be invited to participate.

REFERENCES

AERTSEN, I. (2009), 'Restorative Police Practices in Belgium: A Research into Mediation Processes and their Organisation', in Gunther Moor, L., Peters, T., Ponsaers, P., Shapland, J. and van Stokkom, B. (eds.), 'Restorative Policing', *Journal of Police Studies*, 2009-2, pp 65–82.

BOTTOMS, A. and SHAPLAND, J. (2012), 'Steps Towards Desistance Among Male Young Adult Recidivists', in Farrall, S., Hough, M., Maruna, S. and Sparks, R. (eds.), *Escape Routes: Contemporary Perspectives on Life After Punishment* (London: Routledge), pp 43–80.

BRAITHWAITE, J. (1989), *Crime, Shame and Reintegration* (Cambridge: Cambridge University Press).

BRAITHWAITE, J. (1993), 'Shame and Modernity', *British Journal of Criminology*, 33(1), pp 1–18.

BRAITHWAITE, J. and MUGFORD, S. (1994), 'Conditions of Successful Reintegration Ceremonies: Dealing With Juvenile Offenders', *British Journal of Criminology*, 34, pp 139–71.

CAMPBELL, C., DEVLIN, R., O'MAHONY, D., DOAK, J., JACKSON, J., CORRIGAN, T. and MCEVOY, K. (2005), *Evaluation of the Northern Ireland Youth Conference Service*, NIO Research and Statistical Service Report, 12 (Belfast: Northern Ireland Office), at <http://www.nio.gov.uk/evaluation_of_the_northern ireland_youth_conference_service.pdf>.

CHRISTIE, N. (1977), 'Conflicts as Property', *British Journal of Criminology*, 17, pp 1–15.

Council of Europe (1999), *Mediation in Penal Matters: Recommendation No. R(99)19 and Explanatory Memorandum* (Strasbourg: Council of Europe).

CRAWFORD, A. and NEWBURN, T. (2003), *Youth Offending and Restorative Justice: Implementing Reform in Youth Justice* (Cullompton: Willan Publising).

DALY, K. (2004), 'Mind the Gap: Restorative Justice in Theory and Practice', in von Hirsch, A., Roberts, J., Bottoms, A.E., Roach, K. and Schiff, M. (eds.), *Restorative Justice and Criminal Justice: Competing or Reconcilable Paradigms?* (Oxford: Hart Publishing), pp 219–36.

IIVARI, J., SAKKINEN, S. and KUOPPALA, T. (2009), *Mediation in Criminal and Civil Cases 2008* (Helsinki: National Institute for Health and Welfare).

KANGASPUNTA, K., JOUTSEN, M. and OLLUS, N. (1998), *Crime and Criminal Justice Systems in Europe and North America 1990–1994* (Helsinki: HEUNI), Report no. 32.

MCCOLD, P. (2004), 'What is the Role of Community in Restorative Justice Theory and Practice?', in Zehr, H. and Toews, B. (eds.), *Critical Issues in Restorative Justice* (Monsey: Criminal Justice Press), pp 155–72.

NELKEN, D. (2009), 'Comparative Criminal Justice: Beyond Ethnocentrism and Relativism', *European Journal of Criminology*, 6, pp 291–311.

NERGÅRD, T. (1993), 'Solving Conflicts Outside the Court System: Experiences With the Conflict Resolution Boards in Norway', *British Journal of Criminology*, 33, pp 81–94.

Restorative Justice Council (2011), *Best Practice Guidelines for Restorative Practice* (London: Restorative Justice Council and Ministry of Justice).

ROBINSON, G. and SHAPLAND, J. (2008), 'Reducing Recidivism: A Task for Restorative Justice?', *British Journal of Criminology*, 48(3), pp 337–58.

ROSSNER, M. (2011), 'Emotions and Interaction Ritual: A Micro-Analysis of Restorative Justice', *British Journal of Criminology*, 51(1), pp 95–119.

SHAPLAND, J. (2008), 'Hoe Herstelrecht Evalueren?' (Evaluating Restorative Justice), *Tijdschrift voor Herstelrecht*, 8, pp 26–36.

SHAPLAND, J. (2009), 'Restorative Justice Conferencing in the Context of Community Policing', *Journal of Police Studies*, 2009-2, pp 119–38.

Shapland, J. (forthcoming), 'Desistance From Crime and the Potential Role of Restorative Justice', in Liebling, A., Shapland, J. and von Hirsch, A. (eds.), *Crime, Justice and Social Order: Essays in Honour of A.E. Bottoms* (on file with author).

Shapland, J., Atkinson, A., Atkinson, H., Chapman, B., Colledge, E., Dignan, J., Howes, M., Johnstone, J., Robinson, G. and Sorsby, A. (2006), *Restorative Justice in Practice: The Second Report From the Evaluation of Three Schemes*, The University of Sheffield Centre for Criminological Research Occasional Paper 2 (Sheffield: Faculty of Law), available at <http://www.sheffield.ac.uk/polopoly_fs/1.783!/file/RestorativeJustice2ndReport.pdf>.

Shapland, J., Atkinson, A., Atkinson, H., Chapman, B., Dignan, J., Howes, M., Johnstone, J., Robinson, G. and Sorsby, A. (2007), *Restorative Justice: The Views of Victims and Offenders*, Ministry of Justice Research Series 3/07 (London: Ministry of Justice), available at <http://webarchive.nationalarchives.gov.uk/20110201125714/http://www.justice.gov.uk/publications/research190607.htm>.

Shapland, J., Robinson, G. and Sorsby, A. (2011), *Restorative Justice in Practice* (London: Routledge).

Shapland, J., Willmore, J. and Duff, P. (1985), *Victims in the Criminal Justice System* (Aldershot: Gower).

Shearing, C. (2001), 'Transforming Security: A South African Experiment', in Strang, H. and Braithwaite, J. (eds.), *Restorative Justice and Civil Society* (Cambridge: Cambridge University Press), pp 14–34.

Strang, H. (2002), *Repair or Revenge: Victims and Restorative Justice* (Oxford: Clarendon Press).

Tudor, B. (2000), 'Mediation and the Victim of Violent Crime: A Practitioner's View', in Kemshall, H. and Pritchard, J. (eds.), *Good Practice in Working with Victims of Violence* (London: Jessica Kingsley), pp 119–27.

Tyler, T. (2006), 'Restorative Justice and Procedural Justice: Dealing with Rule Breaking', *Journal of Social Issues*, 62(2), pp 307–26.

Tyler, T., Sherman, L., Strang, H., Barnes, G. and Woods, D. (2007), 'Reintegrative Shaming, Procedural Justice, and Recidivism: The Engagement of Offenders' Psychological Mechanisms in the Canberra RISE Drinking-and-Driving Experiment', *Law and Society Review*, 41(3), pp 553–86.

United Nations (2002), *Basic Principles on the Use of Restorative Justice Programmes in Criminal Matters*, Paper E/2002/INF/2/Add.2.

Van Ness, D. (2003), 'Proposed Basic Principles on the Use of Restorative Justice Recognising the Aims and Limits of Restorative Justice', in von Hirsch, A., Roberts, J., Bottoms, A., Roach, K. and Schiff, M. (eds.), *Restorative Justice and Criminal Justice: Competing or Reconcilable Paradigms?* (Oxford: Hart Publishing), pp 157–76.

Vanfraechem, I., Aertsen, I. and Willemsens, J. (2010), *Restorative Justice Realities: Empirical Research in a European Context* (The Hague: Boom, Het Groene Gras).

Zehr, H. (1990), *Changing Lenses: A New Focus for Crime and Justice* (Scottdale: Herald Press).

Zehr, H. (2010), 'The Development of the Practice of Restorative Justice', paper to the conference on 'Doing Restorative Justice in Europe', Bilbao, 17–19 June 2010, European Forum for Restorative Justice.

Zernova, M. (2007), *Restorative Justice: Ideals and Realities* (Aldershot: Ashgate).

Zinsstag, E., Teunkens, M. and Pali, B. (2011), *Conferencing: A Way Forward for Restorative Justice in Europe?* Report to the European Commission (Leuven: European Forum for Restorative Justice).

5

FACILITATING RESTORATIVE CONFERENCES

Tim Chapman

RESTORATIVE JUSTICE THEORY AND FACILITATION

The very extensive restorative justice literature strives to define process, outcomes, and values (Bazemore and Walgrave 1999; McCold 2000; Pavlich 2007; Pranis 2007; Strang and Braithwaite 2001; Van Ness and Strong 1997), provides a theoretical underpinning for restorative justice (Bazemore and Schiff 2005; Braithwaite 1989), identifies how restorative justice might be institutionalized (Aertsen et al. 2006; Bazemore and Walgrave 1999; McCold 2000; MacKay 2006), sets standards for restorative justice (Braithwaite 2002; Leverton 2008) and evaluates its outcomes (Shapland et al. 2012; Sherman and Strang 2007).

Yet there is very little theory on the actual practice of facilitation other than reference to the 'script' (O'Connell et al. 1999). The script is made up of series of 'restorative questions', which structure the conference and guide the participants through a restorative process. Barton (2003) usefully distinguishes between conferencing *programme models* and *facilitation models*. He recognizes the importance of a skilfully executed process outlining a process to achieve the 'empowerment' of the participants essentially through a more detailed script. Bazemore and Schiff (2005: 22) provide an argument for not defining practice too prescriptively; that, given diverse community, institutional, and ethnic contexts, 'general practice and implementation principles based on replicable theories would seem to be more helpful to practitioners than strict program guidelines.' They set about outlining an intervention theory, which integrates theory with priorities and tasks, and with immediate and intermediate outcomes.

The literature on restorative justice has been part of a process of gaining public and political support for an innovative response to harm. Schon (1983) found that most professions base their claim for professional status on 'technical rationality', or the application of scientific knowledge to problem solving. Technical rationality involves clear definitions of problems, research based methods, and unambiguous solutions or outcomes. This model values control, distance, and objectivity. The skills of professionals being more difficult to define and measure are considered secondary to scientific knowledge. Braithwaite (2002) is concerned that the move towards standardization represents the tendency of the state to maintain control over a process that is meant to transfer power to citizens. This echoes Habermas's (1984) concerns over the colonization of the 'lifeworld' by the state and market systems.

As a result theorizing has tended to exclude the agency of the people involved in restorative conferences: those who offend, those who suffer from offences, their supporters, and the practices of the facilitator. The literature seems to assert that, if the right systems are institutionalized, the right values adopted and the right standards followed, a diverse range of people with a diverse range of needs will be satisfied by scripted practice.

The expert's ability to define another person's problem and to prescribe its solution is an exercise of power (Foucault 1980). Christie (1977) argued that criminal justice professionals steal conflict from citizens and disregard the people affected by crime such as victims. Restorative justice practitioners can also 'steal conflicts' by imposing principles and values that prevent certain people from gaining access to restorative processes through restrictive referral criteria. They can do so by imposing rigid definitions of what constitutes a victim or of the correct level of offender responsibility and remorse. They can exclude vulnerable victims, corporate victims, and victims of domestic abuse or sexual harm. They can exclude people who have difficulty expressing themselves verbally or who find it difficult to understand the process. They can do so by allowing restorative justice to become simply another method for reducing reoffending. They can do so by restricting what is an acceptable restorative outcome.

Such selectivity on the part of the 'experts' can result in 'cherry picking' and significant attrition (Shapland et al. 2011). Criminal justice is a complex and volatile political field. The restorative justice movement is in danger of settling for a marginal role within it, confined to 'safe' contexts such as low level offending and schools, areas that do not pose any political risk to the state.

This chapter aims to make a contribution to the development of a facilitation theory using the experience of youth conferences in Northern Ireland.

YOUTH CONFERENCES IN NORTHERN IRELAND

Northern Ireland has responded to the challenge issued in 1999 by Bazemore and Walgrave (1999: 5) to develop a 'fully-fledged, systemic alternative' restorative youth justice system. The Justice (Northern Ireland) Act 2002 established the availability of restorative youth conferences to all young people who admit any criminal offence other than those who would receive a life sentence in the case of an adult. The significance of this is that the decision to participate in a conference is made by those responsible for the offence and by their victims rather than criminal justice professionals.

This means that conferences can be held to deal with the full range of criminal offences from the trivial to sexual offences and serious violent offences except for murder. People who choose to participate may be vulnerable or may have disabilities which affect their ability to communicate or empathize. The relationship between those affected by an offence may be close or distant. People may feel indifferent towards each other or may be highly antagonistic. Some offences will have no obvious victim.

It was necessary to design a model of restorative justice which was sufficiently flexible and robust to deliver consistent and equitable processes required by human rights and the due process of the law and to be accessible to and effective with a wide range of people affected by a wide range of harmful acts. There are several models available. The victim offender mediation model tends to be prevalent in Europe while the restorative conference model has emerged from experience in New Zealand and Australia. While there is considerable overlap between these two models, mediation tends to imply two parties facilitated by a neutral mediator to resolve private conflicts arising from a criminal offence. This approach was seen as working well with adult parties referred at the discretion of the criminal justice system in cases where there is a relational or financial conflict. However, a restorative justice approach embedded within the criminal justice system cannot disregard the reality that youth crime is a public issue and not simply a private matter between the victim and the offender. Furthermore, to respond to young people involved in crime either by being harmed or by being responsible for harm requires the involvement of and support from family and other carers. Including those people indirectly affected by the harm as well as the principle parties, strengthens both the levels of support and accountability available to the restorative process. Consequently the conference model was preferred. Although the family group conference accommodates victims, its primary focus is on the well-being of the young person responsible for the harm. The Northern Irish approach required a balance between the needs and interests of victims, of the community, and of the young people responsible for harm.

Responsibility for the coordination and facilitation of restorative processes is another area in which there is a range of options. Conferences may be delivered by non-governmental organizations or by statutory agencies and facilitated by full-time professionals or by part-time trained practitioners who may be paid fees or be volunteers. Because of the need to provide an equitable and inclusive service and to maintain consistent standards which would earn public credibility, the government decided that youth conferences should be delivered by the Youth Justice Agency and facilitated by highly trained professionals. These practitioners are not neutral; they are committed to enabling each party to have their voice heard and their needs met. While youth conference coordinators are professionals, their facilitation skills and knowledge are designed to enable the parties to take control of the conference. These arrangements reinforced the commitment to place restorative justice at the centre of the youth justice system.

THE BALANCED MODEL OF RESTORATIVE JUSTICE

The Balanced Model of Restorative Justice (Campbell et al. 2002) in Northern Ireland adopted by the Youth Justice Agency was influenced by the Balanced and Restorative Justice project (BARJ 2000). It is based upon the premise that a harmful act affects three parties: the person who has been harmed, the person who is responsible for the harm, and their communities (see Figure 5.1). The balanced model recognizes the 'ripple effect' of harm caused by the relationships that people have with each other. Crime is seen as both a private problem and a public issue.

Zehr (1990: 24) defines crime as a violation of the self and specifically 'our belief that the world is an orderly, meaningful place, and our belief in personal autonomy.' The model classifies the needs that commonly arise from harmful behaviour under three broad categories: the need to feel safe, the need to experience justice, and the need to regain control over one's life. While these needs are clearly consequences of harm, the same needs, when unmet over a period of time, are also major causes of harmful behaviour. Thus the youth conference process is designed to restore to all parties those needs that have been violated by the harm.

The same needs are as important to the restorative process as to its outcomes. Restoring justice is experienced through accountability to those who have been harmed, through the fair and equitable treatment of all parties, through all parties having their voice heard, through the vindication of the victim (Bennett 2006), through satisfaction with the process and its outcomes, and through legal safeguards regarding rights and proportionality[1] (Bazemore and Walgrave 1999).

Restoring safety is experienced through the preparation process when any fears are raised and addressed, through the parties having confidence in the facilitators' authority, through the presence of supporters, through the explanation of the ground rules and their consistent enforcement, and through the presence of a police officer.[2]

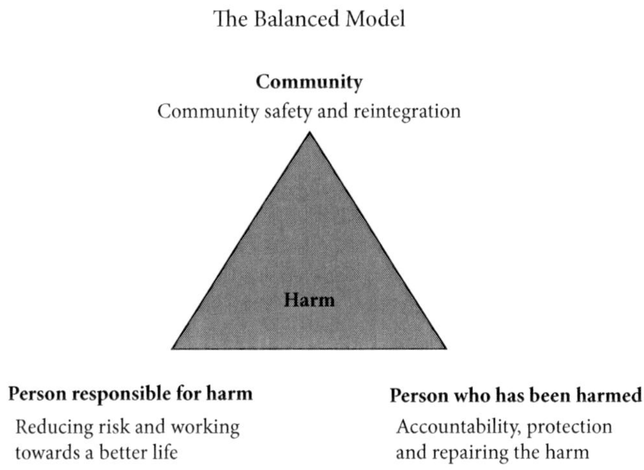

Figure 5.1 The Balanced Model

[1] In Northern Ireland all conference agreements must be ratified by the Public Prosecution Service or the Youth Court. People responsible for harm can bring a lawyer to protect their rights but not to advocate for them.

[2] The presence of a police officer at a youth conference is required by law in Northern Ireland.

Restoring control is experienced through the facilitator's explanation of the process, through the clarity of expectations that each party has, through the presence of supporters, and through a structured yet flexible process which enables the parties to be in control of what they want to say and ask.

The Balanced Model of Restorative Justice provides a framework for practice. But it does not provide a theory of facilitation. In order to understand the process and value of skilful facilitation we need to inquire into storytelling and the concepts of discourse and narrative.

STORIES, NARRATIVES, AND DISCOURSES

Storytelling is critical to the youth conference process in Northern Ireland. In preparation for the conference, facilitators enable each party to tell the story of what happened. The purpose of this process of listening to the story is not to establish the facts but to enable the individual to make sense of what has happened and what they need to do to deal with its consequences. The story is about meaning and the actions that flow from that meaning.

Borrowing from the insights of narrative therapy and mediation (White 2000; 2007; Winslade and Monk 2001; 2008) facilitation is based upon the understanding that, when an individual is recounting what happened, they are not merely reporting on events but constructing a reality. By listening carefully the facilitator will understand what is important to the individual and how the restorative process might work for him or her. Stories contain elements of the individual's identity, beliefs, and values. This can be defined as the individual's personal narrative within which the story of the harmful act is accommodated. Rather than viewing the feelings, needs, and interests of an individual as originating solely as a result of the harm, the facilitator sees them as being sustained by the narrative.

Narratives are in turn a product of cultural discourse. Foucault (1972) defined discourse as a social practice within a cultural context determining the way people see and think about the world. Crime, its detection, and punishment pervade popular culture in western societies through literature, cinema, television, news media, and politics. Various discourses on the problem of crime, its causes, and how to manage it compete within the spheres of public opinion, policy, and practice.

Garland (2001) illustrates how powerful dominant discourses on crime control and criminal justice have been in Britain and the United States leading to populist politics which emphasize public protection, social control, and imprisonment. Such discourses provide people with readymade understandings of the problem of crime and its solutions. However, they simplify complex realities. Once linked to an actual distressing situation, a 'thin' story emerges which neither expresses the full facts or needs arising from the harm nor accommodates other possible narratives. Such a discourse is generally made up of 'totalising descriptions' (Winslade and Monk 2001) and characterized by the exaggeration of some truths and the denial of others. A thin story sustains itself through disengagement and separation from those whom it sees as the 'enemy' or the 'threat', objectifying them rather than seeing them as fellow human beings. The problem with such thin stories is that they rarely have a happy ending. Both the victim and the offender are left with a sense that their stories have not been fully heard or completed.

Zehr (1990) presented restorative justice as an alternative discourse or 'lens' different (and superior) to the legalistic system of retribution. Bazemore (1999) also illustrated the different lenses through which people view delinquency. These writers are developing convincing discourses with which to institutionalize a morally superior and more effective system of doing justice. However, they are doing so from the standpoint of a theoretical model. As if, once the institutional arrangements could be perfectly aligned with the correct restorative principles, 'ordinary people', victims, offenders, and their supporters would abandon the powerful narratives and discourses that they carry.

The 'Social Discipline Window' (Wachtel and McCold 2001) is used to distinguish the nature and superiority of the restorative response over the punitive, neglectful, and permissive approaches to harmful behaviour (see Figure 5.2). Yet many people who will participate in restorative conferences believe in such ideas. Many offenders will have access to 'subcultural discourses' (cf. techniques of neutralization Sykes and Matza 1957).

Campbell et al. (2002) took the liberty of adapting the Social Discipline Window to the model that was being developed in Northern Ireland. The concepts of accountability and social support were used in place of Glaser's (1969) control and support. This configuration links key restorative values, responsibility, relationships, and respect. It

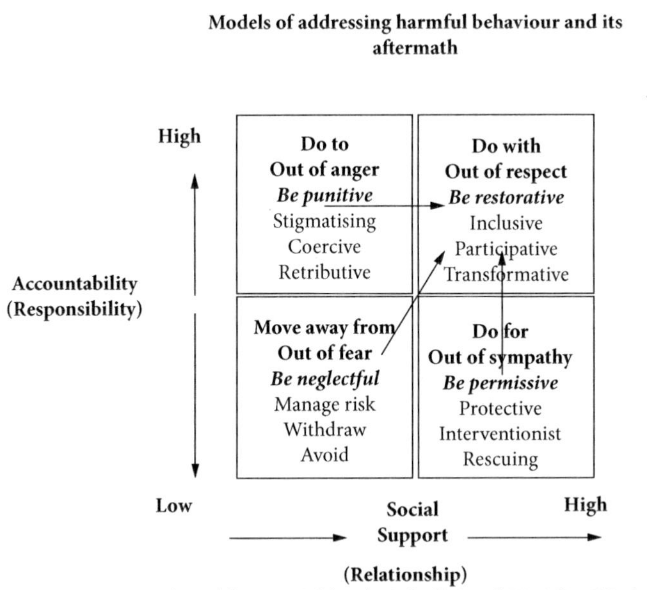

Adapted from McCold and Wachtel's Social Discipline Window

Figure 5.2 Models of addressing harmful behaviour and its aftermath

was important to add an emotional dimension to the model as feelings arise from the underlying needs of each discourse. Finally the arrows signify the restorative process: to respect and include the discourses which each party carries, to enable individuals to express themselves, to listen to others, and to enter into a dialogue which leads to a transformation of thin discourses into thick stories which are satisfactorily resolved or completed.

Restorative processes enable the parties to engage with each other's realities in a safe, just, and controlled space which reduces the need to attack, defend, or avoid. The effectiveness of the conference depends upon the dialogue being based upon a specific direct experience, shared in relationship with others. This allows stories to 'thicken' and to complete. In such a context, difference is not an obstacle to be overcome but a resource (Zernova and Wright 2007) to enable each party to better understand each other and themselves. This requires the facilitator to sustain the conference's respect for each story and the emotions, needs, and interests that it expresses. In doing so the facilitator respects the intelligence and creativity of each member of the conference.

Addressing harm is a respectful act. To choose to act in a way that harms another is disrespectful. It can be experienced by the victim as shameful. 'A moral injury consists of being treated as if you do not really count' (Bennett 2007: 252). Restorative justice is founded on the idea that causing harm to someone creates an obligation to make amends. If that person assumes that responsibility and commits to reparative action, the community should support his or her reintegration. Consequently it is important that the victim's needs are fully addressed before there is any focus on the offender's story and needs. This process is influenced by Braithwaite's (1989) reintegrative shaming theory and Bazemore and Schiff's (2005) concept of earned redemption and is supported by Maruna's (2001) theory of the redemption script as a pathway to desistance from crime.

The facilitation of the stories of people affected by harm within the context of respect is a skilful and professional task which is closer to Schon's (1983) model of 'reflection-in-action' than 'technical rationality'. Professional practice involves numerous judgements and decisions which are rarely based on the conscious application of theory. Through a process of action and reflection the professional improvises a solution through tentatively testing hypotheses in each unique case. Schon found that 'Complexity, instability, and uncertainty are not removed or resolved by applying specialized knowledge to well-defined tasks' (1983: 19). The key to reflection-in-action is engaging in a 'conversation with the situation' (Schon 1983). Through this conversation the facilitator is designing a process that will lead to a solution. This involves the framing of the problem and strategies for addressing it. The relationship between facilitators and those they serve is built upon a dialogue in which meanings are shared and explored until a common understanding emerges. The key premises are that everyone has knowledge to share and that uncertainties may be a source of learning and discovery. In this way facilitators stage conflicts rather than take them over (Christie 1977).

How does one stage a conference? Primarily by being in control of the process, (but not of the participants), which comprises three stages: inclusion, participation, and transformation.

INCLUSION

The purpose of the inclusion process is to gain the informed consent of the appropriate people to participate in a restorative process. The challenge to the facilitator is to engage multiple parties (the person who has been harmed, the person responsible for the harm, their supporters, the community, and the government/criminal justice system) in working together to meet multiple needs and goals (Van Ness and Strong 1997). While there will clearly be differences of approach depending upon whether the facilitator is engaging with an offender or a victim, what follows is a description of the core facilitation processes and skills.

Facilitators may be preoccupied by their own questions rather than those of the parties:

- How do I get these people into a room together?
- How do I make this person more responsible and accountable?
- How do I help this person to feel better?
- How do I meet this person's needs?
- How do I get this person to do the right thing?
- How do I get these people to buy into the restorative vision?
- How do I negotiate a good agreement?

These questions assume that the parties are the problem. The parties are not clients, customers, or recipients of a service but are acting as active citizens. It is important that each party chooses to participate in the restorative process and that they have sufficient information to make that choice. They should not feel that the facilitator is attempting to 'sell' them a service or product.

Inclusion should take the form of a meeting preferably in a private place where the party feels comfortable ie home or place of work. While there are key tasks to be performed in this phase such as developing rapport, explaining the conference process and what is expected of each party within it, the critical task is to facilitate each person's storytelling. This is important because the story will define the issues and goals that each party will want to address. Crucially the stories should not be fitted into the conference structure; rather the conference should accommodate and become part of each person's story, ideally resolving or completing the story and allowing alternative narrative to emerge.

The structure of this process has been influenced by non-violent communication (Rosenberg 2003). The facilitator begins by asking each party what happened. She or he will then tentatively explore the emotional content of the story. Feelings clarify the needs which have been violated by the harm or which may have caused the harmful act. Once the needs specific to each party have been identified, the facilitator explores what each party wants to do about these needs and how the other parties can contribute to addressing the needs.

THE STORY

The facilitator enables the individual to tell the story by simple open questions, perhaps, beginning with 'What happened?'. Respecting the integrity of the story, the facilitator focuses on moving from general statements to more specific views and concrete examples. Listening to a story the facilitator pays attention to what the story teller pays attention to, what is included and what is ignored, what is given depth and what is skimmed over, what is repeated, what is revealed and what is hidden.

This inquiry can be enhanced by 'externalising' (White 2007) the harm as separate from themselves. Externalizing the problem enables people to address it more directly:

- What is the precise nature of the harm to you?
- How long has it been affecting you?
- How has it changed over time?
- How does it make you think about the other person?
- How does it affect your relationships, work, home life, health, etc.?
- If it does not go away, what might happen in the future?
- How is it holding you back from doing what you want to do?

The focus of these questions is on the harm not the person or conditions which caused it. Separating the person from the harmful act can begin the process of freeing the individual from the shame they feel about the incident. This can apply just as much to the victim as to the perpetrator. These questions require 'a tentative, curious and deliberately naïve posture' (Winslade and Monk 2008: 115) from the facilitator.

The care that the facilitator takes to listen to the story and to understand its meaning for the individual is the first step in the inclusion process. The facilitator should resist the temptation to provide a resolution to the issues that arise from the questions. That is the function of the conference and the tension (Fritz 1989) of holding these unresolved issues provides motivation to participate in the restorative process.

THE EMOTIONS

Any story about a harmful situation will contain a range of distressing emotions. The same injury can evoke different emotions in different people. The nuances of the feelings of each individual needs to be appreciated by the facilitator. Such empathy and respect for feelings will aid the inclusion process. Yet, it is important to move on from empathy. Left to their own devices these often distressing feelings will lead people to adopt common public discourses relating to crime.

THE NEEDS

Emotions are a guide to the specific needs of each party. As a general rule if the underlying emotion concerning the harm is anger, people may feel that their need for justice must be restored; if people express fears as a result of being harmed, they need to feel safe once again; if anxiety or worry is predominant, this may indicate individuals' need to regain control over their lives; and if shame pervades the story, the individual needs to reclaim respect.

Once there is a shared understanding of which needs have been violated by the harm, the facilitator enables the individual to move from the general to the specific:

- In what way do you feel that you need justice?
- Can you tell me exactly what you fear might happen as a result of this?
- What do you worry most about?
- How do you feel disrespected?

Some of the needs expressed may not arise solely from the harm. They may be deeper unmet needs reactivated by the experience of harm and may relate to other distressing events or relationships in the past or in their current life. In such circumstances repairing the damage caused by a specific harm may be the beginning of a recovery process and lead to a referral for further support.

The facilitator should resist the temptation to suggest how these needs might be met. Rather she or he should explore with each party how participation in a conference could contribute to restoring what each party needs to move on.

THE WANTS

To engage people's participation in a transformative process requires structural tension (Fritz 1989; Miller and Rollnick 2002) between an undesirable reality and how they would like their life to be. People are motivated by the prospect of meeting their needs and having their interests represented. The facilitator's task is to enable each party to clarify what they want independently of considerations of process (Fritz 1989) and then tailor the process to their needs.

Awareness of needs and wants enables the facilitator to envisage a common ground on which the parties can meet. One area of common ground between the parties is often the wish 'to move on'. Both those who have been harmed and those who have caused harm usually want to stop the story of the harm controlling them. They wish to regain control and to get on with their lives. This is what it means to complete a story. In many cases the parties need each other to resolve issues relating to safety, justice, and control. Zehr (2002: 25) has written about the need to not only retell stories but to transform 'stories of humiliation and shame into stories of dignity and courage'. He speaks of journeys towards justice, towards honour and respect, and towards vindication.

The facilitator is only now beginning to envisage a restorative process which will enable all parties to participate in meeting their needs. Schon and Rein (1994: 172–173) describe such designing as a process of making something out of the materials in the specific situation and under conditions of uncertainty and complexity. The facilitator is not attempting to achieve outcomes but to design a process which will enable the parties to achieve outcomes.

The facilitator shapes the design of the conference to accommodate each of the parties. While a face-to-face encounter is generally the most effective form of conference, there are other options:

1. the victim can be protected by a one way screen;
2. video or telephone conferences (useful when the perpetrator is in custody);
3. the victim can make a video, audio, or written message;
4. the facilitator can 'shuttle' between the parties; or
5. the victim could choose a representative to attend.

Once each party is aware of their needs and interests in relation to the harm and how participation in a conference could enable them to address these needs and interests, he or she is in a position to choose whether to participate. The choice to participate should be made by the parties rather than by the facilitator except in exceptional circumstances. However, the facilitator's ability to both include and to validate the complexity of each party's story increases the likelihood that they will open themselves to a new experience and possibility.

PREPARATION

If the invitation to participate is accepted, the second stage of the inclusion process is to prepare each party so that they can do themselves justice. Some models of restorative practice emphasize the questions that facilitators should ask. This approach focuses on enabling each participant to gain answers to their questions:

- I have been harmed: what protection is available to me?
- I have been wronged: what justice is available to me?
- My life has been disrupted: what support is available to me to regain control of my life?

And:

- I am in trouble: what is going to happen to me?
- I am worried: how can I move on from this?
- Everyone disapproves: will anyone listen to my story?
- I cannot manage on my own: will anyone support me to change what is going wrong in my life?

The skill is to identify and clarify what is the key question for each party and to explain that these questions can only be fully answered at the conference. This enables the parties to begin to realize that they need each other.

The facilitator may spend some time enabling each individual to work out what they want to say to achieve their goals and how to say it in the presence of others. Many young people find it difficult to talk to adults especially when they are aware of the disapproval of what they have done. There is also a higher incidence of language difficulties among young offenders than the norm (Sanger et al. 2001). This can result in the further marginalization of young people (Snow and Sanger 2010). The facilitator takes responsibility for identifying and addressing any obstacle to the full participation of each party in the conference. These may include imbalances of power, low self-worth, lack of confidence in speaking in groups, the expression and control of emotion, and disabilities. Facilitators will also ask individuals to imagine how the other parties may respond to them and, having considered this, ask whether this is likely to produce the desired outcome.

Facilitators will explain what will be expected of each party at the conference. This can be done by describing the key phases of the conference process (Campbell et al. 2002):

1. The person responsible for the harm accounts for what he or she did;
2. The person who has been harmed asks questions;
3. The person who has been harmed recounts what happened and its impact;
4. Other members of the conference comment on the harm;
5. The person responsible for the harm responds to what has been said;
6. The conference engages in a dialogue about how the person who has been harmed can be satisfied;
7. Once this has been agreed, the conference inquires into what can be put in place to support the young person to desist from such harmful behaviour.
8. A plan is drawn up and agreed.

The facilitator's task is to prepare the individual by paying close attention to the challenges and difficulties inherent in this process and inviting her or him to consider how these could be addressed and what support will be needed.

Part of the preparation stage will be to invite appropriate supporters. For the victim, supporters may include others who have been indirectly affected by the harm or a trusted person who will support and encourage. For the person responsible for the harm, supporters can encourage: the young person responsible for the harm to give a good account (Maruna et al. 2006: 64–66), stimulate remorse, and offer suggestions and support to the young person's efforts to desist from harming others. Significant members of the extended family, mentors, and other adults involved in the young person's life can make a positive contribution to the conference.

The facilitator may also invite representatives of the community that has been indirectly harmed and professionals who are currently working with the person who is responsible for the harm. These parties also require preparation so that they are clear about their role in the conference process.

In the balanced model the process must be designed not only to include all the parties but also to accommodate an absent audience or 'gallery of public opinion' (Schon and Rein 1994: 168). Once restorative justice becomes mainstream, it inevitably engages with the discourses of the criminal justice system and the local community. The conference process must then not only meet the needs of the parties but also address institutional interests if it is to survive and remain mainstream. This must be explained to those attending the conference.

If the preparation phase has been effective, participants will trust and feel confident in the authority and competence of the facilitator, will be clear about what they can gain from participation in a conference, will understand their responsibilities and the support available to them, and will feel safe to participate.

PARTICIPATION

Habermas (1984) envisages an ideal speech situation in which public decisions are reached by autonomous citizens in a process of unconstrained communication. This is similar to restorative dialogue (Raye and Roberts 2007: 218). To accomplish this, a safe, just, and controlled space free from domination and deception must be created and facilitated. The role of the facilitator during the conference is to facilitate participation in this space. Facilitators learn to trust the process and focus on ensuring that any obstacles to participation are avoided or overcome, and that includes keeping themselves out of the way of the process.

Ground rules are designed to protect the process and create safety. Other than enforcing the ground rules, the facilitator does not control the participants. The task of the facilitator is to keep the process on track. The authority of the facilitator and the structure of the process as it moves through its phases provide the participants with a sense of safety and control over their participation. This requires an authoritative style combined with an ability to work with a range of emotions. Feelings are a source of energy moving the conference on towards its outcomes. Being sensitive to the energy of the conference is a key skill of facilitation.

The conference addresses the harm caused first. This gives the priority to the needs of the person who has been harmed by the offence. The young person tells the person whom he or she has harmed what he or she did and what they were thinking at the time and what they think about now. The person who has been harmed can then put his/her questions to the young person. Once the questions have all been answered, the victim tells the young person how the harmful behaviour has affected him or her. Other members of the conference can also add their comments regarding the harm.

The young person who caused the harm will then be invited to respond to what he or she has heard. The facilitator may ask him or her to say what were the most important things that the victim said. It is at this stage that an apology is likely to be made. The victim is invited to respond to the apology. It is the young person's responsibility to convince the conference of the sincerity of their remorse. This may involve actions to make amends or repair damage as well as words of regret. The conference enters into a dialogue on how to satisfy the victim's needs.

It is important that the victim feels fully satisfied that their needs have been fully addressed before the conference directs its attention towards the needs of the young person in relation to desistance from causing harm. Once victims feel that justice has been done, they are generally ready to reach out to the young person. Another dialogue addresses the steps that should be taken to reduce the likelihood of further harmful behaviour and how these steps should be supported. The young person and his or her family and supporters should play a major part in this phase. At this stage any professionals present will be invited to offer information and their opinions. This dialogue should lead to another set of agreed actions.

The facilitator then writes up the agreed steps to repair and prevent harm. This will be incorporated into a report to be sent to the prosecution service or the youth court.

This process is facilitated by skilfully enabling the parties' stories to be told, to be enriched or 'thickened' (White 2000), and to be transformed through dialogue. The role of the facilitator is to enable the person or persons who have been harmed to describe the effects of the harm so truthfully that people responsible for the harm cannot evade responsibility for their actions. The victim often needs the accountability of the offender to feel vindicated and the offender needs to develop responsibility in order to work towards a better life.

The restorative process allows different discourses to enter into dialogue. If discourse is a way of organizing meaning about an issue, dialogue is the exchange of meanings. Rather than a debate on who is right and who is wrong, dialogue is a conversation with a centre not sides (Isaacs 1999). The centre of a conference is an act of harm and its consequences. Dialogue seeks to gain access to the collective intelligence and creativity of the group to repair the harm and prevent it from happening again. Block (2007: 11) conceived of conversations which are restorative in that they:

- create *ownership*;
- evoke *commitment*;
- acknowledge *relatedness;*
- identify *possibility;*
- value *dissent* and refusal;
- and *invite* rather than mandate action.

When these conditions are present there is a balance between advocacy and inquiry. Advocacy is speaking about the harm from your point of view. Inquiry is exploring what you do not know and discovering what others think. The complexity of dialogue cannot be facilitated by a simple technique or script.

Following Block (2007), dissent is valued. The facilitator is engaged in double listening (Winslade and Monk 2008) believing that, while each story may have a predominant discourse in conflict with other discourses, there may be another absent but implicit (White 2000) story which may yearn to resolve the situation and move on.

TRANSFORMATION

The restorative process is designed to transform each person's relationship to the harmful event, and like a ritual or a rite of passage (Turner 1969; van Gennep 1960) it may also transform the identity of the 'victim' and the 'offender'. Fritz (1989) distinguishes problem solving, as taking action to make something go away, from creating, as bringing something into being. Block (2007: 4) states that 'we cannot problem solve our way into fundamental change. This is not an argument against problem solving; it is an intention to shift the context and language within which problem solving takes place.' Contexts are created by the nature of the conversations that take place. A restorative context is created by communal accountability and commitment.

The conference process enables its participants to understand more specifically the nature of harm and the obligations that arise from it (Zehr 1990). Such an understanding leads to the possibility, though not the inevitability, of the assumption of personal responsibility for the harm and the consequent commitment to act to repair it.

Responsibility has many dimensions and layers. The assumption of responsibility has benefits for both parties. The person responsible for the harm enables the person who has suffered to complete their story of victimization through vindication and the restoration of justice, safety, and control over their lives. The injured parties are also offered the opportunity to exercise civic responsibility in supporting the reintegration of the wrongdoer. Many victims report that this is a source of satisfaction.

The person who has caused the harm can complete their story of condemnation, shame, and exclusion through the restoration of the respect and the resources and relationships that they need to achieve redemption as a contributing and law-abiding citizen (Maruna 2001). This represents the core social contract underpinning restorative justice: that if people repair the harm that they cause, then society should support them to have a good life.

It is the task of the facilitator to enable the conference to build scaffolding of sufficient strength to complete stories of harm and to create sustainable stories of moving on. The facilitator understands the importance of having witnesses to commitment. A commitment to an agreed course of action is strengthened if it is made to the person whom you have harmed and in the presence of people who are significant to you. Just as these people have earlier expressed disapproval of the harm and vindicated the victim, they now offer support for the commitment to repair the harm and express respect for the person responsible for the harm (Braithwaite 1989).

The history of people's relationships with harm varies. For some people the harm may be an exceptional incident in their lives, which can be resolved relatively briefly. For some victims the specific incident that is being addressed is another event in a history of trauma, which cannot be resolved in one conference. Similarly the act of harm by the perpetrator may not be typical of his or her behaviour. For others it is one offence among many. Such a person may need many restorative experiences before he or she desists from harm. Some offenders may take responsibility at some levels but not all. As Block (2007: 20) states, 'if we cannot say "no", then our "yes" has no meaning.' Above all, agreements must be real. An imperfect plan may still be enough to satisfy some of the victim's needs and be one small step towards desistance. Reparation can be performed effectively even if remorse is not felt or when the apology is not fully meant (Duff 2001).

In this approach to restorative justice, reparation forms the foundation and starting point of the agreed action and reintegration its ultimate outcome. However, in some cases the victim may need further support and rehabilitation to achieve recovery from the harm. Similarly the person responsible for the harm may need rehabilitative support to perform reparation and to work towards reintegration. Van Ness and Strong (1997) argue that the determining goal of resolution between the parties must be balanced by the limiting goal of maintaining safety as required by public policy. Consequently restrictions may need to be placed upon the person responsible for the harm so that he or she can remain in the community and perform reparation. In this way, rehabilitation and restrictions of movement or association become means to the achievement of reparation and reintegration.

In Northern Ireland the agreed plan of action is scrutinized by either the Public Prosecution Service or the Youth Court. This provides legal safeguards in relation to proportionality. The Public Prosecution Service and the Youth Court can amend action plans on the grounds of proportionality or public interest.

CONCLUSIONS

This chapter set out to explain the crucial role of skilful and principled facilitation in the restorative conference process. Shapland et al. (2011: 61) identifying the need to avoid the tendency of professionals to fall back into previous practices that are incompatible with restorative practices conclude that: 'The difference, we think, is the rigorous training, expectations of high quality, constant discussion about difficult cases and internalization of restorative values that happened among facilitators at all JRC sites.'

Much professional training focuses on the 'public face' of professionalism, theoretical knowledge and techniques, jargon and certification,[3] what Schon (1983) calls 'the professional façade'. These components of professionalism are relatively easy to teach and learn. However, there are other elements of professionalism, of which the professional may not be aware but which others see only too clearly: dismissive tone or language, unexamined beliefs and values, and a lack of cultural competence. These negative attributes of professionalism can be identified and 'unlearnt' through exposure and feedback through role-play, reflective practice, or observation of practice by colleagues. Gradually through these processes facilitators embed restorative values in themselves so that their speech and actions are expressions of these values; what Pranis (2007: 60) calls 'the spirit of what we do and how we do it.'

Facilitators understand that cracks in relationships not only cause harm but also offer opportunities to shed light on issues which must be resolved. They learn not to seek in every case a 'perfect offering'. Most conferences do not yield all the possible benefits to both parties. However, even a few 'bells that still can ring' will make a difference.[4]

REFERENCES

Aertsen, I., Daems, T. and Robert, L. (eds.) (2006), *Institutionalizing Restorative Justice* (Cullompton: Willan Publishing).

Balanced and Restorative Justice (2000), *Curriculum* (Washington: Office of Juvenile Justice and Delinquency Prevention).

Barton, C. (2003), *Restorative Justice: The Empowerment Model* (Sydney: Hawkins Press).

Bazemore, G. (1999), 'After Shaming, Whither Reintegration: Restorative Justice and Relational Rehabilitation', in Bazemore, G. and Walgrave, L. (eds.), *Restorative Juvenile Justice: Repairing the Harm of Youth Crime* (Monsey: Criminal Justice Press), pp 155–94.

Bazemore, G. and Schiff, M. (2005), *Juvenile Justice Reform and Restorative Justice* (Cullompton: Willan Publishing).

[3] I am grateful to Kameelah M. Mu'Min, graduate student of the Masters course in Restorative Practices and Youth Counselling, International Institute for Restorative Practices for the ideas in this paragraph.

[4] With thanks to Leonard Cohen for these phrases from Anthem.

BAZEMORE, G. and WALGRAVE, L (1999), 'Restorative Juvenile Justice in Search of Fundamentals and an Outline for Systemic Reform', in Bazemore, G. and Walgrave, L. (eds.), *Restorative Juvenile Justice: Repairing the Harm of Youth Crime* (Monsey: Criminal Justice Press), pp 45–74.

BENNETT, C. (2006), 'Satisfying the Needs and Interests of Victims', in Johnstone, G. and Van Ness, D. (eds.), *Handbook of Restorative Justice* (Cullompton: Willan Publishing), pp 247–64.

BLOCK, P. (2007), *Civic Engagement and the Restoration of Community: Changing the Nature of the Conversation*, available at <http://www.asmallgroup.net>.

BRAITHWAITE, J. (1989), *Crime, Shame and Reintegration* (Cambridge: Cambridge University Press).

BRAITHWAITE, J. (2002), 'Setting Standards for Restorative Justice', *British Journal of Criminology*, 42, pp 563–77.

CAMPBELL, H., CHAPMAN, T. and MCCREDY, S. (2002), *Practice Guidelines for the Youth Conference Service* (Belfast: Youth Justice Agency).

CHRISTIE, N. (1977), 'Conflict as Property', *British Journal of Criminology*, 17, pp 1–26.

DUFF, R. (2001), *Punishment, Communication and Community* (Oxford: Oxford University Press).

FOUCAULT, M. (1972), *The Order of Things: An Archaeology of the Human Sciences* (New York: Pantheon Books).

FOUCAULT, M. (1980), *Power/Knowledge: Selected Interviews and Other Writings* (New York: Pantheon Books).

FRITZ, R. (1989), *The Path of Least Resistance* (New York: Random).

GARLAND, D. (2001), *The Culture of Control* (Chicago: The University of Chicago Press).

GLASER, D. (1969), *The Effectiveness of a Prison and Parole System* (Indianapolis: Bobbs-Merrill).

HABERMAS, J. (1984), *Theory of Communicative Action* (Boston: Beacon Press).

ISAACS, W. (1999), *Dialogue: The Art of Thinking Together* (New York: Doubleday).

LEVERTON, W. (2008), 'The Case for Best Practice Standards in Restorative Justice', *American Journal of Trial Advocacy*, 31(3), pp 501–30.

MACKAY, R. (2006), 'The Institutionalisation of Principles of Restorative Justice—A Case Study from the UK', in Aertsen, I., Daems, T. and Robert, L. (eds.), *Institutionalising Restorative Justice* (Cullompton: Willan Publishing), pp 194–215.

MARUNA, S. (2001), *Making Good: How Ex-Convicts Reform and Rebuild Their Lives* (Washington: American Psychological Association Books).

MARUNA, S., WRIGHT, S., BROWN, J., VAN MARLIE, F., DEVLIN, R. and LIDDLE, M. (2006), *Youth Conferencing as Shame Management* (Belfast: Youth Justice Agency).

MCCOLD, P. (2000), 'Towards a Holistic Vision of Restorative Justice: A Reply to the Maximalist Model', *Contemporary Justice Review*, 3, pp 357–414.

MILLER, W. and ROLLNICK, S. (eds.) (2002), *Motivational Interviewing: Preparing People to Change* (3rd edn) (New York: Guilford Press).

O'CONNELL, T., WACHTEL, B. and WACHTEL, T. (1999), *Conferencing Handbook* (Pipersville: The Pipers Press).

PAVLICH, G. (2007), 'Ethics, Universal Principles and Restorative Justice', in Johnstone, G. and Van Ness, D. (eds.), *Handbook of Restorative Justice* (Cullompton: Willan Publishing), pp 615–30.

PRANIS, K. (2007), 'Restorative Values', in Johnstone, G. and Van Ness, D. (eds.), *Handbook of Restorative Justice* (Cullompton: Willan Publishing), pp 59–74.

Roberts, A. and Raye, B. (2007), 'Restorative Processes', in Johnstone, G and Van Ness, D. (eds.), *Handbook of Restorative Justice* (Cullompton: Willan Publishing), pp 211–227.

Rosenberg, M. (2003), *Non Violent Communication: A Language of Life* (Encinitas: Puddle Dancer Press).

Sanger, D., Moore-Brown, B., Magnusson, B. and Svoboda, N. (2001), 'Prevalence of Language Problems Among Adolescent Delinquents: A Closer Look', *Communication Disorders Quarterly*, 23, pp 17–26.

Schon, D. (1983), *The Reflective Practitioner: How Professionals Think in Action* (New York: Basic Books).

Schon, D. and Rein, M. (1994), *Frame Reflection* (New York: Basic Books).

Shapland, J., Robinson, G. and Sorsby, A. (2011), *Restorative Justice in Practice: Evaluating What Works for Victims and Offenders* (Abingdon: Routledge).

Sherman, L. and Strang, H. (2007), *Restorative Justice: The Evidence* (London: The Adam Institute).

Snow, P. and Sanger, D. (2010), 'Restorative Justice Conferencing and the Youth Offender: Exploring the Role of Oral Language Competence', *International Journal of Language and Communication Disorders*, 46(3), pp 324–33.

Strang, H. and Braithwaite, J. (eds.) (2001), *Restorative Justice and Civil Society* (Cambridge: Cambridge University Press).

Sykes, G. and Matza, D. (1957), 'Techniques of Neutralisation', *American Sociological Review*, 22, pp 664–70.

Turner, V. (1969), *The Ritual Process* (New York: Cornell University Press).

Van Gennep, A. (1960), *The Rites of Passage* (Chicago: University of Chicago Press).

Van Ness, D. and Strong, K. (1997), *Restoring Justice* (Cincinnati: Anderson Publishing).

Wachtel, T. and McCold, P. (2001), 'Restorative Justice in Everyday Life', in Strang, H. and Braithwaite, J. (eds.), *Restorative Justice and Civil Society* (Cambridge: Cambridge University Press), pp 114–29.

White, M. (2000), *Reflections on Narrative Practice: Essays and Interviews* (Adelaide: Dulwich Centre).

White, M. (2007), *Maps of Narrative Practice* (New York: Norton).

Winslade, J. and Monk, G. (2001), *A New Approach to Conflict Resolution* (San Francisco: Jossey-Bass).

Winslade, J. and Monk, G. (2008), *Practicing Narrative Mediation: Loosening the Grip of Conflict* (San Francisco: Jossey-Bass).

Zehr, H. (1990), *Changing Lenses* (Scottsdale: Herald Press).

Zehr, H. (2002), 'Journey to Belonging', in Weitekamp, E. and Kerner, H-J., *Restorative Justice: Theoretical Foundations* (Cullompton, Willan Publishing).

Zernova, M. and Wright, M. (2007), 'Alternative Visions of Restorative Justice', in Johnstone, G. and Van Ness, D. (eds.), *Handbook of Restorative Justice* (Cullompton: Willan Publishing), pp 91–108.

6

CONFERENCING AND VICTIMS

Heather Strang

In the summer of 2011 British people watched news programmes night after night that reported on the trial of the man soon to be convicted of the murder of a 13 year old schoolgirl, Milly Dowler. The details of the murder itself were horrifying but what struck most people as the worst aspect of the trial was the ordeal suffered by Milly's parents at the hands of lawyers for the defence. Because only circumstantial evidence linked the killer to the murdered girl, the defence was instructed to explore all alternative explanations for her disappearance. As a result Milly's father was obliged to discuss, on the witness stand, humiliating aspects of his sex life, and her mother to answer questions about supposed favouritism of her other daughter that might have distressed Milly to the point of suicide. After the public outcry that ensued about the treatment of Milly's parents, the chairman of the Bar Council stated: 'Judges and barristers are required to ensure no victim or a member of their family or friends is put through any unnecessary distress. This was necessary.' (Rayment and Leppard 2011: 19.) In reflecting on the pointlessness of the family's suffering, given that the defendant was already serving a life sentence for the murder of two women, a defence barrister added: 'The Dowlers may well have been given a false expectation of the function of the trial. The trial is not a cathartic exercise or a truth and reconciliation process, however much some people want it to be' (*The Sunday Times* 26 June 2011: 19).

The Dowler trial illustrated in the starkest terms the incompatibility of the formal justice system, at least in the adversarial model, between the expectations and needs of victims and those of all the other players. Whereas Milly's parents had persisted in their understandable wish to see justice done on their daughter's behalf by pursuing prosecution to the hilt of the man accused of the murder, it was in fact they themselves who suffered most as a consequence of the trial. Although the views of the barristers concerned made perfect sense in terms of the law being applied, in terms of a sense of justice being done it was not only the Dowler family who felt the system itself was miserably inadequate to the task before it.

It is this sense of unease felt by so many people about the blunt instrument we know as the criminal justice system that has powered the restorative justice movement over the past two decades. While a great deal can be said about the shortcomings of formal justice from the point of view of offenders, it is victims of crime who, often to their astonishment, are treated with a shabbiness that flies in the face of government rhetoric about their situation. The victim movement that has gathered force over the past quarter of a century, together with scholars who have written scathingly about the plight of victims, has done much to draw attention to the difficulties they routinely face. In 1989, for example, Gottfredson (1989: 210) found that, despite the role and status of victims finally receiving some attention from academics and policymakers, their experience remained 'inconvenience, inattention, anxiety-provoking arrangements...and a lack of information about what is happening in the prosecution of the case.' As McBarnett (1988: 300) observed: 'The state is not just the arbiter in a trial between victim and offender: the state is the victim...If victims feel that nobody cares about their suffering it is in part because institutionally nobody does.'

But governments now often express, at the least, what appears to be a sense of embarrassment about victims. For example, in the British government's response (2011) to the Green Paper entitled 'Breaking the Cycle: Effective Punishment, Rehabilitation and Sentencing of Offenders' (HMSO 2011), there appears the vapid statement that 'We will ensure that victims have a more central role in the criminal justice system' (HMSO 2011: 8). This is followed by an undertaking to make greater use of restorative justice 'as long as it is used appropriately' (HMSO 2011: 8), though without further explanation about what its appropriate use may look like.

Even though through the lens of 20 years observation it is sometimes difficult to tell whether restorative justice around the world is on an ascending or descending trajectory, we must retain a sense of optimism that victims may be on the point of benefiting from some of the most impressive research evidence available about the advantages to them of one particular way of 'doing justice': restorative justice conferencing (RJC). In this chapter I will discuss this concept so as to clarify exactly what we are talking about in a field strewn with ambiguous and overlapping terminology. I will then review the research evidence about the effectiveness of restorative justice in repairing the harm that victims of crime commonly suffer. I will discuss recent findings concerning the long term effects of restorative justice conferencing compared with usual criminal justice processing of cases through the courts, as revealed though a ten-year follow-up of personal crime victims in the reintegrative shaming experiments (RISE). Finally, I will then draw together the empirical data on the experience of victims with RJC to conclude that it offers most victims, willing to take part, significant justice benefits.

RESTORATIVE JUSTICE CONFERENCING

Restorative justice as a justice concept is beset by confusion around its definition. The continuum reaches from the crudest form of 'payback' to the softest kind of 'community resolution' of trivial offences by youthful offenders. The advantage of the term 'conferencing' in RJC is that it narrows the definitional possibilities because embedded in the term are some essential elements of the concept.

It is easiest to define RJC in terms of the way it works and Braithwaite's (2002) description serves the purpose well:

> Once wrongdoing is admitted... [T]he conference is a meeting of... two communities of care. First there is a discussion of what was done and what the consequences have been for everyone in the room (the victim's suffering, the stress experienced by the offender's family). Then there is a discussion of what needs to be done to repair those different kinds of harm. A plan of action is agreed upon and signed by the offender and usually by the victim and the police officer responsible for the case. (p 26)

Braithwaite acknowledges that beyond this core, conferences vary in their character from place to place. Nevertheless, this description articulates the *sine qua non* aspects of the intervention: a *face-to-face* encounter between those responsible for the harm and those harmed by the offence, in the presence of those who care about them; a thoroughgoing and often robust deliberation by everyone in the room about what happened and what the effects have been; an agreement about what should be done to achieve both material and emotional restoration.

The only element missing from this description, I suggest, is the role of the conference facilitator, which is quite different from that of a mediator. Whereas mediators negotiate between the parties, attempting to reach common ground, conference facilitators usually play a much more 'hands off' role. Their job is to ensure that everyone in the room has the opportunity to contribute to the discussion, that the meeting remains civil (while permitting outbursts of emotion that would not be tolerated in a court room), and that the discussion stays on-topic, moving towards a resolution between the parties.

There is another dimension to conferencing though that must be taken into consideration, namely the values upon which the process is based. Meetings that comply with these process conditions could easily agree an inappropriate or excessively punitive outcome without restorative values underpinning the outcome agreement. In the earliest days of conferencing in Canberra an example of such an outcome occurred when a boy who admitted to shoplifting, together with his anxious mother, agreed with the proposal of the aggrieved shopkeeper that he should spend a Saturday morning in the shopping mall where the offence occurred wearing a t-shirt bearing the words 'I am a thief'.[1] Braithwaite (2002) articulates a set of values that would preclude such an outcome, starting with those set out in international human rights covenants, and which are essential for arriving at an agreement based on deliberative dialogue between all the parties. While he acknowledges that these may appear vague and inadequate for guiding how good restorative practices should be done it is clear that the way to arrive at deliberative regulation of restorative justice is via conversations based on these broad principles. Restorative justice advocates, such as the United Kingdom's Restorative Justice Council for example, have worked hard, especially in the last

[1] Students of the Australian National University, outraged at this outcome, which was widely reported in the media, rapidly arranged for several hundred such t-shirts to be printed and a number of people joined him in the shopping mall wearing the same stigmatizing words.

decade, to achieve standards for practice that meet these principles (Restorative Justice Council 2004).

EXPLANATORY THEORIES UNDERPINNING RJC AND CRIME VICTIMS

Explanations for why victims are likely to benefit from RJC embrace several theories. We know, for example, that the main factor influencing victims' satisfaction with the sentence their offender receives is not its harshness but the sense of fair process in the sentencing (Erez 1990). Victimological studies have linked with psychological research undertaken over the past 30 years on procedural justice theory (Tyler 1990, 2000, 2003), to show that people find the justice system more legitimate if they are treated with equality and respect. We know too how much victims value fair and respectful treatment (Shapland et al. 1985; Joutsen 1994; Wemmers 1996; Strang 2002); so the theory predicts that if RJC can offer more fairness and respect than courts do, then this will be a significant benefit for victims.

Another theory about why victims may benefit from the dynamics of RJC as compared with the formal justice system concerns its potential to reduce post-traumatic stress symptoms (PTSS). Emotional processing theory (Foa and Kozak 1986; Foa et al. 2006) offers strong empirical evidence that PTSS can be reduced by discussing, in a safe place, the memory of the victimization. RJC appears to fit the hypothesis of disrupting a crime victim's conditioned response of anxiety whenever the crime is recalled; and strong evidence on its effectiveness has now emerged (Angel 2005).

A third theory which powerfully predicts the effects of RJC on victims, offenders, and everyone else present, is interaction ritual theory (Collins 2004). Drawing on Durkheim, Collins proposes that in successful 'rituals', which he defines as 'the experience of collective consciousness and collective effervescence, insofar as they contribute to a mutual focus of attention' (Collins 2004: 49), a rhythm develops over time between the participants. This rhythm, encompassing a shared focus, leads to a sense of solidarity between the participants that can lead to emotions of shared understanding and empathy. Recent research by Rossner (2008, 2011), based on careful examination of the dynamics of successful and unsuccessful RJCs, strongly supports this theoretical perspective. This work, together with Strang's (2002) exploration of the importance of empathy in successful restorative justice encounters, underpins the importance of the emotional content of conferences as the vehicle for emotional restoration of harm—harm which in crime is often principally of an emotional character.

It is clear that RJC from a victim's perspective has many theoretical components, which is to be expected in such a complex and variable intervention. All of them may be important in determining its effectiveness in delivering what crime victims seek from the justice system to repair the harm they have experienced.

RJC AND CRIME VICTIMS: EVIDENCE FOR EFFECTIVENESS

STUDY DESIGNS AND METHODS

Over the past two decades, conferencing has been the subject of more evaluative research than almost any other criminal justice intervention. Even though the calls for 'more research' remain because of the variability of effects observed on offender recidivism,[2] findings on positive victim effects are so consistent, as we shall see, that 'more research' on victims would probably be unethical.

In this review of the evidence, it is the results from randomized trials in RJC that will be discussed, but it is important to recognize that similar findings have emerged from non-randomized research designs of other kinds of face-to-face restorative justice. These have consistently shown that victims benefit along several dimensions, principally in reducing emotional harm and increasing a sense of fairness. For example, studies of victim-offender mediation report high levels of victim satisfaction arising from the chance to tell their offenders directly about the consequences of the crime and to obtain material and emotional reparation from the meeting (see for example, Nugent et al. 2003; Umbreit 1994, 2001; Umbreit and Coates 1992, 1993; Umbreit, Coates, and Kalanj 1994). Evidence about the effects of indirect or 'shuttle' mediation are not nearly so encouraging (Shapland et al. 2007): it appears that 'face-to-faceness' is essential for the benefits to be experienced.

The programme of research on RJC with which this author has been involved over the past 15 years consists of four experiments conducted in Australia (the Reintegrative Shaming Experiments, or RISE) and a further seven conducted in the United Kingdom. All except two of them involved personal crime victims[3] who in total across the studies numbered over 1,000 people.

In the case of the Australian tests, the research team was responsible for the evaluation (Strang 2002), while the United Kingdom tests were independently evaluated by a team from the University of Sheffield led by Professor Joanna Shapland (Shapland et al. 2004, 2006, 2007, 2008, 2011). All the restorative justice cases in all nine tests in both countries involved a face-to-face meeting of one to three hours duration between people affected by the crime. All offenders had acknowledged responsibility, either by full admissions to the police or by pleading guilty in court.[4] Friends and family of the victim and the offender were present both to support the

[2] Even though *average* effects on offenders are extraordinarily positive and none of the individual results are negative. Data from the Shapland et al. (2008) study of reconviction of offenders in the Justice Research Consortium's 11 randomized controlled trials in the United Kingdom reveal an average reduction, across all experiments, of 27 per cent in reoffending by those assigned to a conference in addition to normal criminal justice processing, compared with those assigned to criminal justice only.

[3] Neither the drinking and driving experiment nor the shoplifting in large stores experiment had personal victims.

[4] An exception to this was the experiment involving violent offenders serving custodial sentences. Some of these had pleaded not guilty in court but all of them admitted responsibility for their crime prior to participating in the test.

principals and, where appropriate, to express opprobrium. All facilitators taking part in all the tests had been trained in the same way by the same restorative justice conference trainer. All conferences required that the participants talk directly to one another, often in highly emotional terms, with the focus always on how people felt rather than what actually had happened.

All these tests employed a randomized research design (Shapland et al. 2007; Sherman et al. 2005; Strang 2002), recognized as the most rigorous method of evaluative research. Randomized controlled trials are the standard in medical research and are required by organizations such as the US Food and Drug Administration for approval of drugs and medical devices (Pocock 1983). This design minimizes the possibility of selection bias in comparing the experimental treatment with the control treatment. Random assignment of all cases reaching the eligibility threshold for a study ensures likely equivalence between the two groups not only on known variables, but also on variables that are unknown and perhaps not even imagined (Gartin 1995). Post-treatment differences between the groups can then be confidently attributed to treatment effects rather than to any pre-existing differences in the individuals making up each group.

In the Australian research, the two tests with personal victims concerned property crime (mostly theft, burglary, criminal damage, and car crime) and violent crime (mostly common assault or aggravated assault). These offences were of moderate seriousness: they were normally dealt with in court but were not so serious that they had to be dealt with in court (Strang 2002). Eligibility for the tests required the offender to be under 18 for the property experiment and under 30 for the violence experiment and to have made full admissions of responsibility for the offence; in addition the offence had to be of a specified type and level of seriousness. These cases were randomly assigned either to court in the usual way or *diverted* to a conference, that is, RJC was used *instead of* formal processing through the courts.

In the United Kingdom research, all seven of the tests involved personal crime victims. One test concerned juveniles who had committed mostly low-harm offences and who were dealt with by the police without prosecution via a 'Final Warning'. The remaining six tests related to serious adult crime, including robbery, burglary, aggravated burglary, and serious violence. All these adult offenders were dealt with in court, many of them in Crown Courts because of the seriousness of their crimes. Half of them were assigned to attend an RJC as well, either before sentencing, in the case of the robbery and burglary tests, or after sentencing, in the case of the tests of violent offenders sentenced either to community supervision or to prison. In all these United Kingdom tests, cases that met agreed eligibility criteria were randomly assigned either to an RJC *in addition* to whatever disposal they would have received anyway (Crown Court, magistrates' court, police Final Warning, community supervision sentence or prison sentence), or to the usual disposal for their offence without such a meeting (Shapland et al. 2004).

Before reviewing the research findings it is important to recognize that conference participation must always be un-coerced, so any benefits can only be available to those victims *who wish to participate*. This issue is important to recognize because of the common report that victims are reluctant to take part (see for example Miers et al.

(2001) who reported on consent rates in the United Kingdom as low as 15 per cent). The great majority of victims (about 90 per cent) in the two Australian RISE diversion tests agreed to participate for a range of reasons including wanting to have a say in the way their case was dealt with (63 per cent of respondents), wanting to express their feelings directly to the offender (56 per cent), and wanting to help the offender (36 per cent) (Strang 2002: 122). Victims were less enthusiastic in the seven United Kingdom tests where RJC was offered in addition to usual justice procedures. This was due in large measure to the much greater level of seriousness of the cases involving adult offenders and the kind of anxiety, fear, and anger that the victims felt, though still well over half of victims invited to take part agreed to do so (Strang et al. 2006: 291). We do not know whether victims who participate in RJC somehow self-select in such a way that they are more likely to benefit than those who decline: what we do know is that those who participate can experience a number of benefits.

RESEARCH RESULTS

It is the consistency of the results for crime victims that provides compelling evidence for the view that victims can reap great benefits from RJC. Despite the variety of offence types, social contexts, age, ethnicity, gender, and race in these experiments, victims have reacted consistently to this way of doing justice. Before–after changes revealed by both qualitative and quantitative findings, as well as comparative findings between the victims who experienced RJC and those who did not, are all in the same positive direction (Shapland et al. 2007; Strang et al. 2006). A review of some specific measures of RJC outcomes allows us to piece together some dimensions of the benefits available to victims.

Apologies

One of the most striking differences between the experiences of victims in RJC compared with court is the opportunity presented for apologies. Victims' desire for apologies from their offenders has in the past received little attention, even though when victims are actually asked about what they want, a sincere expression of remorse from their offender is one of the most frequent responses (Strang 2002). The formal justice system provides little opportunity for offenders to apologize, except in the most stylized way, through their legal representative and directed to the judge or magistrates, rather than personally to the victim. In most restorative justice conferences the discussion moves naturally through the expression of emotions by all parties about the crime and the harm caused towards a resolution concerning what should be done about it. The arc of this discussion almost always presents a moment when it is natural for an apology to be offered in recognition of the emotional restoration needed by the victim. In RISE, around 90 per cent of all victims, regardless of whether their cases had been assigned to court or to RJC, said they should have received an apology from their offender. When they were asked whether their offender has apologized, almost three-quarters of the RJC-assigned said they had done so (and 86 per cent of those who actually experienced RJC), compared with 19 per cent of the court-assigned: none of the court victims said that it was part of the court outcome (Strang 2002).

The quality of the apology is also an important dimension. In RISE there was a significant difference in how victims rated the sincerity of the apology: over three-quarters of the RJC victims said their apology was sincere compared with 41 per cent of the court victims ($p<.001$). Whereas many of the apologies offered to the court victims appeared coerced, those offered in conferences were usually spontaneous and allowed the victim to judge them to be genuine. In the United Kingdom tests there was no direct measure of victims' perception of sincerity of the apology but even though the offences were much more serious than in RISE, 90 per cent of victims reported that their offender has apologized. Furthermore, in 90 per cent of cases offenders said that they believed their victims had accepted their apology; indeed, Shapland et al. (2007: 25) report that 'victims were as likely to say they had accepted the apology in the more serious offence trials (84 per cent of burglary victims; 100 per cent of robbery victims; 86 per cent of Thames Valley prison trial victims) as in the other trials.'

Perceptions of procedural fairness

These perceptions consist of a number of elements around confidence in the process: impartiality, ethicality, lack of bias, the likelihood of being able to correct procedural errors, and the individual's sense of control over the process (Tyler 1990). In RISE, where the RJC-assigned cases were *diverted* from the usual court process, more than 85 per cent of respondents assigned to RJC said they agreed they had experienced all of these elements and were very satisfied about the fair and respectful treatment they had received (Strang 2002: 128). Victims who had experienced restorative justice in the United Kingdom studies were asked a more global question: 'Overall, how fair did you feel the criminal justice process was?' Almost three-quarters responded that they had found it fair, even though, because their cases were dealt with *in addition to* usual justice procedures their mental frame for answering this question was different from that of the RISE victims (Shapland et al. 2007: 29).

Feelings of revenge

The question of whether emotions of vengeance in response to harm are 'instinctive' has been a lively one (see for example, Diamond 2008; Goldschmidt 2008). It may not however be as important as the possibility that it can be remedied. One of the most striking findings from the RISE study concerned the large effects of RJC in reducing victims' desire for violent revenge, especially among victims of violence (Strang 2002). The United Kingdom tests provided another opportunity to test this finding more systematically: in all these tests we found substantially fewer victims expressing a desire to harm their offenders in the RJC-assigned than in the court-assigned cases (Sherman et al. 2005). A review of prospective meta-analysis conducted on the evidence from these tests (Sherman and Strang 2011: 153) concludes that 'the thirst for vengeance is transformable, rather than inevitable.'

These findings should not, however, imply that victims ought to forgive or are often inclined to do so. Much has been said about the benefits of forgiveness for victims in terms of releasing them from the destructiveness of vengefulness (see for example Arendt 1958), but that is different from burdening them with the expectation of forgiveness. Certainly, in the short term, victims in RISE who were assigned to RJC indicated that although many more felt forgiving towards their offender than unforgiving, nearly half of them felt indifferent (Strang 2002: 111). The findings on forgiveness in the United Kingdom tests were less clear: while most victims indicated they accepted their offenders' apologies, as they did in RISE, victims observed in conferences did not show forgiveness (Shapland et al. 2007: 25).

Post-traumatic stress symptoms (PTSS)

Early findings in RISE about the potential for RJC to provide substantial benefits on a range of emotional dimensions led to our pursuing, in the London tests of RJC with burglary and robbery victims, some issues around the psychological aspects of the restorative justice experience. Mental trauma in crime victims tends to be under-reported and under-treated except for special crimes such as rape (Foa and Kozak 1986) and yet even low to moderate levels of PTSS are associated with greater numbers of physical symptoms of illness and more use of medical services (Gillock et al. 2005). Cognitive behavioural therapy (CBT), which can assist with cognitive restructuring of the memory of a trauma and also with desensitizing individuals to things that remind them of it, has been used with some success in post-traumatic stress disorder. We wished to test the theory that an RJC was a type of non-medical treatment that provided many of the conditions required in CBT (Sherman et al. 2005).

About 200 victims in eligible cases for this special study in London were contacted by telephone by a member of the research team, who was a qualified psychiatric nurse, following the finalization of their cases in court (Angel 2005; Angel et al. 2012). A standardized test for PTSS, the 'Impact of Event Scale-Revised' (Weiss et al. 1997), was administered and the results for the experimental and control groups were compared. The results showed that after one month there was a statistically significant difference in the levels of PTSS, with a substantial reduction in the RJC group. This difference was still evident six months later when participants were interviewed again. The difference was particularly clear for women: at six months 20 per cent of the RJC group remained with clinical levels of PTSS compared with 56 per cent of those who had not had the opportunity to participate in RJC (Angel et al. 2012).

Satisfaction with the justice experience

Beyond these specific measures of benefits of RJC to victims, the principal global measure is the subjective view of satisfaction with their experience. For this we have measures comparing the experiences of those who took part in RJC with those who did not.

In RISE, victims whose cases were assigned to RJC were significantly more satisfied than those whose cases went to court (60 per cent vs. 46 per cent, $p < .025$). For many administrative reasons not all cases assigned to RJC actually had a conference take place: for those victims who actually experienced RJC their satisfaction levels were rather higher (70 per cent vs. 42 per cent)[5] (Strang 2002: 133).

5 It is important to note that not all victims whose cases were assigned to RJC actually experienced it: this was sometimes because of administrative problems and sometimes because the offender did not attend the scheduled conference. It was the victims promised RJC but who never experienced it who were the angriest people at interview—significantly more so than victims whose cases had gone to court and who had never heard any more about their case (Strang 2002).

In the United Kingdom tests very similar levels of comparative satisfaction were reported. Of those victims whose cases were assigned to RJC (in addition to 'usual' justice procedures), significantly more reported that they were 'satisfied with what the criminal justice system did about this offence', compared with those whose cases were not assigned to RJC (72 per cent vs. 60 per cent, p = .03) (Shapland et al. 2007: 42). Furthermore, even though the length of time between the offence and the RJC had been highly variable, from a few weeks in the burglary and robbery tests where the RJC took place before sentencing, to several years in the violence study involving offenders serving prison sentences, more than three-quarters of victims said that the RJC had been held about the right length of time after the incident. Satisfaction with the RJC in these United Kingdom tests can also be gauged from the fact that 78 per cent of victims said that they would recommend restorative justice to other crime victims and only 5 per cent said they definitely would not (Shapland et al. 2007: 42). Shapland et al., as the Home Office-appointed evaluators of these experiments, summarized these findings as 'overall, a ringing endorsement of restorative justice' (2007: 43).

LONG TERM EFFECTS OF RJC ON CRIME VICTIMS

One of the most intriguing unanswered questions about RJC has been its effects over the long term. Can this kind of justice change people's lives for better—or worse—over time? Can it help victims with lasting recovery from the harms of victimization, material and emotional? Do the effects persist? Do victims who have experienced RJC fare better or worse in the aftermath of their experience than their counterparts whose cases were dealt with in the formal justice system? Research on the life course of young offenders finds that their experience of crime and the justice system had, in many instances, life-long effects (see for example, Blumstein et al. 1986; Laub and Sampson 2003; Piquero et al. 2003; Sampson and Laub 1993). There has never been comparable research carried out on the life course of crime victims. The aim of our follow-up of RISE victims ten years after their case came into our experiments was to assess whether they may experience long-term effects, and what kinds of effects they may be.

It is important to contribute more knowledge about the long-ignored impact of justice on victims, especially the potential of justice systems to actually provoke crimes of vengeance by failing to give victims what they need to discharge their feelings towards their offenders. Approaching participants in the RISE study randomly assigned to court or RJC allowed us to examine for the first time these long-term effects. Interviews of victims in the seven separate tests in our United Kingdom experiments consistently replicated the effects found in RISE: less anxiety, anger, and inclination towards violence to avenge a violent crime and lower levels of PTSS among those whose cases were assigned to RJC rather than court alone.

In designing the questions to be asked of the RISE victims ten years after their victimization we had these specific aims in mind: what, if any, are the long-term effects of RJC on crime victims' health, employment, relationships, and lawfulness? How long do these effects last and are the effects different from those among victims whose cases were randomly assigned to court as usual?

We began by asking detailed questions about victims' overall physical health and well being, comparing how they feel now with how they felt ten years ago. Then we asked about their emotional well-being, especially in the month before the interview. We enquired about their use of alcohol, tobacco, and prescription drugs, and how their intake compared with ten years ago. We also enquired about their sense of satisfaction with various areas of their lives: family life, relationships generally, their job, their hobbies, their religious beliefs. We then turned to their recollection of their victimization ten years previously and asked many of the same questions they had been asked in the first wave of interviewing immediately after the disposition of the offence, whether by court or by RJC. In this way we were able to map the stability and change in victims' views about what had happened to them.

In the first wave of interviews, which had taken place within a few weeks of the original disposition of their cases, about 90 per cent of the 260 victims of property and violence in RISE agreed to be interviewed. Ten years later 188 or 72 per cent of the original cohort was interviewed. Their average age was now 46: 60 per cent of respondents were male and 80 per cent of them were married or in long-term relationships.

There was only a marginal difference in the response rates between the two categories of victims in the ten-year wave of interviews (70 per cent for property and 74 per cent for violence), and only a narrow difference in the response rate between those assigned to court (52 per cent of all respondents) and to RJC (48 per cent). This relative high response rate, and the small difference between the court victims and the RJC victims, allows us to have a substantial degree of confidence in the generalizability of these responses across all of the original victims.

The results show that while there were few differences between court-assigned and RJC-assigned victims on questions concerning alcohol and drug use, self-harm and hospital admissions, and on the 'life satisfaction' measures, on straightforward well-being measures the RJC-assigned rated themselves more positively than the court-assigned. When asked how they rated their health generally, significantly more of the court victims said that it was only fair or poor (20 per cent vs. 9 per cent, $p = 0.1$). This was especially evident for the victims in the violence experiment (25 per cent vs. 9 per cent). Across several measures of physical and emotional wellbeing, even though differences rarely reached levels of statistical significance (possibly due to the small sample size), the RJC-assigned victims tended to report higher scores than the court-assigned.

We then turned to victims' recollections of their crime and justice experiences ten years previously, and their feelings now about these events. When they were asked whether they were pleased their case had been dealt with in the way it was, a significant difference emerged: 63 per cent of the RJC-assigned were pleased (rising to 74 per cent among those victims who had actually attended a conference), compared with 37 per cent of the court-assigned ($p = 0.001$). These results are similar to the responses in the first wave of interviews shortly after the case was dealt with (69 per cent vs. 37 per cent, $p = 0.003$), though if anything the court-assigned victims appear even less happy ten years later.

We took the opportunity to ask a question which has been repeatedly raised concerning the appropriateness of police officers taking the role of facilitator in the conference. Some maintain that it is not appropriate because the police cannot be unbiased or neutral in the role (Roche 2003), while others maintain that victims only feel secure in the RJC setting in the presence of a police officer. We found an important difference here between victims of property crime and victims of violence: whereas 67 per cent of property victims say they would have attended an RJC if it had been facilitated by someone other than a police officer, such as a social worker or member of the community, only 31 per cent of violence victims would have attended.

It was, however, in the questions around the emotional reactions to crime and justice that some of the most remarkable results were to be found. Some of the clearest differences between the court-assigned and RJC-assigned victims immediately after their case had been dealt with (ten years previously) concerned their feelings of fear, anxiety, anger, and bitterness. Now, ten years later, it was clear that many of the same emotions were at play.

Anxiety about revictimization is a common reaction for crime victims and one that may take many years to recover from. RISE victims who had been assigned to RJC had been asked, a few weeks after their case was disposed of, how anxious they were about the offence happening again, compared with how anxious they had felt before the conference. The percentage feeling anxious had declined significantly after the conference (40 per cent vs. 31 per cent, $p<0.02$). Ten years later both court-assigned and RJC-assigned victims were asked a slightly different question: 'Thinking about how you feel now, in general how anxious are you about the crime happening again?' There was an astonishing difference between the groups: 21 per cent of the RJC-assigned said they were still anxious, compared with 45 per cent of the court-assigned ($p = 0.003$). This difference was especially striking for the property victims, though the difference was statistically significant for the violence victims as well.

Another question asked ten years after the incident explored a different dimension about fear of crime: 'Would you say that you are sometimes afraid to do things because you might be the victim of crime again?' Overall more court-assigned victims said that they were afraid: 22 per cent vs. 34 per cent ($p = 0.1$), but the difference was particularly marked for the victims of violence: 18 per cent vs. 41 per cent were still afraid.

When victims were asked soon after the offence whether they felt bitter about the way they had been treated by the justice system there was little difference overall between those assigned to court and those assigned to RJC, though many more of the violence victims in both conditions agreed. Ten years later interesting differences emerge: overall 74 per cent of the RJC-assigned *dis*agreed, compared with 39 per cent of the court-assigned, with virtually the same results for both the property and violence victims.

Earlier we discussed one of the most striking findings about victims' emotional reactions to crime: their feelings of vengeance towards their offenders. At the first wave of interviews all victims were asked whether 'you would do some harm to your offender if you got the chance.' Overall, 20 per cent of the court-assigned victims said that they would do so, compared with only 7 per cent of the RJC-assigned ($p<0.005$), but the difference was even more conspicuous for victims of violent crime: 45 per cent of the court-assigned said they would harm their offender, compared with only 9 per cent of the RJC-assigned. As one would hope, these feelings are much diminished by the elapse of time but there is still a difference between the groups, driven almost entirely by the violence victims: whereas only 3 per cent of the RJC-assigned said they would harm their offender now, ten years later, 13 per cent of the court-assigned still wanted personal revenge ($p = 0.17$).

All these measures of victims' emotional states so many years after the crime and its disposition give a strong indication of the extraordinary capacity RJC has for resolving the emotional harm that victims suffer, especially victims of violence. This is particularly notable in RISE because the practice of restorative justice was almost in its infancy at the time of these experiments: victims of violence especially were not particularly impressed by their experience of RJC and about one third of them had been dissatisfied with the way their case was dealt with. Restorative justice practice has improved greatly in the interim. The evaluation report on the United Kingdom experiments makes this clear from the extremely high levels of satisfaction expressed by those victims, most of whom had experienced much more serious crime than the RISE victims had (Shapland et al. 2007). These findings are both a reassurance about the long-term benefits of RJC and a warning of the long-term harm victims suffer, even from middle-level offences, when the justice system does not provide them with what they need to resolve their experience and get on with their lives.

CONCLUSION

This review of the evidence leads clearly to the conclusion that the benefits of RJC to victims who agree to participate can be substantial. The shortcomings of the court system for victims have been well rehearsed and despite an apparent willingness in recent times to give greater regard to victims' needs, there are undoubted structural impediments likely to prevent the process ever giving them what they want. These desires are not outrageous. Repeatedly when victims are asked directly what they want they say similar things: information, a participatory role in the resolution of their case, respectful and fair treatment, and material and emotional restoration. But the formal justice system has great difficulty in conducting itself other than as a 'zero sum' game that either victims or offenders are condemned to lose (Strang 2002). Certainly there is strong evidence from the research on diversion of offenders from court that victims can gain more of what they want from RJC than from the court. But even more significantly, for cases with great harm that we do not want to divert from formal justice because of the seriousness of the crime, we find a huge benefit to victims by adding RJC to the justice system. For little additional cost there is the potential for huge victim benefit and indeed substantial cost savings to the justice system and even to the health system (Shapland et al. 2008). There is small doubt that RJC offers victims benefits that no other justice innovation has come close to matching.

REFERENCES

Angel, C. (2005), *Victims Meet Their Offenders: Testing the Impact of Restorative Justice Conferences on Victims' Post-Traumatic Stress Symptoms* (PhD dissertation, University of Pennsylvania).

Angel, C., Sherman, L., Strang, H., Bennett, S., Inkpen, N., Keane, A. and Richmond, T. (2012), *Effects of Restorative Justice Conferences on Post-Traumatic Stress Symptoms Among Robbery and Burglary Victims: A Randomized Controlled Trial* unpublished (Philadelphia: Jerry Lee Center of Criminology, University of Pennsylvania).

Arendt, H. (1958), *The Human Condition* (Chicago: University of Chicago Press).

Blumstein, A., Cohen, J., Roth, J. and Visher, C. (1986), *Criminal Careers and 'Career Criminals'* (Washington: National Academies Press).

Braithwaite, J. (2002), *Restorative Justice and Responsive Regulation* (Oxford: Oxford University Press).

Collins, R. (2004), *Interaction Ritual Chains* (Princeton: Princeton University Press).

Diamond, J. (2008), 'Vengeance is Ours', *The New Yorker*, 21 April.

Erez, E. (1990), 'Victim Participation in Sentencing: Rhetoric and Reality', *Journal of Criminal Justice*, 18, pp 19–31.

Foa, E., Huppert, J. and Cahill, S. (2006), 'Emotional Processing Theory: An Update', in Rothbaum, B. (ed.), *Pathological Anxiety: Emotional Processing in Etiology and Treatment* (New York: Guilford Press), pp 3–24.

Foa, E. and Kozak, M. (1986), 'Emotional Processing of Fear: Exposure to Corrective Information', *Psychological Bulletin*, 99, pp 20–35.

Gartin, P. (1995), 'Dealing With Design Failures in Randomized Field Experiments: Analytic Issues Regarding the Evaluation of Treatment Effects', *Journal of Research in Crime and Delinquency*, 32, pp 425–45.

Gillock, K., Zayfert, C., Hegel, M. and Ferguson, T. (2005), 'Posttraumatic Stress Disorder in Primary Care: Prevalence and Relationships With Physical Symptoms and Medical Utilization', *General Hospital Psychiatry*, 27, pp 392–9.

Goldschmidt, W. (2008), 'An Eye for an Eye', *The New Yorker*, 19 May, p 7.

Gottfredson, G. (1989), 'The Experience of Violent and Serious Victimization', in Weiner, N. and Wolfgang, M. (eds.), *Pathways to Criminal Violence* (Newbury Park: Sage Publications).

Joutsen, M. (1994), 'Victim Participation in Proceedings and Sentencing in Europe', *International Review of Victimology*, 3, pp 57–67.

Laub, J. and Sampson, R. (2003), *Shared Beginnings, Divergent Lives: Delinquent Boys to Age 70* (Cambridge: Harvard University Press).

Lord Chancellor and Secretary of State for Justice by Command of Her Majesty (2011), *Government Response. Breaking the Cycle: Effective Punishment, Rehabilitation and Sentencing of Offenders* (London: HMSO).

McBarnett, D. (1988), 'Victims in the Witness Box—Confronting Victimology's Stereotype', *Contemporary Crises*, 7, pp 279–303.

Miers, D., Maguire, M., Goldie, S., Sharpe, K., Hale, C., Netten, A., Uglow, S., Doolin, K., Hallam, A., Enterkin, J. and Newburn, T. (2001), *An Exploratory Evaluation of Restorative Justice Schemes*, Crime Reduction Research Series paper 9 (London: Home Office).

Nugent, W., Williams, M. and Umbreit, M. (2003), 'Participation in Victim-Offender Mediation and the Prevalence and Severity of Subsequent Delinquent Behaviour: A Meta-Analysis', *Utah Law Review*, 1, pp137–66.

Piquero, A., Farrington, D. and Blumstein, A. (2003), 'The Criminal Career Paradigm', in Tonry, M. (ed.), *Crime and Justice: A Review of Research* (Chicago: University of Chicago Press), pp 359–506.

Pocock, S. (1983), *Clinical Trials: A Practical Approach* (London: John Wiley).

Rayment, T. and Leppard, D. (2011), 'Call This Justice?', *The Sunday Times*, 26 June, p 19.

Roche, D. (2003), *Accountability in Restorative Justice* (Oxford: Clarendon Press).

Rossner, M. (2008), *Why Emotions Work: Restorative Justice, Interaction Ritual and the Micro-Potential for Emotional Transformation* (PhD dissertation, University of Pennsylvania).

Rossner, M. (2011), 'Emotions and Interaction Ritual: A Micro Analysis of Restorative Justice', *British Journal of Criminology*, 51, pp 95–119.

Restorative Justice Council, (2004), available at <http://www.restorativejustice.org.uk/resource/rjc_principles_of_restorative_processes/>.

Sampson, R. and Laub, J. (1993), *Crime in the making* (Cambridge: Harvard University Press).

Shapland, J., Atkinson, A., Atkinson, H., Chapman, B., Colledge, E., Dignan, J., Howes, M., Johnstone, J., Robinson, G. and Sorsby, A. (2006), *Restorative Justice in Practice: The Second Report from the Evaluation of Three Schemes* (Sheffield: Centre for Criminological Research, University of Sheffield).

Shapland, J., Atkinson, A., Atkinson, H., Chapman, B., Dignan, J., Howes, M., Johnstone, J., Robinson, G. and Sorsby, A. (2007), *Restorative Justice: The Views of Victims and Offenders. The Third Report from the Evaluation of Three Schemes*. Ministry of Justice Research Series 3/07 (London: Ministry of Justice).

Shapland, J., Atkinson, A., Atkinson, H., Dignan, J., Edwards, L., Hibbert, J., Howes, M., Johnstone, J., Robinson, G. and Sorsby, A. (2008), *Does Restorative Justice Affect Reconviction? The Fourth Report from the Evaluation of Three Schemes* (London: Ministry of Justice).

Shapland, J., Atkinson, A., Colledge, E., Dignan, J., Howes, M., Johnstone, J., Pennant, R., Robinson, G. and Sorsby, A. (2004), *Implementing Restorative Justice Schemes (Crime Reduction Programme): A Report on the First Year,* Home Office Online Report 32/04 (Home Office: London).

Shapland, J., Robinson, G. and Sorsby, A. (2011), *Restorative Justice in Practice: Evaluating What Works for Victims and Offenders* (London: Routledge).

Shapland, J., Willmore, J. and Duff, P. (1985), *Victims in the Criminal Justice System* (Aldershot: Gower).

Sherman, L., Strang, H., Angel, C. et al. (2005), 'Effects of Face-to-Face Restorative Justice on Victims of Crime in Four Randomized Controlled Trials', *Journal of Experimental Criminology*, 1, pp 367–95.

Sherman, L. and Strang, H. (2007), *Restorative Justice: The Evidence* (London: The Smith Institute).

Sherman, L. and Strang, H. (2011), 'Empathy for the Devil', in Karstedt, S., Loader, I. and Strang, H. (eds.) *Emotions, Crime and Justice* (Oxford: Hart Publishing), pp 145–68.

Strang, H. (2002), *Repair or Revenge: Victims and Restorative Justice* (Oxford: Clarendon Press).

Strang, H., Sherman, L. and Angel, C. et al. (2006), 'Victim Evaluations of Face-to-Face Restorative Justice Conferences: A Quasi-Experimental Analysis', *Journal of Social Issues,* 62, pp 281–306.

Tyler, T. (1990), *Why Do People Obey the Law?* (New Haven: Yale University Press).

TYLER, T. (2000), 'Social Justice: Outcome and Procedure', *International Journal of Psychology*, 35, pp 117–25.

TYLER, T. (2003), 'Procedural Justice, Legitimacy and the Effective Rule of Law', in Tonry, M. (ed.), *Crime and Justice: A Review of Research* (Chicago: University of Chicago Press), 30, pp 257–83.

UMBREIT, M. (1994), 'Crime Victims Confront their Offenders: The Impact of a Minneapolis Mediation Programme', *Research on Social Work Practice*, 4, pp 436–47.

UMBREIT, M. (2001), *The Handbook of Victim-Offender Mediation* (San Francisco: Jossey-Bass).

UMBREIT, M. and COATES, R. (1992), 'The Impact of Mediating Victim-Offender Conflict: An Analysis of Programs in Three States', *Juvenile and Family Court Journal*, 43(1), pp 21–8.

UMBREIT, M. and COATES, R. (1993), 'Cross-Site Analysis of Victim-Offender Mediation in Four States', *Crime and Delinquency*, 39, pp 565–85.

UMBREIT, M., COATES, R. and KALANJ, B. (1994), *Victim Meets Offender: The Impact of Restorative Justice and Mediation* (Monsey: Criminal Justice Press).

WEISS, D. (1997), 'The Impact of Event Scale: Revised', in Wilson, J. and Tang, C. (eds.), *Cross-Cultural Assessment of Psychological Trauma and PTSD*, International and Cultural Psychology Series (New York: Springer), pp 219–38.

WEMMERS, J. (1996), *Victims in the Criminal Justice System* (Amsterdam: Kugler Publications).

PART II

CONFERENCING: INCEPTION, CHALLENGES, AND NEWER DEVELOPMENTS

7

REVOLUTION, DECLINE, AND RENEWAL

RESTORATIVE YOUTH JUSTICE IN NEW ZEALAND

Ashley Shearar and Gabrielle Maxwell

INTRODUCTION

New Zealand's youth justice system owes much of its success to the fact that it was based on principles which emphasized constructive outcomes for victims, young offenders, families, and communities through the creation of the family group conference (FGC). This innovative approach to youth justice helped breathe life into restorative justice theory, although it did not specifically refer to restorative justice in its design. Instead, New Zealand policy makers constructed a youth justice system based on the expressed needs of the community and on principles that affirm the values also expressed in restorative justice theory.

This chapter will provide an overview of how the FGC became a central mechanism for dealing with children in conflict with the law in New Zealand. It will explore the key influences which contributed to the development of this model and explain how the FGC is embedded in law as the primary decision making process for cases of serious offending by children and young people. It will also look at some of the shortcomings in the application of New Zealand's youth justice model and some emerging strategies to address them.

TRANSFORMING THE YOUTH JUSTICE SYSTEM IN NEW ZEALAND

BACKGROUND

During much of the 20th century, New Zealand, like most of the western world, relied on a welfare model for responding to children in conflict with the law. The Children and Young Persons Act 1974 brought in two key amendments to youth justice legislation in New Zealand. One was to distinguish between 'children' and 'young persons', 'children' being below the age of 14 and 'young persons' between the ages of 14 to 17 years. The other was the introduction of the Children's Boards to deal with youth justice matters. These Boards were made up of a police officer, a social worker, and a representative of the Ministry of Māori and Island Affairs to deal with children who committed an offence (Morris 2004).

The intention was for Children's Boards to increase the opportunities to divert children from court processes with some new options at their disposal. These included issuing warnings or referring children for counselling. Serious matters, considered beyond the capacity of the Children's Boards, were referred to the Children and Young Persons' court.

Nevertheless, dissatisfaction with the provisions of the Children and Young Persons Act 1974 from various sectors of society steadily increased. The emphasis on rehabilitation through social work intervention did not appear to be either addressing the causes of offending behaviour or holding young people to account for their actions. Many police officers had lost faith in the Children's Boards' diversion processes and had started to bypass them, making frequent arrests for court prosecution. There was also growing alarm at the conditions in existing welfare residences, as investigations by community based children's advocacy groups into the treatment of children in these residences revealed high levels of neglect and abuse.

In 1984, the Minister of Social Welfare called for a revision of the Children and Young Persons Act 1974. This came during a period when Māori were gaining ground in reclaiming their sense of *mana*[1] and *tino rangatiratanga*[2] which had deteriorated since the signing of the Treaty of Waitangi (Mulgan 1989). A Māori Advisory Committee was established '… to advise the Minister of Social Welfare on the most appropriate means to achieve the goal of an approach which would meet the needs of Māori in policy, planning and service delivery in the Ministry of Social Welfare' (Ministerial Advisory Committee on a Maori Perspective; New Zealand Department of Social Welfare 1988: 5).

The Māori Advisory Committee members consulted widely to consolidate the Māori view on the treatment of children in the New Zealand social welfare system resulting in a report to the Minister of Social Welfare titled '*Puao-Te-Ata-Tu*' meaning 'Day Break'. The report noted that decades of institutional racism had disadvantaged Māori youths and their families, not least of all because of a '… profound misunderstanding of the child in Māori society and of their place in *whānau, hapū* and *iwi*[3] structures' (New Zealand Ministerial Advisory Committee 1988: 7). Many Māori believed that gaining power in matters pertaining to their children through the welfare system would be a significant step towards achieving self-determination (Sharp 1990: 7). The Māori Advisory Committee called for greater empowerment and inclusion of families and communities in decision making around the needs of their chil-

[1] *Mana* is roughly translated as 'honour' or 'prestige', acquired through connection with one's heritage and genealogy, as well as through a character that reflects Māori values and culture.

[2] *Tino Rangatiratanga* is roughly translated as self-determination and authority.

[3] 'Whānau', 'Hapū', and 'Iwi' relate to Maori social structure which defines traditional community connections and belonging. Iwi refers to the tribe, Hapū the sub-tribe, and Whānau the extended family.

dren and young people. A number of social work professionals were also calling for more family and community involvement in child welfare decisions (Renouf et al. 1989).

CREATING A CULTURALLY APPROPRIATE CHILD WELFARE MODEL

The Working Party tasked with drafting the legislation wanted to develop a child welfare system that would account for the stated needs of the people while remaining culturally appropriate for all New Zealanders. The members decided on a process based on the key principles expressed during community consultations. They included the importance of involving families and communities in decisions about their children, empowering communities to support their children's reintegration into society, keeping children in familiar family and community environments wherever possible, and significantly reducing professional involvement in decision making. This formed the foundation of a new approach: the family group conference (FGC).

A form of family group conference based on indigenous Māori practices for dealing with problems affecting children was piloted. Different court processes that relied more on community and cultural input were also piloted in parts of New Zealand with the support of judges who believed in, and advocated for, this approach.[4] These pilot projects provided insight into the possibilities for practically running FGCs and courts that incorporated community input. While Māori voices had the most influence on the design of the FGC, the process was flexible enough to suit the needs of any participants (Daly 2001: 65).

ADAPTING FAMILY GROUP CONFERENCES TO YOUTH JUSTICE

During this period, Mike Doolan, an important member of the Working Party, was on a study tour around the United States of America and the United Kingdom. His report focused on youth justice models that differentiated between justice and welfare needs. The 1984 revision of the Children and Young Persons Act 1974 (Department of Social Welfare 1984: 1) had already acknowledged that '... benevolently intended official measures employed to rehabilitate children in difficulty can violate children's civil rights by introducing a level of interference within their lives that is out of proportion to the seriousness of the behaviour that initially prompted the intervention.'

Doolan concluded that a justice approach helped to make young people in conflict with the law accountable for their actions and provided better assurance for due process. His report following the study tour, *From Welfare to Justice* (Doolan 1988), formed the foundation of the legislative separation of youth justice matters from care and protection matters in New Zealand.

[4] Most notably Judge Mick Brown and Judge David Carruthers, who became the first Principal Youth Court Judges in New Zealand respectively.

The Working Party on the new legislation also adapted the FGC, which was being introduced to deal with care and protection issues, to include justice principles for matters relating to children and young people in conflict with the law. This included holding them to account for their offending and encouraging those involved in making the decisions to seek ways to repair the harm, while promoting the reintegration and rehabilitation of the children and young people through the support of the family or the community.

Initially victims were included in the FGC as a party affected by the offending but it was soon recognized that their presence could enhance the process in a number of important ways. Victim involvement would help children and young people understand the impact of their offending and victim satisfaction in the outcome could serve as a testimony to the success of the model (Doolan 1988). FGCs were also designed to encourage victims to have the support of their families and communities during the process.

Placing emphasis on the importance of family involvement in matters relating to care and protection as well as youth justice led to a new name for the resulting piece of legislation: The Children, Young Persons *and their Families* Act (CYPFA) (our emphasis) (Review of the Children and Young Persons Bill (1987: 34)).

While the new approach to youth justice in New Zealand gave families and communities more responsibility in decision making around children and young people's wellbeing, the system was positioned in more general government structures, including the police, the Ministry of Justice, and the then Ministry of Social Welfare. A branch of social welfare emerged called Child, Youth and Family Services (CYFS) tasked with implementing the legislation. Youth courts were established as a separate branch of the district courts and a principal youth court judge was appointed along with judges to preside over criminal matters pertaining to youths. The FGC became a cornerstone to the decision making for each of these government agencies.

PLACING FAMILY GROUP CONFERENCES AT THE HEART OF THE NEW ZEALAND YOUTH JUSTICE SYSTEM

The Children and Young Persons Bill Review Committee (1987) aimed to provide opportunities for children and young people to be diverted from criminal proceedings and to ensure that their family was consulted at every point once a child or young person enters the youth justice system (Cheyne et al. 2000: 195). This included alerting families to a child or young person's offending behaviour once apprehended, even when the offending is on the more minor end of the scale.

New Zealand made two bold moves when including FGCs in the youth justice system. One was to reserve the FGC for cases of relatively serious or repeat offending rather than as a response to minor offending by children and young people. This was in line with the principle of intervening as little as necessary and for responses to be proportionate to the nature of the offence. The other move was to make FGCs a legal requirement rather than a voluntary adjunct to the youth justice process when young people were referred to the youth court.

The CYPFA states that the youth court must take into account the recommendations of an FGC[5] and that it cannot impose any court orders without an FGC being held.[6] If there is a need for a further appearance on a matter following an initial court outcome, the court may not make any amendments to the initial decision until a new FGC has been convened.[7] The youth court also has the authority to request an FGC at any time during the proceedings if it believes this will assist the decision making process.[8] Therefore, whether a young person admits to the offending or the offending is proven in court, he/she will be referred to an FGC and the outcome of the proceedings must be taken into account in any decision making by the youth court.

Making FGCs a legal requirement for serious cases in the youth justice system ensures that for every case, and at every point in the process, relevant support people (usually from the young person's family) and victims are able to have input into the most appropriate measures to repair harm and address the young person's offending behaviour. It also captures the government's commitment to involving key family members in the decision making process for dealing with children in conflict with the law, thereby responding to the voices of families and communities around the country.

While the overall principles of the CYPFA provide the overarching framework for the youth justice provisions, an additional set of principles were included in the Youth Justice section of the Act to underpin youth justice practice specifically in New Zealand. These principles included that family, *whānau*, *hapū*, and *iwi* should participate in decision making around youth justice outcomes and the views of victims should be taken into consideration when seeking solutions to repair the harm caused by the offending behaviour.

EVALUATING NEW ZEALAND'S FGCS

While New Zealand policy makers did not specifically take into account restorative justice theory when conceptualizing their youth justice legislation, the FGC soon became recognized as a valuable example of applying restorative justice theory in practice following the first in-depth research project conducted by Maxwell and Morris in 1993. FGCs provided a forum for young people to understand the impact of their behaviour on victims and develop plans, with the support of their families, to repair the harm caused by their offending. Restorative justice theorists found that youth justice FGCs incorporated key ingredients required for a restorative justice process. These included the participation of affected parties, reparation of harm, and restoration of those affected by the offending.

[5] Section 279 of the Children, Young Persons and their Families Act 1989.
[6] Section 281 of the Children, Young Persons and their Families Act 1989.
[7] Ibid.
[8] Section 281B of the Children, Young Persons and their Families Act 1989.

Van Ness (1997: 3) explains that: 'The foundation of restorative justice (…) requires that we work to heal victims, offenders and communities who have been injured by crime.' He suggests that early participation by those most affected by the offending is important to restoring justice. Framing of youth justice FGCs as an example of restorative justice in practice helped promote the restorative justice paradigm internationally, giving New Zealanders pride in their innovative youth justice approach.

There have been two significant, large scale studies in New Zealand since youth justice FGCs were introduced (Maxwell and Morris 1993; Maxwell et al. 2004). Additional studies have focused on certain aspects of the FGC process and the responsibilities of some key role players.[9] This research over the past two decades has helped to identify what factors enhance the process for the participants and successful life outcomes for the young people following the conference. The key factors contributing to a successful FGC as identified by the research in New Zealand cited above are described below.

PARTICIPATION

Ensuring that participants are well informed about what is likely to take place and what their role entails, is a key part of ensuring that conferences are successful. The quality of outcomes is also enhanced when the families, victims, and young people are actively involved and are able to express their views and participate in decision making during the conference (Maxwell and Morris 1993).

While the presence of all parties is desirable, victims may choose not to attend. However, finding a way for their views to be reported to the participants, particularly the young person, is important. The FGC coordinator therefore attempts to make sure that the people most affected by the offending are able to have their views heard in other ways, for example a written letter or a contribution from a supporter of the victim.

The role of professionals such as police and social workers is to supply information as needed or to guide the process. It is not intended that they should dominate or dictate the decision making and for the most part the research supports the importance of empowering the young person and their families themselves to take the responsibility for deciding and implementing the outcomes.

EMPOWERMENT

Full participation in the process is likely to empower the participants. Control over one's life can be restored not only to the young people but also to the victims and the family members who take part. However, participants are only likely to gain a sense of empowerment if their views have been listened to, their feelings have been understood, and their concerns have been reflected in the resulting plan.

[9] These include studies that focus on understanding reoffending (Maxwell and Morris 1999), the role of the youth advocate (Morris et al. 1997), and a study of the impact of police responses in relation to diversion (Maxwell and Paulin 2005).

REPAIRING HARM

It is often difficult for the young person to fully compensate for the harm they have caused. However, what is important to both victims and young people is that they both agree on a way to make amends. For many victims, simply knowing that the young person recognizes the impact of what he or she has done, is truly sorry, and is not likely to repeat that behaviour is seen by them as sufficient. Outcomes that have positive results for both the victim, the young person, and for other participants are often valued more highly than curfews, detention, and actions designed to cause pain.

ADDRESSING THE CAUSES OF OFFENDING

The Ministry of Justice's Youth Offending Strategy in 2002 recognizes that young people in New Zealand who are attracted to a criminal lifestyle often come from backgrounds characterized by violence, crime, a lack of parental nurturing or discipline, and substance abuse. These experiences shape their world view from an early age (Consedine 1999). Many have effectively dropped out of the education system and lack both life skills and the vocational skills and qualifications that are needed to find a place in the adult world. To succeed, young people need support in rebuilding their lives. Effective programmes often help and can be the first step towards reintegration. The FGC can therefore be a forum not only to repair the harm caused by the young person but also to repair some of the damage that he/she has suffered.

REINTEGRATION

Rebuilding a new life not only requires appropriate support to meet a young person's needs and opportunities to gain skills and qualifications. It also requires ongoing guidance from people who care about the young person. For most young people genuine commitment and encouragement from their family is an ongoing part of their development. This is enriched by the support and friendship of peers and mentors as they move into the adult world. The successful FGC process will help to locate people who are willing to continue to play a part in the young person's life for some time after this particular episode has been closed, thereby providing a community of care. The effective support of friends, family, and mentors is crucial to any plan for reintegration and the building of a new life.

EFFECTIVENESS

There are many different perspectives on how to measure effectiveness of FGCs. Reducing reoffending is a common criterion. In New Zealand, research has been carried out that compares young people with similar backgrounds, life skills, and experiences who have committed similar offences. The overall conclusion is that the way they are treated in the justice system can make a difference as to whether or not they will reoffend.

Research on FGCs (Maxwell et al. 2004) has focused on assessing factors associated with successful life outcomes. It measures not just reoffending but also the extent to which young people feel good about themselves and have plans for their future. This research found that good life outcomes were considered important features of FGCs. From the point of view of the young people who participated in this research, these included factors such as understanding the victim's views and feeling genuine regret for what happened; feeling able to repair the harm that was done; feeling that others forgive them and give them another chance; and deciding to keep out of trouble in future.

Another key finding was that an FGC tended to be no more effective than diversion in cases of minor offending, but it was more effective than the court system as the offences became more serious (Maxwell et al. 2004).

CHALLENGES TO THE FGC

While the principles of New Zealand's youth justice legislation have generally stood the test of time, some aspects of its practical implementation have fallen short of the vision and full potential of CYPFA 1989. According to Judge Becroft (2009: 30–31):

> Over time, the vision of the Children, Young Persons and their Families Act has been allowed to wither. Too often government agencies decide it is easier to retain a control and monitoring role over a young person's course through the youth justice system rather than relinquishing that control to the community. Too often community agencies have not been supported to enable expertise and experience to develop.

LACK OF RELIABLE RESOURCING FOR YOUTH JUSTICE FGCS

A significant obstacle to the success of FGCs over the years has been the lack of consistent funding and resourcing. At the time the CYPFA was implemented, funding was relatively abundant as a number of residential facilities had closed down making way for the more community based approach to youth justice. Funding for these residences was initially redirected to FGC processes which helped with identifying and locating the most appropriate people to support the young person in repairing the harm and addressing their offending. This allowed for a greater number of participants to attend the conference. It also ensured that FGCs were adequately and appropriately catered for, as providing food and eating together at the end of an FGC is an important part of the social ritual, particularly in the Māori culture. It symbolizes mutual trust, acceptance, and coming together of the parties. Not being able to include this ritual in the process can undermine the potential richness of the gathering.

The requirement to distribute funding allocated to CYFS among both care and protection and youth justice has at times eventuated in various restructures and reconfigurations within the service. When times are tough, care and protection has tended to receive priority over youth justice for funding (Becroft 2003), which can cause tension between them.

DIFFERENCES BETWEEN YOUTH JUSTICE COORDINATORS AND SOCIAL WORKERS

The CYPFA 1989 created a new position of youth justice coordinators. Originally, the youth justice coordinators were recruited for their knowledge of the community as well as their ability to connect with young people and encourage them to take responsibility for their actions. They were appointed for their skills and experience in working with young people and communities. It was expected that their role would be to uphold the principles of the legislation and ensure that the affected parties were enabled to come together to make decisions, rather than for decisions to be determined by professionals.

Youth justice coordinators were given a higher salary and more responsibility than social workers. However, the responsibilities of youth justice coordinators have been reduced over time and the management of youth justice processes has been transferred to managers from a social work background. This practice has underlined the inherent conflicts between a welfare approach, where the state takes responsibility for child care, and justice, with an empowerment approach where the responsibility is devolved to families and communities. This has in part been as a result of funding shortages for CYFS. The former chief social worker, Shannon Pakura (2004: 119) noted that '... the failure to think through the nature of the new position, its relationship to the statutory social work position and the importance of ongoing alignment between the two resulted in a problem of our own making that need never have been.'

REPLACING FLEXIBILITY WITH TICK BOXES

In their research project entitled 'Family, Victims and Culture: Youth Justice in New Zealand' Maxwell and Morris (1993) noted differences between conferences that took place in relatively formal Child, Youth and Family office settings and those held in community settings. When the FGC occurred in the young persons' home, families often felt more at ease and in control, although at times victims felt more uncomfortable. At culturally appropriate venues such as a *Marae*,[10] traditional protocols were more likely to guide the process and the wider communities were more likely to take responsibility for and be an effective part of the follow up. Resourcing constraints have also affected the flexibility of youth justice FGCs to be as culturally appropriate as envisioned. In order to cope with the demands, some youth justice FGCs merely 'tick the boxes' which measure success around the number of FGCs completed, rather than explore the range of solutions and opportunities this forum was designed to offer. Part

[10] A Marae is the traditional Maori sacred meeting place used for community gatherings. Strict protocols are followed when convening gatherings at Marae. Protocols may vary depending on the local people belonging to the Marae. Visitors to the Marae are required to respect and follow these protocols in order to be accepted by the local people, allowing for open discussion and, where necessary, resolution of matters.

of this is the result of limited time and capacity to seek the best or widest range of support people, thereby reducing the community of care for the young person both during and after the conference.

LIMITED FOLLOW UP ON COMPLETION OF FGC PLANS

Another concern has been that often there has been limited follow up to ensure that FGC plans are properly completed and that victims are compensated as agreed at the conference. While the conference itself may provide an opportunity for young people to acknowledge the harm caused to the victim and to apologize, victims can become demoralized if they believe the young people did not follow through on the agreed plan. This sometimes occurs simply because of administrative failure to keep the victims informed but also because the agreed tasks were not completed. However, the responsibility for both of these failures lies largely with the system that has not followed up fully with both the young people and the victims, and also limits the opportunities for FGC processes to be fully restorative.

Restoration in relationships and reconciliation in the actual conference is possible through the open discussions between the key parties. The actual completion of the agreed plan by the young person is a practical indication of their understanding of the impact of their offending, their genuine remorse, and their willingness to compensate for the harm done. Participation in programmes to address underlying factors leading to offending also demonstrates their commitment to avoiding actions that may cause further harm to others. Therefore, not completing plans or not ensuring that affected parties are updated on the progress of plans reduces the benefits of the process. It can potentially be more hurtful to a victim who has been given the expectation that following through on a plan is a gesture of making amends. For these reasons it is also very important to ensure that plans are realistic, appropriate, and manageable for the young person and that young people and their families have adequate support to be able to complete plans.

At the same time, it is very difficult for an FGC plan on its own either to repair the harm that was done or to address the multiple issues facing some young people and their families, which have contributed to offending. An FGC can help to identify these issues, raise awareness about a young person's needs, and consider ways to address these needs through the plan. However, if support for a young person to complete an FGC plans is lacking or fails to continue once the plan has been completed, there is a risk that vulnerable young people and their families feel let down, making it easier for criminal behaviour to recur. Therefore, much of the success of the FGC relies not only on what happens during the conference itself, but also what happens beforehand in terms of preparing parties for the process, as well as afterwards in terms of ensuring that FGC plans are followed up and completed with sufficient support.

PUBLIC PRESSURE FOR HARSHER PENALTIES

Against this backdrop, the youth justice system is also challenged by public pressure for harsher penalties to address serious crimes committed by young offenders. There has often been tension between polarized groups in New Zealand since the implementation of the CYPFA 1989. One main point of difference exists between those who believe that all processes, decision making, and interventions should be handled by professionals versus those who believe that families and communities are best placed to make decisions related to children and young people. The other difference lies between those who believe that diversion and FGC processes and plans are a soft option for children and young people who commit serious violent or sexual offences versus those who are committed to the principles underpinning the FGC process which place value on holding children and young people to account, making amends, and ensuring that families and communities can support their children and young people's positive social reintegration.

As a result of the strength of the view that harsher penalties were needed for young offenders, the New Zealand government re-introduced boot camp like interventions into the youth justice system in 2010. It also lowered the age and increased the range of offences for which children and young people can be sentenced in the adult jurisdiction. These changes were made despite the evidence that indicated that both these strategies are more likely to increase rather than reduce offending by children and young people.

However, many activists, politicians, practitioners, and community members are still strongly committed to the principles of the CYPFA and want to invest in improving outcomes for young people. Honourable Pita Sharples from the Māori Party called for the need to restore confidence and pride in young people during a parliamentary debate on an amendment to the youth justice legislation on 24 February 2010. Arguing against plans for introducing more punitive and restrictive measures for young people such as military style boot camps and electronic monitoring, he stated:

> We need perspectives which provide us with an optimistic view; that remind us of the potential of all our young people; to plan proactively for our future... How do we support these young people, to continue to promote a situation of hopefulness, to focus on their future? We do that by reminding them of their connection to us; that our collective aspirations include them; that they are worthy of work; that they are people we care about. (Sharples 2010: 1)

This view resonates strongly with the objectives of the CYPFA and advocates for a return and a commitment to the principles that guided the development of that legislation.

DEVELOPING NEW APPROACHES TO ENHANCE YOUTH JUSTICE STRATEGIES IN NEW ZEALAND

Most New Zealanders involved in youth justice remain committed to finding strategies that will uphold the vision and principles of the legislation. Below are some approaches which have the potential to increase the effectiveness of community based initiatives to support youth justice FGC processes.

YOUTH OFFENDING TEAMS

Youth offending teams (YOTs) were introduced in New Zealand around 2002 as part of the Youth Offending Strategy. These were made up of members of the CYFS, police, and health and education services, in order to provide a more holistic understanding of youth offending and comprehensive responses. According to a Ministry of Justice evaluation (Harland and Borich 2007: 21), YOTs were designed to have a 'bottom up response to youth justice issues' and that YOTs '... will achieve these aims by strengthening existing relationships between government agencies and local community groups and providers.'

The purpose was for the four key agencies to meet regularly in their local areas to jointly identify and address gaps around youth justice service provision. The way YOTs were established and run has varied across the country. The Ministry of Justice evaluation of YOTs (Harland and Borich 2007) reported that many YOT members were confused about the main purpose of YOTs, including what specific aspects of responding to youth offending they were responsible for, whom from the community the four core agencies should collaborate with, and how YOTs should go about setting up local initiatives to address any gaps identified. However, this research noted that despite the variations in the application of this initiative around the country, the participants who were interviewed from a number of YOTs believed that '... effectiveness and success of YOTs are related to outcomes associated with projects or initiatives and improving outcomes for young people and their *whānau*, rather than with aspects of collaboration' (Harland and Borich 2007: 88).

THERAPEUTIC JURISPRUDENCE

Therapeutic jurisprudence refers to the combining of court sanctions with treatment and rehabilitation initiatives in an attempt to address offending. The concept of therapeutic jurisprudence in New Zealand is still generally associated with initiatives in the Youth Drug Court. The Youth Drug Court was initially piloted in the Christchurch youth court in the South Island in 2002 to respond to the link between young people's use of drugs and alcohol and criminal behaviour. It was recognized that the justice system had to deal with young people's addiction issues if it hoped to reduce their offending. The Youth Drug Court process requires a specialist assessment of the young person's addiction along with other behavioural and environmental factors which may be contributing to the addiction, in order to develop a relevant plan. This plan is then taken to an FGC before a Youth Drug Court hearing to allow for families and victims to be involved in the process. Usually, the offender's ability to address the offending and victim needs increases as the treatment takes effect. Therefore, there could be several FGC hearings as the young person progresses through the plan and is better equipped to contribute to the process (Becroft 2004).

The evaluation of the Youth Drug Court pilot project ironically notes that this initiative puts a lot of emphasis on the role of the court whereas the CYPFA 1989 emphasizes diversion from court process and community based responses. Nevertheless, young people and their families reportedly noted that they '... felt more listened to, supported and respected in the Youth Drug Court than they did going through the Youth Court process' (Carswell 2004: 138).

The apparent strength of therapeutic jurisprudence is that it requires a collaborative approach between the courts, the agencies providing the treatment, the young people, and their families. While the Youth Drug Court has become the recognized model for therapeutic jurisprudence, many FGC plans also require treatment for young people to address factors which contributed to their offending behaviour. However this model is likely to work best if there is funding available to coordinate and implement the most appropriate youth justice programmes to assist with rehabilitation and reintegration, which includes giving community agencies the support they need to manage these cases.

MARAE BASED YOUTH COURTS

Another initiative gaining recognition in parts of New Zealand is the *Marae* based youth court. Otherwise known as the *Ranga Tahi* Scheme (meaning Māori Youth Court), these courts encourage Māori youths in particular to reconnect with their culture, motivating them to address their offending. This approach was first trialled at a *Marae* in Gisborne, on the East Coast of New Zealand's North Island. It has been running there since 2008 and is starting to expand to other parts of New Zealand.

The scheme is not intended to replace the youth court, but allows the local *Marae* to oversee and support the successful implementation of FGC plans which the youth court has agreed to. While a judge still presides over the matter at the *Marae*, emphasis is placed on how Māori cultural values can support young people and their families to complete their FGC plans. Holding these sessions at a *Marae* enables Māori youths to feel that they belong to their wider community and to appreciate the ability for their heritage to offer a more positive direction in their lives.

WHĀNAU ORA

Whānau ora is a policy initiative advanced by the Māori Party. In a budget speech to Parliament on 6 May 2010, Honourable Tariana Turia of the Māori Party explained that *Whānau ora* '. . . . in its most simple expression, is about building and maintaining the capability of whānau to be self-managing.' It is intended to draw on the collective strengths of the community in order to create positive, healthy lifestyles for New Zealanders, as defined by its members.

Whānau ora was not designed to address youth offending specifically. However, the similarities are evident between the principles underpinning this policy and those outlined in the original Report of the Māori Advisory Committee to the Minister of Social Welfare in 1988. While the concept is still in its infancy, *Whānau ora* has the potential to address factors that contribute to offending by children and young people in a more holistic way through community empowerment, and responding to the intergenerational dysfunction that exists in some families and communities. Ideally, this could result in nurturing environments for children and young people that will support their pro-social development and help them discover realistic alternatives to crime.

These various initiatives provide opportunities to better support children, young people, and their families to engage with FGC processes and follow through with plans in order to make amends to those affected by the offending. They can also help to prevent further offending through community and family empowerment and reintegration, and demonstrate that best practice is a continuing concern in a restorative justice system.

CONCLUSION

New Zealand's youth justice model has provided the world with an important model for youth justice systems. It places emphasis on family and community support for children and young people's pro-social development while making them accountable for their actions. The New Zealand experience has shown the need for widespread commitment from the government, communities, families, and agencies for this model to succeed. This can be a challenge when negative public perception of young offenders creates reluctance to invest in them, particularly when government funding is limited.

Nevertheless, most key role players recognize the value of the model and acknowledge that, in principle, it is preferable to removing children and young people from society and placing them in residential homes or prisons. More work is therefore needed to secure funding for youth justice FGCs, which includes the ability to provide adequate rehabilitation programmes and create communities of care around children and young people which will help them desist from further offending. In New Zealand, it may be necessary to ring fence funding[11] for youth justice, to provide better assurance that it is available and can be relied upon when needed (Pakura 2004).

New Zealand takes pride in its ability to assist other countries in establishing similar approaches to youth justice, as well as inadvertently providing a practical approach to restorative justice through the design of the FGC. As such, New Zealand has a responsibility to continue to uphold the principles underpinning its youth justice legislation which have helped to improve outcomes for children and youths in conflict with the law internationally. Increasing public education around youth justice FGCs and seeking ways to mainstream the principles and practice in other types of conflict resolution may increase public recognition, understanding, and support for the model in New Zealand, and cause New Zealanders to consider the approach part of their shared responsibility.

REFERENCES

Becroft, A. (2003), *Youth Justice: The New Zealand Experience Past Lessons and Future Challenge*, paper presented at the Juvenile Justice: From Lessons of the Past to a Road for the Future conference held on 1–2 December 2003 in Sydney, Australia. Canberra:

[11] Ring fenced funding means securing and setting aside funds just for the purposes of youth justice practice, without allowing those funds to be reallocated elsewhere.

Australian Institute of Criminology, available at: <http://aic.gov.au/events/aic%20upcoming%20events/2003/~/media/conferences/2003-juvenile/becroft.ashx>.

Becroft, A. (2004), *Youth Justice in New Zealand: Future Challenges*, paper presented at the New Zealand Youth Justice Conference: *Never Too Early, Never Too Late,* available at: <http://www.lbctnz.co.nz/resources/justice/yj_in_nz_becroft_paper.pdf>.

Becroft, A. (2009), 'Are There Lessons to be Learned From the Youth Justice System?' in Maxwell, G. (ed.), *Addressing the Causes of Offending: What is the Evidence?* (Wellington: Institute of Policy Studies), pp 25–36.

Carswell, S. (2004), *Process Evaluation of the Christchurch Youth Drug Court Pilot* (New Zealand: Ministry of Justice).

Cheyne, C., O'Brien, M. and Belgrave, M. (2000), *Social Policy in Aotearoa-New Zealand-A Critical Introduction* (South Melbourne Vic: Oxford University Press).

Consedine, J. (1999), *Restorative Justice: Healing the Effects of Crime* (New Zealand: Ploughshares Publications).

Daly, K. (2001), 'Conferencing in Australia and New Zealand: Variations, Research, Findings and Prospects', in Morris, A. and Maxwell, G. (eds.), *Restorative Justice for Juveniles: Conferencing, Mediation and Circles* (Oxford: Hart Publishing), pp 59–83.

Department of Social Welfare (1984), *Review of Children and Young Persons Legislation-Public Discussion Paper* (Wellington: Department of Social Welfare).

Department of Social Welfare (1987), *Review of the Children and Young Person's Bill- Report of the Working Party on the Children and Young Person's Bill* (Wellington: Department of Social Welfare).

Doolan, M. (1988), *From Welfare to Justice: Towards New Social Work Practice with Young Offenders* (New Zealand: Ministry of Social Welfare).

Harland, A. and Borich, A. (2007), *Evaluation of Youth Offending Teams in New Zealand* (Wellington: New Zealand).

Maxwell, G., Kingi, V., Robertson, J., Morris, A. and Cunningham, C. (2004), *Achieving Effective Outcomes in Youth Justice* (New Zealand: Ministry of Justice).

Maxwell, G. and Morris A. (1993), *Family, Victims and Culture: Youth Justice in New Zealand* (New Zealand: Ministry of Social Development).

Maxwell, G. and Morris, A. (1999), *Understanding Reoffending* (Wellington: Institute of Criminology, Victoria University of Wellington).

Maxwell, G. and Paulin, J. (2005), *The Impact of Police Responses to Young Offenders With a Particular Focus on Diversion:* Police Youth Diversion—Final Report prepared for New Zealand Police and Ministry of Justice (Victoria University of Wellington), available at: <http://youthjustice.co.nz/sites/default/files/Microsoft%20Word%20-%20Report%20on%20impact%20of%20police%20response%20to%20young%20offenders.pdf>.

Ministry of Justice (2002), *Youth Offending Strategy: Preventing and Reducing Offending and Re-offending by Children and Young People: Te Haonga* (Wellington: Ministries of Justice and Social Development).

Morris, A. (2004), 'Youth Justice in New Zealand', *Youth Crime and Youth Justice: Comparative and Cross-National Perspectives, Crime and Justice—A Review of Research,* 31, pp 242–89.

Morris, A., Maxwell, G. and Shepherd, P. (1997), *Being a Youth Advocate: An Analysis of Their Roles and Responsibilities* (Wellington: Institute of Criminology for Victoria Link).

Mulgan, R. (1989), *Māori, Pākeha and Democracy* (Melbourne: Oxford University Press).

New Zealand Ministerial Advisory Committee on a Maori Perspective for the Department of Social Welfare (1988), *Puao-te-ata-tu (Day break): The Report of the Ministerial Advisory Committee on a Maori Perspective for the Department of Social Welfare* (Wellington: Department of Social Welfare).

Pakura, S. (2004), *The Family Group Conference 14-year Journey: Celebrating the Successes, Learning the Lessons, Embracing the Challenges,* paper presented at the American Humane Association's Family Group Decision Making Conference and Skills-Building Institute, 6–9 June 2004, in Harrisburg, Pennsylvania, United States, available at: <http://www.familypower.org/library/au05_pakura.html>.

Renouf, J., Lagzdins. A. and Angus, J. (1989), *Children, Young Persons and their Families Act 1989—The Process of Social Policy Development* (Wellington: Department of Social Welfare).

Sharp, A. (1990), *Justice and the Maori-Maori Claims in New Zealand Political Argument in the 1980's* (Melbourne: Oxford University Press).

Sharples, P. (2010), *Speech: Children, Young Persons and Their Families (Youth Courts Jurisdiction and Orders) Amendment Bill,* available at: <http://www.maoriparty.org/index.php?pag=nw&id=865&p=speech-pita-sharples-children-youngpersons-and-their-families-youth-courts-jurisdiction-and-orders-amendment-bill.html>.

Turia, T. (2010), *Speech—Whanau Ora: Budget 2010,* available at: <http://www.beehive.govt.nz/speech/whanau-ora-budget-2010>.

Van Ness, D. (1997), *Perspectives on Achieving Satisfying Justice: Values and Principles of Restorative Justice,* A paper presented at Achieving Satisfying Justice Symposium, Vancouver, BC on 21 March 1997.

8

CONFERENCES AND GENDERED VIOLENCE

PRACTICES, POLITICS, AND EVIDENCE

Kathleen Daly

Using conferences in cases of gendered violence (sexual, partner, and family violence) is controversial. Two countries—New Zealand and Australia—have been pioneers in developing appropriate practices. A small body of evidence from the region and elsewhere is available on the topic. In this chapter, I first compare the legal and practice contexts of youth and adult conferencing in Australia and New Zealand, and then summarize debates on the appropriateness of conferences and restorative justice for gendered violence cases. I then review research from Australia, New Zealand, and other countries on practices and victims' experiences[1] with them. I conclude by outlining ways forward.

Here are the key points. In Australia, conferencing centres on youth, not adult offending. New Zealand has made greater advances by introducing conferences for adult cases in 2001, and by having a country-wide network of conference providers and standards of practice. There are differences in the profile of victims who participate in adult and youth justice conferences, which have implications for research and practice. Although there is considerable debate on the appropriateness of conferences for gendered violence in the Antipodes, it is less polarized than in North America. From New Zealand, research is available on adult conferences, and specifically, for partner/family and sexual violence. From South Australia, research is available on youth justice conferences and sexual offences, and on court/conference comparisons, and case studies of youth conferences for family violence. Contrary to those who are critical of using conferences in gendered violence cases, research findings are generally positive for victims. However, movement toward change is slowed by perceptions of conferences as being a 'too lenient' response for gendered violence (particularly those involving adult offenders) or not providing sufficient safeguards to victims. The political and evidential challenges are significant in moving the idea forward, but the ground is softening for change.

[1] Terms such as victim or victim/survivor are used in the literature, but victim is used for simplicity.

YOUTH JUSTICE CONFERENCING IN AUSTRALIA AND NEW ZEALAND

Youth justice conferencing was legislatively established first in New Zealand with the Children, Young Persons, and Their Families Act 1989; it moved to Australia in 1991, with the introduction of police-led diversionary conferences in New South Wales. Youth conferences were first legislated in South Australia with the Young Offenders Act 1993, which based its practices on the New Zealand model of non-police led conferences. Since then, all Australian jurisdictions have established youth justice conferencing, typically using the New Zealand model, and all have a statutory basis.

New Zealand and Australia differ in the profile of youth who participate in conferences. For New Zealand, Maxwell and Hayes (2007: 522, 528) say that 'the family group conference is the key decision-making procedure for the top 25 per cent of offenders, including all serious offending except... murder and manslaughter', and they estimate there have been 100,000 or more conferences since 1989. Family group conferences are referred by the police or the Youth Court, facilitated by coordinators in the social welfare department, and deal with youth aged 14 to 16 years. Although several major reports have been written (Maxwell and Morris 1993, 1999; Maxwell et al. 2004a, 2004b), none has focused on youth cases of family or sexual violence.[2]

In Australia, youth justice conferences are used in relatively less serious cases and deal with a wider age group, youth aged 10 to 17 years.[3] There is considerable variation in youth justice policy across the eight Australian states and territories (see Australian Institute of Health and Welfare 2009: Appendix B; Richards 2010). Using South Australia as an example, data for 1994–95 show that of all offences coming to police attention, 30 per cent were referred to court and 12 per cent to conference; the rest were cautioned, and few were withdrawn (Wundersitz 1996: 29). More recent data for 2009–10 show that while over 2,000 cases were finalized by a conference, most were finalized in court (Courts Administration Authority 2010: 45). Thus, while New Zealand youth conferences deal with the top 25 per cent of offenders, in South Australia, I would estimate that the courts deal with the top 25 to 35 per cent, and conferences are utilized for the next band of offenders.

South Australia and Queensland are the only Australian jurisdictions that permit conferences in youth sex offence cases. Research exists on these cases for South Australia, but none has been reported for Queensland. Across Australia, conferences are used as diversion from court, and to a lesser degree, pre-sentence. One jurisdiction (Tasmania) uses police-led conferences for formal cautions and facilitator-led conferences for court diversion conferences. Another (Victoria) uses pre-sentence conferences only, which are referred by judicial officers. The Australian Capital Territory

[2] Youth family violence normally includes assaults between youths and their siblings or parents. Youth sex offences are intra-familial (often with young victims), extra-familial (among peers), and public indecency types of offences.

[3] There are always exceptions to any general claim. For example, it is reported that in Tasmania, conferences have been used since 2002 in the state's only detention centre for youth, with over 700 conferences having been held from 2002 to 2005 (Llewellyn 2005).

(ACT) has the greatest degree of victim control. Only in this jurisdiction does a victim have veto power, by not consenting to a conference to go forward. Such veto power is unusual in the youth justice conferencing, but typical in the adult context.

ADULT JUSTICE CONFERENCING IN AUSTRALIA AND NEW ZEALAND

In the past decade, New Zealand has established and expanded conferencing for adult offenders to a greater degree than Australia. A national discussion has taken (and is taking) place in New Zealand on developing best practices and standards for restorative justice, including those for gendered violence cases. These developments have been aided by an organization of restorative justice providers, Restorative Justice Aotearoa,[4] incorporated in 2005.

AUSTRALIA

Australia's federated status has limited an ability of practitioners to identify national standards. With eight Australian jurisdictions operating under differing legal regimes and taking different conference approaches, there is relatively less sense of a critical mass of practitioners.[5] Although there is enthusiasm for conferencing within government and the judiciary, it is more dispersed. Importantly, beginning in June 1999, Indigenous sentencing courts for adult offenders began in Australia (see, Marchetti 2009; Marchetti and Daly 2007). Today, these courts exist in all but one state (Tasmania) and in some jurisdictions they are convened for youth offenders as well. The courts aim to harness Indigenous knowledge, forms of authority, and social control to reduce Indigenous offending and criminalization. Here I am speculating, but I suspect that the introduction and popularity of Indigenous sentencing courts in Australia may have displaced government interest to resource other justice forms for adults such as conferencing.[6]

Although conferencing in Australia is used almost exclusively in youth cases, there are exceptions:

[4] Restorative Justice Aotearoa listed 36 providers on its website in July 2011 (see <www.restorativejusticeaotearoa.org.nz/site_user_list>). Its Constitution exemplifies an institutionalization of restorative justice values.

[5] In Australia, conference facilitators are hired on a contract basis or are members of a permanent staff; one jurisdiction uses restorative justice service providers. A few companies provide restorative justice services for schools, workplaces, and communities, but there is not an identifiable national group of restorative justice providers. The Restorative Justice Programs unit in New Zealand's Ministry of Justice shapes national policy and contracts out for research; no national entity like this exists in Australia.

[6] Some Indigenous sentencing courts handle partner and family violence cases. Australian jurisdictions have also created a variety of specialist courts such as drug courts and family violence courts. In New Zealand, the first Rangatahi Court was established for youth in Gisborne in 2008, presided by Judge Heemi Taumanunu. Since then, courts have been established in other locales, including Waitakere, Manurewa, Orakei, Waitara, and Hamilton (Sharpe 2010).

- In South Australia, a pilot project of adult conferencing was carried out in 2004–05; Goldsmith et al. (2005) analysed twelve cases, two for sexual violence.
- In South Australia, a hybrid practice combines adult conferences with Indigenous sentencing court practices. Aboriginal Conferencing began in 2007 and continues to operate when the magistrate is on circuit to Port Lincoln (Marshall 2008).
- In New South Wales, pre-sentence adult conferences (Forum Sentencing) began in two sites in 2005 (People and Trimboli 2007). Initially for those aged 18–24 years, in July 2008, the upper age limit was removed. As of April 2011, Forum Sentencing was operating in nine locations and there are plans to expand it state-wide to all local courts in 2012–13. Sexual assault cases are not eligible.
- In New South Wales, the Restorative Justice Unit in the Department of Corrective Services, established in 1999, carries out meetings between prisoners and victims (or family members), post-sentence and post-release.
- In Victoria, Group Conferencing, established in 2007, includes offenders up to 20 years.
- Legislation for adult conferences was enacted in the ACT in 2005, but conferences have not yet been established.

NEW ZEALAND

The passage of four Acts in 2002 and 2004 gave legitimacy and support for conferences in adult cases: the Sentencing Act 2002, Parole Act 2002, Victims' Rights Act 2002, and Corrections Act 2004 (see Boyack et al. 2004; Proietti-Scifoni 2008). In the Sentencing Act, courts must take into account negotiated outcomes between an offender and victim, eg, actions to make amends. In the Victims' Rights Act, if there is agreement by both victim and offender, and if appropriate resources are in place (eg, a trained facilitator), any legal or court actor (eg, lawyer, judicial officer, prosecutor) can encourage a meeting to 'resolve issues relating to the offence' (s. 9(1)).

In 2001 to 2004, a pilot of adult conferencing was carried out in four New Zealand sites (Auckland, Waitakere, Hamilton, and Dunedin), and an evaluation funded by the Ministry of Justice was carried out by Morris et al. (2005). The pilot excluded partner violence cases[7] and all non-property offences having a maximum sentence of greater than seven years, which effectively excluded all sexual assaults. After a guilty plea, a judge can refer a case to a conference; and for a conference to go forward, both a victim and offender must agree to it. If a conference does go forward, a report of what occurred is given to the judge before sentence (Morris et al. 2005, executive summary, 1). The judge may take into account what occurred at the conference, along with any other reports, in deciding the sentence.

One initially surprising finding was the substantial attrition of cases after referral. Of 539 cases referred, a conference was held for 192 (or 36 per cent) (Morris et al. 2005: Table 3.3). Of the cases that did not proceed, the reasons were victim withdrawn (63

[7] However, some family violence cases were handled by conferences in community-managed programmes in two areas (see Paulin et al. 2005a, 2005b).

per cent), offender withdrawn (29 per cent), and unable to contact the victim or case not suitable (8 per cent) (Morris et al. 2005: section 3.4.1, para 1). For the individual victims who did not participate, they 'did not want to meet the offender' (58 per cent) or could not be contacted (13 per cent) (Morris et al. 2005: section 3.4.1, para 2).[8]

For comparison, I analysed case attrition in the Justice Research Consortium (JRC)-London experiment for adult burglary and street crime offences. Drawing from Shapland et al. (2011: 49, Table 3.1), of 222 eligible burglary cases that did not proceed to random assignment, the reasons were victim refusal (45 per cent), offender refusal (38 per cent), and victim could not be contacted (17 per cent).[9] For street crime (mainly robbery), it was victim refusal (52 per cent), offender refusal (26 per cent), and victim could not be contacted (22 per cent). Victim refusal rates appear to be somewhat higher in the New Zealand pilots than in the JRC-London experiment. I suspect that the reason is that New Zealand victims were asked to participate in a pre-sentence conference, whereas JRC-London victims were asked to participate in an experiment, in which they then would be randomly assigned (or not assigned) to a 'supplemental' conferencing process, in addition to the conventional court process.

The victim refusal figures should not surprise us, in light of other research on victims' reluctance to participate in meetings with offenders or actual participation rates of victims in youth justice conferences: about 50 per cent in New Zealand, somewhat higher in some Australian jurisdictions, very low in England and Wales (Morris et al. 2005: fns. 114 and 115). However, several research and policy implications can be drawn. First, compared to victims in youth conferences (who are typically not asked if they wish to participate), there is substantial selection bias of victims participating in adult conferences. Thus, we would expect to see more positive results from research on victims in adult than youth justice conferences, despite the fact that adult conferences are often for more serious offences.[10] Second, and relevant to debates on the appropriateness of conferences in gendered violence cases, if victims are asked if they wish to participate in a conference, the fact that they have a choice to do so (or not) should allay some critics' concerns.

Adult conferencing was expanded to other New Zealand sites in 2005. Referrals (post-plea and pre-sentence)[11] are made not only by the police and courts, but also by community-based organizations. Depending on the context, varied approaches are used to secure victim consent for conferences to go forward. From 2005 onwards, and unlike the adult pilot, gendered violence cases were not expressly ineligible, although

[8] By comparison, for the individual offenders, the reasons were more dispersed: not wanting to meet the victim (20 per cent), not accepting responsibility for the offence or contesting the facts (21 per cent), not contactable (23 per cent), and failed to attend meetings (11 per cent).

[9] 'Withdrawn' and 'refused' are the terms used by the respective authors (Morris et al. 2005; Shapland et al. 2011).

[10] This selection bias in part explains the differences found in victims' experiences with youth justice conferences in the Re-Integrative Shaming Experiment (RISE) in Canberra and the adult supplemental conferences in the JRC-London experiment (see Sherman et al. 2005). Whereas RISE randomly assigned youth to conferences (or to court), JRC-London randomly assigned victims (from a group of eligible victims and offenders who consented to participate in the experiment) to court or to court plus a conference.

[11] Project Restore-NZ, described below, received court-based referrals and community (self-based) referrals of cases that had not been reported to the police.

the Ministry of Justice said that caution should be exercised. Restorative Justice Aotearoa (RJA) providers began receiving court-referred family violence cases in 2006 (Kingi et al. 2008: 31–39); and their survey published in 2007 revealed that 13 per cent of the cases were family violence matters (RJA 2007). From 1 July 2008 to 30 June 2009, an estimated 1,400 conferences were held, 350 (18 per cent) of which dealt with family violence; by contrast, three sexual violence cases were finalized by a conference (Ministry of Justice official, personal communication, 11 June 2010).

In 2009, the Ministry of Justice announced its intention to review restorative justice in family violence cases, but the review was put on hold, pending a report from Project Restore-NZ. This group, which takes a victim-sensitive approach to conferencing, was created in 2004. It was inspired by the work of Mary Koss and colleagues (Koss et al. 2004), who, in 2001, established the first pilot project in the United States to use restorative justice conferences in adult cases of acquaintance rape and misdemeanour sexual offences (see Koss 2010 for RESTORE; Jülich 2010 and Jülich et al. 2010 for Project Restore-NZ).

DEBATES ON CONFERENCES, RESTORATIVE JUSTICE, AND GENDERED VIOLENCE

Collections by Cook et al. (2006) and by Ptacek (2010a), and a review by Daly and Stubbs (2006), give a good flavour of the debates on conferences and gendered violence. Contributors are typically oriented to the question of appropriateness with partner violence in mind; relatively less is said about sexual violence. Like an early edited collection (Strang and Braithwaite 2002), the 'debate' takes place on principled grounds: few authors can produce research on actual practices or outcomes, victims' experiences, or comparisons of conference and court processes and outcomes. I would emphasize that conducting such research is difficult: it can be hard to gain access to victims; and once contacted, they may not wish to participate in research. The even greater problem, however, is that because so few jurisdictions in the world use conferences (or other types of informal justice practices) routinely in youth or adult cases of gendered violence, there are few sites where it is possible to gather evidence.

Critics identify these problems:

- potential for women's safety to be compromised;
- potential for power imbalances to go unchecked, which can reinforce violent behaviour;
- potential for offenders and bystanders to manipulate the process;
- relevance or meaning of 'genuine apologies' in relationships characterized by violence;
- limited impact of one meeting to change entrenched patterns of abuse and violence;
- potential for victims to be pressured into participating or coerced into agreements and not be able to advocate effectively on their own behalf;

- uncertain role and function of 'the community', when communities are under-resourced or may reinforce, rather than challenge, violent behaviour;
- mixed loyalties of friends and family, who may partly support victims, but also support offenders, and collude with the violence;
- symbolic implications: informal processes reflect a re-privatization of violence; and
- outcomes may appear too lenient and send the wrong message to offenders and potential offenders.

Critics focus on the potentially damaging and negative effects for victims in informal, face-to-face encounters, particularly in intimate relationships characterized by ongoing violence. They fear that protections and penalties that are part of conventional criminal justice will be reduced or minimized.

Supporters see these benefits and potentially positive effects:

- potential for greater victim participation and 'voice' in the process and outcome;
- potential for victim validation and empowerment;
- a greater degree of offender accountability and explicit censuring of violent behaviour;
- a more flexible and less formal environment, which is less intimidating and more responsive to victims;
- greater potential for dialogue and interaction, telling one's story, and checking and challenging an offender's denials or minimizations of harm;
- potential to address violence for those who wish to continue or repair a relationship.

Those who support conferences and restorative justice also emphasize the failures of conventional criminal justice, eg a re-victimization of victims by the legal process and significant attrition of sexual violence cases (Daly and Bouhours 2010; Koss 2006). Interviews of people with a range of views[12] have been carried out in Australia, New Zealand, and Canada. Curtis-Fawley and Daly (2005) found that victim advocates and service providers in two Australian states had different views, depending on their degree of exposure or familiarity with actual practices. Those with greater familiarity were more likely to see the value of restorative justice than those with less exposure or experience. Nancarrow (2006) found a 'racialized split' in the views held by Australian Indigenous and non-Indigenous women. The former were more likely to endorse restorative justice, compared to conventional criminal justice, in partner and family violence cases. Reviewed by Stubbs (2010: 107–8), Canadian professionals and practitioners said that they were not opposed in principle to restorative justice; however, they raised concerns about how well existing protocols could address partner and family violence, along with the adequacy of facilitator training and resources. Kingi et al. (2008) surveyed twenty-four professionals in five New Zealand sites, where adult family violence cases were referred to conferences. The professionals were programme providers, judges, victim advisers, prosecutors, and lawyers. One-third expressed

[12] Most studies asked for views of restorative justice, but in most studies, respondents also had conferences expressly in mind.

unconditional support for using restorative justice in family violence cases, 38 per cent expressed conditional support, and 29 per cent were against it. The conditional supporters said there needed to be better facilitation; those opposed cited problems of coercion and re-victimization of victims and manipulation of the process by offenders.

Proietti-Scifoni and Daly (2011) analysed the views of nineteen Opinion Leaders in Wellington and Auckland on using restorative justice for different types of gendered violence (partner violence, sexual violence, and child sexual abuse [CSA]). The analysis identified three groups, not two: the Supporters, Sceptics, and Contingent Thinkers. Despite their different positions, members of all the groups were concerned with victim safety and voluntariness in participating, and all noted potential problems of power dynamics in on-going relationships. All believed that CSA was the least suitable, although they assumed that a child victim would be present at the conference. Across the three groups, it was recognized that some contexts were more favourable to restorative justice than others: in relationships of roughly equal status (eg, sibling violence), when offenders had little or no previous offending, and when couples wished to maintain a relationship. Their views were shaped by their experiences with restorative justice and current professional role; they correlated with their views on the strengths and weaknesses of conventional criminal justice; and for Māori and Pacific Islanders, they were structured by concerns with state-run practices.

Confirming Curtis-Fawley and Daly (2005), having a more direct experience of restorative justice was related to greater support for its use in gendered violence cases: Sceptics more likely worked as government officials and managers of victim services; and Supporters and Contingent Thinkers, as facilitators, law officers, ministers, or direct victim service workers. The analysis did not find a 'racialized split' as Nancarrow (2006) did, however, the Māori and Pacific Islander participants wanted to see greater 'cultural control' of justice practices, rather than just state control.

Positions on using conferences for gendered violence are more polarized in North America (see, eg, Ptacek's 2010b review for the United States) than in Australia and New Zealand. One reason is a greater degree of exposure and experience with conferences, particularly in New Zealand. In Canada, restorative justice may have been forced too quickly in areas without consultation or sufficient resources (Rubin 2010). In the United States, Linda Mills's work (2003, 2008) on Intimate Abuse Circles (IACs), restorative justice, and partner violence has generated controversy. Those who support restorative justice in gendered violence cases have criticized Mills's analysis of partner violence (emphasizing individual actors' psychology rather than gender-based sources of power) and the principles of IACs, which do not pay sufficient attention to 'normative judgments' about conduct, including that 'domestic [partner] violence is morally wrong' (Coker 2004: 1347, 1349).

Writing with critics of conferencing generally in mind, Morris's (2002: 600–1) comments are especially apt when applied to the gendered violence debate: one may only be able to 'rebut speculation with speculation' and 'positive and negative spins can be put on the same data'. In addition, there is circularity to the debate. Policymakers say there is a lack of evidence on conferences for gendered violence and their impact on victims, but because these offences have been ruled ineligible for conferencing, one cannot gather the evidence. This situation is beginning to change, as we see in the next section.

CONFERENCE PRACTICES AND GENDERED VIOLENCE

Because the evidence base on conferences and gendered violence is small, my review includes practices and research from Austria, Belgium, Canada, Denmark, England, and the United States, in addition to New Zealand and Australia.

ADULT OFFENDERS AND CONFERENCES

For North America, Pennell and Burford (2002) show that a feminist praxis model, which uses family group conferencing, is effective in stopping partner violence and child maltreatment. Elements of family privacy, women's leadership, and state control articulate, they say, to build 'links, interruptions' in stopping the violence (p. 126). Pennell (2006) has also addressed child welfare matters (which often include partner violence) with family-centred meetings, and continues to see benefits of using such meetings to address family violence (Pennell and Kim 2010). For England, the Dove Project reported on a small number of partner violence victims, whose cases were referred to a conference, and who agreed to participate in the research. Of six women interviewed, four rated the conference positively (Social Services Research and Information Unit 2003). In the United States, Koss's RESTORE project in Tucson completed 22 conferences, largely of first-time adult offenders of acquaintance rape and obscene behaviour; however, no in-depth interviews were conducted with victims (Koss 2011). In the South Australia pre-sentence pilot, Goldsmith et al. (2005) found that the two sexual assault cases posed more difficulties for the conference process compared to the other offences. They concluded that 'greater thought' needs to be given to how participation is encouraged and managed in these cases.

Three New Zealand studies report on conferences in family (Kingi et al. 2008), partner (Tisdall et al. 2007), and sexual violence cases (Jülich et al. 2010). In Kingi et al. (2008), nineteen victims who attended conferences were interviewed; they were about half of those for whom contact was attempted (most could not be located); and they were a minority of all those who had participated in conferences (an estimated seventy people) during the research time frame.[13] The offences were typically in 'the less serious to medium seriousness range', eg, assaults not requiring a victim's hospital admission (p ix). Referrals to restorative justice providers came from varied sources; the providers took a cautious, case-by-case assessment of suitability, based on safety; and each site had somewhat different practices. Highlighting the findings, most

[13] Offenders were also interviewed, but the findings are not reported here. Page numbers are not shown on the web-based report, thus, page citations are sourced from the report's table of contents.

victims said the conference was positive, citing 'open dialogue, ... the healing process, and being able to meet the offender in a safe, supportive environment' (p. iv). However, a minority (26 per cent) reported that the offender made up for what they did and 32 per cent believed that the offender understood how the victim felt (p 64). Despite this, most (89 per cent) were pleased they had taken part, 79 per cent said they would do it again if they needed to (p 66), and 74 per cent were satisfied with the process (p 63). Two of the nineteen victims said they felt unsafe at the meeting; for the others, safety did not emerge as a concern.

In Tisdall et al. (2007), eight partner violence victims were interviewed. They were a highly select sample, having been identified from a list of 26 pre-sentence conferences held in Rotorua during 2005–6 that were judged by the service providers to have been successful. Not surprisingly then, in light of sample selection bias, all the victims said they felt safe during the conference (although one reported having been assaulted some months later); the authors concluded that the meetings were 'valuable and positive for most victims' (p 70).

Jülich et al. (2010) focused on ethical and practice matters when preparing for and conducting conferences (or at times, panels)[14] for sexual violence cases. Of 29 referrals, three did not proceed past initial inquiries and two were pending at the time of the report; nine proceeded to a conference (p 25). Although most referrals did not result in a conference, the authors found that a victim's 'sense of justice' could be realized during the pre-conference process. Four conferences were selected for interview purposes and four people (three victims and one offender) were interviewed. All four had a 'high regard for the process ... and appear, at least in part, to have achieved some kind of healing' (Jülich et al. 2010: 48), although the authors recognize that sample selection and a small number of cases limits generalization. The major contributions of this report are two-fold: to identify key principles of best practice in sexual violence cases and to show how the standard restorative justice model would require modification to include victims' perspectives and interests.

ADULT OFFENDERS AND OTHER JUSTICE ACTIVITIES

Other types of related justice activities provide options for gendered violence victims, although they are not called conferences. They include diversionary mediation for partner violence (Pelikan 2010), Community Holistic Circle Healing (CHCH) for child sexual abuse (including historic cases) (Lajeunesse 1996), facilitated meetings for acquaintance rape (Madsen 2008), and prisoner-victim meetings (eg, Miller 2011).

Diversionary mediation for partner violence in Austria is set in motion at the discretion of the prosecutor (Pelikan 2010). The victim-offender meetings, first as dyads with a victim and mediator/social worker, and perpetrator and mediator/social worker, are then followed by 'the talk of four', a mediation session that goes through a

[14] A panel is a restorative process without a victim present. Some victims wanted to confront an offender, but preferred doing so via a victim specialist rather than in a face-to-face meeting (Jülich et al. 2010: 40, 51). The number of panels held was not mentioned in the report.

set of steps to produce 'recognition and empowerment' (p 52). The ultimate aim is to promote 'a partnership free of violence' (p 54). A survey of female victims showed that a high share of the mediators took the violent behaviour seriously (over 80 per cent) and just over half (57 per cent) of the ex-partners understood the extent of hurt and harm caused. For the group of women who experienced no further violence, a high share (80 per cent) credited the mediation.

CHCH emerged in the late 1980s in Canadian First Nations communities in the Hollow Water area in Manitoba. After victim disclosure, the victimizer was confronted by staff members; the police were informed, and the suspect was given the choice of admitting guilt and being sentenced to probation, with the requirement to participate in the 'community way' (circles and intensive therapeutic intervention, which can last for three to five years); or to go through the regular court system. Lajeunesse (1996) found that of 52 victims (or family members of victims), about half said that the CHCH response was appropriate from a justice perspective, but the rest did not think so because the offender was not showing signs of change in that, for example, some continued to abuse alcohol. Two-thirds said they benefited from the CHCH process because it allowed them to talk to others and participate in counselling and circles.

Facilitated 'restorative dialogues' for acquaintance rape cases have been taking place since 2004 at the Centre for Victims of Sexual Assault in Copenhagen (Madsen 2008; Pali and Madsen 2011). The idea evolved when victims expressed an interest to meet or confront the person who attacked them, but did not wish to report the offence to the police. The facilitator (Madsen) used letter writing as an initial step for a victim to express herself to the perpetrator and to broach the possibility of meeting. In 2004, 16 victims came forward; ten wrote letters to the offender and six offenders replied. Some months after the process, Madsen (2008: 7) found that all the victims said 'it was a good thing I did that, and I would do it again.' In a further analysis, Pali and Madsen (2011: 60) reported that the 'procedure provides women with a platform from which to address the men who assaulted them, directly or indirectly, while validating their desire for retribution and rehabilitation.' At the same time, they recognized that 'the restorative dialogues are not a way to end or reach closure [from] a traumatic experience, nor an option for all women', although it is a 'step . . . to take in regaining meaning and dignity in their lives after a sexual assault' (p 60). The Centre continues to receive and respond to requests by victims (about 15 per year), with about one-third of victims eventually having a face-to-face dialogue with the perpetrator (Pali and Madsen 2011: 57).

Victim-prisoner meetings, which can be held post-sentence or post-release, are typically called 'dialogues' not conferences. For rape and child sexual abuse cases that conclude with a court conviction and prison sentence to serve, voluntary meetings can be organized and run by professional facilitators. This has been occurring for some time across jurisdictions in Canada (Gustafson 2005) and the United States (Umbreit et al. 2003).

A feminist-informed study by Miller (2011) analyses cases using restorative justice dialogues that were handled by Victims' Voices Heard (VVH), a programme established in Delaware in 2002. Of the nine victim-offender pairs analysed by Miller, five involved gendered violence (sexual and partner) and four murder or attempted murder. For the gendered violence cases, Miller reports that all the 'victims received immense satisfaction when offenders told them that nothing about the crime was their fault'. In addition, benefits arose from telling offenders of the long-term consequences of the crime and being able to ask offenders questions. In all nine cases, Miller said that victims defined 'their participation as a watershed moment, seeing VVH as essential in breaking the silence and mystery surrounding their victimization and providing a mechanism to combat feelings of being trivialized... and disempowered by the criminal justice process' (p 187).[15] Miller terms this context of restorative justice as 'therapeutic, post-conviction RJ' (p 180), contrasting it to diversionary programmes that 'function in lieu of formal case processing and punishment' (p 206).[16] She argues, and I concur, that post-conviction restorative justice for gendered violence cases is less likely to raise critique or controversy.

In New South Wales, a Restorative Justice Unit (RJU) was formed in the Department of Corrective Services in 1999. As of 2010, there were 145 completed 'restorative justice processes' (out of about 850 referrals). Most are face-to-face, but some are indirect, and they take place post-sentence or post-release. A small number, perhaps three, have been rapes (RJU Acting Manager, personal communication, 12 August 2010). For these cases, RJU's policy is that only victim-initiated referrals are considered. A research project, headed by Janet Chan and Jane Bolitho at the University of New South Wales, began in 2010 to study and evaluate the RJU's activities and outcomes across a range of offence types (Bolitho, email communication, 23 September 2010).

Compared to other contexts of conferences (eg court diversion or pre-sentence), victim-prisoner meetings require significantly more time and intense preparation, which may take several years. Although the offences are very serious, the elements of victim-initiation and offender readiness, coupled with careful preparation, suggest a meeting context that has potential to be highly successful. Indeed, of all contexts in which restorative justice may be used in gendered violence cases, the post-sentence (prison) context is likely to show the highest levels of positive outcomes for victims. At the same time, we should not lose sight of the fact that relatively few cases will ever reach this point in the criminal justice system.

YOUTH OFFENDERS AND CONFERENCES

Research on conferencing for youth sexual offending and family violence, and on court/conference comparisons, is available for South Australia (Daly 2010). In addition, Mercer (2009) and Vanseveren (2010) describe conferences for youth sex offence cases in England and Belgium, respectively.

The South Australian programme of research on gendered violence has several sub-studies: the Sexual Assault Archival Study (SAAS) of 385 sex offence cases

[15] Considerable benefits were also identified for offenders, including 'creating empathy for victims' (p 189), but I do not discuss these here.

[16] Although Miller is right to distinguish diversion from court and post-sentence contexts of restorative justice, she overlooks the fact that 'restorative dialogues' and 'supplemental conferences' may also take place when victims decide not to report an offence to the police (the Copenhagen Centre, discussed above) and when conferences run parallel to the court process (pre-sentence or is supplementary to sentencing).

(1995–2001), in which court-conference comparisons were made of processes, outcomes, and re-offending (Daly 2006, Daly et al. 2011); the In-Depth Study of fourteen conferences of sexual and family violence (Daly and Curtis-Fawley 2006; Daly and Nancarrow 2010); and the Judicial Sentencing Remarks Study (Bouhours and Daly 2007; Daly and Bouhours 2008). Summarizing the findings, youth sex offending was more likely to be admitted to, and more likely to be disposed of by a conference than court, for intra-familial rather than extra-familial sex offending. Of sex offence cases that went to court, nearly half were dismissed. For youths whose cases were proved in court or disposed of by conference, the time to re-offend (specifically, *general* re-offending)[17] was significantly slower if youths were referred to an intensive programme for sex offending, the Mary Street Adolescent Sexual Abuse Prevention Program.[18] However, this held only for youths with no previous offending; for those with previous offending, a referral to Mary Street made no difference in time to re-offend. A similar pattern was evident for youths whose cases were disposed of by conference rather than in court. Reoffending was significantly slowed for conference than court youth, but only for those with no previous offending.

From the quantitative analysis, coupled with case studies of sexual assault victims' experiences, the conclusion is that conferences are better than court from a victim's perspective. The reason is that conferences provide a validating justice mechanism. Further, in a conference, victims (or family members) are able to explain the impact of the offence to an admitted offender and to check and challenge denials or excuses to offending. By comparison, in half of the court cases, there was no validating justice mechanism for victims because the case was dismissed. The analysis of judicial sentencing remarks shows that although the judges admonished intra-familial sex offences strenuously and as 'real rape' (typically, these cases involved young victims), they did not admonish peer sexual assaults. This confirms patterns in adult sexual assaults: those involving acquaintances and peers are not considered 'real rape', and they face more hurdles in the legal process.

In the Greater Manchester (England) area, Mercer (2009) has applied family group conferencing to children and youth who display sexually harmful behaviour (SHB) and victims of SHB. Working with the AIM project (for Assessment Intervention and Moving On), Mercer developed a Restorative Justice Assessment framework to determine if cases (largely intra-familial) are appropriate for restorative processes. The cases are mainly post-sentence, although some are pre-sentence. AIM's justice-therapeutic practice blends a victim, offender, and family focus; it is impressive in the attention given to power dynamics, blame, and shame associated with youth sex offending. As of 2009, 25 referrals were made to AIM; ten had a direct meeting (Mercer 2009:14). In Flanders (Belgium), family group conferences have been used in selected youth sex offence cases (largely intra-familial). It is a pre-sentence option, with a referral by a juvenile court judge (Vanseveren 2010).

[17] The number of cases of sexual reoffending was too low for a separate analysis.

[18] For a comprehensive description and discussion of the Mary Street Programme, see Daly et al. (2011).

WAYS FORWARD

Since the 1970s, second-wave feminism has been challenging 'business as usual' in police and court responses to gendered violence. Some advances have been made, but much remains to be done. A significant thrust of social and legal change is introducing stronger police and court responses to gendered violence offences and to provide greater support for victims. When the idea of restorative justice was introduced in the early 1990s, it was met with critique by those in the domestic violence sector, in part because of well-known failures of mediation in these cases and in part because it sent the wrong message of a 'too lenient' response to perpetrators.

Gendered violence offences pose challenges to conferencing and restorative justice, in part because of a charged political context and in part because these offences require serious reflection on the role and place of victims in a justice process. Victim safety and voluntary participation, and facilitators who are knowledgeable about the dynamics of gendered violence offences, are obvious pre-requisites. If occurring in a legal context, a justice activity cannot be set in motion without an admission by the accused to offending, or at a minimum, by not disputing what occurred.[19] The results from the SAAS project on youth sex offending suggest that in addition to conferences or other types of restorative processes, targeted therapeutic interventions are required. The SAAS project also suggests that conferences and therapeutic interventions aimed at youth sex offending are more effective for first-time offenders.

To move forward, these points should be considered:

1. Distinguish among differing types of gendered violence, by recognizing that some offences and victims may be more amenable to conference processes than others.
2. Be aware that gendered violence is one of several types of offences that cause victims serious distress and potential re-victimization in a justice activity.
3. Move slowly and carefully in developing protocols and practices, and be sure to conduct research on what occurs.
4. Develop a range of responses to gendered violence, some of which are part of a criminal justice process, and others outside of it.

For the first, sexual violence offences, especially historic cases of child sexual abuse, youth and adult peer and acquaintance violence, and youth intra-familial violence are good candidates for conferences. These offences are highly under-reported, associated with high levels of shame and blame among victims, and may involve complex familial dynamics that legal systems handle poorly. In general, sexual violence may be a better starting point than partner violence in developing alternative justice practices: the former offences are more likely to be 'once off' and not involve on-going relations (with exceptions, of course), and many include youth offending.

The second point arises from my research on youth justice conferences, when I discovered that girls' and boys' peer violence created high levels of victim distress and re-victimization (Daly 2008). Although often termed 'school yard squabbles', these

[19] There may be other contexts for conferences, meetings, and restorative justice that are outside a legal context, eg, those for victims when a suspect has not been detected or arrested on a charge (Daly 2011).

female and male peer violence cases are often serious matters of bullying and victimization that require careful handling in a conference process. In addition, youth violence toward mothers and fathers, a type of youth family violence, requires careful handling as well (Daly and Nancarrow 2010). These offences pose as many problems for the standard conference model as the more frequently discussed adult cases of partner violence or peer sexual violence.

For the third, devising more effective justice responses to gendered violence will take some time; there is little to be gained by rushing into ill-considered or poorly resourced practices. New Zealand's history of adult conferencing and gendered violence is a good example of building a strong facilitator base and moving slowly in developing appropriate protocols. For all jurisdictions, practices need to be documented and analysed. Without an evidence base, proposals for change will fall on deaf ears. Such justice practices need to be joined with effective therapeutic intervention programmes.

Even with an evidence base that shows the value of conferences (or similar justice activities), proposals for change may be treated with scepticism. Part of the problem is the politics of justice and gendered violence. There is resistance by some victim and advocacy groups and by government policy makers to entertain alternative justice practices, although there appears to be an increasing openness to the idea. Another part of the problem, and with respect to the fourth point, is the way in which justice alternatives are presented. We need to widen the scope of proposed justice activities beyond conferences and restorative justice. I use the term 'innovative justice' to refer to mechanisms that may be outside a legal process or part of it (Daly 2011). Many victims want something to be done, but they do not wish to call the police or engage a legal process; thus, mechanisms need to be established to assist this group. For those who do engage the legal process, other mechanisms, in addition to conferences, should be considered. The more options there are for victim participation, voice, validation, and vindication in the aftermath of crime, the better. In time, those who are critical of alternative justice practices for gendered violence will come to see their value. Such alternatives cannot replace criminal prosecution and trial, but they offer a larger set of options for victims.

REFERENCES

Australian Institute of Health and Welfare (2009), *Juvenile Justice in Australia 2007–08* (Canberra: AIHW).

Bouhours, B. and Daly, K. (2007), 'Youth Sex Offenders in Court: An Analysis of Judicial Sentencing Remarks', *Punishment and Society*, 9(4), pp 371–94.

Boyack, J., Bowen, H. and Marshall, C. (2004), 'How Does Restorative Justice Ensure Good Practice?', in Zehr, H. and Toews, B. (eds.), *Critical Issues in Restorative Justice* (Monsey: Criminal Justice Press), pp 265–76.

Coker, D. (2004), 'Race, Poverty, and the Crime-Centered Response to Domestic Violence: A Comment on Linda Mills's *Insult to Injury*', *Violence Against Women*, 10(11), pp 1331–53.

Cook, K., Daly, K. and Stubbs, J. (eds.) (2006), 'Gender, Race, and Restorative Justice' [special issue], *Theoretical Criminology*, 10(1), pp 5–138.

Courts Administration Authority (2010), *Annual Report 2008–09* (Adelaide: Courts Administration Authority).

Curtis-Fawley, S. and Daly, K. (2005), 'Gendered Violence and Restorative Justice: The Views of Victim Advocates', *Violence Against Women*, 11(5), pp 603–38.

Daly, K. (2006), 'Restorative Justice and Sexual Assault: An Archival Study of Court and Conference Cases', *British Journal of Criminology*, 46(2), pp 334–56.

Daly, K. (2008), 'Girls, Peer Violence and Restorative Justice', *Australian and New Zealand Journal of Criminology*, 41(1), pp 109–37.

Daly, K. (2010), *Formal and Informal Justice Responses to Youth Sex Offending*, paper presented at the Research-Policy-Practice Symposium on Preventing Youth Sexual Violence and Abuse (Brisbane, Australia), available at: <http://www.griffith.edu.au/professional-page/professor-kathleen-daly/publications>.

Daly, K. (2011), *Conventional and Innovative Justice Responses to Sexual Violence*, ACSSA Issues no. 12 (Melbourne: Australian Centre for the Study of Sexual Assault, Australian Institute of Family Studies).

Daly, K. and Bouhours, B. (2008), 'Judicial Censure and Moral Communication to Youth Sex Offenders', *Justice Quarterly*, 25(3), pp 496–522.

Daly, K. and Bouhours, B. (2010), 'Rape and Attrition in the Legal Process: A Comparative Analysis of Five Countries', in Tonry, M. (ed.), *Crime and Justice: An Annual Review of Research*, vol. 39 (Chicago: University of Chicago Press), pp 485–565.

Daly, K., Bouhours, B., Broadhurst, R. and Loh, N. (2011), *Youth Sex Offending, Recidivism, and Restorative Justice: Comparing Court and Conference Cases*, available at: <http://www.griffith.edu.au/professional-page/professor-kathleen-daly/publications>.

Daly, K. and Curtis-Fawley, S. (2006), 'Restorative Justice for Victims of Sexual Assault', in Heimer, K. and Kruttschnitt, C. (eds.), *Gender and Crime: Patterns of Victimization and Offending* (New York: New York University Press), pp 230–65.

Daly, K. and Nancarrow, H. (2010), 'Restorative Justice and Youth Violence Toward Parents', in Ptacek, J. (ed.), *Restorative Justice and Violence Against Women* (New York: Oxford University Press), pp 150–74.

Daly, K. and Stubbs, J. (2006), 'Feminist Engagement with Restorative Justice', *Theoretical Criminology*, 10(1), pp 9–28.

Goldsmith, A., Halsey, M. and Banfield, D. (2005), *Adult Restorative Justice Pilot: An Evaluation. Final Report* (Adelaide: Flinders University Law School).

Gustafson, D. (2005), 'Exploring Treatment and Trauma Recovery Implications of Facilitating Victim-Offender Encounters in Crimes of Severe Violence: Lessons From the Canadian Experience', in Elliott, E. and Gordon, R. (eds.), *New Directions in Restorative Justice: Issues, Practices, Evaluation* (Cullompton: Willan), pp 193–227.

Jülich, S. (2010), 'Restorative Justice and Gendered Violence in New Zealand: A Glimmer of Hope', in Ptacek, J. (ed.), *Restorative Justice and Violence Against Women* (New York: Oxford University Press), pp 239–54.

Jülich, S., Buttle, J., Cummins, C. and Freeborn, E. (2010), *Project Restore: An Exploratory Study of Restorative Justice and Sexual Violence* (Auckland: Auckland University of Technology), available at: <http://aut.academia.edu/JohnButtle/Papers/221442/Project_Restore_An_Exploratory_Study_of_Restorative_Justice_and_Sexual_Violence>.

Kingi, V., Paulin, J. and Porima, L. (2008), *Review of the Delivery of Restorative Justice in Family Violence Cases by Providers Funded by the Ministry of Justice* (Wellington: New Zealand Ministry of Justice).

Koss, M. (2006), 'Restoring Rape Survivors: Justice, Advocacy, and a Call to Action', *Annals of the New York Academy of Sciences*, 1087, pp 206–34.

Koss, M. (2010), 'Restorative Justice for Acquaintance Rape and Misdemeanor Sex Crimes', in Ptacek, J. (ed.), *Feminism, Restorative Justice, and Violence Against Women* (New York: Oxford University Press), pp 218–38.

Koss, M. (2011), *Restorative Approaches to Sexual Assault*, paper presented at the Third National Restorative Justice Conference (Raleigh).

Koss, M., Bachar, K., Hopkins, C. and Carlson, C. (2004), 'Expanding a Community's Justice Response to Sex Crimes Through Advocacy, Prosecutorial, and Public Health Collaboration: Introducing the RESTORE Program', *Journal of Interpersonal Violence*, 19, pp 1435–63.

Lajeunesse, T. (1996), *Community Holistic Circle Healing in Hollow Water, Manitoba: An Evaluation* (Ottawa: Solicitor General of Canada).

Llewellyn, D. (2005), *Letter from the Tasmanian Deputy Premier to Mary Porter*, Submission Number 15 (ACT Legislative Committee Office).

Madsen, K. (2008), *From Victim to Action*, paper presented at the Associação Portuguesa de Apoio à Vítima (APAV) conference (Lisbon).

Marchetti, E. (2009), *Indigenous Sentencing Courts*, brief 5 (Sydney, Indigenous Justice Clearinghouse).

Marchetti, E. and Daly, K. (2007), 'Indigenous Sentencing Courts: Towards a Theoretical and Jurisprudential Model', *Sydney Law Review*, 29(3), pp 415–43.

Marshall, J. (2008), *Port Lincoln Aboriginal Adult Conference Pilot: Review report* (Adelaide: Office of Crime Statistics).

Maxwell, G. and Hayes, H. (2007), 'Regional Reviews, Section F, Pacific', in Johnstone, G. and Van Ness, D. (eds.), *Handbook of Restorative Justice* (Cullompton: Willan Publishing), pp 519–29.

Maxwell, G., Kingi, V., Robertson, J., Morris, A. and Cunningham, C. (2004a), *Achieving Effective Outcomes in Youth Justice: An Overview* (Wellington: Ministry of Social Development).

Maxwell, G., Kingi, V., Robertson, J., Morris A. and Cunningham, C. (2004b), *Achieving Effective Outcomes in Youth Justice: Final Report* (Wellington: Ministry of Social Development).

Maxwell, G. and Morris, A. (1993), *Families, Victims and Culture: Youth Justice in New Zealand* (Wellington: Department of Social Welfare and Institute of Criminology).

Maxwell, G. and Morris, A. (1999), *Understanding Reoffending* (Wellington: Institute of Criminology, Victoria).

Mercer, V. (2009), *Restorative Justice and Sexually Harmful Behaviour* (Manchester: AIM Project).

Miller, S. (2011), *After the Crime: The Power of Restorative Justice Dialogues Between Victims and Violent Offenders* (New York: New York University Press).

Mills, L. (2003), *From Insult to Injury* (Princeton: Princeton University Press).

Mills, L. (2008), *Violent Partners: A Breakthrough Plan for Ending the Cycle of Abuse* (New York: Basic Books).

Morris, A. (2002), 'Critiquing the Critics: A Brief Response to Critics of Restorative Justice', *British Journal of Criminology*, 42(3), pp 596–615.

Morris, A., Kingi, V., Poppelwell, E., Robertson. J. and Triggs, S. (2005), *New Zealand Court-Referred Restorative Justice Pilot Evaluation* (Wellington: Ministry of Justice).

Nancarrow, H. (2006), 'In Search of Justice for Domestic and Family Violence: Indigenous and Non-Indigenous Australian Women's Perspectives', *Theoretical Criminology*, 10(1), pp 87–106.

PALI, B. and MADSEN, K. (2011), 'Dangerous Liaisons?: A Feminist and Restorative Approach to Sexual Assault', *Temida*, 14(1), pp 49–65.

PAULIN, J., KINGI, V. and LASH, B. (2005a), *The Rotorua Second Chance Community-Managed Restorative Justice Programme: An Evaluation* (Wellington: New Zealand Ministry of Justice).

PAULIN, J., KINGI, V. and LASH, B. (2005b), *The Wanganui Community-Managed Restorative Justice Programme: An Evaluation* (Wellington: New Zealand Ministry of Justice).

PELIKAN, C. (2010), 'On the Efficacy of Victim-Offender-Mediation in Cases of Partnership Violence in Austria, or: Men Don't Get Better, But Women Get Stronger: Is it Still True?', *European Journal of Criminal Policy and Research*, 16, pp 49–67.

PENNELL, J. (2006), 'Stopping Violence or Protecting Children? Contributions From Restorative Justice', in Sullivan, D. and Tifft, L. (eds.), *Handbook of Restorative Justice* (New York: Routledge), pp 286–98.

PENNELL, J. and BURFORD, D. (2002), 'Feminist Praxis: Making Family Group Conferencing Work', in Strang, H. and Braithwaite, J. (eds.), *Restorative Justice and Family Violence* (Cambridge: Cambridge University Press), pp 108–27.

PENNELL, J. and KIM, M. (2010), 'Opening Conversations Across Culture, Gender, and Generational Divides', in Ptacek, J. (ed.), *Restorative Justice and Violence Against Women* (New York: Oxford University Press), pp 177–92.

PEOPLE, J. and TRIMBOLI, L. (2007), *An Evaluation of the NSW Community Conferencing for Youth Adults Pilot Program* (Sydney: NSW Bureau of Crime Statistics and Research).

PROIETTI-SCIFONI, G. (2008), *Restorative Justice in Cases of Gendered Violence: Views from Aotearoa Opinion Leaders*, unpublished honours thesis (Brisbane: Griffith University).

PROIETTI-SCIFONI, G. and DALY, K. (2011), 'Gendered Violence and Restorative Justice: The Views of New Zealand Opinion Leaders', *Contemporary Justice Review*, 14(3), pp 269–90.

PTACEK, J. (ed.) (2010a), *Restorative Justice and Violence Against Women* (New York: Oxford University Press).

PTACEK, J. (2010b), 'Resisting Co-optation: Three Feminist Challenges to Antiviolence Work', in Ptacek, J. (ed.), *Restorative Justice and Violence Against Women* (New York: Oxford University Press), pp 5–36.

Restorative Justice Aotearoa (2007), *Report to the Crime Prevention Unit of the New Zealand Ministry of Justice: A Stocktake of Restorative Justice Providers in New Zealand* (Hamilton: Restorative Justice Aotearoa).

RICHARDS, K. (2010), 'Police-Referred Restorative Justice for Juveniles in Australia', *Trends and Issues in Crime and Criminal Justice*, no. 398 (Canberra: Australian Institute of Criminology).

RUBIN, P. (2010), 'A Community of One's own? When Women Speak to Power About Restorative Justice', in Ptacek, J. (ed.), *Restorative Justice and Violence Against Women* (New York: Oxford University Press), pp 79–102.

SHAPLAND, J., ROBINSON, G. and SORSBY, A. (2011), *Restorative Justice in Practice: Evaluating What Works for Victims and Offenders* (London: Routledge).

SHARPE, M. (2010), 'Rangitahi Courts: A Quiet Revolution in Teen Justice' (Whitireria Journalism School), available at: <http://www.newswirenz.wordpress.com/articles/crime-reporting>.

SHERMAN, L., STRANG, H., ANGEL, C., WOODS, D., BARNES, G., BENNETT, S. and INKPEN, N. (2005), 'Effects of Face-to-Face Restorative Justice on Victims of Crime in Four Randomized, Controlled trials', *Journal of Experimental Criminology*, 1(3), pp 367–95.

Social Services Research and Information Unit (2003), *The Dove Project: The Basingstoke Domestic Violence Family Group Conference Project* (Portsmouth: University of Portsmouth).

Strang, H. and Braithwaite, J. (eds.) (2002), *Restorative Justice and Family Violence* (Cambridge: Cambridge University Press).

Stubbs, J. (2010), 'Restorative Justice, Gendered Violence, and Indigenous Women', in Ptacek, J. (ed.), *Restorative Justice and Violence Against Women* (New York: Oxford University Press), pp 103–22.

Tisdall, M., Farmer, S., Robinson, M., Wells, A. and McMaster, K. (2007), *Review of the Use of Restorative Justice in Family Violence Cases in the Rotorua District* (Wellington: New Zealand Ministry of Justice).

Umbreit, M., Vos, B., Coates, R. and Brown, K. (2003), *Facing Violence: The Path of Restorative Justice Dialogue* (Monsey: Criminal Justice Press).

Vanseveren, B. (2010), *Developments in Flanders and HERGO in Sexual Assault Cases*, paper presented at the Conferencing: A Way Forward for Restorative Justice Conference in Europe (Leuven).

Wundersitz, J. (1996), *The South Australian Juvenile Justice System* (Adelaide: Office of Crime Statistics).

9

DECENTRALIZATION AND PRIVATIZATION

THE PROMISE AND CHALLENGES OF RESTORATIVE JUSTICE IN THE UNITED STATES

Elizabeth Beck and Joan Pennell

The goals of restorative justice are to uphold the obligation of those offending to make amends while collectively addressing the needs of those harmed. Acting on these goals means bringing together the key stakeholders so that they can acknowledge the impact of the wrongdoing, resolve offences (Marshall 1996), address the underlying causes of the harms (Zehr 2002), and recreate relationships (Huntington 2008; Walgrave 2008). The assumption is that people with adequate supports and protections have the moral strength to participate in consensual deliberations, take responsibility for advancing individual and collective welfare, and create peaceful relations. The pursuit of justice as peacemaking is necessarily multi-faceted, including restoration of those victimized, rehabilitation of those offending, and renegotiation of social norms that respect diverse cultures (Villa-Vicencio 2006; Zion and Yazzie 2006).

There are major challenges to realizing the goals of restorative justice in the United States. As a strengths-based, participatory process, restorative justice runs counter to the nation's top-down criminal justice system that focuses on infractions rather than relationships. Moreover, the restorative justice values of inclusivity, collaboration, and respect for all stakeholders conflict with a predominate doctrine in the United States of rugged individualism and its ethic of self-reliance. At the same time, other aspects of the national ethos support a desire to assist those who experience hardship. For example, the United States was the first industrialized country to establish a juvenile court, viewing youth as developing individuals who are in need (Shoemaker 2009). Over the years, however, the general orientation in the United States towards offending by both youth and adults has leaned away from a social welfare model to a crime-control approach stressing public safety and deterrence (Hartjen 2008).

In this chapter, we explore the implementation of conferencing in the United States through the lens of guiding principles. We begin with a discussion of rugged individualism and consider the ways in which the values associated with this belief system in secular society have affected policy formation in the United States and specifically restorative programming. To explore how restorative justice programmes have been initiated and sustained under secular auspices, we interviewed the founders of programmes in four distinct settings. Because the origins of an organization affect its structure, functioning, and beliefs over time (Mintzberg 1979), we saw these founders as offering insights about strategies for instituting restorative programming.

Based on these interviews, we describe four models of how restorative practices have been established under government or non-profit auspices in different regions of the United States. These models are: (1) a state initiative; (2) a non-profit organization; (3) a courtroom; and (4) Native American communities. These examples were selected because they illustrate a wide range of strategies for establishing programmes that have remained steadfast to restorative justice goals. The chapter concludes with a discussion of the strategies used by the model initiators to advance the restorative justice principles of mutual respect, collaborative action, and collective caring within an individualistic society.

'RUGGED INDIVIDUALISM' AND PUBLIC POLICY IN THE UNITED STATES

Many have argued that the national character of the United States is rooted in the doctrine of rugged individualism. In his 1981 essay, Mount (1981: 363) asserts that 'nothing is more American than individualism', and in a 1988 comparative ethnographic study, Hsu (1983) supported Mount's claim and coined the term 'rugged individualism' to describe the attributes unique to the United States. Hsu (1983) identifies that self-reliance is at the core of rugged individualism. The essential features of self-reliance were promulgated by the 19th century American Transcendentalist Ralph Waldo Emerson. In his 1841 essay, Emerson urged individuals to reject conformity to authority and avoid consistency with conventions and instead to trust their own insights, act on their ingenuity, and, thus, fulfil their divine destiny.

The secular and modern doctrine of rugged individualism emphasizes competition and creativity, and these two features can hold a tautological relationship. Specifically, a creative achievement may spur competition, and creativity can be applied to competition. Although seemingly at odds with creativity and Emerson's conceptualization of self-reliance, rugged individualism also involves conformity, and Turner (2008) describes its conformity as typifying maleness and whiteness. Hsu (1983: 11) explicates that through the combination of self-centredness and belief in one's superiority, rugged individualists can distort reality as a 'psychological necessity'. Three significant ways in which rugged individualism is manifest in public policy in the United States include: (1) limited support of public welfare; (2) strong support for hegemony by policy makers; and (3) inability to change direction. Turner (2008: 8) argues that individualism has created a context in which people are able to deny 'their indebtedness to society'. Bruce Jansson (2009) uses the phrase, a 'reluctant welfare state' to describe welfare policy in the United States. He argues that this reticence explains why the United States has limited universal programmes and why existing programmes are fragile. Although Jansson sees the United States' reluctance toward supporting social welfare as morally flawed, he notes the viability of the non-profit sector and the extensive charitable giving of individuals. In many ways, Jansson points to the creative aspects of rugged individualism when he praises the entrepreneurialism and spirit of the non-profit sector.

The notion of rugged individualism is rooted in maleness and whiteness; however, the United States is becoming more multicultural with demographers predicting that by 2050, the white non-Hispanic population will shrink to just over half of the population (United States Census Bureau 2010). For many, the United States is at a precipice. Society is shifting to more support of multiculturalism and yet with each step forward, there appears to be a significant backlash (Hirschman 2003). This interplay is starkly highlighted by the rise of race-based conservatism against the backdrop of the election of the first African American President of the United States.

Although founded by a revolution, the United States has implemented its public policy through incremental change (Laswell 1936/1958). Rather than re-imagining different systems, the tendency in the United States is to keep to existing practices whether or not they yield the agreed upon results. This propensity is especially evident in the country's reticence to address health care. While health care reform had been sought for 50 years, once it was passed, the legislation tinkered with existing mechanisms rather than implementing new approaches, and the backlash has been so intense that it yielded a new political party whose aim is to shrink public welfare drastically (Jacobs and Skocpol 2010).

The implications of rugged individualism and the public policy it supports have profound meaning for the future of restorative justice. The ethos of rugged individualism is antithetical to restorative justice's belief in interconnection and cooperation. Additionally, restorative practices tap into the traditions of diverse peoples from around the globe and affirm indigenous values. Moreover restorative justice requires that fundamental flaws are acknowledged in public policies that led to and then supported mass incarceration of people of colour. Because of this national history, many restorative justice theorists in the United States see the significance of restorative justice on two levels. The first level is as an effective strategy to address harm and perhaps even decolonize prison, and the second is as a way to promote a radical shift in values to emphasize cooperation, caring, and mutuality.

FOUR CASE STUDIES OF RESTORATIVE JUSTICE IN THE UNITED STATES

Although there are vibrant pockets of restorative justice initiatives across the country, (see for example Bazemore and Schiff 2004; Coates, Umbreit, and Vos 2004; International Institute of Restorative Practices n.d.; Umbreit, Coates, and Vos 2004) the slow development of restorative justice in the United States reflects a reluctance to institutionalize human services. While the trend toward restorative justice might be slow, at the same time the success of a variety of initiatives in a variety of states and settings reflect the ingenuity and generosity in figuring out how to create needed programmes. These patterns are illustrated through case studies of the origins of four restorative programmes in quite different contexts—a state-wide implementation across Minnesota, a Midwestern state on the Canadian border; a non-profit centre in Baltimore, Maryland, on the East Coast; a courtroom in Montgomery County, Alabama, in the South East; and incorporation by Alaskan tribal communities in the far North West. The case studies are based on interviews conducted over the spring and summer of 2011 with their founders. These founders identified the impetus for their programme's creation and the challenges in sustaining the programme. We quote extensively from these interviews in order to present the founders' views, examples, and metaphors. Because they were treading new ground, they often relied on anecdotes and symbolic ways of representing their endeavours.

'AN ACCIDENTAL JOURNEY': RESTORATIVE JUSTICE ACROSS A STATE

In 1994, Kay Pranis was hired by the Minnesota Department of Corrections (MDOC) to what was initially a job without a title but with a mandate to promote and support the development of restorative justice throughout the state. Because Pranis believed that restorative justice required democracy, not hierarchy, she did not want her title to be director or coordinator, so she chose the word planner. Years later a colleague suggested her role was that of a 'planter'. Pranis described both the process that led the MDOC to restorative justice and her subsequent role as its planner as 'an accidental journey'. A series of serendipitous events brought the MDOC to restorative justice and Pranis to the MDOC and the planting that occurred in Minnesota.

In the mid-1990s, the MDOC had some unspent money from a federal grant, and with permission from the granting body, MDOC chose to use those funds to develop a strategic plan for the department. The consultant hired to lead the effort had been introduced to restorative justice through her prior work in domestic violence and victim services. As a result, the strategic planning process included a task force on restorative justice.

At this time, Pranis was working with a non-profit organization that supported public policy. In the course of her job, she came across Kay Harris' writing on a feminist version of justice and an early pamphlet by Howard Zehr from the Mennonite Central Committee, both of which made her determined to learn all she could about restorative justice. On learning of the MDOC's interest in restorative justice, Pranis called the department and offered them the resources that she had collected. The task force not only wanted to make use of Pranis' information but also asked her to join them. About a year after its establishment, the task force hosted a conference at which they educated participants from corrections, county leadership, and probation and parole on restorative justice. The conference participants, as Pranis recollected, were 'lit up' by restorative justice and indicated that they wanted to support the programme's implementation. The MDOC then provided money for a position and hired Pranis as a restorative justice planner.

Pranis' orientation to her job was shaped both by her view of restorative justice as a philosophy made up of principles and values and by the skill set of a colleague whose background was in community organizing. Pranis explained, 'I saw the issue as a community issue and not a justice issue, so my approach was to engage the community.' She depicted her approach as shining a light: 'I would put out the energy of this vision and where it got reflected back to me is where I went.' To Pranis, 'going there' meant that she and the others who worked with her would provide resources and assistance to build the capacity of communities to implement restorative justice. For example, when working with probation officers, she emphasized that she was not going to tell them how they might do their job differently. Rather she asked them, 'If you took these ideas, values, principles, how would you do your job differently?' Further clarifying her approach, Pranis stated that if a geographic community wanted a programme, she would work with its members to support it. Support included training and brainstorming ideas about resources. Although the funding streams could include federal, state, local, and community sources, Pranis observed that because of the heavy reliance on volunteers, a number of programmes were started without securing external funding.

In her early work with MDOC, she recounted that the only 'model of restorative practices [that we knew of] was victim-offender mediation. But fairly quickly we learned about conferencing and circles, and we immediately became involved in schools.' The work in schools grew rapidly as the department of education included a strong restorative justice advocate and the state received federal funding to support restorative practices under an initiative called Safe and Drug Free Schools. Reflecting on the totality of the MDOC's restorative justice effort over time, Pranis was clear that 'we were grounded in values and philosophy first, and programmes second.'

After close to ten years of practice, funding cuts resulted in the termination of Pranis' job, but she did not view that as particularly disheartening for the restorative justice movement in Minnesota. She explained that the work had grown well past her time and that the commitment to restorative justice remained strong. She attributed this resolve to the fact that the MDOC's approach 'was so grounded in values that if people [embraced] those values and made the shift, then they found other ways to take these principles in[to] their lives.' Accordingly, people who learned about restorative justice transferred its practices to new positions or to their community, and they were able to succeed in their efforts because of the MDOC's focus on building capacity. Pranis further noted that the same contracting of programmes sometimes occurred at the local level. Nevertheless, Pranis was now seeing renewed growth in some areas where initiatives began and were discontinued. Returning to the metaphor of planting in the quite cold Minnesota climate, Pranis added that when an effort was restarted, it returned stronger, which she was told was the same for the planting of winter wheat. If the wheat survived its first winter, it came back stronger.

Pranis believed that the Minnesota model held lessons for the United States' government support of restorative justice. She did not think that the government should mandate restorative justice legislation, but rather the state should put its resources into supporting processes that enabled the development of restorative work. Pranis' preference was not surprising, given her focus on building community capacity, her belief in grassroots organizing, and her view that restorative justice was fundamentally about values and principles (Pranis 2005; Pranis et al. 2003). She was 'glad that we did not have a lot of dedicated money to programmes and instead focused on process.' Pranis added that it was fortunate the MDOC's effort occurred before today's focus on evidence-based practice. Pranis clarified that an evidenced-based practice does not support outcomes such as basic shifts in individual and organizational philosophy and grassroots processes.

In thinking about the future, Pranis cautioned, 'This is not short term work.' She explained:

> We underestimated how big of a shift we were asking people to make. Restorative justice philosophy is a very, very fundamental shift in how you view the world and human beings. We were all raised with the idea that punishment is effective. Our system is based on fear and the need to hold punishment as a bit of threat over humans. And there is our country's focus on competition [as the best way to achieve a goal].

Rather, Pranis stressed that restorative justice upholds the belief 'that humans collectively are capable of amazing things. Modern scientists are saying it was collaboration, not competition that allowed the species to survive. The fundamental beliefs of our culture are being questioned by this work. I think it is a long term thing.'

'I JUST STARTED CALLING PEOPLE': A NON-PROFIT COMMUNITY CONFERENCING CENTRE

The Community Conferencing Center (CCC) (2008a) was a city-based 'conflict transformation and community justice organization that provides ways for people to safely, collectively, and effectively prevent and resolve conflicts and crime.' As a non-profit organization, the CCC offered no-cost conferencing services to the juvenile justice system, schools, courts, neighbourhoods, and other entities in Baltimore. Since its inception in 1998, CCC (2008b) reported that it had touched over 7,000 Baltimore residents. Despite its productivity, CCC, as is the case with most non-profit organizations in the United States, repeatedly struggled to maintain the resources necessary for its existence. The CCC founder, although not viewing herself as an administrator or fundraiser, remained steadfast in overcoming these financial challenges.

The founder of CCC was a neuroscientist, Dr Lauren Abramson, whose disciplinary background influenced her decision to initiate a restorative programme. In 1994, while attending a conference, Abramson was impressed by the powerful examples of restorative conferencing from Australia. She also noted that her two interests of emotions and communities were integrated in the practice of community conferencing. Specifically, she recognized that community conferencing provided individuals with the opportunity to use their emotions, including those caused by harm, to build communities and reform systems. Following her initial exposure to conferencing, Abramson was excited to 'learn about it and spread it across the land', and her determination led her to develop several Baltimore training sessions, the first of which was facilitated by the Australians who introduced her to conferencing.

In 1998, her efforts to spread conferencing gained momentum when four neighbourhoods in Baltimore obtained a state grant that allowed them to implement the approach. When the project began, Abramson thought it should have a decentralized structure. 'But what we learned that first year,' she reported, 'was that some things needed to stay decentralized like the process itself, but some things really needed to be centralized.' She explained that an organization was required to address referrals, quality control, and outreach. Abramson realized, 'We needed to start an office. I did not want to run a program. I had no interest or skills in management and fundraising, and I resisted. But I realized for the program to reach its full potential, something needed to be done [and] I was the one to do it.'

As founding director of the CCC but an introvert by nature, Abramson began to build support by reaching out to 'neighbourhood peers, the juvenile justice, and criminal justice system, pretty much any place that was dealing in conflict. It got me out of my shell; I just started calling people.' The initial funding for the CCC came from the state grant that was supporting the four-neighbourhood project, a fellowship that Abramson received from a foundation entitled the Open Society Institute, and the state judiciary. The state judiciary emerged as the CCC's most consistent source of funding, starting with an initial grant of $12,000. As Abramson stated, the support of the judiciary had grown to 20 per cent of the CCC's funding base.

Other funding sources, however, did not follow the same upward trajectory. The private foundation money became difficult to obtain because 'they get tired of you after a couple of years.' Abramson further explained while the CCC had received most of its referrals from the State Department of Juvenile Services for 13 years, the programme received only four years of funding from the department. At present, the CCC received no funding from the department, she noted, 'even though we were documenting better outcomes for one tenth the cost.' Abramson did not know why the Department of Juvenile Services cut CCC funding but said that she did not see the department as willing to shift their emphasis from detention to more cost-effective graduated sanctions.

Some of the funding challenges that non-profits in the United States have faced were uniform and could be found in both private sector sources, such as foundations, as well as in public sector support. For example, in the United States, foundations typically have funded programmes and projects only for a period of time. In other words, these private funding bodies supported non-profits as they innovated but did not see their mission as providing operating expenses over the long term (Ostrower 2004). Although it is easy to see why the funding community made these, often difficult, decisions, the process often placed non-profit organizations—especially those that served the poor and did not charge a fee for service—in a vulnerable position. At the same time the public sector had issues, too. When government funded a specific community-based programme, it tended to be in addition to its internal or core programmes or functions. Therefore, when governments—whether federal, state, or local—experienced cuts in their revenues, funding to ancillary programmes or contracted services was also cut.

In spite of her funding experience, Abramson did not believe that the United States should follow the example of other countries such as Australia, which adopted conferencing as public policy and funded it with state funds. She did not 'think legislating conferencing is the answer in this country' because she saw a danger in legislating a programme that was neither fully understood nor funded. Further she noted that 'the culture in the United States is more of cowboy culture—rugged individualism and rugged capitalism.' For large scale conferencing efforts to be successful in the United States, she observed that a shift in values and a deep understanding of ideas like empowerment would be needed. Abramson added, 'I don't think this society psychologically gets what true democratic process is all about, and that we are willing to share power and empower people to make decisions for themselves.' She further stated, 'I think in order for this work to be effective, people have to understand what it is about. If you start legislating it and then you have providers that are providing a service that they don't really understand, and the whole thing is going to get botched.' Thus, not surprisingly, the CCC had put a lot of effort into articulating and educating the community about the tenets that undergirded its work.

The CCC principles, according to Abramson, were that everyone who was involved in the conflict was included in the conference, that the process was voluntary, and that people were empowered to make decisions for themselves. By doing so, she said, the CCC provided a 'structure for people to heal and to learn, and to transform.' The CCC's mission was to find ways to create spaces for people in conflict and provided this methodology to people in Baltimore neighbourhoods as well as the larger society. Without sufficient financial support, though, those goals were hard to achieve. Abramson iterated that 'it is ridiculous, the small amount of money we are trying to get a hold of.' Instead to reshape society, she proposed that the United States 'have a department of peace funded at the same level as the department of defence.'

'IT IS MY COURTROOM': ONE JUDGE'S DETERMINATION TO EFFECT CHANGE

During her interview, Judge Tracy McCooey asserted, 'As a judge, I cannot control anything else but what happens in my courtroom because it is my courtroom.' Judge McCooey had used her judicial autonomy to implement multiple successful restorative justice programmes in the 15th circuit court of Montgomery County, Alabama (Cutting Edge Law n.d.). She did not start off intending to be a judge. Instead she chose a law degree to advance her career goal of becoming a Federal Bureau of Investigation (FBI) agent.

Following a diagnosis of multiple sclerosis, McCooey left the FBI and became an assistant district attorney. She quickly realized that the conventional criminal justice system was not working. 'Criminals were recommitting crimes, and victims were leaving the courtroom upset,' so McCooey knew that practice needed to change. An answer came from a friend who had served as a mitigation specialist on death penalty defence teams. This friend explained to McCooey the principles and values of restorative justice.

In 1998, just elected Judge McCooey was able to begin to put a restorative justice approach into action. Within her first week in her new job as judge, McCooey said to another friend, a sheriff, that her first programme would be 'one that you and I will do, and we are not going to tell anyone until we get this thing going.' She began what she called 'my trash program', in which men and women who appeared before her in court could be sentenced to Saturday morning trash pick-up for community service hours or until they got a job. Initially defence attorneys wondered if the programme would benefit their clients, and district attorneys questioned its impact on victims. Starting with the programme's first Saturday, she took roll to ensure that all those she sentenced to participation were present. Six months later, McCooey publicized her programme, since by that time she was able to demonstrate its value to the community and the people sentenced.

Then McCooey started quilting with individuals who stood before her in her drug court. By that time, sentencing on drug charges to supervized rehabilitation rather than prison had become more popular in the United States and Judge McCooey took rehabilitation into her courtroom. As she explained, 'We know nothing about these people, but we expect them to change, and when they don't, we are upset. When I quilt with them, I know them.' Her approach included a court-ordered check-in on Wednesdays to ensure that individuals were following through on orders. As she put it, 'Saturdays are for talking. It is not a big deal if I am sitting there Wednesdays [during court ordered check-ins] at noon. But when I see you on Saturday, you know I care about your getting off drugs. You have to invest in people.'

With her trash and quilting efforts well established, McCooey's next goal was to offer people in her courtroom the opportunity for a victim-offender dialogue. Acting on this goal, she wrote a grant that allowed about 40 local individuals to receive intensive training in victim-offender dialogue. When the district attorney expressed concern about applying the process to serious crimes, Judge McCooey responded that the 'great thing about being a judge is I can do whatever I want, it is my courtroom.'

When a 19-year-old mentally ill woman appeared before McCooey for having committed a robbery, McCooey postponed the case for a week to gather some information. She learned that the crime occurred when the defendant was not taking the medicine that helped to manage her schizophrenia. McCooey called the victim and after acknowledging that she was so very sorry for the victim's experience, McCooey said that she could sentence the offender to at least 20 years of prison or 'you can let me start a Mental Health Court.' McCooey added she was not a mental health expert, but she could meet with the offender once a week to ensure she was taking her medicine. Without hesitation, the victim responded, 'We need to start a Mental Health Court.' When the case reconvened, McCooey sentenced the young woman to Mental Health Court. The prosecutor pointed out that Montgomery did not have a Mental Health Court, but McCooey replied, 'Sure we do now; I just started it.' Today that court is staffed with case managers and a psychiatrist, and the young woman who committed the robbery has graduated from college with honours. McCooey emphasized to people with mental illness who came before her that 'we just have to take our medications, and we will both be okay.'

Judge McCooey had a repertoire of examples of profound transformation. Fully cognizant that she was responsible for what happened in her courtroom, she acted when she saw an unmet need. Accordingly, she sought consultation and training from national experts including Kay Pranis. To support her innovations, McCooey applied for 22 grants. This support made it possible for her to sustain her initiatives and undertake new ones such as circle sentencing, which she has reported using in 15 cases to date. Grant funding allowed her to track her efforts and to promote her work so she could provide success stories as well as facts and figures.

Over the years, McCooey spoke to many civic groups and found that 'once I am finished talking to a group, I have them on board with restorative justice as they understand it.' Being politically astute, she also shared her work with other judges and confirmed that she had 'never gotten bad press.' She credited her success to the time that she took to explain restorative justice and its being a choice rather than an order: 'The first thing I say is that the programme is voluntary and it is then hard to argue with that.' Every six years, judges in Alabama were re-elected, but McCooey never let re-election fears interfere with her desire to make positive change. 'I think being a judge means you are a public servant,' she said, 'And it is your job to contribute so that when you leave, it is a little better then when you found it...I never cared about things like elections. I believe if you are doing the right thing, then they will work out as they should.'

McCooey would like to see more judges implement restorative justice in their courtrooms. Towards that goal, she has held workshops, developed training videos, and created other resources. 'I tell judges [they] don't have to reinvent the wheel; I will help train your folks. I tell judges that I have never gotten a negative response about anything to do with restorative justice. People say, "Good for you" and "thank you". I tell them, "Don't be scared, this thing is nothing but a positive [contribution]".' She also admitted that her efforts involved a great deal of additive work, as she kept her full traditional docket, and she did not ask her courtroom staff to contribute their time. But for McCooey who loved the law and being a judge, restorative justice was a gift.

'HONOURING ITS OWN COMMUNITY TRADITIONS': CONFERENCING BY ALASKAN NATIVE TRIBES

The implementation of conferencing and other restorative practices in Alaska was a story steeped in tension. On the one hand, conferencing should be facilitated by the familiarity of many of Alaskan Native tribes with conflict resolution strategies that were consistent with restorative justice. On the other hand, the struggle between indigenous authority and state-sanctioned power generated obstacles to conferencing. Additionally, legal questions regarding authority, as well as mandates to support a culturally relevant child welfare system for Alaskan Native children, both helped and hindered the effort to apply conferencing.

The Tlingit and Haida, the largest tribes in Alaska, comprised 24,000 individuals worldwide with the greatest concentration in the Pacific Northwest, Alaska, and Canada (Central Council of the Tlingit and Jaida Indian Tribes of Alaska n.d). In her 2005 *Law Review Comment*, Laverne Hill described the many similarities among the values and beliefs held by Tlingit and Haida tribes and those used in conferencing. Particular areas of overlap cited by Hill included a broad definition of, and a strong belief in, the extended family and ascribing to the principle of shared responsibility by all groups. Hill (2005: 92) explained that Alaskan Natives and Indians 'do not insist that the offender carry the sole responsibility for making the offender whole.'

As was the case for many indigenous people worldwide, the histories of the Tlingit and Haida were replete with efforts by external governments to destroy them, followed by legislation designed to offer some level of protection. In 1978, for example, the United States Congress passed the Indian and Child Welfare Act to stop the removal of American Indian and Alaskan Native children to non-native homes, including boarding schools, which were designed to assimilate the child. The Act required state government and its agencies to make 'active efforts' to preserve the Native family, provide culturally appropriate responses in child welfare cases, and work with tribes in child welfare cases. Seemingly the Act would be bolstered by Public Law 280 passed in 1953, which gave tribes extensive criminal and civil jurisdiction over tribal lands (Hill 2005). However, Hill (2005: 105) pointed out, 'The ability of Alaska Native tribes to govern matters in their own courts has been the source of much confusion, statutory interpretation, and judicial debate.'

A significant statutory and social service issue was the disproportionality of Alaska Native children in the foster care system. According to the 2007 census estimate, although 15.2 per cent of the state's population was Alaska Native, they formed over 62 per cent of the state's out of home foster care population (Alaska Child Welfare Disproportionality Project n.d.). A restorative model might offer an appropriate response for Alaskan Native children. However, state processes to support implementation of restorative practices in child welfare and juvenile justice cases were yet to be realized.

Karen Largent, Mediation and Facilitation Services Manager for the Court System of Alaska, did not know of any group in Alaska that was providing family group conferences in child welfare cases before she received a grant in the early 2000s from the Children's Bureau, a department within the federal government. The grant supported Largent's efforts to influence the practice of child protection in Alaska by bringing the values and practice of family group conferencing (FGC) to child welfare offices across the state. For years Largent travelled the state providing training and engaging stakeholders in the practice of FGC. Using the guidance of American Humane Association's (2010) National Center on Family Group Decision Making, Largent worked to implement FGC as a value driven practice in which families had rights, including the right to maintain their kinship and cultural connections, and the family and state working together had responsibilities. The model used in Alaska's state court-connected programme was based on the New Zealand model of FGC that was legislated after protests by its indigenous people against Eurocentric practices in child welfare and youth justice (Rangihau 1986). By basing her work on this value driven model Largent was seeking implementation of FGC in a way that reflected Alaska Native values and substantively changed the outcome for children and their families.

However Largent found that this level of implementation was most clearly achieved when there was a commitment at the state and regional levels, as well as in local child welfare offices, to embrace FGC. Moreover she noted that a strong level of commitment to the FGC process as well as commitment to the shift in practice FGC required also needed to be realized by child welfare employees that included staff from the top echelons to middle management to line staff. Alaska had yet to firmly make this commitment, but Largent was hopeful as the state made other steps toward collaborative practice and interest in the family driven model of FGC had never been stronger. Although Largent believed that FGC was best practiced when there was a state-wide commitment, she acknowledged the strength of the community commitment in Juneau, Alaska's capital city, where the child protection agency—and community—was 'doing a great job of integrating FGC.'

A second example of conferencing in Alaska was found in the Organized Village of Kake. Although jurisdiction issues still occurred in Kake it was a federally recognized government of the Kake tribe (Harvard Kennedy School 2005). A status that helped to support the circle sentencing that was occurring in Kake. The efforts of Kake in this area were largely due to the work of Mike Jackson and the Healing Heart Council.

Jackson, who in addition to being a magistrate was president of the tribal governance structure the Keex Kwaan IRA l Council, learned about circle sentencing in 1998 at a magistrates' conference on restorative justice. The restorative justice principles resonated with Kake, and he recognized that the approach could have the potential to help with Kake's large problems with alcoholism and suicide (Harvard Kennedy School 2005; 'Healing our community' 2010; Rieger 2001). Kake had implemented a community group to address suicide called the Healing Heart Council. The community brought in restorative justice leaders to train villagers in peacemaking circles, to respond to issues faced by the community as a whole and by its individual members.

The effort continued to expand so that when a youth or adult entered a guilty plea with the state court and when the prosecutor, defence attorney, and offender agreed, the case was handed over to the Healing Heart Council to coordinate a circle. In 2005, 80 circles had been held with youth in Kake, and out of them, only two youths did not agree to the terms ('Healing our community' 2010). In addition, 68 adults who participated in circle sentencing did not repeat their offence (Harvard Kennedy School 2005).

The success of Kake was greater than what was measured by individual participants' successes (Harvard Kennedy School 2005; Rieger 2001). Additional achievements included a visit from the Chief Justice of Alaska to learn from Kake, and efforts by Kake representatives to assist two other areas to bring circle sentencing to their courts. The circle process with its reliance on villagers was re-energizing and strengthening the traditional roots of Kake, and Rieger, the Vice President and General Counsel of the Cook Inlet Tribal Council noted during a phone interview, 'What is fascinating about [the] Kake model is that it is not a blue print, but rather a process that can be changed to traditional community needs.' Finally Kake was able to strengthen tribal sovereignty, and 'has done so in a way that commands the respect of the state judicial system while honouring its own community traditions' (Harvard Kennedy School 2005: 5).

RESTORATIVE PRACTICES IN AN INDIVIDUALISTIC SOCIETY

The interviewees for the four case studies each initiated restorative programmes and came from various disciplines and settings. In adopting restorative approaches, these founders translated the meaning of restorative justice into their own language rather than adhering to the hegemonic discourse. Programme planner Kay Pranis saw restorative justice as planting the capacity of community members to grow solutions together. For neuroscientist Lauren Abramson, restorative justice made sense because it offered a strategy for combining her profound interest in emotion and community. Restorative justice appealed to Judge Tracy McCooey because of her repeated observation of the ineffectiveness of standard justice remedies. And dispute resolution coordinator Karen Largent, attorney Lisa Rieger, and magistrate Mike Jackson promoted restorative practices as a means of re-invigorating community traditions and strengthening the sovereignty of Alaskan Native tribes.

All these founding mothers and founding father were rugged individuals in their non-conformity to conventional justice approaches, their flexibility in responding to emerging concerns, their ingenuity in designing programmes, and their perseverance in overcoming the quite considerable funding, administrative, and legal obstacles. They were decidedly self-reliant and enterprising but not competitive. They did not start with the intention of becoming restorative justice proponents, planners, and least of all managers and fundraisers. Their ventures into restorative programming included considerable risk-taking on their part as well as engaging others through joint planning, grant funding, training, volunteerism, and sharing results.

Although having the state take over the restorative programmes might have assured greater stability, all the interviewees agreed that restorative programmes, whether they were under government or non-profit auspices, needed to stay linked to the community. These organizers worried about hierarchical state programming which they saw as potentially suborning the collective values and participatory principles of restorative justice. In these examples and many others across the United States the values and principles associated with restorative justice largely remain strong and integrated into the practices. However, all of the interviewees expressed concern that restorative processes, as a principled and values based practice, holds some vulnerabilities to the notions of efficiency and cost savings that often trump practice when butting up against the values of rugged individualism. Their views, in part, reflected the general reluctance in the United States toward a social welfare state. Their dedication to restorative justice, however, reflected even more a stance of caring and collaboration.

REFERENCES

Alaska Child Welfare Disproportionality Reduction Project (N.D.), available at: <http://wpicenter.org/docs/AlaskaProjectPlan.pdf>.

American Humane Association and the FGDM Guidelines Committee (2010), *Guidelines for Family Group Decision Making in Child Welfare* (Englewood, Colorado: American Humane

Association), available at: <http://www.americanhumane.org/assets/pdfs/children/fgdm/guidelines.pdf>.

BAZEMORE, G. and SCHIFF, M. (2004), *Juvenile Justice Reform and Restorative Justice: Building Theory and Policy from Practice* (Cullompton: Willan Publishing).

Central Council of the Tlingit and Haida Indian Tribes of Alaska (N.D.), *Welcome of the Central Council of the Tlingit and Haida Indian Tribes of Alaska*, available at: <http://www.ccthita.org/>.

COATES, R., UMBREIT, M. and VOS, B. (2004), 'Systemic Change Toward Restorative Justice in Washington County, Minnesota', *Federal Probation Journal*, 68(3), pp 16–23.

Community Conferencing Center [CCC] (2008A), *Overview of CCC*, available at: <http://www.communityconferencing.org/index.php/impact/>.

Community Conferencing Center [CCC] (2008B), *Impact*, available at: <http://www.communityconferencing.org/index.php/impact/>.

CUTTING EDGE Law (N.D.), *Judge Tracy McCooey: Maverick in Problem-Solving Courts and Restorative Justice*, available at: <http://www.cuttingedgelaw.com/video/judge-tracy-mccooey-maverick-problem-solving-courts-and-restorative-justice>.

EMERSON, R. (1841/2010), *Self-Reliance and other Essays* (New York: Classic Book International).

HARTJEN, C. (2008), *Youth, Crime, and Justice: A Global Inquiry* (New Brunswick: Rutgers University Press).

HARVARD KENNEDY SCHOOL (2005), *Kake Circle Peacemaking*, available at: <http://www.innovations.harvard.edu/awards.html?id=6164>.

HARVARD KENNEDY SCHOOL (2010), 'Healing our community. The Kake peacemaking circle', in *Healthy Alaskans 2010. Creating healthy communities. An Alaskan talking circle*, vol. II, pp 5–12, available at: <http://www.hss.state.ak.us/dph/targets/ha2010/PDFs/Volume%202/01_Kake.pdf>.

HILL L. (2005), 'Family Group Conferencing: An Alternative Approach to the Placement of Alaska Native Children under the Indian Child Welfare Act: Comment', *Alaska Law Review*, 22(1), pp 89–112.

HIRSCHMAN, E. (2003), 'Men, Dogs, Guns and Cars: The Semiotics of Rugged Individualism', *Journal of Advertising*, 32, pp 9–22.

HSU, F. (1983), *Rugged Individual Reconsidered: Essays in Psychological Anthropology* (Knoxville: University of Tennessee Press).

HUNTINGTON, C. (2008), 'Repairing Family Law', *Duke Law Journal*, 57(5), pp 1245–319.

JACOBS, L. and SKOCPOL, T. (2010), *Health Care Reform and American Politics: What Everyone Needs to Know* (New York: Oxford University Press).

JANSSON, B. (2009), *The Reluctant Welfare State* (6th edn) (California: Cengage Learning).

LASWELL, H. (1936/1958), *Politics: Who Gets What, When and How* (New York: Meridian Books).

MARSHALL, T. (1996), 'The Evolution of Restorative Justice in Britain', *European Journal on Criminal Policy and Research*, 4(4), pp 21–43.

MINTZBERG, H. (1979), *The Structuring of Organizations: A Synthesis of the Research* (Englewood Cliffs: Prentice-Hall).

MOUNT, E. (1981), 'American Individualism Reconsidered', *Review of Religious Research*, 22, pp 362–76.

OSTROWER, F. (2004), *Foundation Effectiveness: Definitions and Challenges* (Washington: Urban Institute).

PRANIS, K. (2005), *The Little Book of Circle Processes: A New/Old Approach to Peacemaking* (Intercourse: Good Books).

PRANIS, K., STUART, B. and WEDGE, M. (2003), *Peacemaking Circles: From Crime to Community* (St. Paul: Living Justice Press).

RANGIHAU, J. (1986), *Pau-te-Ata-tu (Daybreak): Report of the Ministerial Advisory Committee on a Maori Perspective for the Department of Social Welfare* (Wellington: Department of Social Welfare, Government Printing Office).

RIEGER, L. (2001), 'Circle Peacemaking,' *Alaska Justice*, 17, pp 6–7 (Anchorage: University of Anchorage).

SHOEMAKER, D. (2009), *Juvenile Delinquency* (Lanham: Rowman & Littlefield Publishers).

TURNER, J. (2008), 'American Individualism and Structural Injustice: Tocqueville, Gender, and Race', *Polity*, 40(2), pp 197–215.

UMBREIT, M., COATES, R. and VOS, B. (2004), 'The Impact of Victim Offender Mediation: Three Decades of Practice and Research', *Conflict Resolution Journal*, 22(1–2), pp 279–303.

United States Census Bureau (2010), *Population Profile of the United States*, available at: <http://www.census.gov/population/www/pop-profile/natproj.html>.

VILLA-VICENCIO, C. (2006), 'Transitional Justice, Restoration, and Prosecution', in Sullivan, D. and Tifft, L. (eds.), *Handbook of Restorative Justice: A Global Perspective* (New York: Routledge), pp 387–400.

WALGRAVE, L. (2008), *Restorative Justice, Self-Interest and Responsible Citizenship* (Portland: Willan Publishing).

ZEHR, H. (2002), *The Little Book of Restorative Justice* (Intercourse: Good Books).

ZION, J. and YAZZIE, R. (2006), 'Navajo Peacemaking: Original Dispute Resolution and a Life Way', in Sullivan, D. and Tifft, L. (eds.), *Handbook of Restorative Justice. A Global Perspective* (New York: Routledge), pp 23–51.

10

CONFERENCING IN SOUTH AMERICA AS AN EXERCISE OF DEMOCRACY?

AN EXPLORATION OF THE 'VERTICAL' ROLE OF RESTORATIVE JUSTICE

Daniela Bolivar, Leoberto Narciso Brancher, Ivan Navarro Papic, and Manyori Vega Gutiérrez[1]

INTRODUCTION

Describing restorative justice in Latin America (LA) is a difficult task, mainly because restorative justice is still a rather recent concept within the field of criminal justice and criminology in LA. In practice, this has been translated into some new, diverse, and frequently isolated restorative justice practices within its territory.

This chapter aims to develop a theoretical exercise focusing on the potential function of conferencing in the promotion of democracy by analysing three concrete practices implemented in Chile, Peru, and Brazil. As a theoretical exercise, this chapter certainly runs the risk of over-generalization. However, we hope that our reflections may help strengthen the debate concerning the social role of restorative justice.

We will first describe some antecedents that could explain the emergence of restorative justice practices in LA. Afterwards, a brief description and comparison between the three practices is offered. In the last part, such descriptions will be linked to the theory of restorative justice and democracy, in order to, in the end, offer some conclusions and reflections on the matter at hand.

[1] We thank Andrea Diaz, Raffaella Pallamolla, and Daniel Achutti for their comments on an earlier version of this manuscript.

THE ORIGINS OF RESTORATIVE JUSTICE IN LATIN AMERICA

We see the emergence of restorative justice in LA as the result of the combination of three factors: (a) an increasing concern for human rights and victim's visibility; (b) social inequality and violence in the region; and (c) the deformalization of most Latin American criminal procedures.

HUMAN RIGHTS AND VICTIMS' VISIBILITY

Human rights became not just relevant but truly central to the Latin American agenda when several countries started their transition to democracy by involving processes of participation in decision-making (Ghiringhelli 2005) and recognizing the rights of victims of mass atrocities (Uprimmy and Saffon 2008). In this context, both ensuring the protection of victims' rights and avoiding impunity, were seen as the two main tasks of the criminal justice systems of countries in transition. In this process, diverse mechanisms were implemented, one of them were truth and reconciliation commissions, usually associated with the restorative justice model (Cortés 2007). In recent years, human rights have been indicated as one of the main fundaments of the implementation of RJ practices in LA (see eg Carta do Recife 2006; Declaración de Costa Rica 2005; Declaración de Lima 2009; Melo et al. 2008).

SOCIAL INEQUALITY AND VIOLENCE

Latin American countries are diverse, but share increasing rates of criminal activity (especially homicides; see for example Briceño-León et al. 2008; Shaw et al. 2003), the extraordinary social and economical inequality of the region (CEPAL 2009), as well as the distrust of the population towards the institutions in charge of solving social and economical problems, especially the criminal justice system (Malaguera and Garrido 2009; Prillaman 2003; Snodgrass 2004).

When combined, poverty, violence, and distrust create a difficult mixture. Some have argued that the need for restorative justice in LA has been related to the necessity of decongesting courts and prisons (Parker 2005) as well as ensuring access to justice for marginalized peoples (Pallamolla 2010; Parker 2005). Restorative justice would also help to avoid situations wherein individuals take justice into their own hands, especially when the criminal justice system is seen as an institution that perpetuates social inequalities (Oxhorn and Slakmon 2005). Restorative justice, therefore, would respond to the need for a more equal, transparent, democratic, and participative justice (Melo et al. 2008).

DEFORMALIZATION OF CRIMINAL PROCEDURES

During the last 20 years, criminal procedures in LA have gone through deep processes of transformation, in which adversarial systems have replaced inquisitorial ones

(Langer 2007), assuming an approach closer to those in continental European countries (Duce 2009). This transformation has allowed a more flexible practice and the introduction of restorative justice principles in criminal procedures for both adults and juveniles (Díaz 2010; Malaguera and Garrido 2009; Maxera 2005; Parker 2005).

RESTORATIVE JUSTICE ON THE LATIN AMERICA AGENDA

The appearance of restorative justice on the LA agenda is very recent. Final elements that boosted the implementation of restorative justice practices in different countries[2] were the United Nations' recommendation concerning the integration of restorative justice in its member states (2002) and the ideal of an 'efficient justice system' promoted by international agencies (Scuro 2005). Consequently, different conferences on restorative justice were organized on the continent in order to encourage the integration of restorative justice, highlighting the importance of justice, peace, and respect for human rights as guiding values (see eg Carta de Araçatuba 2005; Declaración de Costa Rica sobre la Justicia Restaurativa en Latinoamérica 2005; Carta do Recife 2006; Declaración de Lima sobre Justicia Juvenil Restaurativa 2009).

RESTORATIVE JUSTICE IN CHILE, PERU, AND BRAZIL

In the following paragraphs, practices from Chile, Peru, and Brazil will be briefly described. Their description is oriented toward highlighting the institutional context in which they arose, their goals, and the type of intervention they develop.

CHILE: *EL CENTRO DE MEDIACIÓN DE SANTIAGO* (SANTIAGO MEDIATION CENTRE)

The *Centro de Mediación de Santiago* (CMS) was created in 1996 and emerged as the strategic plan of modernization for the *Corporación de Asistencia Judicial de la Región Metropolitana.*[3] The CMS offers mediation in different types of cases[4] though it was in 2007 when, at the initiative of their own mediation service, criminal cases started to be included.

Mediation in criminal offences for adult *imputados*[5] became possible when a reform of the Chilean criminal procedure code (2000–2005) took place. Through such

[2] As far as we know, restorative justice practices have been implemented in Argentina, Brazil, Colombia, Chile, Costa Rica, Nicaragua, Mexico, and Peru.

[3] CAJ (<www.cajmetro.cl>): a public organization whose mission is to provide legal representation to individuals in situations of poverty.

[4] These include civil and commercial matters as well as family and community conflicts.

[5] '*Imputados*': those who are being investigated—but not prosecuted yet—for the commission of a crime. For the staff of this programme, the word 'offender' (in Spanish: *ofensor*) implies a label neither appropriate for, nor coherent with the philosophy of mediation.

reform, and without mentioning the word 'mediation', the new code introduced the possibility of resolving the conflict through a procedure external to the criminal system (see eg Díaz 2010).

The CMS, whose team is composed of five mediators, aims for the development of a model focused on both victim and *imputado*, with special emphasis on the victim, and the generation of conditions for a direct (face-to-face) encounter between parties. So far, the programme works mainly with referrals from the prosecutor's office. Involvement of other actors of the criminal procedure is still in progress.

Within this programme, mediation takes place mainly at the beginning of judicial procedures, specifically during the period of investigation.[6] The target population comprises adult[7] *imputados* and victims of all ages who are referred by the prosecutor.

In terms of the intervention[8], once the case is referred, the mediator contacts both parties who are invited to attend an individual meeting. In this pre-mediation phase, the mediator explains both the context in which the referral is produced and the principles of mediation. The possibility of a personal encounter with the other party is explored. The option of inviting other participants to the encounter is considered when a party proposes it spontaneously. In these pre-mediation sessions, interests, opinions, and needs are all explored.

During the mediation phase, the parties participate in one or more face-to-face encounters in order to repair the damage that has been done. The session starts with an introductory explanation by the mediator who refers to the context in which the session occurs. Afterwards, the parties (first the victim and then the *imputado*) express their opinions, visions, and concerns. If an agreement is achieved, it is signed by both parties as well as the mediator.

Immediately after a mediation session takes place, the agreement is sent to the prosecutor who can interrupt the criminal procedure. At the same time, a survey to evaluate the overall sense of satisfaction is completed by the participants. Follow-up of the agreement is informal and usually relies on the interested parties to re-contact the mediator if the agreement is not accomplished or its implementation faces difficulties.[9]

PERU: *PROYECTO DE JUSTICIA JUVENIL RESTAURATIVA* (RESTORATIVE JUVENILE JUSTICE PROJECT)

In 2002, the Foundation Terres des Hommes Lausanne (Tdh)[10] carried out a study in order to diagnose the situation of juvenile justice in Peru. Results indicated several

[6] Mediation could also take place at other points within the criminal procedure. However, this possibility does not constitute a practice yet.

[7] Mediation with juvenile offenders is possible administratively (since 2005: Law 20.084) but such a practice has not been implemented yet.

[8] Until 2010, 427 direct encounters were carried out, from which 68 per cent achieved an agreement and 31 per cent did not. From the total of agreements, 31.5 per cent were cases involving physical injury, 31.5 per cent threats, 14 per cent negligence, 11.5 per cent economic crimes, 3 per cent property damage, and 2 per cent thefts, among others (6.5 per cent) (data provided by the programme).

[9] The programme is still lacking stronger institutional coordination within and outside the criminal justice process. Despite these limitations, the level of agreements fulfilled is considered positive by its staff.

[10] <www.tdh.ch>

relevant problems, such as arbitrary detentions, irregular due processes, excessive use of imprisonment, and lack of involvement of the victim, among others (Alvarez 2002). This diagnosis motivated and recommended a progressive application of restorative justice principles in juvenile justice.

In 2005, Tdh and the Peruvian NGO *Encuentros* implemented a pilot project in two regions of Peru: El Agustino (Lima) and José Leonardo Ortiz (Chiclayo). The legal context facilitated the process: even though the Peruvian normative framework does not refer to the concepts of mediation and restorative justice, the law allows for the use of diversion (*remisión*)[11] in which the prosecutor or the judge, respectively, have the option to avoid (prosecutor) or interrupt (judge) the judicial process by referring it to a socially-educative programme.

The objective of the *Proyecto de Justicia Juvenil Restaurativa* (PJJR) is to offer an efficient and timely defence to juveniles (that is, as soon as the adolescent is detained by the police), promoting the de-judicialization and diversification of non-custodial measures as well as developing mechanisms for the reparation of the victim.

The intervention[12] of the PJJR, implemented by an interdisciplinary team (two lawyers, two psychologists, two social workers, and a mediator in each district), concretely offers different types of services oriented to the juvenile that may last the whole judicial process. One of them is mediation. In practice, this service offers both orientation and information to the juvenile offender as well as legal defence to juveniles during the judicial process. Professionals also evaluate whether the adolescent has fulfilled certain requirements for participation in a non-custodial sanction programme. In addition, the programme offers the victim information concerning the case.

When considered suitable, the case is referred to the mediator, who—as said—also belongs to the PJJR team. The mediator contacts the parties and explores the possibility of a face-to-face encounter (indirect mediation can also be offered). The option of mediation is therefore always offered as a suggestion by the PJJR team.

The type of mediation developed by the PJJR is often referred to as a form of 'broad mediation' (*mediación amplia*). This means that both victim and offender may attend the meeting in the company of supporters. These supporters act as allies to the party they accompany, participating actively in the search for solutions to the conflict.

BRAZIL: '*JUSTIÇA PARA O SÉCULO 21*' (JUSTICE FOR THE XXI CENTURY)

The programme, *Justiça para o Século 21*, which aims to establish a restorative justice practice for the pacification of conflicts and violence that affect children and juveniles, is the result of the consolidation of a pilot project that started in 2005 in Porto Alegre,

[11] *Remisión*: in the case of young offenders, the judge or prosecutor can replace the criminal justice procedure with a socio-educative measure (art. 206, *Código del niño y del adolescente*).

[12] Until 2010, 609 adolescents and 140 victims have taken part in the whole programme, while 43 mediations (face-to-face encounters) have taken place. Although these numbers are not high, they represent an important achievement for its practitioners, since this is a unique project in the country.

capital of Rio Grande do Sul, in the south of Brazil. The project, in its initial stage, was financed by the United Nations Development Programme and the Brazilian government through the *Secretaria da Reforma do Judiciário* (Secretary of Judicial Reform) of the Ministry of Justice. From the very beginning, the team was composed of staff members of both judicial and extra-judicial institutions involved in the intervention of juvenile offenders.[13]

With regard to the judicial context of the programme, Brazilian legislation allows for a broad application of restorative justice. The children and juvenile laws were initiated in 1990 and were completely inspired by the United Nations' Convention of the Rights of the Child (1989). Based on the principle of diversion promoted at an international level, Brazilian legislation accepts the principle of *remissão*[14] in juvenile cases, which allows for different mechanisms that give flexibility to the juvenile justice system.

With regard to their intervention, the programme, *Justiça para o Século 21*, applies restorative justice within and outside the criminal justice system. Within the judicial sphere, the programme has implemented 'Restorative Circles'[15] for juvenile offenders.[16] In this type of practice, the prosecutor, the defence, the court, or the professional in charge of the case can take the initiative of the procedure. The procedure itself is carried out by the staff of the Juvenile Court, referred to as 'coordinators of the restorative procedure'. The coordinator meets every party with his/her own community of care. Members of institutions related to the treatment of the juvenile can also be included. In the final encounter, the victim may or may not participate.

When the circle takes place, all the participants meet face-to-face to talk about the harm done and to discuss the various ways to repair it, in essence originating a restorative plan. When the circle occurs before the sentence, if approved by the judge, the plan can substitute the sentence and be implemented as a socio-educational sanction.[17] When the circle takes place after the sentence, the objective is to promote participation and involvement among the juvenile's primary social networks (family, friends, and local community) within the socio-educative plan already elaborated by the professionals of the Juvenile Court.

Restorative conferences (*círculos*) have also been implemented within the extra-judicial sphere in order to contribute, under judicial supervision, to the re-educational process of the youth. Because these practices remain outside of the judicial process

[13] The objective of such a 'hybrid' team was to serve as a 'laboratory of experiences' and a permanent source of training for all its members, promoting the integration of restorative justice at different levels, institutions, and spaces within the community.

[14] Brazilian '*remissão*' differs from the Peruvian '*remisión*'. Here, 'remissão' refers to the judicial discretion of judges or prosecutors to interrupt the criminal procedure.

[15] Here, the name 'circles' is a translation from the Portuguese 'círculos'. These 'circles' refer to conferencing and not to 'Sentencing Circles' because they do not include the participation of judges or prosecutors in their meetings.

[16] In the period 2005–2007, 380 conferences took place.

[17] The socio-educative sanctions can be either custodial (restriction of freedom, such as detention or semi-detention) or non-custodial (warning, reparation of the harm, community services, and assisted freedom).

and, therefore, have an administrative character[18], the direct victim does not participate in these encounters. In his/her place, indirect victims (or members of the victim's community) may attend. In other words, the victim is invited only to those circles that count on the judge's authorization.

Three main types of intervention have been developed within the extra-judicial context.[19] A first type is *Círculo Restaurativo Familiar* (Restorative Family Circle). This practice focuses on transforming the guilty-approach implicit in the sentence into a logic of responsibilization. The final objective is to find ways to repair the damage and facilitate the offender's process of social reintegration.

A second type is the *Círculo de Compromisso* (Commitment Circle) which takes place when the juvenile finishes his/her custodial sentence. It serves as a 'rite of passage' to freedom. The meeting takes as its starting point the originating offence, but the discussion is focused on jail time experiences and future commitments for the period of freedom about to begin. Here, relatives and other members of the community, as well as organizations that will be related to the juvenile in the near future (for example, a school or the future juvenile's employer), may participate.

Finally, since 2010, a new practice has been developed. Four *Centros de Justiça Juvenil Restaurativa na Comunidade* (Community Juvenile Centres of Restorative Justice) have been created and installed in areas of major violence in Porto Alegre. This is an innovative project oriented towards a new field of application for restorative justice. It is proposed and managed by the prosecutor's office of the region Rio Grande do Sul (*Procuradoria General de Justiça do Estado*), financed by the federal government and implemented by two NGOs associated with the programme. These centres work with juveniles who have committed minor offences[20] and function as an alternative to the judicial system. This practice responds to a pilot agreement reached among the authorities involved, allowing that a case registered in one of these centres replaces a referral to the judicial system. This way, through an innovative procedure, the case will be managed by a restorative intervention even before reaching the judicial sphere. If an agreement is not possible or the restoration plan is not accomplished, authorities will be informed in order to evaluate the need for further action.

THREE PRACTICES, THREE APPROACHES

So far, we have described in general terms three RJ practices implemented in South America. In the following paragraphs we will discuss such practices and compare them, keeping in mind those elements that could be useful to further develop our central topic, that is, conferencing as a tool to promote democracy. To facilitate the comparison, we have summarized the main characteristics of the three programmes in Table 10.1.

[18] In Brazil there is a clear separation between the justice system sphere (called jurisdictional sphere) and the governmental one (called administrative sphere). In reality, the administrative sphere takes over the re-education task of the youth after the judicial process.

[19] Within the extra-judicial sphere, in the period 2005–2007, 722 people have participated in these restorative practices.

[20] This project is part of a set of actions supported by the federal government and mainly has a preventive character. Major offences are still to be dealt with by the juvenile criminal justice system.

Table 10.1 General comparison of the three countries/programmes

	Chile	Peru	Brazil
Title programme	'*Centro de Mediación de Santiago*' (Santiago Mediation Centre)	'*Proyecto de Justicia Juvenil Restaurativa*' (Restorative Juvenile Justice Project)	'*Justiça para o Século 21*' (Justice for the XXI Century)
Origin of the programme	Reform of the criminal procedure	Negative evaluation of the Peruvian juvenile criminal procedure by an international NGO	Based on pre-existent experiences of socio-educative measures in juvenile criminal procedures Stimulated and financed as a pilot project by United Nations through UNDP and the Brazilian Ministry of Justice
Target population	Adult offenders Victims all ages	Juvenile offenders Victims all ages	Juvenile offenders Victims all ages
Type of crime	Minor crimes (so far)	Minor and moderate crimes	All type of crime
Legal context	Restorative justice not explicitly mentioned, but allowed by concrete mechanisms described by the law		

Organization	Governmental organization	Terres des Hommes Lausanne Peruvian NGO 'Encuentros'	Justice system and NGOs lead by the Magistrates' School
Relationship CJS	Diversion mediation takes place at the beginning of the procedure (so far)	Diversion	Diversion[21]
Focused on a specific territory	No	Yes El Agustino (Lima) José Leonardo Ortiz, Chiclayo (north Peruvian coast)	Mixed (Community Juveniles Centres of Restorative Justice work in a number of areas in Porto Alegre)
Type of intervention	Victim-Offender Mediation Participation of supporters is not encouraged but accepted when asked for by the parties	'Broad mediation' in the context of a more general intervention oriented to the juvenile offender. Participation of family members is encouraged	Conferencing ('circles') in both judicial and extrajudicial contexts. Participation of members of the community is encouraged

[21] Primary networks involve individuals that have an emotional link to the victim or the juvenile. Secondary networks involve educative or social organizations and community, sport and religious leaders; in sum, everybody who can contribute to the juvenile's educative programme.

The programmes described above are similar in some aspects but differ in others. A first element to take into account is their origin. While the Chilean mediation programme had a more exclusive origin in procedural reform, Peru and Brazil locate their origins in the need to improve the conditions under which juvenile offenders were handled by the juvenile justice system. From that point of view, the Peruvian and Brazilian restorative justice programmes were conceived from the beginning, and therefore implemented, as programmes focused on juvenile offenders (offender-oriented approach).

Their institutional origins reveal something else: not coincidentally, the three programmes involve a 'social justice element' in their intervention by promoting among socially disadvantaged people the exercise of their rights. While the Peruvian and Brazilian programmes attempt to protect the rights of (usually deprived) juvenile offenders, the Chilean mediation service is inserted in an institutional context whose mission is to ensure access to justice to individuals in situation of poverty.

Another relevant element to consider is that the intervention from Brazil and Peru has a territorial component which suggests a community-based character. In fact, the territories in which these two programmes have been implemented (both regions in the case of Peru and the Community Juvenile Centres of Restorative Justice in the case of Brazil) were chosen precisely because of the high rates of poverty and violence. A territorial intervention, as opposed to a non-territorial one, may allow for a better coordination of efforts and the creation of networks between institutions, NGOs, schools, police, judges, and so on. It may in fact facilitate the creation of conditions for a more community-based restorative intervention by having more direct access to the community in which the offender and the victim are inserted.

In terms of the type of intervention, the three programmes seem to constitute a 'continuum'. In one extreme, the Chilean programme performs mediation in its strict sense: *imputado* and victim speak face-to-face in order to find ways to repair the damage caused by the crime. Its approach promotes the importance of a personal meeting, restoration of the harm, and the reintegration of the offender into the community. Meetings are attended by the individual parties, but other supporters within the community of care (McCold 2004) are rarely included. These characteristics belong to what has been described as victim-offender mediation (Roberts 2004; Umbreit 2001).

In the middle, we could locate Peru. They describe their practice as 'broad mediations', indicating that victims' and offenders' supporters can also take part in the mediation process. This 'broad mediation' is part of a more general intervention oriented to the juvenile.

Finally, in the other extreme, we could situate Brazil. In this country, restorative conferencing ('circles') have been developed as a main strategy of intervention in which the meeting itself is not just oriented toward detecting the harm done to the victim but also to any other need originated by the offence. The richness of the final plan or agreement will increase in proportion to the number of participants. According to the staff, the 'circles'—in their different modalities—have been highly inspired by Marshall Rosenberg's model of non-violent communication. Furthermore the circles are designed according to the values and principles of the New Zealand model of conferencing which intends 'to empower and value participants, while building upon the resources of the extended family and community' (MacRae and Zehr 2004: 11). Indeed, the programme *Justiça para o Século 21* considers the community, in addition to the victim and the offender, as a relevant stakeholder within their intervention. In this case, community is understood in a broad sense. In their 'circles', participants belong to the primary and secondary social[22] networks of both victim and juvenile.

RESTORATIVE JUSTICE AND DEMOCRACY

The relationship between restorative justice and democracy, and restorative justice and, in particular, deliberative democracy, has been mentioned, among others, by Braithwaite (2000); Dzur and Olson (2004); and Kurki and Pranis (2000). Parkinson and Roche (2004) argue that restorative justice may be considered as an example of small-scale exercises of deliberative democracy since it fulfils the requirements of inclusiveness, equality, transformative power, decisiveness, and accountability. It is inclusive because restorative justice aims to include in the decision-making process all the parties affected by a crime. Equality is involved in terms of power: 'if people are unable to speak or to be heard, the process becomes simply an exercise in oppression, while viewpoints critical to a rational outcome will be missed' (Parkinson and Roche 2004: 512). Transformative power can be seen as the fact that the outcome is expected to be the result of an agreement rather than that of an imposition. In addition, restorative justice would allow a broader scope of decisiveness since victims may participate and have a role in someone else's case (the offender). Finally, accountability refers to the mutual accountability of restorative justice participants in terms of transparency within the decision-making process. Based on Parkinson and Roche's arguments, we will develop our discussion of conferencing and democracy by focusing on three main topics: restorative justice and inclusiveness, the horizontal-vertical role of restorative justice, and the territorial issue.

RESTORATIVE JUSTICE AND INCLUSIVENESS: REACHING VICTIMS AND COMMUNITY

One of the differences usually mentioned between mediation and conferencing is the number of participants: while in the former, victim and offender are the main participants, the latter also relies on the participation of members of the community. Possibly, several people would agree that, from a numeric point of view, conferencing seems to fulfil the democratic element of inclusiveness better than mediation, especially when 'community' is understood in a broad sense. However, we argue, inclusiveness is not just about how many people are included in the practice but also whether the

[22] Sometimes, it can also take place in parallel to the procedure.

community as a whole is actively considered as a beneficiary of restorative justice practices.

We see inclusiveness as a concept composed by two dimensions. A first dimension is availability. From this perspective, we are aware of the limited availability of the programmes described here. Firstly, none of the three countries offer restorative justice for both adults and juvenile offenders. To develop democratic restorative justice practices, all types of victimization should be recognized and heard (Pranis 2001); the invisibility of (certain types of) victims maintains the status quo (Aguinsky et al. 2008a). Secondly, the offer of mediation or conferencing takes place within an institutional context in which professionals or law practitioners are evaluating the suitability of mediation or conferencing. We wonder, therefore, to what extent such procedures are limiting access to restorative justice, especially for those cases that remain outside the criminal justice system.

A second dimension of inclusiveness is *true* involvement of all stakeholders. In this regard, there are two issues that seem to be relevant. The first one refers to the degree in which inclusiveness can be fully promoted for all parties, including the victim, when restorative justice programmes are offender-oriented—as the Brazilian and Peruvian programmes are. Indeed, some scholars have already argued that conferencing runs the risk of becoming an offender-oriented practice since it may take place without the participation of the victim (see eg Dignan 2007). The second issue is that restorative justice (including conferencing) is still an approach whose main focus of intervention is the 'case' (Crawford and Clear 2001), because the election of potential participants in a restorative justice meeting is still based on the needs of the case—and not on the needs of the community. The question therefore arises as to whether a participative-case-approach can actually have an effect on the whole community in terms of promoting democracy. Kurki and Pranis (2000) argue that restorative justice produces, without a doubt, collective effects, since it strengthens communities by building social capital and social control. How can restorative justice achieve this at the 'community level' when it starts from the 'case'? Some have argued that micro- and face-to-face practices of deliberation can be strong experiences since they are based on concrete problems that make the experience meaningful (Gordon 2006), engaging individuals more deeply (Kurki and Pranis 2000; Pranis 2001). Education in democracy, argues Gordon (2006), can go beyond citizens' roles, influencing social relationships and increasing civic consciousness. Naturally, despite its importance, such effects are difficult to research because they concern variables difficult to measure (Kurki and Pranis 2000).

Our, perhaps not surprising, conclusion is that inclusiveness could be resolved in these two dimensions (availability and involvement) when restorative justice is understood as a practice that considers the whole community as a potential beneficiary of restorative justice. In this task, the Brazilian experience is taking a step forward. On the one hand, their practitioners argue that their programme, inspired by Levinas' philosophy of alterity, aims to go beyond the resolution of the conflict between the two individual parties: it is a process of community empowerment, an experience of 'social pedagogy', in which participants learn not just to co-exist or to develop a culture of peace but also to participate 'politically' by exercising their citizenship. On the other hand, offering restorative justice conferencing in criminal cases before involving the criminal justice system, as the Community Juvenile Centres of Restorative Justice do, can be an innovative way to reach cases that otherwise would remain unknown.

Nevertheless, further study of the community as a beneficiary of the intervention at both theoretical and practical levels is needed. A way to do so, in addition to promoting the use of conferencing, is by incorporating community dimensions into restorative justice evaluations. The Brazilian and Peruvian experience have included the participation of several social actors in their practice as indicators of community involvement, but when evaluating the practice, individual criteria remain dominant (eg Aguinsky et al. 2008b; Nexos Voluntarios 2008).

FROM HORIZONTAL TO VERTICAL?

Pranis comments on how victims and offenders usually come from 'the most disenfranchised groups in society' (2001: 293). They feel powerless to resolve issues that concern their lives and have limited access to social and economic resources. This is especially true in the Latin American context, one of the most unequal regions in the world. If restorative justice gives power back to the people (Braithwaite 2002) then restorative justice could certainly serve as a tool to fight social injustice. How can relationships of power be democratized? If we consider crime as a situation in which one person imposes power over another one, the first level that needs to be democratized is the relationship between victim and offender. This is not a simple task, however, as structural inequalities can be defining in such a relationship (Cunneen and Hoyle 2010; Strang 2002).

A second level corresponds to the participants of the restorative justice meeting in general. Restorative justice can enforce equal relationships among them, which, in concrete terms, means equal weight in the decision-making process (Kurki and Pranis 2000). At this point, it is important to consider not just the 'numeric weight' of the parties' supporters but also the fact that all visions of the problem are voiced and taken into account.

A third, and final, level would correspond to the relationship between citizens (participants), authorities (criminal justice system) and society in general. This is, in our opinion, the most problematic level. Could it be argued that, by democratizing the horizontal level, giving equal access and voice to every participant, we are in effect trying to reach the societal-vertical level? One argument could be that, when the criminal justice system takes into account the agreement achieved by the participants of the encounter, the horizontal and vertical levels interact (Aertsen 2006), causing the latter to take part in the micro-space of deliberative democracy. Another view is represented by Aguinsky et al. (2008b): according to them, one of the intentions of the Porto Alegre restorative justice programme is to promote the capacity of the community to criticize institutional practices, by allowing horizontal relationships of power to develop.

But when the general legal-social contexts in which Latin American restorative justice practices are inserted is taken into account, a more pessimistic evaluation arises: restorative justice seems to have limitations in democratizing its relationship with the state. Unfortunately, social inequalities in the criminal justice system still persist. 'Restorative justice lacks praxis—in the sense of a constantly reflexive, dialectical relationship between theory and action. It lacks an analysis of its significant shortcomings; it lacks an analysis of political power and social power; it lacks a transformative politics' (Cunneen and Hoyle 2010: 186).

THE COMMUNITY MIGHT BE A PLACE: THE TERRITORIAL ISSUE

Restorative justice literature has tended to define community by stressing the sense of connectedness among individuals which allows for the building of bonds among people and the sharing of interests and activities (McCold and Wachtel 1997; Van Ness and Strong 2006). The territorial aspect has been avoided in RJ literature, in part because it is difficult to establish 'its existence' in reality (Walgrave 2008: 76).

Yet, is territory an important element in the definition of community? Let us introduce the definition of community offered by a Latin American community psychologist, Maritza Montero. She argues that community is a concept in constant evolution as its interrelationships create a sense of belonging and social identity as well as an awareness among its members about its existence as a group. Community, she adds, is a social group that shares history and culture. It counts on a certain organization and involves frequent interaction among its members characterized by action, affection, knowledge, and information (Montero 2004). As it can be observed, Montero's definition does not mention territory but highlights dimensions that can be found with more probability in a territorial community. From a Latin American perspective, this definition may better meet our needs, especially when a special relevance is placed on the fact that, as argued by Fattah (1991), victim and offender usually belong to the same community.

The South American experiences explored here, and in particular those in Peru and Brazil, indicate that these practices have been conceived with a territorial component in mind. In this sense, and following the distinction offered by Crawford and Clear (2001), these practices would have a 'community justice component', since the 'place' plays an important role in the design and implementation of these programmes. Our conclusion on this point is, therefore, that even though democracy can be promoted through micro-experiences (such as mediation in its classical sense), the impact of restorative justice practices, and, in particular conferencing, on processes of democratization might be stronger when these practices are located, inserted in existent, concrete communities.

FINAL REMARKS: THE NEED FOR A LATIN AMERICAN RESTORATIVE JUSTICE?

Latin America offers a singular context for restorative justice: it is a continent characterized by inequality, poverty, and, in several countries, a history of civil war or authoritarian regimes. In LA, minorities (under-empowered social groups) are, in numeric terms, not the minority but the majority (Montero 2004). In this reality full of exclusion and experiences of victimization, the need for a better and serious development of the collective dimension of restorative justice is a fact. For this reason, it is not surprising to find in this continent restorative justice practices involving social justice components or developing community-based approaches—as the programmes described here. Community-based conferencing seems to be a promising alternative in this regard. However, to further develop restorative justice in LA, several limitations need to be resolved. Most of the practices remain undocumented, programmes usually function with instable funding, and important (material or ideological) distances separate practitioners, researchers, and policy makers.

We would like to conclude this chapter by arguing that restorative justice seems to face a special challenge on our continent: to promote social change by not just *restoring* but also *transforming* communities (Crawford and Clear 2001). This transformation not only refers to the relationship between victims and offenders, or among members of the community, but also to the relationship between community and state, including the criminal justice system. This implies to conceive crime as a phenomenon embedded in both the social context in which it is produced, and the institutional context in which it is controlled.

REFERENCES

Aertsen, I. (2006), 'The Intermediate Position of Restorative Justice: The Case of Belgium', in Aertsen, I., Daems, T. and Robert, L. (eds.), *Institutionalizing Restorative Justice* (Portland: Willan Publishing), pp 68–92.

Aguinsky, B., Baldini, C., Gonçalves, S., Tejadas, S., Kullmann, A., Vecchi, K., Battisti, T. and Fonseca, T. (2008a), *A Invisibilidade das Necessidades das Vítimas no Sistema de Justiça da Infância e Juventude: Achados Preliminares do Observatório de Vitimização e Direitos Humanos*, available at: <http://www.justica21.org.br/j21.php?id=263&pg=0>.

Aguinsky, B., Hechler, A., Comiran, G., Giuliano, D., Davis, E., da Silva, S. and Battisti, T. (2008b), *A Introdução das Práticas de Justiça Restaurativa no Sistema de Justiça e Nas Políticas da Infância e Juventude em Porto Alegre: Notas de um Estudo Longitudinal no Monitoramento e Avaliação do Projeto Justiça para o Século 2*, available at: <http://www.justica21.org.br/j21.php?id=262&pg=0>.

Alvarez, A. (2002), *Informe Sobre la Consultoría Realizada en Lima, Peru*, para Terre des Hommes, unpublished (Lima).

Braithwaite, J. (2000), 'Repentance Rituals and Restorative Justice', *Journal of Political Philosophy*, 8, pp 115–31.

Braithwaite, J. (2002), 'Setting Standards for Restorative Justice', *British Journal of Criminology*, 42, pp 563–77.

Briceño-León, R., Villaveces, A. and Concha-Eastman, A. (2008), 'Understanding the Uneven Distribution of the Incidence of Homicide in Latin America', *International Journal of Epidemiology*, 37, pp 751–7.

Carta de Aracatuba (2005), available at: <http://www.idcb.org.br/pdfs/cartadearacatuba.pdf>.

Carta do Recife (2006), available at: <http://www.idcb.org.br/documentos/simposio270406/CARTADORECIFE.pdf>.

Comisión Económica para América Latina y el Caribe (CEPAL) (2009), *Panorama Social de América Latina*, available at: <http://www.eclac.org/publicaciones/xml/9/37839/PSE2009-Cap-I-pobreza.pdf>.

Cortés, F. (2007), 'Los Derechos de las Víctimas de la Violencia Política a la Verdad, la Reparación y la Justicia. Reflexiones Sobre Cuatro Casos en América Latina', *Estudios Políticos*, 31, pp 61–86.

Crawford, A. and Clear, T. (2001), 'Community Justice: Transforming Communities Through Restorative Justice?', in Bazemore, G. and Schiff, M. (eds.), *Restorative Community Justice: Repairing the Harm and Transforming Communities* (Cincinnati: Anderson Publishing), pp 127–49.

Cunneen, C. and Hoyle, C. (2010), *Debating Restorative Justice* (Oxford: Hart Publishing).

Declaración de Costa Rica (2005), available at: <http://www.justiciarestaurativa.org/news/crdeclaration>.

Declaración de Lima (2009), available at: <http://www.opcion.cl/word_press/?p=170>.

Díaz, A. (2010), 'La Experiencia de la Mediación Penal en Chile', *Política Criminal*, 5 (9), pp 1–67.

Dignan, J. (2007), 'The Victim in Restorative Justice', in Walkate, S. (ed.), *Handbook of Victims and Victimology* (Cullompton: Willan Publishing), pp 309–31.

Duce, M. (2009), 'Reformas a la Justicia Criminal en América Latina: Una Visión Panorámica y Comparada Acerca de su Gestación, Contenidos, Resultados y Desafíos', in Dammert, L. (ed.), *Crimen e Inseguridad, Políticas, Temas y Problemas en las Américas* (FLACSO-Chile), pp 189–224.

Dzur, A. and Olson, S. (2004), 'The Value of Community Participation in Restorative Justice', *Journal of Social Philosophy*, 35(1), pp 91–107.

Fattah, E. (1991), *Understanding Criminal Victimization* (Scarborough: Prentice Hall).

Ghiringhelli, R. (2005), 'Criminalidade e Justiça Penal na América Latina', *Sociologias Porto Alegre*, 7(3), pp 212–41.

Gordon, D. (2006), 'Public-Empowering Justice. Arguments From Effectiveness, Legitimacy and Democracy, and the South African Case', *Punishment and Society*, 9(1), pp 49–66.

Kurki, L. and Pranis, K. (2000), *Restorative Justice as Direct Democracy and Community Building* (Saint Paul: Minnesota Department of Corrections, Community and Juvenile Services Division).

Langer, M. (2007), 'Revolution in the Latin American Criminal Procedure: Diffusion of Legal Ideas of the Periphery', *The American Journal of the Comparative Law*, 55, pp 617–76.

MacRae, A. and Zehr, H. (2004), *The Little Book of Family Group Conferences: New Zealand Style* (Intercourse: Good Books).

Maxera, R. (2005), *Mecanismos Restaurativos en las Nuevas Legislaciones Penales Juveniles: Latinoamérica y España*, paper presented at the 11th United Nations Congress on Crime Prevention and Criminal Justice, 2005, available at: <http://enj.org/portal/biblioteca/penal/penal_juvenil/35.pdf>.

McCold, P. (2004), 'What is the Role of Community in Restorative Justice Theory and Practice?', in Zehr, H. and Toews, B. (eds.), *Critical Issues in Restorative Justice* (New York and Cullompton: Criminal Justice Press and Willan Publishing), pp 155–72.

McCold, P. and Wachtel, B. (1997), *Community is Not a Place: A New Look at Community Justice Initiatives*, paper presented at the International Conference on Justice without

Violence: Views from Peacemaking Criminology and Restorative Justice A Albany, New York 1997, available at: <http://www.iirp.edu/article_detail.php?article_id=NDc1>.

Malaguera, J. and Garrido, N. (2009), 'Justicia Penal Alternativa (Reparatoria): Breve Análisis de Algunos Sistemas Latinoamericanos', *Revista Cenipec*, 28, pp 183–206.

Melo, E., Ednir, M. and Yazbek, V. (2008), *Justiça Restaurativa e Comunitária em São Caetano do Sul. Aprendendo com os conflitos a respeitar direitos e promover cidadania*, Secretaria Especial dos Direitos Humanos da Presidência da República, available at: <http://www.tj.sp.gov.br/Download/CoordenadoriaInfanciaJuventude/JusticaRestaurativa/SaoCaetanoSul/Publicacoes/jr_sao-caetano_090209_bx.pdf>.

Montero, M. (2004), *Introduccion a la Psicologia Comunitaria. Desarrollos, Conceptos y Procesos* (Buenos Aires: Paidós).

Nexos Voluntarios (2008), *Análsis Costo/Beneficio Económico y Social de los Modelos de Justicia Juvenil en el Perú*, available at: <http://www.encuentroscj.org/facipub/upload/cont/813/cont/file/est-y-analisis-sobre-costo-beneficio-de-los-modelos-de-just-juv-en-el-peru.pdf>.

Oxhorn, P. and Slakmon, C. (2005), 'Micro-Justiça, Desigualdade e Cidadania Democrática. A Construção da Sociedade Civil Através da Justiça Restaurativa no Brasil', in Slakmon, C., De Vitto R. and Gomes Pinto, R. (eds.), *Justiça Restaurativa* (Brasília—DF: Ministério da Justiça e Programa das Nações Unidas para o Desenvolvimento—PNUD), available at: <http://200.169.22.139/justica21orgbr/webcontrol/upl/bib_190.pdf>.

Pallamolla, R. (2010), 'A Justiça Restaurativa e o Acesso à Justiça: Em Busca da Efetivação dos Direitos Fundamentais', in Bertoldi, M. and Santos de Oliveira, K. (eds.), *Direitos Fundamentais em Construção—Estudos em Homenagem ao Ministro Carlos Ayres Britto.* (Belo Horizonte: Fórum), pp 361–75.

Parker, L. (2005), *Developing Restorative Practices in Latin America. Restorative Justice in Emerging Countries*, paper presented at the 11th United Nations Congress on Crime Prevention and Criminal Justice, available at: <http://www.restorativejustice.org.uk/resource/developing_restorative_practices_in_latin_america_by_lynette_parker/>.

Parkinson, J. and Roche, D. (2004), 'Restorative Justice: Deliberative Democracy in Action?', *Australian Journal of Political Science*, 39(3), pp 505–18.

Pranis, K. (2001), 'Restorative Justice, Social Justice and the Empowerment of Marginalized Populations', in Bazemore, G. and Schiff, M. (eds.), *Restorative Community Justice: Repairing the Harm and Transforming Communities* (Cincinnati: Anderson Publishing), pp 127–49.

Prillaman, M. (2003), 'Crime, Democracy, and Development in Latin America', *Policy Papers on the Americas*, 15 (6), pp 1–30.

Roberts, A. (2004), 'Is Restorative Justice tied to Specific Models of Practice?', in Zehr, H. and Toews, B. (eds.), *Critical Issues in Restorative Justice* (Cullompton: Willan Publishing), pp 241–52.

Scuro, P. (2005), *Chances e Entraves Para a Justiça Restaurativa na América Latina*, available at: <http://www.justica21.org.br/j21.php?id=201&pg=0>.

Shaw, M., van Dijk, J. and Rhomberg, W. (2003), 'Determining Trends in Global Crime and Justice: An Overview of Results from the United Nations Surveys of Crime Trends and Operations of Criminal Justice Systems', *Forum on Crime and Society*, 3(1–2), pp 35–63.

Strang, H. (2002), *Repair or Revenge: Victims and Restorative Justice* (Oxford: Clarendon Press).

Snodgrass, A. (2004), 'When "Justice" is Criminal: Lynchings in Contemporary Latin America', *Theory and Society*, 33(6), pp 621–51.

Umbreit, M. (2001), *The Handbook of Victim-Offender Mediation: An Essential Guide to Practice and Research* (San Francisco: Jossey Bass).

United Nations (2002), *Basic Principles on the Use of Restorative Justice Programs in Criminal Matters,* Economic and Social Council, available at: <http://www.pfi.org/cjr/about-cjr/un-initiatives/ecosocresolution>.

Uprimmy, R. and Saffon, M. (2008), *Usos y Abusos de la Justicia Transicional en Colombia,* Anuario de Derechos Humanos, available at: <http://www.cdh.uchile.cl/anuario04/6-Perspectivas_regionales/Rodrigo_Uprimny_Maria%20Paula_Safon.pdf>.

Van Ness D. and Strong, K. (2006), *Restoring Justice: An Introduction to Restorative Justice* (3rd edn) (London: LexisNexis/Anderson Publishing).

Walgrave, L. (2008), *Restorative Justice, Self Interest and Responsible Citizenship.* (Cullompton: Willan Publishing).

PART III

CONFERENCING: EUROPEAN PERSPECTIVES

11

CONFERENCING IN NORTHERN IRELAND

IMPLEMENTING RESTORATIVE JUSTICE AT THE CORE OF THE CRIMINAL JUSTICE SYSTEM

Estelle Zinsstag and Tim Chapman

INTRODUCTION

Youth conferences in Northern Ireland have become one of the most successful examples of the possibilities presented by conferencing at a European and international level. The Northern Irish model has recently been endorsed by a succession of reports within the United Kingdom.[1] This model has also become an exemplar of good practice in Europe (Zinsstag et al. 2011).

The experience in Northern Ireland illustrates what restorative conferencing fully integrated within a criminal justice system might look like and how it could work. Therefore this chapter captures the origins and context in which this ground-breaking restorative justice practice was developed and then presents some of the unique characteristics of this successful programme. The chapter outlines the historical context of the development of restorative justice in Northern Ireland, describes the legislative mandate and institutional structure for the delivery of youth conferences, explains the Northern Irish conference model, reports on the outcomes of the programme, and examines some of the challenges that putting conferencing at the centre of the youth justice system presents.

[1] *Rules of Engagement: Changing the Heart of Youth Justice*, The Centre for Social Justice (2012); *A Review of the Youth Justice System in Northern Ireland*, Department of Justice NI (2011); *Time for a Fresh Start*, *Independent Commission on Youth Crime and Anti-social Behaviour* (2010); *Making Amends: Restorative Youth Justice in Northern Ireland*, Prison Reform Trust (2009).

HISTORICAL CONTEXT

To understand the policy and practice issues relating to youth conferences in Northern Ireland it is necessary to know something of its history of both violent civil conflict and peace building over the past 40 plus years. Inevitably in doing so in such a brief way, we have to simplify the complexity of this history.[2]

THE CONFLICT

From the late 1960s until the late 1990s this conflict took the form of civil disorder and violence involving the Protestant, unionist and loyalist majority, the Catholic, nationalist and republican minority, and the British Government. Northern Irish politics have been formed by conflict over the legitimacy of the Northern Ireland state. While republican and nationalist politics aspire to a united Ireland, ie the withdrawal of British sovereignty over Northern Ireland, the struggle for civil rights and equality were the driving forces of the conflict over recent years. Thirty years of violence have resulted in over 3,000 deaths, and many more maimed, traumatized, and bereaved.

In addition to the use of the British army, the state needed to deploy the police, courts, and prisons to manage the violence. The criminal justice system, designed to process and control criminal offenders, was adapted to manage people who are organized to break the law for political purposes.

Many of the most bitter and violent struggles focused on the institutions of the criminal justice system. These include the use of emergency legislation to arrest and interrogate suspects, the security forces releasing confidential information to loyalists, the use of internment, 'Diplock' no jury trials and the 'supergrass' trials, special category status, segregation, and hunger strikes in the prisons (McEvoy 2001). This was compounded by the fact that police officers and prison officers were predominantly from the Protestant community. Many judges, magistrates, police officers, and prison officers were targeted and killed by paramilitary organizations.

There were positive responses to the conflict. A vibrant network of community organizations—delivering services to the unemployed, to women, to the elderly, and to youth—emerged in the most deprived and politically alienated areas. Many groups sought to divert young people from offending. They were motivated by the perception that the criminal justice system had failed to protect them and to contain youth crime. They were also concerned about the vicious punishments for anti-social behaviour being inflicted on young people by paramilitary organizations (Feenan 2002; Knox 2002). These included warnings to young people and parents, exclusion from the community, beatings, bullet wounds through various limbs ('knee-cappings'), and killings (in the case of drug dealers). While these draconian measures were supported by many beleaguered members of the public, they proved no more effective in reducing offending than the state's system of punishments.

Eventually paramilitary organizations realized that this punishment system was not working and restorative justice initiatives emerged in both republican and

[2] For more information see eg McKittrick and McVea (2001).

loyalist communities. Two organizations were formed, Community Restorative Justice Ireland and Northern Ireland Alternatives. They have been working mostly with volunteers. These initiatives were not supported by the state due to their association with paramilitary organizations. The organizations secured funding from a foreign philanthropist. The initiatives used informal forms of conferencing adapted to local conditions (McEvoy and Mika 2002). Eventually they came to an arrangement with the government through strict protocols which seriously constrained their activities (Northern Ireland Office 2006; Eriksson 2009).

Restorative justice was also developing within the formal criminal justice system. The police force was the first criminal justice agency to embrace restorative justice practices in Northern Ireland (O'Mahony et al. 2002). They replaced their traditional method of cautioning juveniles in 2001 with a restorative caution delivered by specially trained youth diversion officers. Restorative cautions emphasize the importance of the young person taking responsibility for their actions and encourage empathy for the victim.

PEACE BUILDING: THE GOOD FRIDAY OR BELFAST AGREEMENT[3]

After many years of violence a peace agreement was announced on Good Friday 1998.[4] This created a 'road map' for building peace, human rights and equality, and established a system of government based upon power sharing between previous adversaries. Given the contentious part that the criminal justice system played during the conflict the Agreement included a major review thereof.

Given the political commitment to a more participative democracy based upon respect for difference and non-violent conflict resolution, restorative justice soon became the focus of reform in the youth justice system. Members of the Criminal Justice Review Group visited restorative programmes in New Zealand and the United States. They recommended a model of conferencing adapted from the New Zealand family group conferencing model. The Justice (Northern Ireland) Act 2002 implemented the recommendations made in the Criminal Justice Review (Criminal Justice Review Group 2000) to introduce restorative justice to the youth justice system (Campbell et al. 2005).

THE LEGISLATIVE MANDATE AND INSTITUTIONAL STRUCTURE FOR CONFERENCING IN NORTHERN IRELAND

The Justice (Northern Ireland) Act 2002 provided for the introduction of youth conferences and youth conference orders. The legislation empowers the Public Prosecution

[3] For a general overview of the events that led to the Good Friday agreement, the main players, and the conflict in general, etc., see eg O'Connor (2002).

[4] For information on the Good Friday Agreement, see eg Bell (2003).

Service (PPS) to arrange restorative youth conferences for virtually every young person charged with a criminal offence in Northern Ireland. Young people who have committed less serious offences and have not developed a persistent pattern of offending will be cautioned in a restorative manner by the police (O'Mahony et al. 2002). Those who have been cautioned and have continued to offend will be referred for a diversionary youth conference. Diversionary conferences avoid court prosecutions and result in voluntary agreements made by young people to make reparation and to prevent reoffending. If they do not comply with the agreement made at the conference, they may be prosecuted in court for the original offence. Young people who have committed serious offences or have developed a pattern of offending will be prosecuted in the youth court. In all cases except for those criminal offences which attract mandatory sentences (eg murder) the District Judge must offer the young person the opportunity of a youth conference.

Youth conferences are facilitated meetings of all those affected by the harmful action and their supporters. No one can be compelled to attend a youth conference. For a conference to take place the young person who has admitted the offence, his or her parent or carer, a police officer, and a youth conference coordinator must be present. The police officer, normally a 'youth diversion officer' trained specifically for participating in conferences, is responsible for stating the facts of the crime and may then later take an active part in the discussions on the agreement.

A conference can be arranged if there is no victim present though every effort is made to enable the person who has been harmed to participate. The young person responsible for the harm can bring a lawyer who is responsible for ensuring that his or her clients' rights are observed. The lawyer should not speak for, or advocate on behalf of, the young person. The young person responsible for the offence and the person who has been harmed can bring supporters to the conference. Depending upon the nature of the offence members of the community may be invited to express the community's views on what should happen. If the young person has a social worker or probation officer, he or she will be invited.

The statutory objectives of the youth conference are to engage young people who have offended in making amends to their victims and to undertake actions which will prevent their further offending. Youth conferences are facilitated by trained facilitators (youth conference coordinators) employed by the Youth Justice Agency (YJA). Youth conference coordinators must have a qualification that equips them to work with young people. They include qualified social workers, youth workers, probation officers, teachers, and police officers.

The youth conference coordinators facilitate dialogue between the participants and enable them to come to an agreement on what the young person should do to repair the harm and to avoid causing further harm. Actions specified in a plan may include a verbal or written apology, reparation directly to the victim or indirectly to the community in the form of unpaid work, financial compensation, supervision by an adult, participation in activities or programmes to address offending, restrictions on actions (may include curfews, prohibitions from entering certain places, eg a shop, electronic monitoring, and custody), and treatment for a mental health condition or for alcohol or drugs. The conference process should be completed within 30 days of a referral.

If the conference has been referred by the PPS, the agreement must be sent to the PPS for authorization. They may insist on changes to the agreement on the basis of proportionality or if the public interest has not been respected or taken into account enough. If the youth court has referred the conference, the agreement must be authorized in the court and again may be amended by the court. Once it is endorsed it becomes an enforceable court order, the youth conference order. This order is supervised by the YJA.

YJA staff support the young person to complete the agreed plan in full and hold the young person accountable if he or she does not comply with the agreed actions. The YJA has also negotiated service level agreements with a range of organizations in the community and voluntary sectors to deliver programmes and services to support action plans agreed at conferences. These programmes are designed not only to support young people to desist from harmful behaviour and to improve their lives but also to make sense to victims. For example, a young person who has offended against an elderly person may be asked to volunteer in a centre for the elderly. A young person who has committed a racially motivated hate crime may be asked to attend a programme delivered by an organization for ethnic minorities.

Practice is governed by a few clear statutory rules and by detailed practice guidelines (Campbell et al. 2002) rather than prescribed standards. Compliance with conference agreements is addressed through restorative processes rather than through a standardized or bureaucratic process. Remarkably few orders have been returned to the youth court due to non-compliance.

The youth conferencing service became operational in late 2003, first in the Greater Belfast area. Following a favourable internal evaluation in 2004 the service gradually expanded its work to other regions within Northern Ireland (Campbell et al. 2005). By 2006, youth conferences were available to the whole of the country.

THE NORTHERN IRISH CONFERENCE MODEL[5]

Campbell et al. (2005) explain that the Northern Irish youth conference, while based upon the New Zealand model of the family group conference, was designed differently from the outset to give more importance to the victim. Therefore a 'balanced model' (Campbell et al. 2006) that gives equal attention to the rights, needs, and interests of the person who has been harmed by the offence, the young person responsible for the harm, and the community. The model was also influenced by the Balanced and Restorative Justice project (BARJ 2000). Figure 11.1, proposed in Campbell et al. (2002) represents the model.

Campbell et al. (2002: 17) explain the thinking behind the Balanced Model:

> For a crime to take place there must be a person who chooses to offend, an opportunity to offend, and a person or institution who suffers harm or loss. A BALANCED

[5] A number of the points and comments made in the following sections are based on observations and interviews made by the authors in the context of their professional activities.

Figure 11.1 The Balanced Model, based on Campbell et al. (2006)

> APPROACH to managing a crime should address: the motivation of the person who chooses to offend; the opportunities to offend and stop offending; the harm caused by the offence.

The key idea behind the Northern Irish model is that a formal state system of justice must balance the need to repair the harm to the victim, to protect the community, and to reduce the need for the offender to harm others. Unless each party—victim, offender, and community—believe that their needs and interests have been addressed, it cannot be said that justice has been served.

The model is based upon the premise that while these needs and interests will be specific to each individual and to each conference, there will be general areas of need common to all parties arising from harmful acts: the need to restore one's safety, the need to experience justice, and the need to regain control over one's life. Facilitators are crucial to the process of enabling each person to clarify what they need and want from the conference. Their role includes making arrangements for the conference, preparing all those who will take part, facilitating the conference, and working with all those present to work out a plan which will be acceptable to all those concerned and to the referring authority. The practice manual for facilitators (Campbell et al. 2002) has adapted the social discipline window (Wachtel and McCold 2001). It illustrates the principle that an appropriate balance between supporting someone and holding them accountable creates the respectful relationship that allows a restorative process to take place. The process involves three phases, which must be facilitated skilfully. Inclusion involves creating a relationship based upon safety, respect, and empathy that encourages people to see the value of the conference to them and to agree to attend. Participation requires the coordinator to enable the parties to prepare to take an active part in the restorative process. Transformation occurs through storytelling, dialogue, and agreeing a plan. These phases correspond generally, though not exactly, with the three stages of the conference process:

> 1. Pre-conference; in which the coordinator engages the parties in choosing how they wish to participate in the process, and to prepare for their contribution.
>
> 2. Conference; in which the coordinator facilitates the parties to meet, to tell their stories, to express their emotions, to enter into a dialogue with each other, to arrive at a shared understanding, and generate a plan to repair the harm and to prevent further offending.
>
> 3. Post-conference; in which Youth Justice Agency staff work as a team with external partners to support the implementation of the plan and to hold the young person accountable (Campbell et al. 2002: 36).

The pre-conference preparation stage is crucial to the successful coordination of a conference. The facilitator prepares and coordinates all the people who will take part. First he or she needs to make sure that the offender is ready, willing, and able to take part. The victim will be contacted only after this is confirmed so as to ensure that no further victimization takes place. As Campbell et al. (2002) explain, it is very important that the facilitator makes clear to all parties at this stage the voluntary nature of participation. Facilitators are trained to engage each party to explore how a restorative process could be in their interests. They do not attempt to 'sell' the conference. The facilitator may meet with the main protagonists a number of times to ensure that they have all the information they need to make an informed choice. She or he will offer explanatory as well as preparatory material and may also show individuals a DVD of a conference.[6]

The coordinator will also prepare the other persons who will take part, such as the adults who will accompany the youth or the supporters for either party. He or she will also organize a convenient date and time for the parties, a safe and neutral venue for the conference, and all other practicalities of the conference and make sure that everybody is informed, invited, and committed to attend.

Conferences are run in a semi-structured way by a facilitator who has the responsibility for its smooth unfolding (Campbell et al. 2002). The duration of a conference depends on each case and may therefore be quite different. It can last from just under an hour up to three hours but on average will take about one hour (Jacobson and Gibbs 2009).

The facilitator opens the conference by reminding everyone of the purpose of the process and reiterating the ground rules which are written up and visible throughout the conference. The rules include: fairness, everyone will be heard; respect, listen, avoid interrupting, and respect confidentiality; engage, participate actively and honestly in the process; safety, no one will be abused or attacked verbally or physically; and harm, the conference focuses on the harm caused and how to repair it, not on the individuals who are present. There will also be a reminder to switch off mobile phones.

The police officer recounts the facts of the offence that has caused the harm. The young person responsible for the harm is then invited to account for what he or she did. The Northern Irish model does not employ the 'script' approach (O'Connell et al. 1999). The preference is for people to tell their stories in their own way. Questions may be used to support young people to tell their story but only if they are having difficulties. In general the participants' questions are considered more important than the facilitator's. So once the young person has fully expressed their account, the injured party is invited to ask him or her questions. These may include asking about details of what happened. Common questions include:

[6] A questionnaire, which is available on the website of the service, allows the victim to prepare and anticipate some of the problems, emotions, hopes, etc. that they could face during the conference (at <http://www.youthjusticeagencyni.gov.uk/document_uploads//Victim%20leaflet.pdf>). There are also leaflets explaining to the youth what it is about, what they are to expect, and what it involves (at < http://www.youthjusticeagencyni.gov.uk/document_uploads//Youth_conference_Your_Decision.pdf>).

Why did you do it?
Why did you choose us to harm?
Are you going to harm us again?

Once the facilitator is satisfied that all the questions have been answered, the person who has been harmed will be invited to tell his or her story of the offence and its impact. After this, the supporters will be asked to say how the incident has affected them. Throughout this process the participants are encouraged to speak to each other rather than through the facilitator.

Once the full extent of the harm caused has been expressed, the facilitator will ask the young person to say what they have heard and what they feel about it. At this stage in most, but not all, cases the young person will apologize, though this is not a prerequisite. The victim will then be asked to respond. Sometimes the injured party is not convinced and the dialogue continues until the young person demonstrates that he or she really feels remorse. The facilitator may ask: what are you sorry about? Or, how can you show you really are sorry?

When the facilitator reckons that either the victim is satisfied with the apology or that a satisfactory apology is not going to be given, he or she will initiate the crucial discussion about how to repair or make amends for the harm. In addition to an apology the young person may agree to repay some money to compensate for material loss or make some direct or indirect reparation through unpaid work. The victim may ask for some restrictions on the young person's movement so as to feel safe. These could include not entering the victim's shop or street for a set period of time. The local police will be informed of any agreed restrictions.

When the coordinator is sure that the victims' needs have been addressed and that they have experienced justice, the coordinator will direct the conference's attention to the young person's needs in relation to desisting from harming others. The timing of this is important. If, on the one hand, the offender's needs are addressed too soon, victims and their supporters will conclude that the conference is designed for the person who has harmed them. This realization will amplify whatever feelings they have about the harm, (anger, fear, anxiety, shame, etc.) and lead them to become frustrated or to withdraw from the process. On the other hand, when they feel that their story, their feelings, and their needs and interests have been respected, they can show great concern for the young person.

This second phase of the conference invites the conference to consider what the young person needs to do to desist from offending and what support he or she might require to do this and to have a good life. The views of the young person responsible for the harm and his or her parents or carers are particularly important. At this stage any professionals present may be asked to provide their opinions and suggest programmes or services appropriate to the young person's needs. The victims may also have some ideas. The different parties must agree on a fair and proportionate plan which deals directly with the causes of the harm and which has a realistic chance of being completed.

The final plan is a combination of the action steps agreed earlier to repair the damage to the victim and the actions steps agreed to reduce the risk of further harm. These action steps must be specific, measurable, achievable, relevant to the reparation of and prevention of harm, and time bound so as to constitute an enforceable contract or court order. This plan is sent to the PPS or presented to the youth court for approval. The YJA has developed a holistic approach to its work with young people who offend. It is based upon managing risk of harm, upon building young people's resilience, upon the obligation to repair harm caused, and upon the reintegration of the young person within their family and community. This enables the YJA to respond to whatever the conference determines.

Once the plan is approved the post-conference stage commences. The commitments that the young person has entered into as a result of the conference must be honoured to the letter. This is of critical importance to the victim's sense of justice, to the young person's future well-being, and to the community's confidence in restorative justice. The YJA will allocate a trained worker to support the young person and to deliver some programmes addressing offending, to arrange for other agencies to provide reparation, rehabilitation and reintegration services, and to hold the young person accountable for the completion of the plan. It should be stressed that the effectiveness of the youth conference process relies as much if not more upon the post-conference support as upon the conference itself.

OUTCOMES

Since 2003 when youth conferencing began in Northern Ireland, there have been over 10,000 conferences. This is a substantial number in a population of approximately 1.8 million. A conference can comprise of between five and 15 people. To the 10,000 we can add the thousands of restorative processes which the community based schemes have facilitated for over 10 years. This means a significant and increasing proportion of the population has participated in restorative justice. This approach could very soon become part of 'the way we do things here', an integral part of the Northern Irish culture.

This, of course, assumes that restorative justice is viewed positively. Consequently the quality of the conference experience and its outcomes must be positive though not necessarily perfect. As McCold (cited in Mirsky 2004: 1) commented: 'There is a tendency to compare new programs to perfection and to criticize them when they fail to reach the ideal. To succeed, restorative justice does not need to be perfect. To be preferred, it need only demonstrate superiority, on average, to traditional adjudicatory approaches.'

In Northern Ireland the previous system, of court disposals informed by pre-sentence reports, continues to operate in parallel with the new restorative system because some young people who have admitted to an offence will not consent to a youth conference. This offers a comparison group.

Since the youth conference became available throughout Northern Ireland in 2006 the restorative response to youth offending quickly became the primary youth justice disposal. Diversionary youth conference plans and court ordered youth conference orders increased by 141 per cent and 38 per cent respectively over the five year period from 2006/07 to 2010/11 (Lyness and Tate 2011).

Previously in addition to fines and conditional discharges, combination orders, community service orders, probation orders, attendance centre orders, reparation orders, and community responsibility orders were available to young people who offended. In 2005 there were 323 such orders made and 172 diversionary or youth court ordered youth conferences. In 2006 there were 438 youth conferences and 265 of the other non-custodial orders. By 2007 the figures were: 905 youth conferences and 152 other orders. In 2008 there were 890 youth conferences and 105 other orders. These figures suggest that the PPS and the youth court and young people who had offended preferred a restorative response in most cases.

Diversionary youth conferences were designed to divert young people who had not committed serious offences from prosecution in court. However, the statistics show an overall increase in non-custodial disposals (combining the previous disposals with the youth conferences) from around 1,100 in 2005 and 2006 to 1,458 in 2007. This suggests that as many as 70 per cent of young people who participated in diversionary youth conferences would not have been prosecuted in the youth court. This may indicate the attraction of a restorative response. But it also indicates the risk that restorative justice can pull too many young people into the formal youth justice system. Nevertheless the statistics do demonstrate that perhaps around 150 young people are being diverted from prosecution by youth conferences.

A key measure of the effectiveness of conferences is the participation and satisfaction of victims. However, we must bear in mind that the youth conference scheme in Northern Ireland addresses the full range of offences, many of which may have no obvious direct victim. The YJA coordinates conferences for drug offences, motoring offences, disorderly conduct offences, vandalism, and theft or damage of property of corporate bodies. In these cases there is rarely a 'personal victim' though many people are harmed indirectly. Nevertheless, youth conference coordinators are committed to having a strong victim dimension to as many conferences as possible. They may invite people who have been harmed by drug use, people who have been severely disabled by road accidents, local community representatives, and senior managers of organizations. Victim participation was measured by the YJA in 2009/10 as occurring in 74 per cent of all conferences. Personal victims, defined as those directly affected by the offence, were present in half of all youth conferences in 2010. Victims' satisfaction has been measured through an independent evaluation (Campbell et al. 2006) as 90 per cent. Since then it has been routinely measured after conferences by the YJA. In 2009/10,84 per cent of victims were satisfied with their conference experience. Satisfied victims are a very important source of support for restorative justice. It is crucial that these figures are sustained and, if possible, improved.

The fact that the conference plan has been endorsed by a victim and sometimes by community representatives as well as freely entered into by the young person and his or her parents or carers has made it a popular order with most district judges in Northern Ireland. Another benefit is that the court can see exactly what the young person has committed to doing to make amends and to stay out of trouble. Its specificity increases transparency and accountability and also offers the opportunity for achievement in the young person's life. Perhaps for these reasons there is a very high completion rate (over 90 per cent) of conference plans. It may be that these factors have encouraged courts to sentence very few young people to the Juvenile Justice

Centre, the custodial institution for young people in Northern Ireland. The figures since the introduction of youth conferences have been fairly stable ranging from 45 in 2006/07 and 2007/08 to 37 in 2009/10. The most recent figure 2010/11 was 40. This rate of detention in Northern Ireland in 2009/10 was 2.2 per 10,000 population aged 10–17. It was 5.4 per 10,000 population aged 10–17 in England and Wales during the same period. It is also less likely that a young person subject to a youth conference order will receive a custodial order after reoffending than a young person supervised under a probation order, community service order, or a combination order (Lyness and Tate 2011).

Official reoffending rates are calculated over a one-year follow-up period. They are measured through both convictions and out of court sanctions such as cautions or diversionary youth conferences. The latest figures are for the calendar year 2008 (Lyness and Tate 2011). There are two custodial institutions in Northern Ireland, the Young Offenders Centre (YOC) and the Juvenile Justice Centre (JJC). Their combined reoffending rate was 68.3 per cent. More 10 to 17 year olds go to the JJC and its reoffending rate was slightly higher at 81.5 per cent. The rate for the probation order was 58.8 per cent and the attendance centre order's rate was 56.2 per cent. The reoffending rate for the (court ordered) youth conference order was 45.4 per cent. The rate for diversionary youth conferences was at 29.4 per cent. Given that perhaps only 30 per cent of young people who participated in a diversionary youth conference would have been prosecuted in the past, this low figure is understandable. Nevertheless, there is a clear trend that restorative responses to youth offending have generally been more effective in reducing reoffending than the long established court orders.

The statistics suggest that many young people who offend prolifically are offered youth conferences. About 20 per cent of young people have participated in between three and 30 youth conferences. A significant number of these are persistent offenders who are struggling with serious difficulties in their lives and demonstrate little will or capacity to change. It is unlikely that the other non-custodial orders attract a similar group in such numbers. Indeed, their equivalent would be those who are in custody. Although a detailed analysis has not been undertaken, it is probable that if this group were excluded the reoffending rates for youth conference orders would be lower. One final point: youth conference reoffending rates for violent offences are significantly lower than for offences against property.

In summary, over a short period youth conferencing in Northern Ireland has established itself at the heart of the youth justice system, it has gained the confidence of victims of crime, and it has supported young people to work towards better lives and to reduce their offending. What has contributed to this success and what are the challenges ahead?

CHALLENGES AHEAD

The Northern Irish experience has demonstrated that any restorative justice approach, which is designed to operate at the centre of the justice system, will require a robust and flexible practice model. The YJA commissioned the University of Ulster to produce a practice manual (Campbell et al. 2002). This was based upon a literature review into best practice internationally and included the legislative regulations, restorative principles and values, an explanation of the needs of people who have been harmed, of young people responsible for harm and of communities, an outline of the restorative process and the skills it requires, and detailed step by step practice guidelines.

This provided practitioners and managers with an evidence based and outcome oriented process with which to engage victims, young people, and their supporters and to structure and organize practice. The strong value base and rationale was also critical in promoting youth conferencing and responding to the resistance that the service encountered from many quarters. Bearing in mind that youth conferencing is available to all victims and offenders who consent to participation, it soon engaged with a much wider variety of people and harmful behaviours than were originally envisaged. The strong value base and the flexibility of the designed process enabled coordinators to adapt the conference to fit the needs of individuals rather than develop criteria to determine who is suitable for conferencing. This is at the heart of the youth conference's inclusive and participative ethos. Coordinators have created guidelines for engaging people with learning disabilities or autism. A practice model has also been produced for conferencing in cases of sexual harm.

A practice model is only as effective as the people who implement it. Youth conferences are facilitated by full-time specialists, youth conference coordinators. The YJA recruited a high calibre of staff with experience of working with people. The training, which was delivered by the University of Ulster, contributed to developing committed and competent practitioners.

Training consisted of an intensive nine day course which covered the balanced model; understanding what needs to be restored to victims for them to recover from being harmed; understanding what needs to be restored to young people who offend if they are to desist from harmful behaviour; understanding what needs to be restored to the community if they are to support and reintegrate offenders and victims; and six days of rigorous role play when participants practice the skills required at every stage of the process. Participants found this training challenging but very valuable once they began to undertake youth conferences. The key to training experienced professionals, particularly those who have worked primarily with young people, is to enable them to 'unlearn' their previous role and the skills and knowledge that supported that role. In order to learn to 'be restorative', students must become conscious of their incompetence before they can learn new skills and techniques. This is an uncomfortable experience which must be facilitated sensitively. It is particularly challenging for young person centred practitioners to balance the needs of the victim with the young person. Professionals also find it difficult to resist the urge to 'steal the conflict' (Christie 1977) from the parties rather than to 'trust the process'. Students then complete five further modules to gain a Diploma in Restorative Practices. This investment in learning has resulted in highly creative practitioners who are prepared to take on the many challenges of facilitating youth conferences. The challenge for the YJA will be to sustain this investment during a period of severe constraints on funding.

One consequence of the investment in developing a high quality youth conference was that similar attention had not been given to the post conference support and supervision by the other division within the YJA, Community Services. This division had employed a practice model which was family oriented, systemic, and therapeutic. This approach was not easily integrated into a restorative framework. The YJA has recently restructured its service delivery integrating youth conferencing and community services into one area team. This provides the YJA with the opportunity to create a unique synergy between restorative and systemic practices which, if implemented to a consistently high standard, could generate even better results for young people who offend and for their families and communities.

The quality of supervision and service post conference is critical to another challenge that the YJA faces, multiple conferences. The fact that courts have to offer young people the opportunity to participate in a conference has resulted in a small group of individuals experiencing many conferences. The facts are that 63 per cent of young people experience just one conference. A further 17 per cent have a second conference. Fifteen per cent have had three to six conferences. This leaves actually less than 5 per cent who have more than six conferences.

Nevertheless, this can have an appreciable impact upon the public credibility of the youth conference. Some have argued that the law should change or that coordinators should use their discretion to limit the amount of conferences that one young person can be offered. This argument, while understandable, has not been fully thought through. It is based upon the assumption that a youth conference is another method of reducing reoffending. It is in fact a means of engaging those most affected by a crime in determining what should be done to repair the harm and to prevent it occurring again. It is important to emphasize that a primary objective of youth conferences is to meet the victims' needs. People who have been harmed by crime should be offered the opportunity to meet the person who harmed them whether that person is a prolific offender or not. The conference should be owned by the parties not the professionals. While the experience of participating in a conference can, as we have shown, be very satisfying to a victim and can motivate a young person to accept support to change his or her behaviour, the actual outcomes of the conference depend upon what happens after it has been completed. To curtail conferences is to exclude the victim and the community from the process of justice. Furthermore, as McCold (in Mirsky 2004) asserted, to prove its worth restorative justice does not have to be perfect, just preferable. The alternative to a youth conference is a court appearance and either a custodial order or another non-custodial order and each of these options have proved less effective in preventing reoffending than the youth conference order.

The YJA will need strong leadership to resist attempts to dilute or distort its restorative values and practices. Fortunately it has been excellent at collecting data which provide evidence of its effectiveness. Its strategy should be to improve the effectiveness of its post-conference practice in relation to supporting young people to have lives in which they have no need to harm others.

In partnership with the University of Ulster the YJA has designed a priority young offenders programme (Chapman 2010) designed to engage those young people who have committed serious sexual or violent offences or have developed a pattern of persistent offending. As explained in the Independent Commission on Youth Crime and Antisocial Behaviour's report (2010: 58) these youths may be:

> [...] intensively supervised, with up to seven days a week contact, and helped to complete their restorative plans through an approach known as 'circles of support and accountability'. This creates a network of constant communication between the people in the community and professionals that are most involved in their lives.

The Circle of Support and Accountability was developed in Canada to support adult sex offenders in the community. It has been adapted for young people in Northern Ireland. It aims to bring all those people who care about a young person together to work as a team. These include the extended family, friends, mentors, youth workers, sports coaches, social workers, teachers, and other professionals. The aim is to have more people from family and community in the circle than professionals. The circle becomes something like an ongoing conference which meets regularly to support, to encourage, to problem solve, and hold the young person accountable to his or her commitments to the victim and to changing behaviour. Between meetings the young person is in contact with at least one member of the circle each day. This provides an intensive and restorative method of supporting young people. A small scale study (Murray 2011) of 20 young people who were persistently offending and participating in a circle of support and accountability found that 55 per cent had desisted from offending or were significantly reducing their offending. It is by delivering such programmes that the YJA will reduce multiple conferences.

Maruna et al (2006) interviewed a sample of young people after they had completed their conference plans. One recurring view was that, while a great deal of attention and care is taken over the conference process, not much happened at the successful completion of the plan. This research recommended an ending ritual that recognized the effort the young person had made to make amends and to stop harming people.

The final challenge facing youth conferencing is to avoid being a victim of its own success. There is some evidence that diversionary youth conferences may not be diverting young people from the formal justice system. This may be because they are seen as effective and, thus, attractive to the PPS. However, there are excellent community based organizations which could provide restorative conferences and divert more young people from the formal youth justice system. This course of action would be less costly, more effective, and ultimately more restorative.

CONCLUSIONS

The Northern Ireland youth conference has demonstrated that restorative justice can be effective at the heart of the criminal justice system. It has taken a dedicated group of practitioners and managers to restore to victims, young people who offend, and their supporters and community the right to participate actively in the process of justice. However, there still exists that tendency of the system and its experts to steal the conflict from ordinary people (Christie 1977). To resist this, the YJA must continually improve its ability to engage victims in a process which satisfies their needs and to engage young people in a process that enables them to have a better life and provide evidence that these processes work.

REFERENCES

Balanced and Restorative Justice (2000), *Curriculum* (Washington: Office of Juvenile Justice and Delinquency Prevention).

Bell, C. (2003), 'Dealing with the Past in Northern Ireland', *Fordham International Law Journal*, 26, 1095–147.

Campbell, H., Chapman, T., McCready, S. and the Northern Ireland Office for the Youth Conference Service (2002), *Practice Manual* (Belfast: Youth Justice Agency).

Campbell, C., Devlin R., O'Mahony, D., Doak, J., Jackson, J., Corrigan, T. and McEvoy, K. (2005), *Evaluation of the Northern Ireland Youth Conference Service* (Belfast: Northern Ireland Statistics and Research Agency).

Chapman. T. (2010), *Priority Youth Offender Project Manual* (Belfast: University of Ulster and Youth Justice Agency).

Christie, N. (1977), 'Conflict as Property', *British Journal of Criminology*, 17, 1–26.

Criminal Justice Review Group (2000), *Review of the Criminal Justice System in Northern Ireland* (Belfast: HMSO).

Department of Justice NI (2011), *A Review of the Youth Justice System in Northern Ireland*, (Belfast: Department of Justice NI).

Eriksson, A. (2009), *Justice in Transition: Community Restorative Justice in Northern Ireland* (Cullompton: Willan Publishing).

Feenan, D. (2002), 'Researching Paramilitary Violence in Northern Ireland', *International Journal of Social Research Methodology*, 5(2), pp 147–63.

Independent Commission on Youth Crime and Antisocial Behaviour (2010), *Time for a Fresh Start: The Report of the Independent Commission on Youth Crime and Antisocial Behaviour* (London: The Police Foundation).

Jacobson, J. and Gibbs, P. (2009), *Out of Trouble—Making Amends: Restorative Youth Justice in Northern Ireland* (London: Prison Reform Trust).

Knox, C. (2002), "See No Evil, Hear No Evil: Insidious Paramilitary Violence in Northern Ireland", *British Journal of Criminology*, 42(1), pp 164–85.

Lyness, D. and Tate, S. (2011), *Northern Ireland Youth Re-Offending: Results from the 2007 Cohort Statistical Bulletin 2/2011* (Belfast: Statistics & Research Branch, Youth Justice Agency).

Maruna, S., Wright, S., Brown, J., Van Marle, F., Devlin, R. and Liddle, M. (2006), *Youth Conferencing as Shame Management: Results of a Long-Term Follow-Up Study* (Belfast: Youth Justice Agency/Youth Conferencing Service (ARCS)).

McEvoy, K. (2001), *Paramilitary Imprisonment in Northern Ireland: Resistance, Management and Release* (Oxford: Oxford University Press).

McEvoy, K. and Mika, H. (2002), 'Restorative Justice and the Critique of Informalism in Northern Ireland', *British Journal of Criminology*, 42(3), pp 534–62.

McKittrick, D. and McVea, D. (2001), *Making Sense of the Troubles* (London: Penguin).

Mirsky, L. (2004), *A Summary of: A Survey of Assessment Research on Mediation and Restorative Justice, by Paul McCold*, at <http://www.iirp.edu/library/rjsurvey.html>.

Murray, D. (2011), *An Investigation into the Priority Youth Offender Project and the Impact of Circles Of Support and Accountability on the Enhancement of Social Capital* (Masters dissertation, University of Ulster).

Northern Ireland Office (2006), *A Protocol for Community-based Restorative Justice Schemes: Consultation and Equality Impact Assessment* (Belfast: Criminal Justice System Northern Ireland).

O'Connell, T., Wachtel, B. and Wachtel, T. (1999), *Conferencing Handbook* (Pipersville: The Pipers Press).

O'Connor, F. (2002), *Breaking the Bonds: Making Peace in Northern Ireland* (Edinburgh: Mainstream Publishing).

O'Mahony, D., Chapman, T. and Doak, J. (2002), *Restorative Cautioning: A Study of Police Based Restorative Cautioning Pilots in Northern Ireland* (Belfast: Northern Ireland Office, Research and Statistical Series No. 4).

The Centre for Social Justice (2012), *Rules of Engagement: Changing the Heart of Youth Justice* (London: The Centre for Social Justice).

Wachtel, T. and McCold, P. (2001), 'Restorative Justice in Everyday Life', in Strang, H. and Braithwaite, J. (eds.), *Restorative Justice and Civil Society* (Cambridge: Cambridge University Press), pp 114–29.

Zinsstag, E., Teunkens, M. and Pali, B. (2011), *Conferencing: A Way Forward for Restorative Justice in Europe?* (Leuven: European Forum for Restorative Justice).

12

CONFERENCING AT THE CROSSROADS BETWEEN REHABILITATION AND RESTORATIVE JUSTICE

Inge Vanfraechem, Katrien Lauwaert, and Mélanie Decocq[1]

INTRODUCTION

Several countries have introduced conferencing as a means of dealing with youth delinquency, albeit mostly common law countries.[2] Belgium started a pilot project in 2000, the practice of conferencing (called 'hergo') was evaluated by the KU Leuven (Vanfraechem 2003, 2005), and conferencing was included in the revised Youth Justice Act (YJA 2006) in 2006 (Put et al. 2012). This chapter first describes the set-up of conferencing in Belgium, both in legislation and in practice. It then identifies the bottlenecks that arise from implementing a restorative justice practice in a welfare oriented, rehabilitative youth justice system. In the conclusion, findings are evaluated and lessons are drawn which may inspire other (civil law) countries when implementing conferencing.

CONFERENCING IN BELGIUM

A PILOT PROJECT: PRACTICE AND RESEARCH PIONEERING CONFERENCING

In 2000, a pilot project introduced conferencing in Flanders, the Flemish speaking part of Belgium.[3] A youth justice coordinator from New Zealand trained experienced

[1] The authors wish to thank especially Antonio Buonatesta, Riet De Cuyper, and Bie Van Severen for their input from practice and feedback on earlier drafts.

[2] Research in Europe has shown that conferencing is in practice more widespread than commonly assumed, even though the difference with mediation is not always clear cut (Zinsstag et al. 2011).

[3] Belgium is a federal country, with three communities (the Flemish-speaking, French-speaking, and German-speaking community) and three regions (Flanders, Wallonia, and Brussels). The federal Ministry of

mediators: since victim-offender mediation had already been practised for several years (Claes et al. 2003), the decision was taken to have mediators implement conferencing. Furthermore, conferencing was to be oriented towards more serious juvenile delinquency since victim-offender mediation focused mostly on less serious crimes.[4] The New Zealand model was thought to be most beneficial for this, due to its central position in the youth court handling of cases, the presence of the police, and the private time for the young offender and supporters during the conference (Vanfraechem 2003; Walgrave 1999).

Five mediation services in five judicial districts in Flanders participated in the pilot project. Judicial actors were involved from the beginning in order to adapt the procedure to the peculiarities of the Belgian justice system, for example, the referral by the youth judge and the role of the police. Furthermore, the judicial actors were informed about the pilot project in order to get referrals. A steering committee guided the research and included representatives from the actors involved: lawyers, prosecutors, youth judges, social services, victim support, and mediators. A methods group consisted of the mediators and the researcher to discuss practical issues, such as getting enough referrals, how to invite and motivate parties to participate, and how to deal with group dynamics (which proved to be quite different from one-on-one mediation).

Although referrals came in rather slowly (98 young people were referred in the period 2000–03, of which 58 youngsters participated in 53 conferences[5]), the seriousness of the cases increased over time and referral agencies became more confident about the possibilities of conferencing in comparison to both mediation and other measures. The research showed that: (1) conferences can be implemented in a civil law country, which requires certain adaptations such as the police participating to symbolically refer to the societal consequences of the crime (and not representing society, since this is the role of the public prosecutor) and the attendance of the youth lawyer; (2) the implementation at the youth court level ensures that crimes are serious and that legal safeguards can be secured; (3) the participants were generally satisfied with the proceedings and results when the conference was well-implemented; (4) although difficult to measure, recidivism tended to be lower for those young people having participated in a conference compared to those who were referred but did not have a conference;[6] and (5) judges interviewed concluded that conferencing might be an alternative for, or an add-on to, a placement in a closed institution (Vanfraechem 2003, 2005).

These results were viewed as positive and the research therefore suggested continuing the practice of conferencing. The Minister of Welfare at the time decided to await

Justice is competent for legislation, while the communities are to implement the legislation in practice (Lemonne and Vanfraechem 2005). The translation of 'Family Group Conferences' led to 'herstelgericht groepsoverleg' or 'hergo'. In French the term 'concertation restauratrice en groupe (CRG)' is most common.

[4] This is not to say that mediation can only be used in less serious cases. It has been used in sexual assault cases, murder, etc., also in Belgium, but mostly for adult offenders (Suggnome 2005).

[5] Cooffenders may participate in one conference.

[6] This was only checked through a dossier study and no control group was set up, so the results should be read with care.

federal legislation to have a legislative framework to generalize the conferencing practice throughout Flanders. In the meantime, some mediation services continued to provide for conferencing: 39 conferences took place involving 51 young people in the period 2004–05.

LEGISLATION: PERPETUATING AND GENERALIZING PRACTICE

Belgium was one of the first countries to implement a welfare-oriented youth justice system in 1912. The law was adapted in 1965 but still upheld a welfare focus. This Youth Protection Act (YPA 1965) was relatively quickly criticized, as was the case for other welfare-oriented youth justice systems, because it did not achieve rehabilitative effects; legal safeguards were not upheld; the measures were too soft for serious crime; and the victim was not taken into account (Walgrave 2004). After years of debate, the YPA 1965 was adapted and restorative justice was integrated in what may be called the YJA 2006 (Put et al. 2012). The Explanatory Memorandum explicitly refers to existing practices and research as grounds for including a.o. conferencing in the YJA 2006 and the title includes the damages to the victim.[7]

The public prosecutor and youth judge/court are to first consider a restorative offer (mediation and conferencing) before taking another decision. There is no obligation to refer a case to mediation/conferencing, but the prosecutor has to motivate his/her decision not to offer mediation in order for the referral of the case to the youth judge to be allowed (art. 45*quater* §1 YJA 2006). The youth judge/court may offer mediation/conferencing under the condition that a victim has been identified (art. 37*bis* §1 YJA 2006).[8] The youth judge/court can offer a conference to the young person when he/she appears before court. A letter is then sent to the victim. The youth judge/court sends a copy of the decision to the service for conferencing.[9] When the parties have not contacted the conferencing service within eight days, the service will repeat the offer. The offer of conferencing can only start and continue when all parties voluntarily accept to participate (art. 37*bis* §1 YJA 2006).

When conferencing has taken place and an agreement has been reached, it needs to be signed by the young person, the parents, and the victim, and it is added to the judicial file. A so-called 'declaration of intent' is also to be added.[10] The judge/court

[7] 'Wet betreffende de jeugdbescherming, het ten laste nemen van minderjarigen die een als misdrijf omschreven feit hebben gepleegd en het herstel van de door dit feit veroorzaakte schade' (Law concerning youth protection, charging youngsters that committed an act defined as an offence and restoration of the harm caused by the acts—our translation). Reform of the 1965 YPA by the acts of 15 May 2006 and 13 June 2006, published in the Belgian Bulletin of Acts, Orders and Decrees of 2 June 2006 and 19 July 2006, with errata rectified in the Bulletins of 28 June 2006 and 25 August 2006.

[8] The Act also included two other conditions, namely 'serious indications of guilt' and 'the person charged does not deny his/her involvement in the facts' but these were not upheld by the Constitutional Court because they impede the presumption of innocence (judgment of 13 March 2008).

[9] In practice, these are called mediation services: in 2007, existing mediation services received additional funding to also implement conferencing. In the YJA, these are referred to as 'services for conferencing' in the section on conferences.

[10] The agreement entails the elements the young person will undertake for the victim; the declaration of intent includes the young person's engagements vis-à-vis society and to prevent reoffending, which may for example include community service, engagements with regard to school, or following a treatment programme.

homologates the agreement, without changing its contents: he/she can only refuse the agreement when its content is contrary to public order (art. 37*quater* §1 YJA 2006). The conferencing service delivers a concise report with regard to the proceedings and result of the restorative offer, which is to be handed over to the parties beforehand for their advice (art. 37*quater* §2 YJA 2006). The conferencing service draws up a short report with regard to the execution of the agreement and hands it over to the youth judge/court and its social service (art. 37*quinquies* §1 YJA 2006). If the agreement is executed before the court's decision, the court is to take the agreement and its execution into account when coming to a decision (art. 37*quinquies* §2 YJA 2006). If it is executed after the court's decision, the measure can be reviewed and possibly lightened (art. 37*quinquies* §3 YJA 2006).

If no agreement could be reached, neither the recognition of the facts, or the process and outcome of the conference can be used in detriment of the young person. Furthermore, all documents and communications are confidential, unless the parties agree to communicate these to the judicial authorities. These documents cannot be used in subsequent proceedings or as proof (art. 37*quater* §2 and 3 YJA 2006).

Through the inclusion, as a restorative offer, in the YJA 2006, conferencing is now available throughout Belgium. It has not been thoroughly evaluated through research following the implementation of the YJA 2006, but some findings from practice are available, which may offer a view on its implementation: did legislation advance conferencing practice?

ECHOES FROM PRACTICE: GENERALIZATION AND EXPANSION AFTER LEGISLATION?

In 2009, 144 young people in Flanders were referred to conferencing and 33 of them actually participated in a conference. Nine cases were still in the preparation phase at the time of data collection and for 72 young people a conference did not take place, most frequently because the victim did not want to take part (OSBJ 2010: 30). In comparison, the number of young people having committed a crime and receiving a measure at the youth judge/court level in Flanders amounts to about 3,520 young people in 2009.[11] This leads the authors of the OSBJ report to state that except for the judicial districts of Brussels, Leuven, and Antwerp (three districts that participated in the pilot project) the number of referrals remains low (OSBJ 2010: 29).

In the French-speaking part of Belgium there was no pilot project previous to the introduction of conferencing in the YJA 2006. For justice practitioners it was a totally new concept. A central and uniform registration system for restorative practices for young people was not developed. A research project (Decocq and Lauwaert 2011) revealed that in the four year period 2007–10 only 145 minors were referred to a conference. These cases were unequally spread over the 13 judicial districts. In five of the districts, no cases were referred at all. The district of Liège and Charleroi referred

[11] These figures stem from the data supplied by the social services of the youth courts (Johan Peeters, Agentschap Jongerenwelzijn, personal communication, 9 September 2011).

respectively 77 and 27 cases, the other six districts referred between two and 11 cases each.

For 126 of the 145 referred cases, the judicial file was analysed. Although the information in the files was often rather limited, it is possible to indicate—with caution[12]—some tendencies concerning the conference process, the type of facts, and the profile of the offender. The initial willingness to participate was rather high for victims (55 per cent, 50 of 91 cases) and very high for offenders (89 per cent, 81 of 91 cases). In about one third of the referred cases a conference actually took place (31 of 91 cases). Where we only count the cases where the victim was willing to participate, the proportion of conferences taking place increases to 62 per cent. The (un)willingness to participate on the side of the victim thus seems an important explanatory factor for the (non-) execution of the conference. Interestingly, in more than half of the cases in which the youth judge offered a conference to the juvenile offender (54 per cent, 46 of 85 cases), the public prosecutor had requested a placement in a (open or closed section of a) youth institution.

The majority of the acts committed concern offences against persons (69 per cent, 86 on 125 cases) and are committed in group (59 per cent, 74 of 125 cases). The seriousness of the offences is variable and ranges from verbal aggression, tagging, and simple theft to arson, burglary, assault, and robbery to sexual offences such as collective rape. The 'community' dimension of the case (conflict between neighbours, verbal aggression, and intimidation in a school context, theft in a local football cafeteria, etc.) seemed to have been an important factor for selection. In the judicial files reference is made to ongoing tensions between the parties, feelings of insecurity in the neighbourhood since the facts, victims and offenders from the same family or neighbourhood, or going to the same school (75 per cent, 95 of 125 cases).

The predominant profile of the young offenders referred to a conference is a young male of around 16 years old, coming from a rather positive, stable family context, and with regular school attendance. Only a minority (21 per cent, 26 of 123 cases) presents troubled conduct at school (violent behaviour, lack of discipline, impulsive behaviour, etc.). Almost all have Belgian nationality. Minors of non-Belgian origin[13] are nevertheless overrepresented in comparison to their presence in the overall population of young people under 18 years old.[14] The great majority of the offenders appeared before the youth judge for the first time (89 per cent, 111 of 124 cases). The described profile points towards a possible dualization in which mainly first offenders with a good social network would have access to conferencing.

One may distinguish a two-tracked development: on the one hand, mediation services that participated in the pilot project (in Flanders) or had a well-established mediation practice before the introduction of conferencing in the YJA (in Wallonia), do not only generally receive more referrals, but the cases also tend to be more serious.

[12] The collected information was not available in all the examined files.

[13] The criterion used was the parents' country of origin. A youngster was considered of non-Belgian origin if at least one of the parents was not born in Belgium.

[14] It is interesting to note that this overrepresentation is less important than the overrepresentation observed in a study of Vanneste (2001) concerning the profile of juveniles in judicial files at the level of the prosecutor and the juvenile judge.

The mediation service in Brussels, for example, deals with sexual assault cases (Vanseveren 2010). Both the facilitators and judges become more confident over time in dealing with more serious cases. On the other hand, mediators and judicial actors starting with conferencing tend to question the model with regard to, eg the role of the police and victims, issues that were already addressed during the pilot project (Vanfraechem 2003, 2005, 2007a).[15]

Due to the fact that referrals have been rather slow, coordinators of the mediation services in Flanders have, in 2011, decided to appoint a person to stimulate and inspire practitioners and referral agencies to make more use of the possibilities of conferencing. A working note has been written.[16] It describes the aims of 'hergo'; indicators for referral; the procedure; communication between the facilitator and referral agency; hergo in combination with other measures such as a placement in a closed institution; and the role of the various actors and parties in a conference. The note ends by referring to local initiatives on sensitizing the referral actors and it aims to further sensitize actors at a Flemish level. The coordinators appealed to a researcher to take the lead in further action to improve the number of referrals. The cabinet of the Ministry of Youth of the French-speaking community has launched a similar initiative by subsidizing an action research.[17] The researchers in both Flemish and French communities will organize round tables with practitioners in order to further develop the Flemish working note and turn it into a real manual of good practice. A national conference will be organized during which the results of the whole process will be presented.

From these developments, we may conclude that legislation has enhanced the generalization of conferencing throughout Belgium, since it is now available in all judicial districts. In practice however, the number of referrals has been rather low and slow, and has been—in Flanders—mostly limited to those judicial districts where mediation services played a leading role in developing conferencing. Although the YJA 2006 puts restorative justice practices forward as the first response to youth crime, this has not led to a sharp increase of conferencing referrals. Without concrete research results at hand, we may nevertheless formulate some possible explanations.

Firstly, the law refers to mediation as the first measure to be considered by the prosecutor. In Flanders this has led to an increase of mediation referrals at the prosecutor's level from 1,587 in 2005 to 4,050 young people in 2009 (Put et al. 2012).[18] Since in those cases, mediation has already been offered to the parties, the youth judge might not consider a conference to be useful.

[15] This may indicate that the people working on the ground are not familiar with the research outcomes, even though these were written down in a hands-on book (Vanfraechem 2007a).

[16] Nota Herstelgericht groepsoverleg, 23 March 2011.

[17] The action research is titled 'Recherche-action concernant la concertation restauratrice en groupe en Communauté française' and is carried out at the department of Criminology of the University of Liège.

[18] A first comparison of the total number of cases at prosecutor's level show that six to seven per cent of the registered decisions entail an offer of mediation (Detry et al. 2010). The number of referrals to mediation may in practice be higher, due to registration problems (Eef Goedseels, researcher at NICC, personal communication, 05.09.2011). Furthermore, these figures include both Flanders and Wallonia. The degree of mediation referrals tends to be higher in Flanders: 74 registered mediations per 1,000 incoming cases, compared to 16 for French-speaking prosecutors' offices (Detry et al. 2010).

Secondly, Belgium has, as explained, a tradition of a welfare-oriented youth justice. For judicial actors, it might be hard to let go of their habits in dealing with cases in this manner (Put et al. 2012). Furthermore, they give away part of their decision making power by handing over the case to the parties and only being able to check afterwards whether the agreement is in conflict with public order. Although judges may still add other measures to the case after a conference, it could be that they feel hesitant to really include the parties in the proceedings.

Thirdly, exploratory interviews indicate that there is a real lack of knowledge about conferencing (the practice and the philosophical underpinnings) amongst judges in the French speaking community, which can partly be explained by the fact that no pilot project had been developed before the introduction of conferencing in the YJA 2006. Even in the Flemish community it is not always clear for judges what the distinction is between mediation and conferencing. When the magistrates feel uncertain about how to put a conference in practice, they seem reluctant to propose it.

And lastly, mediators may also need the time and experience to be convinced of the added value of conferencing: practice has shown, as said, that new facilitators utter the same concerns as when the pilot project had just started. Without adequate training and follow-up, they might not regard conferencing as being different from mediation and therefore stick to what they know, namely victim-offender mediation.[19]

REHABILITATION AND RESTORATIVE JUSTICE: BOTTLENECKS

With regard to the implementation of conferencing as a restorative justice practice within a rehabilitative, youth protection system, we distinguish some bottlenecks which prove to be a challenge because of the tensions the YJA 2006 has created.

WORKING PRINCIPLES

Restorative justice practices are—in Belgium explicitly—based upon three working principles: voluntariness, confidentiality, and neutrality (Lauwaert 2008, see also Aertsen et al. 2004: 33–34, UNODC 2006: 33–34). The question arises whether legalizing the conferencing practice influenced these working principles.

Voluntary participation

The voluntary nature of the participation of all parties is considered to be important in order to come to a genuine communication process. The YJA 2006 stipulates that all parties have to agree with their participation throughout the whole process

[19] Although in theory conferencing is rather different from mediation, through eg the role of the police, the presence of support people, and the focus on the community/society aspect of the case (see also Bazemore and Umbreit 1999; McCold 2006; Walgrave 2008: 33–36), the difference in practice may not always be clear-cut and practitioners may use elements of both in order to adapt the method according to the parties' needs (see also Zinsstag et al. 2011; Shapland in Chapter 4).

(art.37*bis* §1 YJA 2006). Thus parties may withdraw their consent at any stage. Furthermore, the Minister of Justice stated that mediation and conferencing are formulated in the law as a 'restorative offer' to exactly emphasize that parties may only participate on a voluntary basis.[20]

Nevertheless, this voluntariness might not be respected so strictly. Firstly, the YJA does not refer to the possibility of self-referral to conferences: the youth judge/court has to take the initiative by offering the possibility of conferencing (art.37*bis* §1 YJA 2006). Secondly, the conferencing service has to send a report to the youth judge/court, who will evaluate whether the agreement goes against public order and will take the outcome into account when coming to a decision (art.37*quater* §1 and art.37*quinquies* §2/3 YJA 2006). Knowing that the judge/court will evaluate the agreement may, as such, influence the parties' choice to participate in a conference or determine the outcome.

The young person's voluntary participation becomes relative when he/she knows that the youth court/judge will evaluate the result. Maybe this is not a problem, since the young person can still be motivated to participate, but it could also lead to young people making a calculated decision. The facilitator is to evaluate the young person's motivation so the victim is not confronted with an offender who does not empathize at all, or to at least inform the victim of the young person's attitude. The victim may, on the one hand, agree to something he/she is not totally convinced of, knowing that the judge/court will have to evaluate the outcome. On the other hand, the victim may also be happy to leave the final decision power to the judge/court: victims want to have a say, but not necessarily make the final decision on the outcome (Strang 2002; Wemmers 1996).

Confidentiality

The YJA 2006 recognizes the principle of confidentiality by stating that when the restorative offer does not yield a result, neither the process, the outcome, or the recognition of the facts can be used against the young person (art.37*quater* §2/3 YJA 2006). Furthermore, all documents and communications remain confidential, unless the parties want to communicate certain elements to the youth judge/court. But the YJA 2006 also requires the facilitator to submit a brief report on both the process and outcome of the case. Parties are only required to give their advice with regard to this report (art.37*quater* §2 YJA 2006). Furthermore, the conferencing service is to draw up a small report with regard to the execution of the agreement (art.37*quinquies* §1 YJA 2006).

Further regulation by the Flemish community puts focus on the fact that the report needs to be brief.[21] With regard to not being able to hold a conference, the report only refers to the fact that one of the parties could not be reached; one of the parties does

[20] Commissieverslag Senaat (I) Jeugdwet, 38 (report of the Senate Commission—our translation).

[21] Samenwerkingsakkoord van 13 December 2006 tussen de Federale Staat, de Vlaamse Gemeenschap, de Franse Gemeenschap, de Duitstalige Gemeenschap, en de Gemeenschappelijke Gemeenschapscommissie, betreffende de organisatie en de financiering van het herstelrechtelijk aanbod bedoeld in de wet van 8 April 1965 betreffende de jeugdbescherming, het ten laste nemen van minderjarigen die een als misdrijf omschreven feit hebben gepleegd en het herstel van de door dit feit veroorzaakte schade (Agreement of cooperation between the communities and the federal state—our translation).

not want the conference to take place; the parties already came to an agreement; or one of the legal conditions for holding a conference (namely identification of the victim) could not be met. In a case where the conference started but did not lead to a concrete result, the report mentions the name of the people that were contacted and the fact that no agreement could be reached, as well as any other information the parties deem important to communicate. The tension created in the YJA 2006 is thus moderated through this regulation by stressing the fact that the report ought to be brief.

Neutrality

The neutrality and independence of the facilitator are considered as essential for the communication process. Conferencing services are therefore set up independently of the Ministry of Justice. The YJA 2006 puts the neutrality of the facilitator forward as an important principle without entering into detail, which leaves ample room for practice to develop a deontological code in this regard (Vandebroek and Vanfraechem 2007).

Working principles and the YJA 2006

The legalization of conferencing has clearly created a field of tension with regard to at least two of the working principles of restorative justice practices. This tension seems to be born out of the concern to maintain judicial control over a process which was handed over to the parties. The mediation law for adults[22] leaves more room to the parties and shows greater confidence in the dynamics of the restorative justice process (see also Vandromme 2006). We could therefore conclude that the YJA 2006 shows a tendency to pocket restorative justice in the traditional vision of a youth welfare system, a tendency which is nevertheless tempered by the concretization of certain elements through the implementing regulation,[23] such as stressing the briefness of the report and the importance of deontology for the facilitators (Vandebroek and Vanfraechem 2007).

THE POSITION OF THE VICTIM

Since restorative justice gives the conflict back to the parties (cf. Christie 1977), the position of the victim becomes central in restorative justice practices. The definition of hergo/CRG in the YJA 2006 refers to the victim as one of the central parties to whom the possibility of conferencing should be offered:

> The conference aims at offering the person suspected of having committed an act defined as an offence,[24] the victim, their social surroundings, and other possible serviceable persons, the possibility of considering solutions worked out during communi-

[22] Wet 22 juni 2005 tot invoering van bepalingen inzake de bemiddeling in de Voorafgaande Titel van het Wetboek van Strafvordering en in het Wetboek van Strafvordering, *B.S.*, 27 July 2005.

[23] The Agreement of Cooperation, cf. footnote 21.

[24] Since the youth protection law considers young people to be in need of protection, they are not regarded as having committed a crime, but 'an act defined as an offence' (Put 2007).

> cation, in group and with the help of a neutral mediator, with regard to the way the conflict stemming from the acts defined as an offence, can be solved, taking into account, among others, the relational and material consequences of the act defined as an offence. (art. 37*bis* §3 YJA 2006—our translation)

In practice however, debate has been ongoing with regard to the position of the victim. It is agreed that a conference runs best when a victim is present, but could also be held when the victim is represented eg through a representative (most likely a partner or family member), a letter, or the co-facilitator (Vanfraechem 2007a).[25] Discussion arises when a victim chooses not to be physically present during the conference, but furthermore does not want to have anything to do with the conference: does the victim then have a *de facto* veto-power on the conference taking place? Some would argue the conference can then still make sense by addressing the harm done to the community/society and any elements the young people need to address in order to get on with their life. Although we agree with this reasoning, we would then opt not to call it a 'restorative conference' ('herstelgericht groepsoverleg') anymore, since one of the key parties is no longer involved in the process. One could then think of installing a 'care conference' ('hulpverlenend groepsoverleg'), in order to address the young person's issues—as is the case in New Zealand where both types of conferences exist (Hudson et al. 1996; Shearar and Maxwell in Chapter 7). The question remains what to do with the restorative aspect towards the community/society:[26] should it get a place in such a 'care conference'? Or would that be a reason to still call it a 'restorative conference'? If the latter option is taken, we believe this would reside under a welfare-oriented philosophy, where the main focus lies with the offender and what to do with him/her, rather than being a fully restorative practice (McCold and Wachtel 2002).

THE ROLE OF PROFESSIONALS

Police

During the pilot project, a conference was defined as follows:

> a guided communication process between (1) the offender and his/her family, sometimes also members of the broader network, (2) the victim, eventually his/her networks, and (3) a specialized police officer, aimed at finding a constructive solution for the consequences of the crime (damages, relationships, society) (Walgrave 2000: 1—our translation).

In the YJA 2006, the role of the police officer is not specified anymore: the Act refers to 'serviceable persons' (art. 37*bis* §3 YJA 2006, cf. supra). There were some doubts, especially in the French-speaking community, on the usefulness of having the police present and whether this presence would prevent the young person from speaking up.

[25] Most conferences are run by two facilitators: the main facilitator takes the lead, the co-facilitator ensures that everybody gets their say and that all aspects discussed are reflected in the discussion and agreement.

[26] A specific element of conferencing is the fact that it not only addresses the harm toward the victim and possibly the offender, but also towards the community/society (see Vanfraechem 2007b).

Although other reasons might have also played a role—such as financial issues (who would pay for the police officers' presence?) and distribution of competences (police fall within the remits of the Ministry of Interior affairs, while regulation of youth justice is the competence of the Minister of Justice and its execution of the communities)—the argument brought to the fore refers to the youth protection philosophy, by focusing mostly on the young person.

The police were included in the pilot project in order to symbolically represent society: since conferencing addresses serious crimes, broader consequences than the ones for the victim come into the picture. Order and peace are threatened by crime and warrant a public response (Walgrave 2008). By involving the police officer in a conference, parties might become aware that a broader issue is at stake. This public/societal harm may be addressed through eg a community service (Vanfraechem 2007b). If a conference is to be fully restorative (McCold and Wachtel 2002), then the community/society aspect should not be lost out of sight.

Lawyer

According to the first version of the YJA 2006, a youngster could be supported by a lawyer before a conference and when the agreement is determined. The YJA 2006 thus tended to exclude the presence of the lawyer during the conference, while this presence was considered to be important during the pilot project to preserve the young persons' rights. This exclusion was the result of some negative experiences with regard to the lawyers' presence during mediation, especially in the French-speaking community. In Flanders, on the contrary, experiences in the pilot project were 'quite positive' to 'very positive', especially with the so-called 'youth lawyers' who were experienced in youth justice matters and therefore already played a more mediating role (Vanfraechem 2003). Involvement of the lawyer is now also possible during the conference and ensures that the young persons' rights are protected—a critical element in the welfare approach (Walgrave 2004).

In the YJA 2006, nothing is mentioned about the lawyer of the victim. In practice he/she can be present. During the pilot project, a lawyer was seldom present for the victim, which may be linked to the fact that the victim has to pay for his/her lawyer, while the youngster will get a lawyer appointed. Furthermore, victims did not think their lawyers' presence was needed, or sometimes they received support of the youngster's lawyer during the conference, eg when he/she clarified certain elements (Vanfraechem 2007a).

Social service

In every district, a social service for the youth court is established which is initiated and organized by the communities. The social service carries out necessary investigations to assess the personality of the young people and their environment, to determine what measures would be in their own interest, and what means are appropriate for their education and treatment (Put 2007). During the pilot project, social service representatives were often involved in the conference. They can take up possible problems the young person may have and follow up after the conference. In this sense, the welfare approach is brought into the conference. It might be important for the victim that those issues are addressed, since victims may participate in order for the young person to get his/her life back on track. At the same time, these social issues do not overwhelm the communication process since they will be followed up afterwards. The YJA 2006 does not explicitly refer to the role of the social service: the tension between the restorative justice approach (focusing on the harm) and rehabilitation (including the social service in order to address the young person's personal problems) is rather created in practice.

CONCLUSION

Although the Belgian YJA 2006 offers room for conferencing by putting the offer of restorative justice practices forward as the first step to think of when dealing with juvenile delinquency, it also creates certain tensions between a restorative justice and a rehabilitative, welfare approach. Since conferencing is an offer by the juvenile judge/court it is, in principal, voluntary. But the youth judge/court will evaluate the outcome and may add another measure; therefore the young offender will take this into consideration when deciding whether or not to participate. Also for the victim, this judicial overview may have an impact on the voluntariness. The YJA 2006 also mentions the report the facilitator is to make of the process, which could impede the confidentiality, but this matter is resolved in practice by ensuring that the reporting remains brief.

Since the young offender is the focus in a welfare system, debate arises with regard to the victim: does he/she have a veto-right with regard to the conference taking place? Firstly, when deciding to go on with the conference without the victim's involvement, it may be better to rename a 'restorative conference' into 'a welfare conference' in order to avoid confusion and only talk about a restorative conference when a victim is somehow involved. Secondly, and related to this first issue, a victim may decide to not physically participate in the conference, but send a representative or a letter in order for his/her view to be taken into account.

Questions also arise with regard to the role of the professionals in a conference. The police are present to symbolically represent society—this presence may be viewed as problematic because of the possible effect on the communication: the question arises whether the young person will be able to talk freely. The presence of the social worker may offer an added value because he/she can deal with matters related to the young person and his/her problems. But it can also take away the focus on the harm and put too much emphasis on the young person, thus moving from a restorative to a rehabilitative approach. The presence of the lawyer for the young offender may create an imbalance towards the victim, who has to pay for his/her lawyer to take part in the meeting. Working with youth lawyers who are familiar with a mediation approach may offer a solution in that regard.

In practice, the focus on or attention for the rehabilitative aspects does not necessarily always create problems, firstly because the victim may find it important that the youngster's problems are dealt with, secondly, it is also important for society that these issues are addressed in order to get to a long-term solution to the problem, and thirdly because practice is creative in looking for solutions for the tensions discussed. But we believe the focus should nevertheless remain with the restorative approach, in order to ensure restoration of the harm and attention to the victim.

Legislation generally helped to generalize the conferencing practice in Belgium, but doubts in practice nevertheless remain—both for judicial actors and facilitators—and therefore the number of referrals remains rather low. This entails that legislation as such is not enough to ensure an increasing practice. When looking at New Zealand (see Shearar and Maxwell in Chapter 7) and Northern Ireland (see Zinsstag and Chapman in Chapter 11), a standardized model by which all young offenders go through a conference, may on the one hand offer a better lead to 'success' and higher number of cases. On the other hand, one can wonder whether this leads to a more offender-oriented system since the conference will take place anyway, regardless of the victims' will to participate.

A last element which needs further consideration entails the difference between mediation and conferencing: in theory this difference is clear-cut but in practice this is not always the case (see also Walgrave in Chapter 3 and Shapland in Chapter 4). Since mediation is offered at the prosecutor's level, youth judges do not always see the possibilities for conferencing. A possible solution in serious cases is that prosecutors refer the case to the youth court, and suggest a conference when referring. Also for mediators the differences between the two practices are not always clear—more empirical research on the actual dimensions and dynamics in the meetings may offer more insight into the matter.

REFERENCES

Aertsen, I., Mackay, R., Pelikan, C., Willemsens, J. and Wright, M. (2004), *Rebuilding Community Connections—Mediation and Restorative Justice in Europe* (Strasbourg: Council of Europe).

Bazemore, G. and Umbreit, M. (1999), *Conferences, Circles, Boards, and Mediations: Restorative Justice and Citizen Involvement in the Response to Youth Crime* (Minnesota: OJJDP).

Christie, N. (1977), 'Conflicts as Property', *The British Journal of Criminology*, 17(1), pp 1–15.

Claes, M., Spiesschaert, F., Van Dijk, C., Vanfraechem, I. and Van Grunderbeeck, S. (2003), 'Alternative Practices for Juvenile Justice in Flanders (Belgium): The Case for Mediation', in Walgrave, L. (ed.), *Repositioning Restorative Justice: Restorative Justice, Criminal Justice and Social Context* (Cullompton: Willan Publishing), pp 255–70.

Decocq, M. and Lauwaert, K. (2011), *Recherche Portant sur l'Utilisation par les Magistrats de la Jeunesse des Concertations Restauratrices en Groupe en Communauté Française* (Liège: Service de Criminologie, Université de Liège).

Detry, I., Goedseels, E. and Vanneste, C. (2010), 'Les Chiffres des Parquets de la Jeunesse au Grand Jour', in Gazan, F., De Craim, C. and Traets, E. (eds.), *Jeugddelinquentie op zoek naar Passende Antwoorden, Congresboek* (Antwerpen/Apeldoorn: Maklu), pp 41–65.

Hudson, J., Morris, A., Maxwell, G. and Galaway, B. (eds.) (1996), *Family Group Conferences. Perspectives on Policy and Practice* (Monsey: The Federation Press-Criminal Justice Press).

Lauwaert, K. (2008), *Herstelrecht en Procedurele Rechtswaarborgen* (Antwerpen: Maklu).

Lemonne, A. and Vanfraechem, I. (2005), 'Victim-Offender Mediation for Juveniles in Belgium', in Mestitz, A. and Ghetti, S. (eds.), *Victim-Offender Mediation with Youth Offenders in Europe* (Dordrecht: Springer), pp 181–209.

McCold, P. (2006), 'The Recent History of Restorative Justice: Mediation, Circles, and Conferencing', in Sullivan, D. and Tifft, L. (eds.), *Handbook of Restorative Justice* (New York: Routledge), pp 23–51.

McCold, P. and Wachtel, T. (2002), 'Restorative Justice Theory Validation', in Weitekamp, E. and Kerner, H.-J. (eds.), *Restorative Justice: Theoretical Foundations* (Cullompton: Willan Publishing), pp 110–42.

OSBJ (2010), *HCA, Cijfernota 2009*, available at: <http://www.steunpuntjeugdhulp.be>.

Put, J. (2007), 'The Juvenile Justice System in Belgium' in Giostra, G. and Patanè, V. (eds.), *European Juvenile Justice Systems, vol. I* (Milano: Giuffrè Editore), pp 3–37.

Put, J., Vanfraechem, I. and Walgrave, L., 'Restorative Dimensions in Belgian Youth Justice', *Youth Justice*, 12(2), 2012, pp 83–100.

Strang, H. (2002), *Repair or Revenge* (Oxford: Clarendon Press).

Suggnomè vzw (2005), *Waarom? Slachtoffer-Dader Bemiddeling in Vlaanderen* (Antwerpen-Apeldoorn: Garant).

UNODC (2006), *Handbook on Restorative Justice Programmes* (New York: United Nations).

Vandebroek, M. and Vanfraechem, I. (2007), 'Bemiddeling en Hergo', in Put, J. and Rom, M. (eds.), *Het Nieuwe Jeugdrecht* (Gent: Larcier), pp 147–82.

Vandromme, S. (2006), 'En Iedereen gaf Elkaar de Hand…de Introductie van Herstelbemiddeling in het Wetboek van Strafvordering', *R. W.*, (69)35, pp 1361–70.

Vanfraechem, I. (2003), 'Implementing Family Group Conferences in a Legalistic System: The Example of Belgium', in Walgrave, L. (ed.), *Repositioning Restorative Justice: Restorative Justice, Criminal Justice and Social Context* (Cullompton: Willan Publishing), pp 313–27.

Vanfraechem, I. (2005), 'Evaluating Conferencing for Serious Juvenile Delinquency', in Elliott, E. and Gordon, R.M. (eds.), *Restorative Justice: Emerging Issues in Practice and Evaluation* (Cullompton: Willan Publishing), pp 278–95.

Vanfraechem, I. (2007a), *Herstelgericht Groepsoverleg* (Brugge: die keure).

Vanfraechem, I. (2007b), 'Community, Society and State in Restorative Justice: Some Reflections', in Mackay, R., Bosjnak, M., Deklerck, J., Pelikan, C., van Stokkom, B. and Wright, M. (eds.), *Images of Restorative Justice Theory* (Frankfurt am Main: Verlag für Polizei und Wissenschaft), pp 73–91.

Vanneste, C. (2001), *Les Décisions Prises par les Magistrats de la Jeunesse: Rapport Final* (Bruxelles: INCC).

Vanseveren, B. (2010), *Developments in Flanders and HERGO in Sexual Assault Cases*, paper presented at the seminar 'Conferencing: A Way Forward for Restorative Justice in Europe' (Leuven).

Walgrave, L. (1999), 'Restorative Justice Conferences: Een Nieuwe "Parel aan de Herstelrechtelijke Kroon"?', *Tijdschrift voor Criminologie*, 41(3), pp 268–84.

Walgrave, L. (2000), *Naar een Experiment met Herstelgericht Groepsoverleg (Family Group Conference) in Vlaanderen. Stand van zaken* (Leuven: KU Leuven), unpublished.

Walgrave, L. (2004), 'Restoration in Youth Justice', in Tonry, M. and Doob, A. (eds.), *Youth Crime and Youth Justice. Comparative and Cross-National Perspectives* (Chicago: University of Chicago Press), 31, pp 543–97.

WALGRAVE, L. (2008), *Restorative Justice, Self-Interest and Responsible Citizenship* (Cullompton: Willan Publishing).

WEMMERS, J.-A. (1996), *Victims in the Criminal Justice System* (Amsterdam: Kugler Publications).

ZINSSTAG, E., TEUNKENS, M. and PALI, B. (2011), *Conferencing: A Way Forward for Restorative Justice in Europe* (Leuven: European Forum for Restorative Justice).

13

RESTORATIVE JUSTICE IN THE WELFARE STATE

CONFERENCING IN THE NORDIC COUNTRIES

Anna Eriksson

INTRODUCTION

Restorative justice has often been portrayed as an alternative to punitive and adversarial criminal justice practices, providing a more explicit focus on victims of crime and paths to offender reintegration. This usually does not mean that the aim is to replace an existing retributive system, but to offer an alternative route within that system for certain victims and offenders, a route characterized by an emphasis on repair, reintegration, and inclusion as opposed to punishment, alienation, and exclusion. We know that the models of restorative justice differ depending on the context in which it is implemented, for example victim-offender mediation, family group conferencing, and the more inclusive circles. 'Context' in this instance, refers both to the target population for the programme, for example young or first time offenders, domestic violence, adult offenders and so on, but also to the type of justice system, eg adversarial or inquisitorial, and the national context of any one country, such as Australia, Belgium, England, or Sweden.

In this chapter, I want to focus in particular on the latter—the national context—and explore the impact this can have on the model and aims of a restorative justice programme. I will argue that this 'bigger picture approach' is one we need to employ if we want to understand the use of restorative justice in different environments, an understanding that is crucial if we want to engage in comparisons along such elusive variables as 'effectiveness' and ask questions as to 'what works'. It also highlights the difficulties one might have when trying to export a particular model of restorative justice, for example the New Zealand model, into a different context. The model and practice of restorative justice 'must be adapted' to its new environment, and the needs and constraints of that particular environment. And as I have argued elsewhere (Eriksson 2009), restorative justice 'can' be modified in this way, without losing its underlying value and philosophy, which is an important strength of restorative practices such as conferencing.

This first part of the chapter will briefly describe the development and current practice of conferencing in Sweden, Norway, and Finland before moving on to the substantive discussion about restorative justice in the welfare state. Importantly, this is not a comprehensive discussion of the features of the welfare state or all the variables within its criminal justice system. The aim is rather to initiate a discussion about the importance of national context, shaped by significant cultural, social, political, and historical factors, and how such contexts affect restorative justice practice. The point is that restorative justice initiatives are often introduced based on the needs of victims and offenders in any one jurisdiction. However, those needs do not materialize in a vacuum, nor are they solely determined by a particular crime, but the position of victims and offenders—the support structures available, the existing or non-existing routes to repair and reintegration—are determined by cultural, political, and social constructions that vary significantly between different jurisdictions. Hence, in some countries, offenders are often stigmatized, labelled, and excluded, whereas in others, the routes towards reintegration and inclusion are much clearer. Such over-arching factors will arguably have a tangible, but often unacknowledged, impact on restorative justice practice. This chapter aims to bring them if not to the forefront then at least out of the closet.

CONFERENCING IN THE NORDIC COUNTRIES: A SHORT HISTORY

Norway and Finland were the first Nordic countries that began using mediation in relation to criminal cases in 1981 and 1983 respectively. Sweden followed in 1987 and Denmark in 1994. The term 'restorative justice', in its literal translation, is rarely used in these jurisdictions. Instead, 'reparative justice' is used as an umbrella term and 'mediation' is the most common form it takes. However, these mediations almost always include several other people, such as parents of offender and victims, and other support people. Norway in particular practices a more inclusive model, based on principles of community ownership of both conflict and solutions, following on from Nils Christie's (1977) scholarship. Hence, the term 'conferencing' is not necessarily used in the Nordic countries, but the practice of mediation in these jurisdictions are similar enough—when a larger group of people comes together to discuss a crime and its effects—to be able to be compared with conferencing practices in Continental Europe and beyond. I will use the term 'mediation' when discussing these practices, since that is the terminology used in the respective country's legislation. However, it is important to note that mediation in the Nordic countries is much more inclusive than the classic victim-offender mediation, with processes that can accurately be seen to reflect those of a restorative conference.

Restorative justice initiatives also exist in Denmark, where mediation run by so-called conflict councils, modelled on Norway, are still being trialled. However, there is no legislative framework or guidelines from the Department of Justice, perhaps a reflection of the Conservative right holding power in government in the period 2007 until mid-September 2011. Indeed, the Danish government voted to *not* introduce conferencing as an alternative within the criminal justice system in 2008, but it has been practised in some local police districts previously. Iceland only introduced restorative practices in 2001 in the form of mediation, where the police run the initiative, and the explicit aim is to mediate complaints towards police as opposed to the more traditional victim-offender mediation (Paus 2008). Hence, the initiatives in these two countries are much more limited than those in the other three, and since both use Norway as a model of practice I leave them out of the more in depth discussions below. Importantly, only conferencing initiatives that have a direct relationship with the criminal justice system will be discussed in this chapter. Conferencing, following restorative justice principles, is however used in other instances by social services and community based organizations, for example around child abuse and neglect, homelessness, and sexual assault (see Engel 2009; Pali and Madsen 2011; Sundell and Häggman 1999; Sundell and Vinnerljung 2004), but these fall outside the scope of this chapter.

SWEDEN

The first attempts at mediation in Sweden started in 1987, but until 1998 it was only practised sporadically through various smaller projects aimed at young people and focused on criminal damage, theft, and the like. These few projects were generally organized through partnerships between police, school, and social services; a common approach in Sweden with regards to juvenile offenders and children who break the law. The minimum age for participants was set at 11, the lowest in any of the Nordic countries (Paus 2008). Up until 1998, the mediation activity was rather ad hoc, and even though the Chief Prosecutor had been tasked with providing a proposal for a more widespread model in 1994, the resulting activities were limited. Run through the social services, the 10 most active programmes only dealt with around 20 cases per year. However, the decision to expand the use of mediation was eventually made, and the main underlying rationale was the promise of victim-offender conferencing as a 'pedagogical' and 'preventative' tool, especially in relation to young offenders.

In 1998, the Swedish Crime Prevention Council was given the mandate to explore the possibilities of an expansion of the practice of reparative (restorative) justice and tasked with establishing 32 conferencing projects across the country. In 2003, the government allocated more funds to the Crime Prevention Council, with the aim of having a mediation programme in every local municipality. The mediation service should be part of the municipalities' social welfare activities and not run through the criminal justice system per se. From 1 January 2008 onwards, all 290 municipalities in Sweden are able to offer mediation to offenders under the age of 21. The process shall be voluntary for both parties and the offender must have admitted guilt for a mediation process to be initiated (Brottsförebyggande Rådet 2008; Lag om medling 2002; Paus 2008).

Mediation takes place during the evidence collection phase of the investigation or just after its completion but has to take place before a court process is under way. The prosecutor shall be consulted to ensure that a mediation before trial does not interfere with the evidence or other aspects. This prominent role of the prosecutor is due to the Swedish criminal justice system being a mix between the inquisitorial and the adversarial models. Mediators in the Swedish initiative are a mix of paid professionals, employed by the local social services, and volunteers.

According to a law enacted in 2002 about mediation in relation to crime (Lag 2002: 445), the overall aim of the reparative meeting is to minimize the negative consequences of crime. For the offender, the aim is to achieve a better understanding/ insight with regards to the consequences of the crime and for the victim, the opportunity to work through his/her experiences. The law emphasizes this dual focus and states that mediation can never be used simply as a crime prevention tool for the offender or as a rehabilitation method for the victim, since both of those carry the risk of one party's interests being promoted at the expense of the other. Conferencing 'has' to be available to every offender under the age of 21 since 1 January 2008, the offer to attend is put to the offender either offered by police or social services. About 3,000 mediations have been completed across the country since the end of 2003. By far the most common category has been shoplifting, followed by minor assault, criminal damage, and theft. The age of the offender ranged from 6 to 54, with an average age of 15 (Brottsförebyggande Rådet 2008).

When the offender is under age, the legal guardian of the child shall be given the opportunity to attend unless there are particular reasons not to, a decision taken by the mediator. Other persons can also be invited to attend if that is seen to be helpful, however, legal representation should not attend since the aim is not to investigate a crime or solve complicated issues of damages and compensation (Brottsförebyggande Rådet 2007: 18). The facilitator can also work with other partners such as schools, local victim support and crime prevention programmes, counselling services, and so on. No offence categories are excluded according to the law, but it is recommended that cases of sexual abuse and victimless crimes such as drug use are normally not subject to such processes. Research conducted by the Crime Prevention Council (Brottsförebyggande Rådet 2008) also discovered that a certain resistance exists in Sweden against using mediation in more serious and violent crimes.

Hence, in Sweden, restorative justice is not used as an 'alternative' to other criminal justice sanctions, such as a fine or formal caution, diversion from court or police prosecution as is the case in many other jurisdictions. Instead it is used as a 'supplement' to the criminal justice process, and organized mainly through the social services, which means that it does not constitute a penal sanction or an alternative to the criminal justice system (Rytterbro 2003).

Evaluation of restorative justice in Sweden is scant, and overall, the discipline is marked by comments such as 'new practice', 'lack of knowledge about usefulness and effects in Sweden', and 'more research needed' (Rytterbro 2003). Moreover, whereas the practice of restorative justice in Norway and Finland (see below) is based on the arguments by Nils Christie and his seminal article published in 1977, *Conflict as Property*, Sweden largely ignored these developments when they took off in neighbouring countries and instead based its gradual introduction of restorative justice on existing practices primarily in the United States and New Zealand, but also England and Australia (Albrecht 2010).

NORWAY

Discussions about using mediation in criminal matters dates back to 1978, when the then Minister of Justice, Inger Louise Valle, put out a call for alternatives to imprisonment for young people and she also suggested raising the age of criminal responsibility from 14 to 15. A proposal was produced in close cooperation with child protection services and the social services, and the first pilot projects began in 1981. After an evaluation in 1990 and pressure from the Chief Prosecutor, mediation practices were expanded to include more types of cases and also to be used for people over the age of 18. However, mediation would not be used for offences that qualified for imprisonment. Importantly, the pressure to establish mediation came from government, statutory agencies, and the academic elite (Paus 2008: 8–9), as opposed to pressure from NGOs and community organizations which is the case in many other jurisdictions.

Mediation was given a statutory framework in 1991 (*Lov om megling i konfliktråd*). The law allows for mediation in both criminal cases—for which a fine or a suspended sentence would normally have been the outcome—and civil matters. There is no age restriction for participation, even though it is presumed that mediation will be most effective for those under the age of 25. Consequently, cases can be referred by both police and prosecutor, and by individuals themselves, the community, or other civil entities (Albrecht 2010; Paus 2008). The programme is called *Konfliktråd*, which can be translated as the Norwegian Mediation and Reconciliation Service. The aim of the service is to strengthen local communities to resolve minor law breaking and civil conflicts themselves, thereby contributing to local crime prevention (Albrecht 2010; Paus 2008). This reclaiming of conflicts and localized ownership of solutions is clearly based on the scholarship by Nils Christie (1977). Importantly, for the discussions in this book, mediation meetings in Norway are often large affairs and the service reflects conferencing practices much more closely than the more limited victim-offender mediation processes (Hydle and Kemény 2010). But, as mentioned earlier, the legislation regulating the practice uses the term 'mediation' and hence the adoption of the term in this section.

The number of cases mediated tripled between 1994 and 2007, from 3,272 to 9,120. The split between civil and criminal matters is almost 50/50, but police or prosecutors referred more than 80 per cent of all cases. The majority of those cases involved criminal matters but because the offender was below the age of 15, it becomes classified, and is dealt with, as a civil offence (Paus 2008: 19). The largest category of cases dealt with in 2007 was violence (17 per cent), arguments/defamation/bullying (12 per cent), property damage (17 per cent) and shoplifting (15 per cent). The majority of offenders were between 15 and 17 years of age, followed by 12 to 14 year olds, and men over 35. There are currently 22 Mediation and Reconciliation Services across Norway, employing 600 to 700 volunteer mediators. The lowest age for mediators is 18 and they may also have previous criminal convictions as long as it was more than five years ago, or ten years ago if the offence carried a prison sentence. The service is administered by the civil branch of the Department of Justice (Paus 2008: 15–17).

FINLAND

Mediation in Finland emerged during the 1970s, as a response to the high imprisonment numbers, which at the time was as high as all the other Nordic countries combined. Initiators in this jurisdiction were socially engaged academics, criminal justice practitioners, and representatives from the Lutheran church. As in Sweden, the responsibility of conducting mediations was placed with local social services and by the year 2000 mediations took place in 255 of Finland's 452 municipalities (Paus 2008: 9). Up until 2006, mediation took place without legal regulation and financial support from the state, and its practice relied on volunteers, arguably an indication of the level of community ownership of restorative justice in Finland.

Legal frameworks came into force in 2006 (*Lag om medling i straff- och civil saker 2006*). Its philosophy is very much grounded in restorative justice, with emphasis placed on repairing emotional and material harm. Referrals are made directly from the parties, from police or prosecutor, or other statutory agencies and mediation can take place both before and after police, prosecutor, and court processes. The restorative justice model in Finland is much more closely integrated into the criminal justice system than is the case in Sweden and Norway, and the outcome of mediation can have an impact on the continuation of a case. For example, the prosecutor can decide if a complete diversion from any court processes should take place (Paus 2008: 13). Mediation is run through the social services, in cooperation with the Department of Justice. There are around 25 mediation offices across Finland, with 100 employees and 900 volunteers. The number of mediations in 2008 was 9,583, which was almost two per cent of all reported crimes in the country. In contrast to many other countries, mediations in domestic violence cases are relatively common and have been deemed to be a successful intervention, but in such cases, referrals can only come from the police, not the parties themselves (Paus 2008: 16–21, Slög and Kurikka 2008).

By way of summary at this point, it is a 'particular feature of mediation in the Nordic countries that initiatives are mainly proposed by the authorities, with support from academic researchers and activists' (Paus 2008: 11). Norway and Sweden have a greater focus on young offenders, whereas Finland employs a broader remit and has a particular focus on the prison population. Moreover, mediation in Finland and Sweden fall under the social services, in cooperation with the justice sector, whereas Norway's *Konfliktråd* is managed by the justice sector (Paus 2008). Key features of restorative justice in all the Nordic countries are education, ownership, diversion, and reintegration.

CRIMINAL JUSTICE AND CONFERENCING IN THE WELFARE STATE

As mentioned in the introduction, an exploration of the use of restorative justice in Nordic countries and in any other jurisdictions arguably requires a discussion that includes a socio-cultural explanation of punishment. Restorative justice initiatives are not implemented in a vacuum and even though certain models more often than others act as blueprints, such as the New Zealand one, these still need to be adapted to local conditions (Eriksson 2009). In the Nordic countries, crime is largely viewed as having its roots in inequality, lack of education, unemployment, and social exclusion (Andersson and Nilsson 2009). Hence, responses to crime tend to focus on these larger social and structural causes, and punishment is generally less inhumane and stigmatizing than in many other countries. The consequence is arguably that restorative justice in the Nordic countries is far less controversial than in many other jurisdictions, such as the United Kingdom, Australia, and New Zealand. This largely stems from the social-democratic welfare state, which characterizes the Nordic countries, which encompasses a particular value base, reflected in their criminal justice systems *and* in their approach to restorative justice. Hence, I would argue that crime in the Nordic countries is largely viewed as having a social aetiology, with the solution to be found in educational and inclusive measures, as opposed to the criminalization of social problems, with corresponding punitive and exclusionary responses.[1]

This is an important distinction when comparing restorative justice initiatives between countries. In most jurisdictions, restorative justice is aimed in particular at young people, often as an alternative to more punitive measures, including imprisonment, operating as part of the juvenile justice system. The significance of the difference emerges when we consider that the age of criminal responsibility in England is 10 years of age, and in Ireland 7, for example. So even though the age groups involved in restorative justice in these various countries may be largely similar, the consequence of not having access to such a process varies considerably. Hence, in many jurisdictions with a low age of criminal responsibility, such as 10 years of age, restorative justice signifies an important alternative within a punitive justice system, whereas in Nordic countries, it is viewed as a pedagogical and preventative tool for those who are not normally subjected to criminal sanctions.

The majority of law-breakers that take part in a restorative justice mediation in the Nordic countries are under the age of 15, particularly in Sweden. This is significant, since the age of criminal responsibility in these countries is 15 and hence restorative justice is not an alternative to harsher sentences in the criminal courts, but one way of addressing offending behaviour of those groups who fall *outside its remit*. For example, in Sweden and Norway, child welfare legislation makes no strict distinction between child protection and youth justice. Asocial behaviour of young people under the age of 20 is seen as a child welfare problem, outside the realm of criminal justice. Neither are there organizational dividing lines between different means of intervention. Local authorities shall mainly work with social support to, and in partnership with, families, regardless of the age of the child or the reason for the intervention (Hassle and Vennerljung 2000).

By design then, restorative justice in the Nordic countries exists on the fringes of the criminal justice system, a supplement, as opposed to being integral to it. I would

[1] This may also be true for other European countries, such as the Netherlands and Belgium (see for example Aertsen et al. 2004; European Forum for Victim-Offender Mediation and Restorative Justice 2000; Vanfraechem et al. 2010), but since the focus on the chapter is on the Nordic countries, I will confine my discussion to that area.

argue that there are three reasons for this. Firstly, the age of criminal responsibility as mentioned above. Secondly, the historical and long-term influence of the welfare state viewing crime as social problems with social solutions, and thirdly—which flows on from point two—a less punitive justice system overall than in many other jurisdictions, which provides more recognition for victims, diversion from imprisonment for the absolute majority of offenders, and clearer routes to reintegration. Such a system, constructed around principles of inclusiveness, repair, and reduced stigmatization, arguably has less need for a non-punitive alternative. These different views of crime and offenders can be traced back to the particular model of welfare state that operates in the Nordic countries and can be compared with the anglophone model of welfare that will aid in illustrating these differences.

Firstly, the dominant view in Nordic countries contains that crime and victimization have their roots in social inequalities, problematic family dynamics, lack of education and meaningful employment. In essence, crime is largely viewed as a social problem that needs to be met with social solutions as opposed to punishment. This stems from long-standing cultural values of 'inclusion' that were institutionalized, embedded, given a materiality and sharpened by the particular model of social democratic welfare state that emerged in Nordic countries, particularly in the post-1945 period (Esping-Andersen 1990; Pratt 2008; Pratt and Eriksson 2012). In effect, the Nordic model helped to increase solidarity between citizens and led to high levels of trust—between citizens who do not regard each other as potential welfare 'cheats' or rivals for contested welfare benefits, as happened under the liberal model of welfare in the anglophone countries; and between individuals and the state because of the tangible benefits the universalism of this model provides (Rothstein and Uslaner 2005). Nineteenth century distinctions between deserving and undeserving poor maintained their place in anglophone societies, but much less so in Nordic countries. Meanwhile, state power came to be seen as something unwanted and restrictive in the anglophone countries—individuals should be left to make their own way in the world as far as possible, and take responsibility for their own actions (Pratt and Eriksson 2012). As this has occurred, so the role of the state in the governance of everyday life has increasingly come to be punitive and repressive. By contrast, in the Nordic countries, the power of the state is a largely accepted feature. This, in conjunction with a prominent role given to academic and justice experts, and a clear division between criminal justice policy and day-to-day politics, have allowed for a largely non-punitive approach to crime and offenders, in sharp contrast to many other countries outside of the western European context. The consequences have been that the Scandinavian welfare model, notwithstanding recent modifications and restrictions to it, has reinforced the inclusionary capabilities of these societies. It has done so by enhancing their ability to absorb, rectify, and reintegrate problem populations. In contrast, the anglophone welfare model reinforced the exclusionary tendencies of these societies, by ultimately weakening rather than strengthening social cohesion, and by further setting individuals against each other (Pratt and Eriksson 2011, 2012). Within such an inclusionary, non-punitive approach to crime in the Nordic countries, the key tool of prevention is education. Not only within the school environment but it also takes place in many spheres of life, including inside the prisons. Mediation then is used not only as a preventative tool, but a 'pedagogical' one, highlighting the importance placed on education in a broad sense, to address and prevent social problems such as offending behaviour by young people.

However, even though restorative justice in the Nordic countries is a largely uncontroversial affair (in comparison to Northern Ireland for example, see Eriksson 2009), there are two issues I would like to raise here: that of unintentional labelling children as offenders, and the role of victims. The former may arguably constitute a challenge for restorative justice in the Nordic countries, particularly for Sweden that relied on the New Zealand model and other Anglo countries as providing the blueprint for practice, and that is the labelling of young people—who would normally fall outside the net of formal intervention—as offenders. These models, designed to operate *within* a criminal justice system, or be an 'alternative' to such punitive interventions have to, by default, use the labels of 'victims' and 'offenders'. This is a reflection of operating in such close proximity to the formal criminal justice system. For Swedish practice however, this means that children who are under the age of criminal responsibility are labelled as 'offenders' when participating in mediation processes. Hence, there is a possibility that the very labels that restorative justice is trying to counteract are introduced inadvertently. Norway and Finland, relying as they are on Christie's (1977) framework, arguably employ a more inclusive and 'neutral' model, where people are 'participants', not necessarily 'offenders'.

However, even though more attention might be paid to reintegration, avoidance of labelling and education with regards to offenders in the welfare state, it is still argued that 'victims' of crime have been largely 'ignored, invisible, hidden, forgotten and even abused' (Snare 2008: 42). The victims' movement has been a key contributing factor to the establishment of restorative justice in many jurisdictions, but it has been much less vocal in Nordic countries until recently.[2] However, there are several statutory provisions for victim support in these countries, for example the Crime Victim Compensation and Support Agency (*Brottsoffermyndigheten*), established in Sweden in 1994. Much of the funding to the Agency comes from offenders, and anyone sentenced to prison has to pay 54 Euros to the fund, for the direct benefit of victims. It also coordinates research on victimology and support to victims before, during, and after their case (<http://www.brottsoffermyndigheten.se>). Moreover, if the offender is unable to pay (too young, has no money) or is unknown, the state will compensate the victims through so-called crime compensation (*brottsskadeersättning*). The law introducing such compensation came into force in 1978 even though the actual Agency took longer to be established. So, victims in Sweden have a right to compensation, but, as the government recognized, there is still a need to address the emotional harm of crime and the needs of those victims whose offender falls outside the remit of the criminal justice system.

Hence, even though Nordic countries are arguably doing better than most anglophone countries, with legislation around mandatory compensation for victims of crime, this does not apply to those whose offender is under age. And because of the relatively high age of criminal responsibility, 15, this leaves many victims without any

[2] Particularly in relation to domestic violence and so-called 'honour killings', receiving much attention in the early 2000s.

kind of compensation, be it monetary or symbolic. Nor can they apply to the Crime Victim Compensation and Support Agency, since it only compensates in relation to personal injury, leaving victims of theft, burglary, and other property crimes on the wayside. However, such monetary compensation can be paid as a result of mediation, even if the offender is under age. Moreover, and perhaps another feature of the welfare state, if the offender is under the age of 12, insurance companies can cover the money to be paid to victims (Byström 2008: 54). These paradoxical features—little support for victims whose offender is younger than 15 years of age and a relatively strong position of victims within the traditional criminal justice system—are arguably another reason why restorative justice was introduced in the first place, but remains on the periphery.

CONCLUSION

As noted in the introduction to this chapter, there is a need to view restorative justice initiatives—their form, scope, and effectiveness—within the particular socio-cultural environment in which they have been implemented. This chapter raised the argument that restorative justice processes will differ quite significantly within jurisdictions that are characterized by a punitive approach to crime and to offenders, in contrast to countries characterized by much more inclusive and non-punitive responses. Criminal justice practitioners in the different Nordic countries may very well not view their own system as non-punitive, but when viewed through a comparative lens, particularly in relation to anglophone countries, such differences emerge starkly. Hence, the form of restorative conferencing in a jurisdiction will not only depend on needs of victims, offenders, and their families in relation to crime and victimization, but also reflect the over-arching socio-cultural context of any one criminal justice system.

Importantly, crime in the Nordic countries is largely viewed as having its roots in inequality, poverty, a lack of education, and exclusion. Hence, crime 'prevention' tends to focus on these larger social and structural causes. Crime is seen mainly as a social problem in the Nordic countries and this should be put in contrast to countries like the United Kingdom and Australia, where many social problems are criminalized. The point is this: in a jurisdiction where social problems stand a greater risk of being criminalized is where restorative justice—which emphasizes the larger social context of crime and its consequences—will be most needed. And in a jurisdiction where the reverse is true—crime is seen largely as a social problem—there will arguably be less need for and excitement around restorative justice. Basically, there is less need for an alternative to a punitive criminal justice system when that system is not punitive in the first place.

REFERENCES

Aertsen, I., Mackay, R., Pelikan, C., Willemsens, J. and Wright, M. (2004), *Rebuilding Community Connections—Mediation and Restorative Justice in Europe* (Strasbourg: Council of Europe).

Albrecht, B. (2010), 'Multicultural Challenges for Restorative Justice: Mediators' Experiences from Norway and Finland', *Journal of Scandinavian Studies in Criminology and Crime Prevention*, 11(1), pp 3–24.

Andersson, R. and Nilsson, R. (2009), *Svensk Kriminalpolitik* [Swedish Criminal Justice] (Stockholm: Liber).

Brottsförebyggande Rådet [The Crime Prevention Council] (2007), *Medling Vid Brott* [Mediation in relation to crime] (Stockholm: Brottsförebyggande Rådet).

Brottsförebyggande Rådet [The Crime Prevention Council] (2008), *Medling Igår, Idag Och i Morgon: En Kort Skrift om Medling Vid Brott* [Mediation yesterday, today and tomorrow] (Stockholm: Brottsförebyggande Rådet).

Byström, M. (2008), 'Medlingsverksamheten i Örnsköldsvik, Sverige: Ett Arbetssätt Vid Höga Skadeståndskrav på Underåriga', in *Restorative Justice in the Nordic Countries: NSfK's 22nd Contact Seminar 2008*, Reykjavik, Iceland 31 October–2 November, pp 53–5.

Christie, N. (1977), 'Conflict as Property', *British Journal of Criminology*, (17), pp 1–15.

Engel, C. (2009), *Fran Utopi till Praktisk Handling: En Studie av Reparative Rattvisa i Arbetet Med Hemlosa pa Bostallet* (Stockholm: Ersta Skondal Hogskola).

Eriksson, A. (2009), *Justice in Transition: Community Restorative Justice in Northern Ireland* (Cullumpton: Willan Publishing).

Esping-Andersen, G. (1990), *The Three Worlds of Welfare Capitalism* (Cambridge: Polity Press).

European Forum for Victim-Offender Mediation and Restorative Justice (ed.) (2000), *Victim-Offender Mediation in Europe. Making Restorative Justice Work* (Leuven: Leuven University Press).

Hassle, S., and Vennerljung, B. (2000), *Child Welfare in Sweden: An Overview* (Stockholm University: Sweden).

Hydle, I. and Kemény, S. (2010), 'From Local Trial Projects to State Owned Services—Empirical Research on Restorative Justice in Norway', in Vanfraechem, I., Aertsen, I. and Willemsens, J. (eds.), *Restorative Justice Realities: Empirical Research in a European Context* (The Hague: Eleven International Publishing), pp 207–17.

Lag om medling (2002), *Om Medling Vid Anledning av Brott* , Justitiedepartementet, Sweden.

Lag om medling i straff- och civil saker (2006), Justitieministeriet, Finland.

Pali, B. and Madsen, K. (2011), 'Dangerous Liaisons?: A Feminist and Restorative Approach to Sexual Assault', *Temida*, 14(1), pp 49–65.

Paus, K. (2008), 'Restorative Justice i Norden: Regelverk og Iverksettining', in *Restorative Justice in the Nordic Countries: NSfK's 22nd Contact Seminar 2008*, Reykjavik, Iceland October 31–2 November, pp 6–26.

Pratt, J. (2008), 'Scandinavian Exceptionalism in an Era of Penal Excess: The Nature and Roots of Scandinavian Exceptionalism', *British Journal of Criminology*, 48, pp 199–37.

Pratt, J. and Eriksson, A. (2011), '"Mr Larsson is Walking Out Again": The Origin and Development of the Scandinavian Prison System', *Australian and New Zealand Journal of Criminology*, 44(7), pp 7–23.

Pratt, J. and Eriksson, A. (2012), *Contrasts in Punishment: An Explanation of Anglophone Excess and Nordic Exceptionalism* (Oxford: Routledge).

Rothstein, B. and Uslaner, E. (2005), 'All For One: Equality, Corruption and Social Trust', *World Politics*, 58(1), pp 41–72.

Rytterbro, L. (2003), 'Victim and Offender Viewed from the Perspective of Mediation', *Journal of Scandinavian Studies in Criminology and Crime Prevention*, 4(1), pp 101–22.

Slög, P. and Kurikka, K. (2008), 'Situational Aspects and Experiences from Mediation: Practical Examples and Observations Based on Research', in *Restorative Justice in the Nordic Countries: NSfK's 22nd Contact Seminar 2008*, Reykjavik, Iceland, 31 October–2 November, pp 56–61.

Snare, A. (2008), 'Recidivism and Restorative Justice', in *Restorative Justice in the Nordic Countries: NSfK's 22nd Contact Seminar 2008*, Reykjavik, Iceland, 31 October–2 November, pp 42–52.

Sundell, K. and Häggman, U. (1999), *Familjerådslag i Sverige* (Stockholm: Stockholms stad FoU rapport).

Sundell, K. and Vinnerljung, B. (2004), 'Outcomes of Family Group Conferencing in Sweden: A 3-year Follow-Up', *Child Abuse & Neglect*, 28, pp 267–87.

Vanfraechem, I., Aertsen, I. and Willemsens, J. (eds.) (2010), *Restorative Justice Realities: Empirical Research in a European Context* (Den Haag: Eleven International Publishing).

14

MOST THINGS LOOK BETTER WHEN ARRANGED IN A CIRCLE

FAMILY GROUP CONFERENCING EMPOWERS SOCIETAL DEVELOPMENTS IN THE NETHERLANDS

Rob van Pagée, Jan van Lieshout, and Annemieke Wolthuis

INTRODUCTION

In the Netherlands, restorative justice developments took off rather modestly, but the success of family group conferencing (FGC) increases year by year. Conferences are mainly organized by the 'Eigen Kracht Centrale', an independent foundation that operates nationwide. Over the years, the organization has constructed an effective infrastructure for the use of FGC. The Dutch name for FGC, *Eigen Kracht*, reflects the capacity that people have to harness their own (*eigen*) strength (*kracht*) when it comes to taking responsibility and making a plan, summoning the resources of their own family, friends, and other people in their social environment (<http://ww.eigen-kracht.nl>). Eigen Kracht-conferences are employed in multiple areas, as each situation that requires a plan to be made and decisions to be taken, deserves a conference. About 1,000 conferences are organized per year in the Netherlands. They are organized for parents, juveniles, families, students, patients with severe and chronic illnesses, homeless people, school dropouts, patients in mental health care, tenants, prisoners, people who are at risk of being evicted, neighbourhood residents, mentally or physically challenged people, and perpetrators and victims of a crime. Eigen Kracht-conferences are available to individuals as well as to groups, neighbourhoods, and communities (Van Pagée 2003).

Since 2003, the Eigen Kracht Centrale has strived to obtain a legal mandate for FGCs in the Netherlands. In March 2011, the Dutch Parliament voted unanimously in favour of an amendment that gives citizens the opportunity to construct a plan of action when state intervention in relation to child protection is imminent. Families are allowed six weeks to come up with their own plan or to adapt an existing plan. To achieve this, they will make an appeal to relatives, in-laws, and others who are part of their social network (Handelingen 2011).

Politicians emphasize the appeal that is made on citizens. Citizens can shoulder responsibility in their circle of friends and they can help to find a solution for conflict situations. This will result in citizens who take control over their own problems. Moreover, social cohesion will increase. This can also contribute to the well-being of children, for example when people who care offer support, when out-of-home placement can be avoided, or when foster care within their own network is promoted. Currently the relationship between government and citizens is under discussion in the Netherlands and elsewhere. For bureaucratic reasons and because of the enormous costs of public services, the welfare state requires more responsibility from the side of citizens to contribute more to public provisions that are available by right.

This chapter focuses on a conferencing scheme that enables social systems like families, school communities, and neighbourhood groups to instigate their own solutions for problems, mutual tensions, and conflicts. It deals with problems or conflicts which are often a precursor for, or related to, criminal behaviour, but are (mainly) taking place outside of the criminal justice system. At first the main restorative justice developments in the Netherlands over the last decades will be discussed. This is followed by an explanation of how conferencing operates, with a special focus on the mission, vision, and the history of the 'Eigen Kracht' organization and its working methods. Furthermore, new developments and strategies in the Dutch context of restorative justice and conferencing are described. After that results of evaluation research are shown to get an insight into the numbers and satisfaction rates. The whole process makes it possible to address the meaning of conferences for citizenship: what do participants have to say about their role? Finally, the relationship between the provisions of the welfare state and social systems, such as families, networks, and neighbourhood groups is discussed.

RESTORATIVE JUSTICE DEVELOPMENTS

Restorative justice developments in the Netherlands started slowly, but there are positive restorative developments in different social fields. The EU Framework Decision on the status of victims in criminal procedures of 2001 as well as project evaluations have contributed to a policy decision in 2007 by the Minister of Justice that all victims of a criminal offence get an offer to participate in a so-called 'victim-offender conversation'. This is a form of victim-offender mediation (VOM), mainly focused to bring the offender and the victim together with an independent mediator. The responsible organization is 'Slachtoffer In Beeld (SIB)', an independent institution linked to the victim support organization in the Netherlands (Slachtofferhulp Nederland). The public prosecutor can refer offenders to SIB for a victim-offender conversation. Officially this form of mediation operates outside the criminal justice system, since its results cannot have an impact on the criminal procedure. In practice, a short overview of the conversation is sent to the public prosecutor and shows that prosecutors and judges do take this into account when making further decisions (Van Burik et al. 2010).

About 1,000 victim-offender conversations are conducted per year. At the same time, many other restorative justice initiatives that have been started and were evaluated positively, have been discontinued or have had to find financial means on their own (Blad 2011; Wolthuis and Wiersma 2010). These experiments included well appreciated and positively evaluated pilots with conferencing. The Dutch government is still reluctant in making more long term decisions on continuation of successful projects and experiments done for example in the youth detention centres (Wolthuis and Vandenbroucke 2009) or at the level of the public prosecutors (Dierx 2010). However, restorative justice initiatives are slowly becoming more visible in the Netherlands. They mainly started from a bottom up approach since many initiatives and pilots with VOM and conferencing have started locally.

A project for restorative mediation was started in 1997 by probation officers and the Dutch victim support organization. After a judgment had been passed, they offered well prepared discussions between victims and offenders, especially to allow them to come to terms with what had happened. Four years later, the introduction of conferences happened independently. 'Real Justice' initiators in the Netherlands have been very active since the 1990s and introduced the Real Justice method based on the American example with roots in Australia (http://www.realjustice.org; Wachtel 1997). The Real Justice method of conferencing (working with a large network in a circle by following a certain script) was successful especially when implemented in schools and in criminal cases of first-time juvenile offenders. In the Netherlands, when young persons have committed misdemeanours or certain types of minor crimes, they are given the chance to keep a clean record by accepting a task or an activity that is aimed at restoration (so-called 'Halt'). Taking part in a conference can be such an activity. Within five years, with financial contributions from the government and thanks to some enthusiastic school boards, (Real Justice) conferences were organized in about ten regions of the Netherlands in connection to misbehaviour and criminal behaviour of young persons, in parallel to a possible legal procedure.

Other initiatives involving restorative justice are taking place at the level of the police, public prosecutor, and courts, and locally at detention centres. The police had local initiatives in different cities or provinces such as Tilburg, Amsterdam, and Friesland. Sometimes these initiatives are very successful, but often they are run by one or two active persons. If these key persons move on, initiatives tend to disappear. Since there is no structural embedding or finances, many are also depending on local funding. This resulted in the development of local projects which often disappeared again after a few years due to lack of funds. In 2002, a Decision by Public Prosecutors was filed which stated openness towards mediation, but it was not accompanied by active policies. Therefore, not much is happening at this level, although there are some active prosecutors who are involved in mediation, for example in Maastricht. The office in Utrecht had a specific pilot, but this stopped after a few months only, due to lack of funds and no concrete government policy.

In the closed youth detention centres (Youth Custodial Institutions) one initiative is also looking for ways on how to address issues such as shame, guilt, and taking responsibility. Experiments with developmental restorative justice skills for delinquent youth have been carried out in several detention centres. One of them (Teylingereind in Sassenheim) has been working with victim-offender mediation for several years now. They also run restorative justice courses in which the actual offence and talking about shame and responsibility take a central place (Wolthuis and Vandenbroucke 2010). There is also a successful restorative justice pilot in the adult prison in Nieuwegein (Van Rhijn 2007).

CONFERENCING

From its creation in 2000 the Eigen Kracht Centrale mainly contributed to Real Justice conferences in some (mostly local) pilots. Real Justice operated in the beginning mainly in the field of criminal offences. Unlike Eigen Kracht-conferences, in cases of Real Justice conferences coordinators from within the system were employed: school officials and police officers for example. The strategy was aimed at introducing restorative justice in the criminal justice system. That strategy did not work, mainly because the Minister of Justice decided on the development of victim-offender conversations in criminal cases and Real Justice projects were not funded any longer. In 2004, 2006 and 2007 research results on the Dutch conferencing projects with youth were published. The recommendations of the researchers imply that conferences offer an important supplement to youth criminal law, but the researchers also note the lack of structure in relation to criminal law (Hokwerda 2004; Steketee et al. 2006).

The foundation for most of these conferences was laid by the Eigen Kracht Centrale. In the period 2001–2006, 542 cases were registered by the coordinators. The data might have served as a foundation for a broader approach and a firmer implementation in criminal law, or in education (Van Beek and Grambergen 2007). This broader implementation did not happen: all government investment in the local projects was stopped, including the earlier restorative justice project from 1997. A choice was made to focus mainly on victim-offender conversations.[1] Because the Netherlands are bound to the Framework Decision (2001) of the European Union with regard to the position of victims in criminal justice, mediation in criminal cases has to be promoted. The core of these discussions is a dialogue about consequences, motives, and questions regarding the crime (Blad 2011). On condition of voluntary participation, this conversation may supplement the criminal lawsuit. Possibly, the result of the conversation has an impact when a criminal procedure has yet to take place. Conferencing is thus currently not a serious option in the Dutch criminal law policy despite the research on conversations which gives a positive image of the practice that has been built (Van Burik et al. 2010).

[1] A letter of the Ministry of Interior and Kingdom Relations d.d. 18-9-2006 (5400790/06/DSP) to the Parliament about achieving the Dutch policy regarding agreement 2001/220/JBZ (juridical position of the victim) of the European Union.

From 2009 onwards, the Eigen Kracht Centrale stated its independent position and made use of independent coordinators for restorative conferences, which were then called Eigen Kracht-conferences. The restorative character was built in a community development strategy. Eigen Kracht-conferences focus on people, inclusion, and participation. Some of the main messages are: 'People need people', 'Inclusion is the starting point', 'Participation is the key', and 'Mutual self reliance of citizens is the sky-line'. In that framework citizens are able to retain maximum control over their own lives, which means that they decide and they make the plans. Conferencing is a decision model. It is common knowledge that citizens have access to a lot of 'strength'—through their social network, their own circle of people.

The Eigen Kracht Centrale has an infrastructure of coordinators spread throughout the country. The coordinators are fellow-citizens who support families in the organization of their conference. On top of their everyday activities, they organize at least one conference a year. Citizens applying for a conference indicate what kind of coordinator would best suit their situation. Gender, religion, and age are some characteristics they may ask for (Van der Horst et al. 2011). Facilitating conferences does not require knowledge of the social care system, nor the educational or criminal justice system. People who are interested may be of all ages; have higher, average, or hardly any education; and have very different professional backgrounds. At each conference, they are coached by the project manager, a member of the Eigen Kracht Centrale. At regional and national meetings they improve their skills. Currently 500 coordinators are available in the Netherlands, speaking 89 languages and dialects, including sign language. In general, coordinators find their work satisfactory and are often active over a long period of time (Eigen Kracht Centrale 2011). Coordinators receive a fee based on the number of hours that they spend on facilitating a conference. Conferences including a large number of people may take up to 30 hours.

Eigen Kracht-conferences occur in a number of ways. There are conferences for individuals and families with social problems. There are also restorative conferences where victims and perpetrators, each with their own network, discuss what happened and try to restore the damage that resulted from a misdemeanour or a crime. In addition, there are conferences within neighbourhoods and districts, to discuss mutual tensions and exclusion or problems within schools. The purpose of each conference is that participants make a plan together, which enables them to tackle their problems. The coordinator helps to widen the circle. He/she contributes to the preparations by explaining the model to all participants, by inviting them, and by asking them what they need to do in order to participate safely. The coordinator also asks if they need certain information for making a plan and sees to it that such information is available at the conference. The coordinator also takes care of some practical matters, like a room for the conference, food, and drinks.

A conference meeting is divided in three parts. During the first part of the conference, the Eigen Kracht-coordinator explains to the group the problematic situation which is the cause for the gathering. Government officials, or professionals speaking on their behalf, attend the first part. They express their concerns about the situation but also make their knowledge available to the participants. The issues may range from health to welfare, justice, education, labour, and other topics. During this part of the conference, the professionals share information and they explain why a plan has to be made and, if necessary, what kind of help is available. The second part is called 'private time', during which the plan is actually made. Neither the professionals nor the Eigen Kracht-coordinator are present during this section of the conference. The person involved and his/her family and friends, the support persons then discuss their feelings and viewpoints concerning the problem at hand. They negotiate restorative plans, take decisions, and come to agreements about what to do to resolve the problem which has brought them there. In the third part of the conference, the plan is presented to the coordinator and sometimes professional workers, representing the society, or to a statutory representative in cases of child protection. Support from professionals may be part of the plan, if required by the family group. Finally, agreements are made among all the participants as to who does what, who will meet with whom if the plan does not work out as intended, and when an evaluation meeting will be held. The coordinator has the responsibility to put the plan in writing and to send it to all those concerned (Van der Horst et al. 2011: 67).

When restoration is needed in case of criminal behaviour or school incidents, or if a large group of people who hardly know each other are asked to participate in a conference, the work method may differ slightly. These conferences follow a fixed script. Usually there is no private time. In these conferences, the first part is about sharing opinions and feelings about what happened. In the second part, the participants formulate a plan that contributes to restoring relations or a solution to the problems that exist. They also make agreements about, for instance, the way in which damage can be repaired. The third part is informal. While the coordinator puts the plan in writing, the participants are invited to have a drink and then to sign the plan. The main principles, such as the position of the independent Eigen Kracht-coordinator or the 'ownership' of the plan, are the same in all types of conferences. Four weeks later, the coordinator contacts the main participants of the conference to inquire about the progress in the completion of the agreements. Three months after the conference an independent research bureau interviews participants in order to gather information on the progress and execution of the plan. This is done in the framework of continuous research into the functioning of the conferences (Gramberg 2011; Van Beek 2007).

NEW DEVELOPMENTS AND STRATEGIES

A RESTORATIVE JUSTICE FORUM

In November 2010, a forum named Restorative Justice Nederland was officially founded (<http://www.restorativejustice.nl>). It actually started in 2001, but mostly led a dormant existence until 2010. The Dutch and Flemish Journal of Restorative Justice (*Tijdschrift voor Herstelrecht*) on the contrary featured a successful discussion on restorative justice theory and practice. This is partly due to input from Belgium, where access to the criminal justice system and/or judge is complemented with access to restorative justice (Blad 2010). The foundation of the new Dutch forum gave a renewed boost to restorative justice in the Netherlands. This happened through introducing restorative practices in the full array of conflicts: in neighbourhoods, at school, at work, right up to penal justice, and spreading and sharing information between these fields.

Within a few months, over 50 persons, usually as delegates from their organizations, participated in periodical meetings that are characterized by the ideas 'connection, innovation, broader approach, and dynamic' (Leijten 2011). Although criminal justice is not ignored, the interest in introducing restorative justice at schools, neighbourhoods, and prisons is more prominent. It seems that this approach creates fertile bedding for restorative justice in general in the country. An important goal for the new forum is developing support from various social organizations and bringing persons together who, with strength and creativity, 'take their own responsibility for their conflicts'. Most crucially it is about the embedding of restorative practice systematically.

A THREEFOLD GROWTH

The increase of conferences is characterized by a threefold growth. Firstly, there has been an increase in numbers. The yearly growth was never less than 20 per cent and often over 30 per cent. We can now draw from experience with conferencing from about 4,000 registered examples. Secondly, the number of domains in which families become active increases. As in international developments, the safety of children was the main issue in the Netherlands: a court order for child protection was initially the most common instance to initiate an Eigen Kracht-conference. Presently, there are other issues that lead to conferences, such as the disturbed development of children, neighbourhood nuisance, a lack of security in the social environment, or domestic violence. Most conferences still focus on the problematic situation of a child, but more and more adult cases are referred.

Thirdly, there is a growing conviction that the conference model strengthens the position of citizens in need of care. The present government policy intends that a family requiring care from the government will first search in its own network to find what help is available. This results in a more equal sharing of rights and responsibilities in the relationship between state, institutions, and citizens: responsibility for the public domain in society is shared by all.

FOUR STRATEGIES

Against this background, four strategies to promote conferencing were used by the Eigen Kracht Centrale. Originally the growth of conferences took place through hearsay. In a number of places across the Netherlands a high number of conferences were organized in order to gain experience and to develop good practice. The information gained through those conferences, about the running of conferences as well as about the results achieved, was passed from the bottom up by professionals and experts. Until 2007, this strategy prevailed. In that year, the landmark of 1,000 conferences was passed.

In the meantime, a second strategy was developed: embedding the conference model in the procedures of subsidized institutions (social work, youth care, child protection). The decision making about the help that is offered to clients/participants in the care system is dominated by professionals. This makes it hard for citizens in need of help to voice their own opinion on what help they need. Furthermore once they have become a client, this professional dominance is maintained by a combination of diagnostics and therapy as defined by protocols. The individual fades into the background as far as decision making is concerned. Nevertheless, it seems possible to make the conference a turning point in the procedures within institutions. Boards of youth care organizations and especially the government proved to be able to make this second strategy successful. In 2009, in Overijssel, one of the Dutch provinces, a vision statement was drawn up, in which the government and the executing organizations name the conference model as a starting point for initiating care by the system. The youth care and child protection organizations offer a conference with a standard procedure, which means: 'The family has a right to choose to make their own plan in case of problems. This right does not change (provided it remains within a safe and legal framework) at the time that the community and/or the family indicate that problems exist that require support or intervention of third parties' (Province Overijssel 2009: 4).[2]

This is a major step toward a third strategy: finding a legal mandate for the right of citizens to make a plan in their own circle first, before outsiders/representatives of the law or civil institutions, impose *their* plans. Actually, this strategy is an extension of the second, meaning that when the conference has been embedded structurally in the care that is offered at various places, a formal order or a legal regulation is a logical consequence. The legal amendment that was accepted in March 2011 (as mentioned before), is a big step forward in achieving this approach.

The fourth strategy consists of registration of the conferences for research purposes. This strategy has been employed from the very beginning and supports the other three. It facilitates the support of organizations when they want to make a shift in their policy from offer-orientated thinking to demand-orientated thinking.

RESEARCH AND RESULTS

After five years of research into the actual data, the general lines concerning the usability, procedures, and results of the conferences have become clear. New research questions arose: what are the long term effects of family plans? Does it make a difference whether or not a conference was held, with regards to the care that was offered and the result of that care? Does a conference change the cost of the care offered? Does the conference model contribute to active citizenship?

[2] Unofficial translation of the relevant paragraph of the vision statement made by the province of Overijssel.

Gradually, such research has been initiated or activated by the Eigen Kracht Centrale. Results showed that the safety of children remains intact over the years and that the number of care items in the family decreases drastically after a conference, much faster than without a conference (Wijnen-Lunenberg et al. 2008). The research also provided remarkable insights in the relationship between professionals and the social network. For instance, citizens and professionals use the same criteria in relation to safety. Professionals get to know more people in the network of the client and there is a greater chance of cooperation. During the first year following the conference, the family often grows stronger and gradually starts pulling the strings which are needed to cope with the previous problems.

Because of the strategy of continuous research, the Eigen Kracht Centrale produces a yearly report on the data of Eigen Kracht-conferences. The last report (Gramberg 2011) illustrates the overall trend of the previous reports (2001–2009), therefore we present the most important findings from 2010 below.

WHAT AND HOW IN 2010?

A total of 826 conferences were registered in 2010 (Gramberg 2011).[3] After the first contact with a coordinator, 72 per cent of all cases end in a formal conference. In 19 per cent of the cases, activating the family system is enough: a formal conference is no longer necessary. Only nine per cent of the conferences come to a halt. Overall there were 7,191 persons involved in 593 conferences in 2010.

The initiative for starting a conference was mainly taken by organizations (80 per cent). In 20 per cent of the cases the initiative was taken by a family, from which 9 per cent by the main person him-/herself (Gramberg 2011: 16). Over the last five years, the proportions gradually changed: the number of applications from outside organizations doubled. Families and citizens in general seem to have discovered the model. They get increasingly familiar with the possibility of making their own plan when they enter the care system (Gramberg 2011: 77). Furthermore almost all families that participated in a conference in 2010 have had experiences with social workers, some of them (18 per cent) for over five years. In half of the families this concerns youth care and situations in which intervention measures are or have been considered. Only 11 per cent of the families had never had any involvement with social care before (Gramberg 2011: 17).

Children are the main protagonists in nearly half (49 per cent) of the conferences. The other conferences are about problems of adults in combination with worries about the children (32 per cent). The remaining conferences deal exclusively with problems of adults (19 per cent). The fact that the conferences focus not solely on children, means that often multiple problems are involved (an average of three per conference) (Gramberg 2011: 17). This is what makes conferences special from the social care point of view: the people in the social environment of the family are usually aware of these multiple problems. They have their (unique) history with the family and often

[3] The number of referrals is a lot higher, but for many conferences the results and hence the statistical data were only available in 2011.

see the connection between, for instance, behavioural problems of the child and over-burdening, divorce, or unemployment and/or addiction of a parent (Van Beek and Muntendam 2011).

Social workers and other professionals, who generally deal with family problems from the point of view of their own specialized field, logically consider mostly the aspects that belong to their specialization and do not have the knowledge to see the connections that are known to the network. Furthermore, and more importantly however, is the fact that a majority of the professionals exclusively deal with the 'client' or the 'nucleus family'. This implies that they seldom (want to, or can, or are allowed to) get in touch with the other family members and with others in the neighbourhood of that family. Social workers mainly work for their own specialized organization and lack a platform where they can make decisions on cooperation at another (joint) level. When surveying the registered problems that are dealt with in conferences, it becomes apparent that much is to be gained in the field of cooperation between professionals in the care system (Van Beek 2007).

Each conference starts with a number of concrete questions. In 2010, as in preceding years, the questions concerning children were mainly about their education and their behaviour. Other subjects are their residence, sometimes in conjunction with visitation arrangements of parents or others. School related problems occur frequently as well. Where adults are concerned, there is more emphasis on independence issues often in combination with housing and financial management (Gramberg 2011: 18).

During the preparations, children take part in discussing these questions. Unless it is absolutely impossible, they are preferably present at the (their) conference. A mere 21 per cent are younger than four years old and 35 per cent are older than 13, the remainder are in between (Gramberg 2011: 22). In 2010, 901 (14 per cent) minors attended a conference. They were either (part of) the issue for which a conference had been started or came along as a supporter (Gramberg 2011: 44).

OUTCOME AND FOLLOW UP

It is an exception for a conference to end without unanimity about a plan. In 2010, 95 per cent of the families made a plan. They laid down the agreements in writing. In 4 per cent the plan was not yet finalized, because it was unclear what resources would be available. It is not necessary for the whole group to be involved in the agreements: sometimes only a part of the social network shoulders the plan. In a very limited number of cases (1 per cent = 4 cases) the questions were returned without a plan (Gramberg 2011: 75).

Per plan, families can make a large number of agreements. A plan holds an average of 18 agreements, spread out over a number of interconnected areas: housing and care, finances, leisure time, and therapy. As far as children are concerned, one of the frequent questions is whether the child can stay at home (with the parents) or if they should move to another place. A change of residence often occurs: 28 per cent of the plans contain a change of address. There are some indications that families choose less intensive (41 per cent) or equal (25 per cent) care in comparison to professional agreements. Research shows that families and professionals use the same criteria on safety of children. Professionals indicate that they appreciate the plans as equally valuable or more valuable and more creative. In about 34 per cent of the cases the families decide on more intensive help than before (Gramberg 2011: 45).

The majority of the families set a date for a meeting where (a part of) the family reconvenes to see to what extent the agreements have been kept and if some of them need to be adjusted. Such a meeting is lacking in only 7 per cent of the cases. Furthermore, 87 per cent of the plans provides for contingencies in case the matter runs a different course than was expected (Gramberg 2011: 46).

Participants are contacted twice after the meeting. First, a month after the conference to speed up the family when there seems to be a slow start of the execution of the plan. The second time it is mainly for research purposes. The follow up of the proceedings is handed over to the researchers. During the follow up, contact has been made with an average of over three persons and 93 per cent of these interviews took place within six months following the conference.

Regardless of the position of the respondents, 37 per cent reply that the plan has been executed in its entirety and 49 per cent explain that at least parts of the plan have been executed. About 9 per cent reply that the plan has not been executed at all (Gramberg 2011: 50). The families that were interviewed, and their social network, think the situation after the conference is better than before (69 per cent) or is the same (17 per cent). Only 6 (main persons/family) or 8 per cent (people who refer) say the situation is worse than before (Gramberg 2011: 52).

LOOKING BACK AT THE CONFERENCE

After the conference, the participants are given a questionnaire. They are asked to indicate whether they, each from their own position and viewpoint, were sufficiently prepared for the conference and whether they were able to realize their objectives. The positive responses to these questionnaires were 52 per cent of professional social care workers, 60 per cent from the part of the families and social networks (Gramberg 2011: 55) and 48 per cent of the minors (p 69).

In the past, research has been done to find out what professionals who propose a conference to a family are interested in. The result showed that they want to know what role they can play, what the proceedings are at a conference in general, and at their own conference in particular, and what it means for families to contribute to the solution with their own resources. Professionals look back with satisfaction on all these items. They get sufficient information on their role (98 per cent) and know enough about the subject matter of the conference (99 per cent) (Gramberg 2011: 55). On average, they rate the conference 7.6 on a 1 to 10 scale. The plan gets an average rate of 7.4. The professionals pay attention to the feasibility and the clarity of the plan, as well as to the safety and the cooperation from the social network. The marks 7 and 8 are given most (p 56). From the beginning in 2001, the plans are valued between 7.2 and 7.6. The coordinator and the region manager, the person who accepts the plan and who coaches the coordinator, get high marks from the professionals, respectively 7.7 and 8.1. What matters in the contact with both is clarity, speed, and patience (p 58). 273 minors gave their opinion on the conferences that were registered in 2010. Three quarters of the children mention that they have been well listened to. They rate the conference, the plan, and the coordinator 7.9 or higher (Gramberg 2011: 69–71).

The members of the families and the social networks that participated in the conference give high marks as well: 7.8 for the conference, 7.8 for the private time, 7.9 for the plan, and 8.1 for the coordinator (Gramberg 2011: 65–67). These ratings are given by people around the main person, such as parents, brothers, and sisters (28 per cent), but also grandparents, uncles or aunts, cousins (25 per cent), or friends (22 per cent) (p 61). In the classical and traditional forms of care (youth care, psychiatry) these categories seldom occur in the contact between social care worker and client.

In the conferences, these connected persons indicate that they have contributed to the conference by providing their own information (67 per cent), by having been able to ask what they wanted (93 per cent), by having been able to say what they wanted to contribute (92 per cent), and by being able to be part of a solution (85 per cent yes, 13 per cent partly). These outcomes indicate a large strength in the social environment of people or families who experience problems. Questioning whether they felt at ease during the conference, 87 per cent showed to be positive and 10 per cent rather positive (Gramberg 2011: 62–65).

CONCLUSION: CONFERENCING BUILDS A BRIDGE

As mentioned before, the family system and the professional system do not mesh easily. During the last ten years, Eigen Kracht-conferences have been able to connect the two systems increasingly. This happens by making use of fellow citizens who, from an independent position, make a connection between people in trouble on the one side and a professional institution on the other side. This also includes criminal matters. Although the conferences so far are mainly used outside the criminal justice setting, they often deal with matters that are a starting point for or are in fact already criminal offences (think about violent incidents, domestic, in the neighbourhood, or in schools). At the same time the conferencing method described is able to fit into the current criminal justice system; what is lacking is a clear political choice on this matter.

Finally a 'plan by all' emerges. The independent coordinator balances the professional system with the capacity of the family or social system. In fact, the family's responsibility for the problems that have arisen, or that of a perpetrator (group) for the misbehaviour or crime is returned to its source. This means a shift in perception: people, who were considered earlier to be the cause of the problem, now provide the solution in the form of an agreed plan (Ghaeminia 2010).

At the same time it is no less than a shift in power. Often professional institutions take hold of the problems of their clients and then steer them towards a solution. The independent coordinator strives to divide the power equally between structured formal bureaucracy and its procedures on the one side, and the unique family or social system which functions informally and knows its own ways to settle matters on the other. Conferencing enables dialogue and gives a meaning to solutions in the form of a shared plan. Implementing conferencing is reclaiming the decision rights of citizens where it concerns their own problems or conflicts.

Increasingly, people recognize the way in which they, by means of a conference, exercise human rights and practice democracy. Conferencing gives people the opportunity to discuss together what is going on, to share opinions and feelings, and to understand each other. It enables the claiming of rights and taking responsibility. It connects people and makes social cooperation possible. The circle proves to work.

REFERENCES

Blad, J. (2010), 'Tien jaar Tijdschrift voor Herstelrecht, editorial', *Tijdschrift voor Herstelrecht*, 10(4), pp 7–13.

Blad, J. (2011), 'Herstelrecht in Nederland? Voorlopig veel Nadruk op Gesprekken', *Tijdschrift voor Herstelrecht*, 11(1), pp 40–53.

Dierx, J. (2010), '"De Blauwe Plekken Moeten Liefst Nog niet Zijn Verkleurd": Strafrechtelijke Bemiddeling in Maastricht', *Tijdschrift voor Herstelrecht*, 10(3), pp 53–8.

Eigen Kracht (2011), *Jaarverslag 2010* (Zwolle: EKC).

Eigen Kracht Centrale (2011), *State of Affairs Eigen Kracht Centrale* (Zwolle: EKC).

Ghaeminia, S. (2010), 'In een Eigen Kracht-Conferentie Bedenken Familie en Vrienden Zelf Oplossingen voor een Familielid in Nood', *Dagblad Trouw*, 20 January 2010.

Gramberg, P. (2011), *Eigen Kracht-Conferenties voor Families en Individuen: Jaarcijfers 2010* (Voorhout: WESP).

Handelingen Tweede Kamer der Staten Generaal (2011), *Amendement 32 015 of Book 1 of the Civil Code, the Law on Civil Rights, Requisitioning, The Law on Child Welfare and the Law on Foster Child Care Law, in Connection with Revised Child Care Measures*, by MOP J. Voordewind c.s.

Hokwerda, Y.M. (2004), *Herstelrecht in Jeugdstrafrechtzaken* (Den Haag: Boom Juridische uitgevers).

Horst, H. van der, Joanknecht, L. and Van Pagée, R. (2011), *Handleiding voor Eigen Kracht-Coördinatoren* (Zwolle: EKC).

Leijten, M. (2011), 'Restorative Justice: Vooruitzichten', *Tijdschrift voor Herstelrecht*, 11(1), pp 3–4.

Province Overijssel et al. (2009), *Shared Vision: Successfully Supporting Children and Families* (Zwolle: Province Overijssel).

Steketee, M., ter Woerds, S., Moll, M. and Boutellier, H. (2006), *Herstelbemiddeling voor Jeugdigen in Nederland* (Utrecht: Verwey-Jonker Instituut).

Van Beek, F. (2007), *Het Zit Nog Niet in Ons Systeem* (Voorhout: WESP).

Van Beek, F. and Gramberg, P. (2007), *'Gewoon Normaal Tegen Elkaar Doen'*. Herstelbijeenkomsten Echt Recht 2000–2006 (Voorhout: WESP).

Van Beek, F. and Muntendam, M. (2011), *De Kleine Gids; Eigen Kracht-Conferentie 2011: Moeilijke Zaken Makkelijk Uitgelegd* (Alphen aan den Rijn/Deventer: Kluwer).

Van Burik, A., Heim, M., Hoogeveen, C., de Jong, B., Slump, G. and Vogelvang, B. (2010), *Evaluatie Slachtoffer-Dadergesprekken. Een Onderzoek Naar de Landelijke Implementatie van Slachtoffer-Dadergesprekken* (Van Montfoort Collegio for WODC, Den Haag: Ministerie van Veiligheid en Justitie).

Van Pagée, R. (ed.) (2003), *Eigen Kracht (Family Group Conference in Nederland): Van Model Naar Invoering* (Amsterdam: SWP).

Van Rhijn, A. (2007), 'Een Kei met Datum, Herstelbemiddeling in de P.I. Nieuwegein, 2004–2007', *Tijdschrift voor Herstelrecht*, 7(4), pp 53–61.

Wachtel, T. (1997), *Real Justice* (Pennsylvania: Piper's Press).

Wijnen-Lunenberg, P., Van Beek, F., Bijl, B., Gramberg, P. and Slot, W. (2008), *It's the Family's Move* (Duivendrecht/Voorhout: PI-Research/WESP).

Wolthuis, A. and Vandenbroucke, M. (2009), *Schade Herstellen Tijdens Jeugddetentie: Een Evaluatieonderzoek Naar Herstelgericht Werken in Forensisch Centrum Teylingereind* (Utrecht: Verwey-Jonker Instituut).

Wolthuis, A. and Vandenbroucke, M. (2010), 'Schade Herstellen Tijdens Jeugddetentie', *Proces*, 3, pp 150–64.

Wolthuis, A. and Wiersma, E. (2010), 'Welk Spoor Volgt Nederland?', *Tijdschrift voor Herstelrecht*, 10(4), pp 105–11.

15

CONFERENCING

CONCLUDING COMMENTS

Ivo Aertsen

INTRODUCTION

The origins of this book are situated in a European project entitled 'Conferencing: a way forward for restorative justice in Europe', which was conducted in the period 2009–2011. To which extent can we now conclude that conferencing programmes and developments indeed show the way forward for restorative justice in Europe? Showing 'The Great Leap Forward', I am afraid, cannot be attained. Luckily most people working in the field of restorative justice—be they practitioners, policy makers, or researchers—do not believe in 'only true' models. They would fully agree with what the recently deceased Tony Peters wrote in his introduction to the first book of the European Forum for Restorative Justice in 2000, and which is certainly still valid today:

> The attractiveness of mediation and restorative justice stems from the multitude of aims. It seems easy to consider the many practices to be a success for at least one and often for several reasons. (…) It is a challenging task to look far beyond these points of convergence translated in what one can call 'the restorative justice movement'. Many and often different concrete projects of mediation and restorative justice bring us together in an optimistic mood, with strong expectations about the future opportunities of these approaches. Nevertheless, we have to be careful in developing a clear vision and in defining the most essential elements of the concepts, in analysing the structure and coherence of the aims, in prescribing the principles and standards to evaluate practices and in identifying the fields of tension in which these practices are implemented. (…) The greatest danger is the illusion of the existence of a common language in this field. We need some more time to develop a common restorative justice and mediation language which pays full respect to the different cultural backgrounds of the countries and regions involved in these developments. (Peters 2000: 15)

The diversity of the restorative justice landscape is fully reflected in this volume. Lode Walgrave takes off in Chapter 3 by stating that 'there is not just one story' in restorative justice, not even within the conferencing model. Confronted with the variety of 'models and versions', he asks for clarity in concepts and terminology. We should develop our knowledge not in order to discover 'whether restorative justice works or not', but to learn 'which model of restorative justice conferences may work for what purposes and under what conditions'. Therefore, he pleads for 'a second generation programme of research on restorative justice', with more differentiation according to distinct variables, steered by theory and more frequently including close observation of restorative justice processes. Diversity is also the starting point for Joanna Shapland in Chapter 4, where she again draws our attention to the necessity of making things more explicit: restorative justice programmes (and policy makers and funders) should clarify the schemes' aims and, through the development of theoretical models, be clear on the desired outcomes. Careful analysis of the processes of victim-offender mediation and conferencing should allow us to conclude which elements of practice fit a theoretical model. She warns of certain risks when one tries to compare different forms of restorative justice. The most difficult is to understand the differences in cultural and historical background in which programmes operate in different countries. This is precisely the focus of Anna Eriksson in Chapter 13 where she explains how different approaches of 'the welfare state' globally, but also within Europe, lead to different options on which types of programmes should be developed and how (not) to implement them nationwide.

FACTS AND FIGURES

The origins of this book lie in an international survey and a seminar which were organized in the framework of an EU co-funded project granted to the European Forum for Restorative Justice. The project deliberately focused on the model of 'conferencing', knowing that in Europe the predominant model of restorative justice was (and mainly still is) victim-offender mediation, be it in various forms. The initiators of the project expected the model of conferencing to offer an added value, that it thus could achieve more or at least particular results that victim-offender mediation was not able to reach (European Forum 2008). This assumption mainly derived from restorative justice literature and theoretical insights. The model of conferencing, it was believed, could help develop the community dimension in restorative justice practices, whereas mediation was criticized because of its over-individualizing approach and de-contextualization of the crime and its solutions. Moreover, conferencing seemed to be a more promising model in terms of effectiveness mainly with respect to its impact on satisfaction of participants and degree of reoffending, as was shown in various meta-studies (Latimer, Dowden and Muise 2001; McCold and Wachtel 2001; Sherman and Strang 2007; Vanfraechem 2005). In short, the project was another logical step in the conceptual and practical development of restorative justice in Europe, promoted by the European Forum which in the years before had initiated practice oriented or evaluative projects to train restorative justice practitioners and legal professionals, to support and implement restorative justice in particular parts of Europe (Central and Eastern Europe, Southern Europe), to study EU policies in the field of restorative justice, to build societal support for restorative justice, and to study the crime prevention mechanisms of restorative justice processes.[1] The new project would focus on a better understanding of *conferencing* practices and models internationally, its processes and outcomes as compared to victim-offender mediation, and under which conditions conferencing could be developed in a European legal and cultural context. Both the victim's position and the community dimension in restorative justice programmes were important themes for the European Forum, as this came to the fore even more explicitly in recent projects of the organization, including a European empirical research project on the experiences of victims when participating (or not) in mediation and conferencing, and on the practical relevance of the model of 'peacemaking circles' in a European environment.

Some of the main findings of the conferencing research project are presented by Estelle Zinsstag in Chapter 2 of this volume. An important merit of this research is the delivery of a whole series of factual data on the practice of conferencing (and mediation) in about 25 countries. This is not about how or what restorative justice is supposed to be, but about its functioning in reality. It therefore helps to combat and correct inaccurate and stereotypical images (see also Shapland, Chapter 3), or mere assumptions about restorative justice internationally. So it was found that conferencing—of which a definition was given in the survey—is generally more developed and widespread internationally than initially thought. Also the range of crimes that can be dealt with by conferencing seems to be very wide, including cases of sexual violence. Not surprising was the finding that the majority of programmes address juvenile offenders and that only a few exclusively deal with adult cases. Referring authorities in European countries are mainly judges and public prosecutors, whereas in non-European countries police play a more important role. The latter refers to the existence of different legal systems, which is obviously also relevant for the finding that in many common law countries guilt of the offender must be proven before a referral to a conference can be made, whereas in most civil law countries referrals are possible before and after the establishment of guilt. Furthermore the survey provides detailed information on who are the required and allowed participants in conferencing practices and who can represent the victim; on the status of the so-called supporters for both victim and offender; on the role, status, and training of the facilitator; on the preparation of parties before the conference; on the agreements reached and complied with and the legal consequences of (non-fulfilment of) the agreement; and on the follow-up information given to the victim. Against the background of these and other findings, the survey demonstrates that also in the field of conferencing 'practice is much more advanced than theory'. This might be reflected in the diversity of types of conferences which are applied in the field of crime and criminal law worldwide: family group conferencing, restorative conferencing, Real Justice conferencing, police-led conferencing, community conferencing, etc., not to mention the even much wider spread of conferencing models when dealing with dispute, conflict, and tensions in other social

[1] All reports of the projects can be downloaded from the Forum's website: <http://www.euforumrj.org>.

contexts such as schools, workplaces, neighbourhoods, and youth organizations. However, the different types of conferences often show considerable overlap in the way their objectives and processes are conceived. 'These typologies do not seem as important in practice', Zinsstag concludes in her overview. Most striking in the conferencing research project (on the basis of the survey, seminar, and interviews with practitioners and other experts) was the finding that—in practice—the distinction between the models of conferencing, on the one hand, and victim-offender mediation, on the other hand, is not always so clear. What in some countries is called 'conferencing', might be defined in other countries as a form of 'extended mediation'. In many mediation practices indeed, support persons for victim and/or offender take part in the process. This is shown in the project's final report (Zinsstag et al. 2011) and is mentioned in several of this book's chapters. It leads Shapland, in Chapter 4, to conclude that 'old stereotypes of conferencing being Anglo-Saxon but mediation being more 'European' now need drastic re-examination'.

FACILITATION

The critical role of the mediator, facilitator, or coordinator has always been recognized in restorative justice processes. Restorative justice programmes may differ in respect to initial options to work with professional mediators, unpaid volunteers, or paid lay persons. There is, however, a large consensus on the requirements for mediators or facilitators in terms of required knowledge, attitudes, and skills. No one will question the importance of training, be it initial training, continuous training, or training 'on the job'. The international survey however, as reported in Chapter 2, reveals considerable differences in extent and nature of training. Another result of the survey concerns the status of the facilitator in conferencing programmes: much more than is the case in mediation programmes, facilitators in conferencing models are paid employees. There seems to be less room for volunteers (although the model of the Netherlands—operating with lay facilitators, see Chapter 14—should be kept in mind). Furthermore, the facilitator in conferencing programmes seems to have a crucial role in the preparation of the parties to take part in the conference. The role of the empowering facilitator in conferencing is highlighted in detail by Chapman in Chapter 5, starting from the Northern Irish case: 'The facilitation of the stories of people affected by harm within the context of respect is a skilful and professional task which is closer to [a] model of "reflection-in-action" than "technical rationality"'. Restorative justice cannot be understood from an external point of view. The role of the mediator or facilitator can only be captured through close observation and participation.

Compared to victim-offender mediation, the role of the facilitator may be more hands-off (Strang, Chapter 6), although also within mediation practices important differences exist in terms of mediation styles. Practices can be characterized by a more directive mediation style, where the outcome and effect (on the offender) prevails on the one hand, or a more 'independent' mediation style, which offers more room for initiative by the parties (Marshall 1996), on the other hand. In the same way, conferencing can be guided according to a script model (which might be a safe option for larger groups) or following a more open and flexible approach. Various chapters in this book deal with the tension in decision-making power: should the focus be on professionals to decide, or rather should family and community members be in power? We believe that both tendencies exist in victim-offender mediation practices and in conferencing. But we feel attracted by the Northern Irish approach, where in the training of professional facilitators, a central task is to enable them to 'unlearn' their previous role (eg as social worker) and the skills and knowledge that supported that role (Zinsstag and Chapman, Chapter 11). This also demonstrates why combi-roles in restorative justice (doing probation work in the morning and leading a conference in the afternoon) might be problematic.

IMPACT AND VALUES

Comparing different restorative justice models, and comparing victim-offender mediation with conferencing in particular, remains a difficult exercise. Nevertheless, 'there is unity within restorative justice practice which enables comparison' (Shapland, Chapter 4). Restorative justice is indeed more than just an umbrella term. Both in practice and theory common elements can be identified, defined, compared, and analysed across different models. There might be, on the one hand, different definitions of 'restorative justice' and divergent theoretical underpinnings (as this is certainly also the case for criminal justice in general and its very diverse justifications), which partly reflects differing opinions and priorities. On the other hand, there might be more in common than in difference. The practice of victim-offender mediation is a clear example of the existence of a broad consensus on the core conditions and elements of good mediation practice. International instruments such as the Council of Europe Recommendation R(99)19 on Mediation in Penal Matters and the UN 2002 Basic Principles on the Use of Restorative Justice Programmes in Criminal Matters provide guidance and further explanation of the key elements of restorative justice. The operational principles for conducting *mediation* and organizing programmes are agreed on in many countries, often supported by national policies, whereas this might be less the case, in a uniform way, for conferencing.

Common ground in restorative justice, however, can best be found in the shared *values* that underpin practice. This book offers a remarkable example of a common direction—although showing different accents—when looking at the *aims and objectives* that are attributed to conferencing practices and programmes. The international survey (Zinsstag, Chapter 2) is very clear in this respect: both in programmes with juvenile and adult offenders non-instrumental objectives are considered as the most important. Meeting victims' needs and offering reparation, increasing the offenders' sense of responsibility, reaching an agreement which is acceptable for all parties, and, to a lesser degree, providing opportunities for family and community members to participate, form the top priorities according to the large group of experts that responded to the international survey. 'Reducing reoffending' does *not* figure in the

'Top Five', and totally at the end of the list are objectives such as 'reducing the caseload of the court', 'reducing prison population', and 'reducing financial costs'. These prioritized aims and objectives might reflect respondents' aspirations more than restorative justice realities in their countries, although, given the careful selection of respondents, their answers should be considered as reliable and well founded in practice. Of course, 'influencing reoffending' might be chosen less frequently by respondents because of the lack of theoretical models so far, or uncertainties and difficulties related to measuring such effects, as also wider community involvement does not appear as a priority, maybe because of the non-availability of practical scenarios to realize broader participation. What, on the basis of the survey and other book chapters, is certainly clear, is that experts' opinions on the aims and objectives of conferencing stand in sharp contrast with the political discourse on restorative justice in many countries which heavily relies on effectiveness and crime reduction. This discrepancy is reinforced from the non-expert side: when one looks at the objectives of participating in restorative justice practices as expressed by victims and offenders themselves, aspects related to mutual (future oriented) *communication* seem to be the most important, both in conferencing and mediation practices as researched in England and Wales (Shapland, Chapter 4).

The non-instrumental approach of restorative justice in general and conferencing in particular is demonstrated extensively in Tim Chapman's chapter on facilitating restorative youth conferences in Northern Ireland (Chapter 5). In the Balanced Model of Restorative Justice the needs and interest of victim, offender, and community are addressed in an open, non-directive way. 'Agency' of all is an important aim to be achieved on itself, for which the role and the skills of the facilitator are crucial. Restoring justice, safety, and control all require essential processes of communication and dialogue, allowing for, *inter alia*, expressing needs and opinions and creating mutual accountability and commitment. Restorative justice, as convincingly explained in the chapter, is about storytelling and giving meaning, and therefore allows for (re-)constructing realities. In Northern Ireland, a model of conferencing has been developed to bring this into practice, following the stages of inclusion, participation, and transformation.

Elizabeth Beck and Joan Pennell in their chapter on conferencing in the United States (Chapter 9) demonstrate, on the basis of four case studies, once more the value-driven nature of many restorative justice initiatives. Programmes often depend on a strong personal commitment of initiators. Restorative justice is 'a principled and values based practice' and we should not forget how big the shift towards another basic attitude is when people are asked to participate in such processes, the authors argue.

COMMUNITY

There is little discussion about who are the key actors of a conference: victim, offender, and their support persons, helped by a facilitator. Support persons usually include family members or friends. Other persons may participate as well, such as a police officer, a lawyer, a community worker, etc. The presence and the role of these 'other persons'—all professionals—show considerable variation according to the type of conference and the country where it is applied. The support persons represent the 'community of care'. Together with the 'other persons' they often have a double, partly overlapping role: offering personal support to victim and/or offender and to the process of dialogue on the one hand, and taking up responsibilities from within the community on the other hand. Furthermore, family and community members can participate on the basis of their own personal or common needs or interests because they feel affected by the crime in one or another way, and because of their feelings of concern about the future. Finally, as we know from other criminal justice related practices such as victim support and probation, *volunteers* can play an important role in representing and valorizing the community. In this way, volunteers take a central position in victim-offender mediation models in several countries, as is highlighted in Chapter 13 on the Nordic countries. However, the discussion on involving volunteers in *conferencing* programmes remains largely absent in this volume, maybe because of the difficulty that might be experienced in practice when trying to reconcile the requirements related to methodological skills on the one hand with the nature and limitations of unpaid volunteer work on the other hand, as suggested by Walgrave in Chapter 3. However, in this respect the experiences with lay facilitators in the model of Eigen Kracht-conferences in the Netherlands as largely applied mainly in non-criminal, family, and other disputes is remarkable. Rob Van Pagée, Jan Van Lieshout, and Annemieke Wolthuis in Chapter 14 report extensively on the emergence and development of this model, initially based on the United States' Real Justice format. They explain how the model empowers personal communities and social systems in order to let them make their own plans on how to deal with the problem, and how through such processes cooperation between citizens and professionals is put in a totally new light. In this model, facilitators are not specifically skilled and trained persons, but 'fellow-citizens who support families in the organization of their conference'. The 500 facilitators are coached by professional project managers, and they receive a fee on the basis of the number of hours they have spent in a conference.

An interesting observation relates to the *focus* of the community participation. All the possible types of community involvement as presented in the previous paragraph mainly reflect an *individualizing* approach. Members of the community participate—*grosso modo*—in line and in function of the wellbeing and treatment of victim and/or offender. Often, the group of community members remains rather small. Heather Strang, in Chapter 6 on 'Conferencing and Victims', adds to this overview, on the basis of empirical research in Australia and the United Kingdom, the community's function of 'expressing opprobrium' where appropriate, which recalls the possible (re-integrative) shaming element in conferences (Braithwaite 1989). Indirectly, one might argue, community members participate because of the larger community's or society's interest. It is, however, not clear at all whether this is the same as the so-called 'public dimension' which is often envisaged as a necessary element and added value at the same time in conferencing models. The public dimension might be personalized through the presence of a police officer, as is for example the case in the Belgian situation (see Chapter 12 by Inge Vanfraechem, Katrien Lauwaert, and Mélanie Decocq, who mention that the police refer symbolically to the societal consequences of the crime, without necessarily 'representing society'). In New Zealand, the role of the police (and other professionals) in conferences is to supply information or to guide the process, without 'dominating' or 'dictating' the conference (see Chapter 7 by Ashley Shearer and Gabrielle Maxwell). The police officer's *presence* might be a sign of support and recognition for the victim, as is shown in the Belgian experience (Chapter 12), while in Australia victims (mainly of violent crime) report positive experiences with the police in its role as *facilitator* even 10 years after the conference took place (Chapter 6). We do not know precisely how this presence of the police is perceived by the offender and whether the policeman's role has a supportive function for genuine dialogue. Much might depend on how the police in general are perceived by youngsters or by some social groups or minorities in a given city or region. The public image of police forces can differ a lot across localities, and therefore generalizing a conferencing model (heavily) depending on the role of the police might be risky. But if it also remains true that 'crime is a public issue and not simply a private matter between the victim and the offender' (Chapman, Chapter 5), then the very challenging question is who will decide on who can or must participate in a conference. Mediators tend to leave this to the decision of the direct stakeholders, thus victim and offender; they would often not invite persons in the process against the will of victim or offender. But can we agree, taking into account the public dimension of a crime, that victim and offender have a monopoly position in deciding who should participate? In short, it seems to me that—for the time being—including 'the public dimension' in conferencing is more a matter of rhetoric than actual experience. We are in need of models where the societal dimension can be integrated more fully in restorative justice processes, be it in the form of official representation by police or judicial authorities, or in the form of participation by community actors and organizations making use of more informal mechanisms.

Notions of community and the role of the community in restorative justice practices differ a lot between countries and regions (Karp and Clear 2002; Pranis 2000; Vanfraechem 2007). Instructive in this respect is the analysis made by Eriksson in Chapter 13, where she comments on the 'inclusive model' of mediation in Nordic countries. These countries do not need to talk about community, since community ownership of conflict and problem solving is so self-evident. Different from anglophone countries, the author argues, culture in Nordic countries is less individualistic (see also Chapter 7) and the role of the state and the criminal justice system is much less threatening to citizens. The roots of crime have always been situated, also by representatives of the criminal justice system, much more in factors of 'inequality, lack of education, unemployment, and social exclusion'. Therefore 'responses to crime tend to focus on these larger social and structural causes', which also makes approaches such as restorative justice much less controversial in these countries. In practice, mediation almost always includes several other people besides victim and offender, 'hence, the term "conferencing" is not necessarily used in the Nordic countries'. However, it seems that the police are not participating in these mediation processes (although referrals are often coming from the police), whereas it has been argued that the presence of a police representative 'in its typical roles of informant and guardian of public order' probably makes the most important difference between conferencing and mediation (Walgrave, Chapter 3).

There is a remarkable parallel to be drawn between the chapter on the wealthy Nordic countries and the chapter on the economically poor South American countries, as presented by Daniela Bolivar, Leoberto Narciso Brancher, Ivan Navarro Papic, and Manyori Vega Gutiérrez (Chapter 10). In both regions, responding to societal and structural needs seems to be important in criminal justice and restorative justice approaches. However, restorative justice in the Nordic countries operates thanks to, and on the basis of, the existing democratic orientation of a legitimate criminal justice system. In contrast Latin American restorative justice appears to be in competition with a criminal justice system, which is experienced as illegitimate by most of the population. There is a high level of trust of citizens in public institutions in the one region, and a high level of distrust towards institutions in the other region. In Latin America, according to the authors of Chapter 10, criminal justice tends to perpetuate social inequalities, not to fight them. Therefore, restorative justice and in particular conferencing, through practices such as restorative circles, are not the expression of a democratically founded criminal justice system, but a tool for challenging this system and at the same time a strategy for promoting basic democracy and social justice. Establishing a democratic system of restorative justice in a Latin American context requires, according to Bolivar et al., inclusiveness not only for the victim and the offender but also for the community. The difference with forms of restorative justice in industrialized countries might be that in the South the community is considered much more as an important co-beneficiary of restorative justice practices. Real inclusiveness in restorative justice means that the needs of the community are taken as a full starting point for setting up a conference, and not only the needs of victim and offender with their personal communities of care. Seen from a social-pedagogical angle, restorative justice processes in order to reach social justice must allow for political participation and community empowerment. Therefore, restorative justice practices and programmes should be 'located and inserted in existing concrete communities'.

We can learn a lot from initiatives and concepts of restorative justice as they are emerging in Southern countries. Reference can be made to experiments such as the Zwelethemba model in South Africa, where the idea is also to bridge between the individual (micro-)level on the one hand and the societal-structural level on the other hand (Shearing and Froestad 2007). Such experiences at least make clear how different the role, function, and place of 'the community' can be in society and also in the framework of restorative justice practices. The main endeavour of developing restorative justice in many countries probably is to be situated in between the two extreme situations of the North and the South as we have discussed them in the previous paragraphs: on the one hand, restorative justice programmes are to be developed and implemented on the basis of existing legal structures; on the other hand, these programmes should be conceived and organized in such a way that existing structures can be challenged constantly and that restorative justice's societal and democratic potential can be fully realized.

JUSTICE

As is the case for different approaches to 'community', the notion of 'justice' also appears very differently in the previous chapters dealing with conferencing models. Restorative justice is about 'doing justice', but what this precisely entails and how this 'justice' can be reached, is less clear. Most restorative justice practitioners and advocates believe in the role that direct stakeholders have in contributing themselves to 'justice'. 'Justice' is no longer considered as something that can be 'delivered' or imposed by the court, but it is now much more seen as a process that requires active participation by those immediately involved or by community members in order to make justice decisions acceptable, credible, and legitimate. Therefore, it should not come as a surprise that restorative justice research has been set up from the socio-psychological theoretical perspective of 'procedural justice'; these studies shed a light on perceptions of justice by citizens when they go through a process of restorative justice (see, amongst others: De Mesmaecker 2011; Strang 2002).

But how is 'justice' conceptualized in *conferencing* practices more concretely and how does it differ from mediation practices? Some observations and reflections on the basis of the foregoing book chapters might be the following. First, one must remark that conferencing in pioneering New Zealand strongly represents a welfare model. The starting point was the position of the (aboriginal) child or youngster, for whom one wished to develop a more culture-sensitive type of intervention with the help of his/her (extended) family. In recent years, the welfare approach has even become stronger and conferencing practices might now become less oriented to community resources, since the responsibilities of the youth justice coordinators have been reduced and, partly because of funding shortages, transferred to managers with a social work background (Shearar and Maxwell, Chapter 7). It seemed that initially Australia had adopted a conferencing model based on a criminal justice (and police) approach, but as Kathleen Daly clarifies in Chapter 8, all Australian jurisdictions have now legally established youth justice conferencing using the New Zealand model. This model also formed the basis for the introduction of conferencing in countries as Belgium and Northern Ireland. Belgium, however, is struggling with a lack of cases in practice, notwithstanding the strong formulation of conferencing (and mediation) in the new Youth Justice Act 2006. Vanfraechem et al. in Chapter 12 refer to possible explanations for this paradoxical situation, one of them being the simultaneous offer of mediation which for legal professionals is less complicated to apply, and another 'the tendency to pocket restorative justice in a traditional vision of a youth welfare system'. Both restrictions could apparently be avoided in the implementation of conferencing in Northern Ireland, which might explain its major success in a quantitative way since 2002. Zinsstag and Chapman in Chapter 11 report on the implementation processes of restorative justice for juveniles 'at the core of the criminal justice system' in Northern Ireland. Without any doubt, a lot can be learnt from the Northern Irish experience for the development of restorative justice in other countries. The authors report how from the outset the national programme was designed differently compared to forerunner, New Zealand. More importance was given to the victim and, as already mentioned, a balanced model was developed. In this model, the justice approach becomes more prominent, in the sense that the formal state system of justice 'must balance the need to repair the harm to the victim, to protect the community, and to reduce the need for the offender to harm others'. 'Unless each party, victim, offender, and community believe that their needs and interests have been addressed, it cannot be said that justice has been served' (Chapter 11). Restoring 'justice' must be *experienced*: through exchanges of accountability, through the fair and equitable treatment of all parties, through the fact that all parties must have their voice heard, through the vindication of the victim, through satisfaction with the process and its outcomes, and through legal safeguards regarding rights and proportionality (Chapman in Chapter 5, referring to Bennett, and to Bazemore and Walgrave). For Walgrave (Chapter 3), 'doing justice' implies 'justice that restores' and therefore restoration *as an outcome* must be examined at the material, psychological, relational, and social level. Specific aspects related to justice experiences are reported by Strang (Chapter 6) on the basis of her follow-up research in Australia with victims 10 years after their participation in conferencing: compared with a court-group, conferencing-victims still felt more satisfied with the criminal justice system and were significantly less revengeful towards the offender. How the experience of justice can or should be shaped according to social-structural needs and how thus restorative justice can meet social justice, has been discussed in the previous section starting from ideas and findings in Latin America.

What we can conclude on the basis of the accounts above, is that the notion 'justice' in restorative justice processes relates to very different elements indeed and that different functions can be given to it. It might make sense to consider 'justice' in restorative justice processes both from a bottom-up and a top-down perspective. On the one hand, justice is a process that must be experienced as such by all involved, including members of the wider community. There are both substantial and procedural elements in justice experiences. Compared to mediation, a conferencing model can offer an added value in this respect: wider support and recognition for both victim and offender can be offered in direct meetings, social disapproval or 'censure' can be mobilized in a more effective way (through informal processes and—possibly—the presence of a public authority), and more social resources to implement and follow-up the agreement or plan can be explored. On the other hand, the justice system should play an active role top-down: in providing and safeguarding the right of equal access to restorative justice programmes for all, in referring cases, in exercising the function of legal protection and control, and in being committed to listen to justice perceptions from those participating as protagonists in the dialogue.

REFERENCES

Braithwaite, J. (1989), *Crime, Shame and Reintegration* (Cambridge: Cambridge University Press).

De Mesmaecker, V. (2011), *Perceptions of Justice and Fairness in Criminal Proceedings and Restorative Encounters: Extending Theories of Procedural Justice* (doctoral dissertation) (Leuven: KU Leuven).

European Forum for Restorative Justice (2008), *Application Specific Programme on Criminal Justice—Conferencing: A Way Forward for Restorative Justice in Europe* (Leuven: European Forum for Restorative Justice).

Karp, D. and Clear, R. (2002), *What is Community Justice? Case Studies of Restorative Justice and Community Supervision* (London: Sage Publications).

Latimer, J., Dowden, C. and Muise, D. (2001), *The Effectiveness of Restorative Justice Processes: A Meta-Analysis* (Ottawa: Department of Justice).

Marshall, T. (1996), 'The Evolution of Restorative Justice in Britain', *European Journal on Criminal Policy and Research*, 4(4), pp 21–43.

McCold, P. and Wachtel, T. (2001), 'Restorative Justice Theory Validation', in Weitekamp, E. and Kerner, H.-J. (eds.), *Restorative Justice: Theoretical Foundations* (Cullompton: Willan Publishing), pp 110–42.

Peters, T. (2000), 'Victim-Offender Mediation: Realities and Challenges', in European Forum for Victim-Offender Mediation and Restorative Justice (ed.), *Victim-Offender Mediation in Europe: Making Restorative Justice Work* (Leuven: Leuven University Press), pp 9–17.

Pranis, K. (2000), 'Conferencing and the Community', in Burford, G. and Hudson, J. (eds.), *Family Group Conferences: Perspectives on Policy, Practice and Research* (Hawthorne: Aldine de Gruyter), pp 120–30.

Shearing, C. and Froestad, J. (2007), 'Beyond Restorative Justice—Zwelethemba, a Future-Focused Model Using Local Capacity Conflict Resolution', in Mackay, R., Bosnjak, M., Deklerck, J., Pelikan, C., van Stokkom, B. and Wright, M. (eds.), *Images of Restorative Justice Theory* (Frankfurt: Verlag fur Polizeiwissenschaft), pp 16–34.

Sherman, L. and Strang, H. (2007), *Restorative Justice: The Evidence* (London: The Smith Institute).

Strang, H. (2002), *Repair or Revenge: Victims and Restorative Justice* (Oxford: Clarendon Press).

Vanfraechem, I. (2005), 'Evaluating Conferencing for Serious Juvenile Offenders', in Elliott, L. and Gordon, R. (eds.), *Restorative Justice: Emerging Issues in Practice and Evaluation* (Cullompton: Willan Publishing), pp 278–95.

Vanfraechem, I. (2007), 'Community, Society and State in Restorative Justice: Some Reflections', in Mackay, R., Bosjnak, M., Deklerck, J., Pelikan, C., van Stokkom, B. and Wright, M. (eds.), *Images of Restorative Justice Theory* (Frankfurt am Main: Verlag für Polizei und Wissenschaft), pp 73–91.

Zinsstag, E., Teunkens, M. and Pali, B. (2011), *Conferencing: A Way Forward for Restorative Justice in Europe?* Report to the European Commission (Leuven: European Forum for Restorative Justice).

INDEX